BOCCACCIO
The Man and His Works

VITTORE BRANCA

BOCCACCIO
The Man and His Works

Translated by
RICHARD MONGES

Cotranslator and Editor
DENNIS J. McAULIFFE

Foreword by
ROBERT C. CLEMENTS

New York: NEW YORK UNIVERSITY PRESS
1976

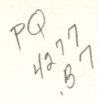

Contents

BOOK I
Boccaccio's Life

BOOK II
The *Decameron*

FOREWORD

It is a pleasure and honor for New York University Press to present this definitive study on Boccaccio's life and works during this anniversary year 1975. For no such book on this important subject has appeared in the English language for many decades. The present work is not the direct translation of a single book done by Branca in Italian, but rather a carefully constructed volume designed by the author from his important and basic *Boccaccio Medievale* and some complementary writings appearing in encyclopedias and other important sources. The resulting pages assemble the most important updated information on Boccaccio, correcting earlier information—on even so basic a matter as his birthplace—and incorporating the best scholarship on Boccaccio's vernacular and Latin works undertaken by Branca and his associates around the review *Studi sul Boccaccio.* Just as Branca's annotated edition of the *Decameron* (Le Monnier, 1960) will long remain the most widely used edition, the editors hope that the present volume will similarly remain for years the authoritative source for Boccaccio's biography and publications. The definitive autograph of the *Decameron,* as discovered recently by Branca, has been issued by the Accademia della Crusca.

Vittore Branca's preëminence in Italian studies is attested by his election in 1973 to the presidency of the International Association for the Study of Italian Language and Literature (AISLLI), succeeding his old friend Umberto Bosco. Branca's academic posts have been distinguished ones: Rome, Catania, Bergamo (where he served as rector), and currently Padua. He holds honorary degrees from Budapest, Bergamo, and New York, as well as many citations from other institutions and academies. He has held two major offices in UNESCO. Born at Savona in 1913, he is now a Venetian at heart. His administrative talents have won him the post of Secretary General and Vice-President of the Cini Foundation of Venice, where his charming offices face across the water the Byzantine splendors of St. Mark's Square. His comfortable, art-filled home faces across the canal the imposing Accademia, witness to the special character of the Venetian Renaissance. As Secretary General he organizes each year several meaningful international conferences on contemporary or historical phases of culture, and oversees publication of many volumes on aspects of Venetian history.

Because of his dynamism and initiative, I called him for a while "the American Italian" until finally conceding that he outdistances even the most enterprising academician on this side of the Atlantic.

His many books include studies of Saint Francis, Petrarch, the *Decameron,* Politian, Alfieri, Manzoni, Emilio de Marchi, the *Conciliatore,* Sebastian Ciampi, among others. *Lettere Italiane,* which he edits, is one of the most solid philological reviews in Italy.

As a man Branca is endowed with great personal charm, generosity, and warmth. In a profession where rivalries germinate easily, he seems a man without enemies. At one of his receptions in the Cini Foundation, where a throng of some sixty disparate guests had gathered for sherry after a lecture, I remember remarking to a friend that Branca was inconspicuously making contact with everyone in the room. And, to recall Confucius' definition of education, Branca brushed off a bit of himself on each. I met him in 1961 at a round-table in the Casa di Boccaccio at Certaldo, and within two days I knew that I had made a new life-long friend.

During his sixty years Branca has created a school of young critics and philologists dedicated more to traditional values than to fluctuating schools and tastes and thrusts. He works actively to help younger men, whether his own disciples or others, move ahead in the profession. When he was awarded an honorary doctorate at New York University in 1973, the citation read in part: "You are admired by scholars and students the world over by reason of the publication of your literary and philological works on four continents and through your ubiquitous teaching and lecturing, whether in Tokyo, Istanbul, Zagreb, Montevideo, or here in New York.

"You have been infallibly true to the severest demands of your discipline. You have inspired younger scholars to seek historical understanding and critical evaluation of literature through the application of a vigorous, philological method." The pages which follow demonstrate this method in a felicitous way.

Robert C. Clements
Co-President, AISLLI

Part I

Boccaccio's Life

CHAPTER I

The Days of His Early Youth
between Florence and Certaldo
(1313-1327)

The family of the "father" of the European narrative belonged to the petty landowning middle class of the rural area around Florence, specifically to that of a village in the Valdelsa, Certaldo. Certaldo is always mentioned by Boccaccio in the course of his literary career as his little home town. He referred to it this way since the time when he was pleased to exalt it with a pretty, etiological fable:

> . . . a lovely plain, in which . . . not very far from the river stood a little hillock on which a very high and very old grove of oaks grew . . . "Why does Filocolo not found the new town on this hillock, where this grove stands? No spot have I seen in these parts so suitable for such a purpose: this place rises above all the surrounding countryside; this is a strong place, and beautiful, here there is water in abundance" . . . *(Filocolo,* III, 33, 12; V, 42, 2).[1]

But in the twilight of the thirteenth century the family of Boccaccio escaped the toilsome and weary life of the petty land-

3

owners of Valdelsa by moving to Florence and trying the great mercantile venture which attracted such a great part of the Tuscan community between 1200 and 1300. By 1297 Vanni, a son of Boccaccio's grandfather, Ghelino or Chelino (diminutives of Michele) di Buonaiuto, appeared established among the inhabitants of the San Frediano quarter of Florence, where there were several families of Boccacci,[2] and it is very probable that the father of Boccaccio, Boccaccio or Boccaccino di Chelino, was already with him there at that time.[3] The turnover of business of the sons of Chelino must have increased considerably in the first decade of the fourteenth century, for around 1313 or 1314 they moved to the San Pier Maggiore quarter (one of the centers of Florentine mercantile life) "with their families and engaged in business there"[4] and because by 1318 they were burdened with onerous taxes and duties. They then declared that they should no longer pay these taxes to Certaldo and Pulicciano but only to Florence because they had been living in the San Pier Maggiore quarter of that city (Vessilo della Chiave) much longer than the four years required by law ("iam sunt quattuor anni et ultra").[5]

In this same period Chelino's sons must have extended their mercantile activity beyond the Florentine circle to the European sphere, for "Boccasin Lombard et son frère" appear in the "livre de la Taille" as lodging in Paris near the church of Saint-Jacques-la-Boucherie in the first quarter of 1313 (probably towards the end).[6] Indeed Boccaccino must have made more than one journey to Paris in those years, as the son seems to refer to recollections or impressions, direct or indirect, of the father's travels. In the *De casibus* (IX, 21), he tells of the sending of the Templars to the stake (May 12, 1310) and the torture of Jacques de Molay (March 18 or 19, 1314): "Ut aiebat Boccaccius genitor meus, qui tunc parte Parisius negotiator honesto cum labore rem curabat augere domesticam et se his testabatur interfuisse rebus." (The testimony however is rather uncertain because the narration seems to be taken from Villani or at least from a common source.)[7] Boccaccio's father, then, carried on his business between Florence, the banking fulcrum of the European economy, and Paris, the greatest commercial emporium of the West, and he carried it on quite possibly as an associate of the powerful "compagnia" of the Bardi.[8]

Boccaccio's life was deeply affected by this turning point in the activities and in the very conditions of his family, a development which moreover was decisive for Tuscan and Italian society between the age of Dante and that of Boccaccio. Forsaking a prevalently agricultural and landowning existence, necessarily municipal or at most regional, the middle class rapidly and overpoweringly penetrated into European and Mediterranean life; it became a candidate for the position of ruling class of the world; it imposed economic power on political power. Only later, towards the middle of the fourteenth century, did it become apparent to what ruin this rapid and magnificent expansion had condemned its most characteristic and productive civilization: the communes.

The Boccacci family (and Boccaccio himself) participated actively in this great development, which left a deep impression on the young Boccaccio.

During the very time when Boccaccino was achieving his first successes on the European level, there was born to him in Tuscany, in Florence, more probably than in Certaldo,[9] in June or July 1313,[10] the offspring of an illicit love, the son who was to make his name forever world famous. At the baptismal fount he named him Giovanni out of affection for his business partner, his brother, who shared his home.[11]

The month of Giovanni Boccaccio's birth, with some approximation, is indicated by a passage in one of Petrarch's *Seniles* (VIII, 1: "ego te in nascendi ordine novem annorum spatio antecessi"), and by a mention in the epistle to Mainardo Cavalcanti of August 1372 (ep. XX: "sexagesimum annum ago"). To the contrary, the birthplace and identity of his mother, as well as the early events of his life, have been the subject of much discussion due to the lack of documents or of reliable information as is well known.[12]

Boccaccio's biographers based their work on typically romantic, fanciful, and often cryptic accounts, scattered through his early works, of some half-score different characters which they considered autobiographical. Such data, often contradictory, were chosen arbitrarily, combined in an artificial narrative mosaic and presented as a valid reconstruction of a biography narrated by the writer himself (material was drawn indiscriminately from the *Filocolo,* especially from the episodes of Idalogo and Caleone and Fileno; from the *Filostrato;* the *Teseida;* the *Comedia delle Ninfe,* particularly from the episodes of Ibrida and of Caleone; from the *Amorosa Visione* and its mysteriously scrupulous chronological indications; from the *Rime,* arbitrarily arranged to correspond with that imaginative romance; from the *Elegia di Madonna Fiammetta,* which presented a reverse situation, and so on). Having set foot on this path, these biographers doggedly continued to give disproportionate prominence to an equivocal mention of Giovanni's birth to a Parisian woman. This allusion was inserted in the second edition of Filippo Villani's account of the life of Boccaccio, whereas in the first edition of 1380, revised and approved by a well-informed friend of Boccaccio, Coluccio Salutati, Certaldo was said to be the birthplace of the author of the *Decameron.*[13] Thus a fabulous "vie romancée" was invented for Boccaccio; according to the *Filocolo,* he was born to a king's daughter who had been seduced by Boccaccino in far-away storied Paris, the medieval citadel of science and the Western mecca of European commerce. In that version, she had the lofty rank of queen, and was portrayed as the pure woman in love, and mother of the fabled pair of twins. In the *Comedia delle Ninfe,* however, Boccaccio's mother was reduced to the rank of a lady of the petty nobility, to a widow in her lonely bed, susceptible to desires and to regrets; she was the mother of an only son, abandoned by her faithless seducer. Finally, in Villani (and in a certain way, in the *Fiammetta*) Boccaccio's mother appeared as a plain unknown Parisian girl ("quandam iuventulam parisinam"), whom, however, Boccaccino married (disregarding the authentic documents on the illegitimacy of Giovanni's birth, beginning with the pontifical: see p. 119).

By now this pretty fable constructed in the last century on some literary or enigmatic allusions hidden in Boccaccio's early writings has lost all biographical credit. Perhaps Boccaccio had hoped to profit from the notoriety resulting from the Parisian sojourns of his father, and thus painted in alluring colors the bleak dawn of his own life. At the time he was ambitious to call attention to himself and to shine in a literary and worldly way at the court of Naples. Instead, today, we can and we must outline the boyhood of Boccaccio from the scanty reliable information available, and within the picture of the new and adventurous life which had opened up to his family.

Outside of his beautiful literary fables, Boccaccio never refers to his mother, and she is also never mentioned in family documents.[14] However, a few recollections of his childhood emerge from the placid and tender memories of the old writer engrossed in his great learned works. Reference to his mother is made when he catches himself thinking of the boy Giovanni on the bank of the Arno watching the flow of the city's river which, thanks to these memories, is awarded first place in the *De Fluminibus* ("Longo agmini dux dabitur Arnus, Florentie civitatis fluvius, non quidem tamquam ob litterarum ordinem meritus, sed quia *patrie* flumen sit et *mihi ante alios omnes ab ipsa infantia cognitus*"); or when, in the lonely house in Certaldo, alone and ill, with touching nostalgia he relives the domestic rites of New Years' Day, when as a child he marveled at the patriarchal actions of the *paterfamilias:*

> Habemus autem Florentini et sic forsan nonnulle alie nationes, ut plurimum, in aulis domesticis, ubi fit communis ignis toti familie domus, ferrea quedam instrumenta ad lignorum igni appositorum sustentationem apposita, que Lares vocamus, et in sero precedente Kalendarum Januarium die a patre familias omnis convocatur familia, et replete lignis igne stipes magnus apponitur, cuius caput unum igne crematur, in reliquo insidet ipse pater familias ceteris circumstantibus, et vino sumpto bibit ipse pater primo, et inde capiti stipitis incense superinfundit, quod vini superfuerat in calice, et deinde cum in circumitu potaverint ceteri, quasi perfecta solennitate ad officia consur-gunt sua. *Haec sepe puer in domo patria celebrari vidi a patre meo, catholico profecto homine. (Genealogia,* XII, 65.)

Always in these recollections of childhood (from which, natur-ally, Paris is completely absent) Florence appears as the city of his birth *(Gen.,* XV, 7; epistles VI, VIII, XIV, XXIV) as it is also unani-mously defined by his contemporaries (see for example Petrarch,

Sen., I, 4; F. Nelli, ep. XXIII; Sacchetti, canzone CLXXI); and it is contrasted sometimes with Certaldo, the origin and seat of the family (see *De Fluminibus,* ep. XXIV). And indeed it must have been in Certaldo that the boy received his first impressions of the Tuscan countryside, in the outings and in visits there with his father and other relatives. Perhaps he amused himself then hunting and collecting "mid barren hills rising almost midway between Corito [Fiesole] and the land of the foster-mother of *Romulo* [Siena]" (*Comedia,* XXIII, 25) and on the "little hill" the "marine snails" left there by the "vengeful waters of the just wrath of Jove" in such abundant quantities that "one cannot dig much or little in it [the hill] without finding some of those [fossil shells] shining white" (*Filocolo,* IV, 8, 1).[15]

"Pascua sunt nobis Cerreti montis in umbra" he sang also in the sixteenth eclogue, referring to the family farms; but as though alluding to the reasons for the emigration of the preceding generation he added:

> heu! sterili nimium, nullis frondentia lucis;
> nec salices capris surgunt, nec surgit ybiscus.
> Lambere muscosas silices rarumque vetustis
> immixtum conchis serpillum carpere cogit
> egra fames miseras; illis hinc squalida pellis,
> hinc macies tristisque color seteque cadentes
> Elsa brevis fluvius post his precordia saxum
> fecit, et attonitas vacuavit sanguine fibras.
>
> (*Bucc.,* XVI, 52 ff.)

Boccaccio spent his childhood in Florence, in the house in San Pier Maggiore. He was quickly claimed and legitimized by Boccaccino: "who had of his own free will, and gladly, nourished me as a son, and I had called him and do call him my parent" (*Amorosa Visione,* XIV, 42 ff.). Probably the legitimation had taken place before the wedding of Boccaccino and Margherita de' Mardoli, and before she bore him his son Francesco (towards 1320).[16]

The house of the Chelini was a prosperous and luxuriously appointed middle-class house, brightened by patriarchal customs and cheered by the financial and civic success of the head of the family. Indeed in those years Boccaccino pursued his career as a businessman and important citizen. We see him not only engaged in important contracts but, supported by the faith of his colleagues, he was called in the first half of 1322 and the second half of 1324 to be consul of the Arte del Cambio, finally reaching the high magistracy of the priors for a two-month term between December 15, 1322 and February 15, 1323.[17]

In this situation of economic prosperity and civic importance it was natural for the father to provide for a sound and useful education for Giovanni, beginning with his earliest years. Thus when he was six years old the boy already possessed the first elements of reading and writing ("satis memor sum, nondum ad septimus etatis annum deveneram . . . vix prima licterarum elementa cognoveram . . ." *Gen.,* XV, 10). As Filippo Villani recounts, he was entrusted to a good teacher, Giovanni di Domenico Mazzuoli da Strada, father of the more famous Zanobi, who (after having initially followed his father's profession) would later be both friend and competitor of Boccaccio for the favors of the Angevin court (". . . qui posita ferula qua ab incunabulis puellulos primum gramatice gradum temptantes cogere consuerat . . ." ep. XVIII). Together with the most elementary rules of Latin grammar, and some encouragement from the feared "ferula," the boys learned to spell from the children's psalm-book and, later—just like Florio and *Biancifiore* as children (*Filocolo,* I, 45, 6)[18]—from the texts of Ovid then most currently used for teaching. These provided the opportunity to learn something about mythology and Roman history (*Metamorphoses*). Perhaps Mazzuoli, attuned also to the first voices of literature in Italian, did not refrain from introducing Dante, whose fame was already widespread and assured in the last years of his life, and whose ideal presence was already dominant in Tuscan culture. It was a "presence," moreover, which the boy encountered in his own home: his stepmother was a relative of the family of Beatrice, and his stepmother's own mother, Lippa de' Mardoli, was in all probability the "trustworthy person who from very close blood relationship with her" talked at length to Boccaccio of Beatrice and of Dante himself.[19] It was not by mere chance that when writing to Petrarch in 1359 Boccaccio could affirm that Dante had been "primus studiorum dux et prima fax" (see *Fam.*, XXI, xv, 2). His first notions or first impressions of Dante go back to these very years. The tracings in the *Caccia* and in the *Filostrato,* in the scholastic exercises of the epistles of 1339 to the *Esposizioni,* and in the last sonnets were to be developed all through his life in a cult and veneration which would be at the bases of the passionate poetical and human credo of Boccaccio.

Alongside this grammatical and literary education his father, who was an expert merchant, aimed at consolidating the family business. As a result he very soon proposed to provide his son with an education which would train him to become an effective co-worker: "Satis enim memini apposuisse patrem meum a pueritia mea conatus omnes, ut negociator efficerer, meque adolescentiam nondum intrantem arismetrica instructum maxime mercatori dedit discipulum." *(Gen.,* XV, 10.) In accordance with the scholastic customs of the time, after having taken the courses of the trivium (which preceded mathematical education),[20] Boccaccio, still *puer* but close to *adolescentia,* presumably about eleven years old, was already "arismetrica instructus," that is to say, skilled in the art of reckoning ("calculis" is how Villani puts it); from then on there was practical apprenticeship in commercial activities and money matters, probably under the supervision of his father and uncle, and other relatives or associates.[21]

Boccaccio's change of domicile to Naples falls in this period of mercantile apprenticeship, at a date difficult to establish precisely.[22] It evidently came at the end of a whole series of contacts and business affairs which, increasing in importance, must have dotted the years immediately preceding. As we have previously mentioned, some years earlier Boccaccino had probably become an associate of the Bardi, the "company," which, together with the Peruzzi and the Acciaiuoli, had monopolized the financial affairs of the kingdom since 1312.[23] Perhaps because of relationships with the Angevin court, Boccaccino had to perform welcome services for King Robert's son, Carlo, Duke of Calabria, called in 1326 to assume the seigniory of Florence, for he was appointed by the latter to be one of the three councillors of the Ufficio di Mercanzia (March through May 1327; he had previously served in that capacity in January 1326).[24] In Carlo's retinue were Barbato da Sulmona and Giovanni

Barrili, who later became two of the most important and faithful friends of Boccaccio in his Neapolitan period and remained such throughout the rest of his life. It is not difficult to believe that these two illustrious persons of rank at the Angevin court, both cultivated and highly literate men (they were to popularize Petrarch's writings in Naples) [25] became acquainted with Boccaccino and his family during their sojourn in Florence, and perhaps admired the thirteen-year-old boy who even then was showing a powerful and inescapable inclination for literature. Those useful services to the duke and these relationships with influential personages of the Court were precisely the things which might have resulted in Boccaccino's appointment as representative of the Bardi in Naples, at first together with Bentivegna di Buonsostegno and later in his place.[26]

That was a particularly delicate period for the kingdom; it was threatened to the north by the coming of Ludwig the Bavarian, who—called by the "Ghibellines and tyrants of Tuscany and Lombardy" (Villani, X, 18)—in the summer and autumn of 1327 was preparing to set out from Pisa towards Rome and Naples; it was threatened in the south by Federico d'Aragona, a traditional enemy of the Angevins, who, from Sicily, was looking toward joining his forces with those of the emperor. The banking "trust" of Florence had to support the defensive and offensive effort of the king, the political and military head of that Guelf party of which Florence was the economic pillar. Needed, then, were able, shrewd representatives, well vouched-for and well accepted at Court, and experienced in affairs on the international plane. Boccaccino must have been such a man, whom we see between November 1327 and March 1331 drawing up noteworthy agreements of an economic (but also political and military) character, at first at the side of Bentivegna (until April 1328) and then alone as the responsible director of the Bardi firm in Naples.[27] His activity must have been esteemed by the "compagni," the partners who, a few months after his arrival, entrusted him with full supervision of the very important branch house and permitted him to make increasingly important engagements (up to hundreds of thousands of ounces of gold). Also he must have been highly regarded at court, for already by March 22, 1328 King Robert in an official document called him "familiaris et fidelis noster," and then on June 2

named him his counselor and chamberlain, "de nostro hospitio . . .
retinendum" (titles empty of substance, but signs of esteem and of
fondness, with which those Florentine merchants, in their middle-
class late-Gothic yearning for knightly insignia and decorations,
loved to decorate themselves and to boast).[28] Henceforth Boccaccino
had a stable and authoritative position at the Angevin court. Moreover, the Florentine seigniory pressed him, together with Acciaiolo
Acciaiuoli, to act as their intermediary with the King (April 12,
1329).[29]

Boccaccio must have reached Naples during the summer or fall
of 1327, at the time of his father's transfer.[30]

NOTES

1. And again in the *Filocolo,* with a prophetic gesture: "Honor this place
   [Certaldo] for from here will depart he whom thy happenings with
   memorable poetry will make known unto men, and his name will be
   filled with grace" (IV, 1, 13). Then in the *Decameron:* "Certaldo . . . is a
   castle in Val d'Elsa situated in our district, which, although small,
   formerly was inhabited by noble and wealthy men" (VI, 10, 5). Finally
   in the *De fluminibus:* "Elsa fluvius est Tuscie . . . et cum oppida plura, hic
   inde labens, videat, a dextro modico elatum tumulo Certaldum vetus
   castellum linquit: cuius ego libens memoriam celebro, sedes quippe et
   natale solum maiorum meorum fuit antequam illos susciperet Florentia
   cives" *(De Fluminibus,* Elsa).
2. Doc. cit. by D.M. Manni, *Istoria del Decameron,* Firenze, 1742, p. 10; and
   by A. Della Torre, *La giovinezza di G.B.,* Città di Castello, 1905, p. 8.
   Documents on the various Boccacci families are cited by V. Branca in
   Studi sul B., II, 1964.
3. In those years in fact we see the two brothers constantly associated in
   their various enterprises. For the second we shall use the less frequent
   and less certain form of the name, Boccaccino, only to avoid confusion
   with his famous son. A. Della Torre, pp. 10–12; V. Branca, *B. medievale,*
   Florence 1970[3], pp. 245 ff. V. Crescini, *Contributo agli studi sul B.,* Torino,
   1887, pp. 40 ff., supposes flatly a Chellini firm.
4. Doc. pub. by V. Branca, p. 246.
5. Doc. pub. by A. Della Torre, p. 11. It seems indeed that four years was
   the minimum period required to establish the fiscal domicile in the city

and in the quarters. The declaration therefore does not rule out the possibility that the two brothers had lived more than four years in Florence.

6. See the documents cited by E. Longnon, "La famille de Boccace," *Bull. Soc. Histoire de Paris,* 1878; by M. C. Piton, *Les Lombards en France,* Paris 1892; and then, with various additions, by H. Hauvette, "Pour la biographie de B," *Bull. It.* XI, 1911. O. Schultz-Gora, "B. vater ur-kundlich in Paris." *Z. Rom Phil.,* XLVII, 1927 determined the month. See the profile on Boccaccino Di Chelino by Z. Zafarana, *Dizionario biografico degli italiani* X. Naturally, since the name Boccaccio (and its derivatives) is not very unusual, the identity remains somewhat in doubt.

7. G. Billanovich, *Restauri Boccacceschi,* Rome, 1945, p. 43.

8. We find him associated with several persons for various enterprises of a certain importance (Della Torre, pp. 9 ff.). However, because we find him as a "socio" of the Bardi in 1327, it is probable that he was already in contact with that firm earlier.

9. The reasons for this greater Florentine probability are given in my report to the Primo Convegno di Studi Boccacciani; see *Misc. Stor. Valdelsa,* LXIX, 1963.

10. The date has recently been determined with exactitude by P. G. Ricci, "Studi sulle opere latine e volgari del B." *Rinascimento,* X, 1959; XIII, 1962.

11. The exact form of the name constantly used by him is, therefore, in vernacular "Giovanni di Boccaccio" and in Latin "Johannes Boccaccii" and even simply "Boccaccius."

12. I include the basic, original studies, omitting the host of lesser ones and the repetitions: G. B. Baldelli, *Vita di G.B.,* Florence, 1806; G. Körting, *B's Leben und Werke,* Leipzig, 1880; G. Körting, "B. Analekten." *Z. Rom. Phil.,* V, 1881; M. Landau, *G.B.,* Leipzig, 1880; A. Gaspary, *Geschichte der italienischen Literatur,* Berlin, 1885; V. Crescini, op. cit.; H. Cochin, *G.B.,* London, 1910; F. Torraca, *Per la biografia di G.B.,* Milan, 1912; H. Hauvette, *Boccace,* Paris, 1914; G. Lipparini, *La vita e le opere di G.B.,* Bologna, 1927; N. Sapegno, *Il Trecento,* Milan, 1934. The undoing of this romanticized biography was accomplished in these last few years and especially by V. Branca (ed. *Rime,* Bari, 1939; ed. *Amorosa Visione,* Florence, 1944; "Schemi letterari e schemi autobiografici nell'opera del B." *Bibliofilia,* LXIX, 1946) and by G. Billanovich (*Restauri boccacceschi,* Rome, 1945).

13. The mention of Paris is repeated in Domenico Bandini's close copy of

Villani, but it is ignored or even contradicted by all the other earliest biographers, who place Boccaccio's birthplace in Tuscan territory, in Florence or Certaldo. The early biographies have been diligently collected by A.F. Massera, "Le più antiche biografie del B." *Z. Rom. Phil.*, XXVII, 1903 and again by A. Solerti, *Le vite di Dante Petrarca Boccaccio scritte fino al secolo decimosettimo* (undated, but 1905).

14. Perhaps because she died very early or was of very humble origin? Certainly she was not married because the pontifical dispensation (see p. 119) speaks of Boccaccio as being "de soluto genitus et soluta."

15. And on a more learned and exact plane in the *De Fluminibus,* loc. cit. "Multas preterea et diversarum specierum maritimarum tamen omnium radens cursu solum detegit [Elsa fluvius] concas vacuas et vetustate candidas, atque ut plurimum aut fractas aut semesas. Quas ego arbitror diluvium illud ingens, quo genus humanum fere deletum, dum agitatu aquarum magno terras circumvolveret fundo, illis reliquit in partibus." See also *Filocolo,* III, 33, 11; *Bucc.*, XVI, 55 ff.; *Gen.* proemio 7; *Esposizioni,* XIV, 1, 19.

16. On August 21, 1333 Boccaccino freed his son Francesco of subjection to him as a father, "maiorem decennio et proximum pubertati" (doc. in Della Torre, pp. 24-25): he must then have been about thirteen years old. His marriage with Margherita then must have taken place before 1320. Margherita is mentioned later in documents of 1336 or 1337 as Boccaccino's wife (Della Torre, pp. 306 ff.).

17. In May 1324 he was also one of the "adjuncti pro arte cambii" for the election of five councillors of the Mercanzia. Documents published or republished by R. Davidsohn, *Forschungen zur Geschichte von Florenz,* Berlin, 1901, III p. 253 and by Della Torre, pp. 9-15.

18. "dum puer Johanne Magistro, Zenobii poete, non plene gramaticam didicisset . . ." (Solerti, *Vite cit.*, p. 672).

19. M., Barbi, *Problemi di critica dantesca,* Florence, 1941, II, pp. 415 ff. The quotation is from the *Esposizioni,* II, 1, 83.

20. Petrarch, for example, spent four years after reading, to learn grammar, dialectics, rhetoric (*Posteritati, Sen.*, X, 2; XVI, 1).

21. It seems to me vain and useless to argue about the identity of the "maximus mercator": evidently a vague and generic indication.

22. In 1327, on March 27, Boccaccino figures as a witness in an act (doc. published and discussed by E. Carrara and V. Crescini in the *Rassegna bibliografica della lett. it.* I, 1893, p. 245); then a document shows him already in Naples on November 30 (Davidsohn, *Forschungen*, III, p. 181). According to a document cited by Torraca as a résumé of

Davidsohn, but which I have been unable to identify, Boccaccino appeared in Florence on September 1. Concerning the sale of the house see the documents cited by Gherardi in the "illustration" published by F. Corazzini, *Le lettere edite e inedite di Messer Giovanni Boccaccio,* Florence, 1877, pp. IC ff.

23. See documents in Davidsohn, op. cit., p. 123; G. Yver, *Le Commerce et les marchands dans l'Italie méridionale au XIII et au XIV siècle,* Paris, 1903, pp. 305 ff.; A. Sapori, *Studi di storia economica,* Florence, 1955, p. 689.

24. Documents cited by F. Torraca, "G.B. a Napoli." *Arch. Stor. Prov. Nap.,* XXXIX, 1915, p. 3; and by Davidsohn, *Forschungen,* III, pp. 172, 181, 184 (for more bonds with Carlo in 1328).

25. F. Torraca, art. cit., p. 34; N. Faraglia, *I miei studi storici sulle cose abruzzesi,* Lanciano, 1893, p. 107.

26. F. Torraca, *art. cit.,* pp. 3 and 13; Davidsohn, *Forschungen,* III, p. 174. Sapori, op. cit., p. 735, has drawn from the documents of the Company of the Bardi the information on the appointment on October 12, 1327 with a salary of lbr. 145. Bentivegna had been the chief agent of the Bardi from 1306 to 1315; then, sent to Florence by Robert on his business, he reappears in Naples in March 1326.

27. See doc. cit. by Torraca, pp. 4-8. And see R. Caggese, *Roberto d'Angiò e i suoi tempi,* Florence, 1922-1931, I, p. 128.

28. Documents cited by Davidsohn, *Forschungen,* III, pp. 151, 167, 5 for other merchants; 182, 184, 187 for Boccaccino: on February 4, 1329 "consiliarius, cambellanus, mercator, familiaris et fidelis."

29. Doc. cit. by Davidsohn, "Il padre di G.B." *Arch. Stor. It.,* S. V, xxiii, 1899, p. 144.

30. It is the only hypothesis possible and credible, in the absence of any precise document or memoir in this connection, and in the absolute inconsistency of the dates proposed in the past even by the most earnest scholars, musing in one way or another on the romance of love composed of the various fragments of the biographies of Idalogo, of Caleone and of Ibrida: Körting and Crescini decided on the end of 1329; Della Torre: December 1323; Hauvette: December 1328; Torraca and Sapegno: end of 1325; Massera: December 1327; Villani still more absurdly gives 1338 in the first edition, and 1341 in the second.

CHAPTER 2

Adolescence in Naples
and Social and Mercantile
Experiences (1327-1341)

Boccaccio must have traveled from Florence to Naples along one of the routes customarily followed by the merchants, who made the trip in about fifteen days *(Fiammetta, V, 2, 7)*. These routes passed through Siena, Perugia, Rieti, Aquila, Sulmona, Isernia, Teano and Capua, or went by way of Siena, Rome, the forest of Aglio, "silva latrociniis incolarum accomoda *(De Silvis:* it is the one in V, 2 of the *Decameron)*, Cassino, and Gaeta.[1] Boccaccio had crossed the Tiber with its many "gentle waves," the Volturno which drags the stones along in its rapid current, "the few waves which, between Falerno and Vesevo, wearily reach the sea," and finally the Sebeto, "brook rather than river, nameless"; he had crossed the pleasant hills of Siena, the wild and cold Alpine mountains of Abruzzi or of the Ciociaria region, the forests of Sabina, the vast fertile lands of Campania. And so he had come, between "Falerno covered with vineyards producing excellent wine" and Vesevo [Vesuvius] "everywhere abounding in vineyards and orchards" at last to the "never before beheld streets" of Naples, which "with delight won his heart."[2]

Perhaps the Boccacci went to live, at least in the beginning, in

16

the *fondaco* of the Florentines ("in quo Florentini consueti sunt hospitari") [3] it was not far from the "Laurentii sacram edem" (ep. XVIII), that is, from that "pleasant and beautiful temple" of San Lorenzo, noteworthy for the preference of the Angevins and the solicitude of the Franciscans. It was there that, according to an illustrious tradition, confirmed, for the vernacular, by Dante and Petrarch, right on a holy sabbath "there appeared to his eyes the marvelous beauty" of the mythical Fiammetta (*Filocolo*, I, 1, 18).

But the life of the young man during these years—of which there is no precise record in reliable documents—was spent in another quarter, in the neighborhood of the Castel Nuovo then recently finished; that is, in the region of Portanova where, between the walls and the breakwater, warehouses, banks and merchants' offices were crowded together. Among them, in the "Ruga Cambiorum," "juxta Petra Piscium," was the Neapolitan office of the Bardi firm (next to that of the Frescobaldi), previously allotted to the company, without charge, by Carlo II as a token of gratitude.[4] That was the very place where Boccaccio, barely adolescent, spent the days of his long and apparently fruitless apprenticeship in banking and merchandising, between approximately the ages of fourteen and eighteen : that is, almost to the age when—by the rules of the Arte del Cambio—one could become an active "cambiatore" (money-changer) with an independent "tavola" (changer's table) of one's own, whereas before they became nineteen only those who, like Giovanni, were working with a father, uncle, or brother, could engage in the "arte del cambio." [5]

Like the other young "apprentices" or co-workers, Boccaccio stayed at the bank, greeted and directed the customers, weighed and exchanged the various gold, silver, and copper coins he received, and—after having carefully checked—paid letters of credit and bills of exchange. Already well educated in literature and accounting, he took care of the heterogeneous correspondence, or, as an "*arismetrica instructus*," he managed the "exchequer" and kept the registers of accounts ("ragione"), of property and other wealth possessed ("asse"), of cash ("cassa"), drafts ("tratte"), purchases ("compre"), and sales ("vendite"); he prepared audits and final balance sheets for the use of the partners in the settling of accounts ("saldamento della ragione"). Certainly he also went out often on various errands, especially in the commercial and port zone, towards Sant' Angelo a Baiano ("the holy temple named by the prince of the heavenly birds," where he was to imagine a meeting with Fiammetta and her request to narrate the story of Florio and Biancifiore: see *Filocolo*, I, 1, 23). Or perhaps he headed toward the Castel Nuovo, where he would pass right through that Rua Catalana and in front of that Malpertugio, which would later become the delirious background of the picaresque novella of Andreuccio of Perugia. He certainly went often to the port, to the warehouse, or the customs to take note "of all the merchandise (and of the price of it)" deposited and registered by some merchants who had asked the bank for exchanges, barter, or sales. On these errands he would come in contact with customs officers, with ships' masters, with brokers and middlemen, and even with "women very beautiful of body but enemies to honesty," astute deceivers ("pettin-atrici": hairdressers!) of inexperienced young men like Niccolò da Cignano (a contemporary of Boccaccio who, with an authentic friend, Pietro Canigiani, was to become in the *Decameron* the prota-gonist of the novella VIII, 10).

This singular close-up of mercantile proceedings and dealings was scrutinized day after day through the loupe of a youth who had to weigh and evaluate coins and letters and men in order to close each transaction scrupulously, to make each entry properly; he was in ever new contact with people from the most diverse countries of Occident and Orient, who gathered in the warehouse not only to discuss business but to await mail and news coming from a variety of European, Asiatic, and African markets, which they compared and expounded. Here the bright visions and fabulous echoes of the economic saga of Florence and all Italy, gleaned from the conversa-tions of friends and relatives, became strengthened and humanly real in the run of the day's work; strengthened, that is, by a feeling of their truth and reality, which little by little became clear and strong in the imagination and mind of the youth who was to be the impassioned extoller of those knights-errant of commerce. And those very exper-iences in the animated quarter of Portanova, the daily contacts with businessmen both petty and great, with honest and with faithless

moneychangers, with adventurous seamen and with port adventurers, with substantial citizens and with capricious Neapolitan
commoners, with women, both homebodies and seductive women of
easy virtue (as were Fiordaliso and Jancofiore, *Decameron,* II, 5, and
VIII, 10), surely aroused in Boccaccio that penetrating humane spirit
requisite to a great storyteller. And they gave him that knowledge of,
and taste for, characters of the most varied social strata from the most
diverse Mediterranean countries, from Catalonia to the Levant,
which in Naples had one of their great political centers and great
commercial emporiums.

Beyond that training in the Bardi bank (and perhaps, also in the
Frescobaldi company nearby, and that of his friends, the
Acciaiuoli),[6] for Boccaccio life in Naples opened other horizons and
experiences. He was not just another learner, an ordinary apprentice,
the illegitimate but promptly acknowledged son of a partner of the
Bardi company who, after having reached the highest offices in the
Florentine commune, was one of the arbitrators of the finances of the
Angevin court.

> I have lived [he could write, thinking back on those years] from
> my childhood to man's estate, nourished in Naples and amongst
> noble youths of my own age who, although noblemen, were not
> ashamed to enter my house nor to visit me. They saw me . . .
> living in a very refined way, the way we Florentines live; in
> addition they saw my house, its furnishings and fittings, very
> splendid, within the measure of my means. Many of these friends
> are still living, and having grown old along with me, they have
> attained dignity and high office (ep. XII).

The portrayal of this existence and of these courtly customs,
prompted and spurred by association with the best mercantile and
court society, grows broader in the shining frescoes in which he lives
over again the joyous life of the Neapolitan nobility and bourgeoisie.
Boccaccio witnessed the contrasts between the aristocratic urban
opulence, adorned by gallant festivities and recreations, and the
care-free and voluptuous leisure of the countryside and the seashores

of the Neapolitan gulf. Certain pages of the *Filocolo,* the *Comedia,* and the *Fiammetta* convey the immediacy of an experience lived with deep feeling.

Our city, more than all other Italian cities, abounding in gladsome festivities, not only causes its citizens to rejoice with nuptials or with baths or with the seashore but, open-handed with many amusements, often gladdens its inhabitants with an alternation of these. But among the many things in which she makes a splendid show, there are the frequent jousts and tournaments. This is an old custom of ours, that when the rainy time of winter has gone by and the spring with its flowers and new grass has given back to the world its lost beauties, the youthful spirits stimulated with all this and more than customarily eager to show their desires, summon on the finest days to the loggias of the knights the noble ladies who, adorned with their most precious jewels, gather there. Nor, I think, was it a more rich or noble spectacle to look upon the wives of Priam's son gathered with the other Phrygian women, than it is to behold in several places in our city those fair ladies, its citizens. When they are seen as in great numbers they flock to the theaters, each of them showing her beauty in its highest degree perfected, I doubt it not that any foreign connoisseur who might appear, viewing the proud countenances, the splendid costumes, ornaments royal, rather than fitting for ordinary women, would deem us to be, not moderns, but some of those magnificent women of old come back upon the earth. . . . There, . . . there are no long periods of idle sitting, no voices silent or barely audible, but, while their elders stand watching, the illustrious youths, holding their ladies by their delicate hands as they dance, sing aloud their love. When the gay group had shown themselves to the onlookers as their mounts caracoled around the lists with short, prancing steps, the tilts began: erect in the stirrups, protected beneath their shields and holding their light lances so that the tips almost grazed the ground, they spurred their steeds to run faster than the wind; the air, resounding with the voices of the spectators, with the many harness-bells, with the many musical instruments, with the shock of the clanging armor of horses and riders, urged them on to still greater speed. And as the watchers saw them thus, not once but many times, right worthily they made themselves laudable in the hearts of the beholders (*Fiammetta,* V, 27, 1-6 and 9; V, 29, 1-3).

Tournaments were introduced by Charles d'Anjou and continued—especially at Carbonara and at Le Corregge near Castel Nuovo—by his successors, who surrounded themselves with feudal courts of a military nature, in the aristocratic and warlike custom of France.[7]

While such spectacles prompted those gallant nostalgias in the late-Gothic taste, which endured so long in the Florentine middle class and in Boccaccio the writer himself, the gay life of a refined society found softer and more Epicurean rhythms in sojourns along the delightful Parthenopean shores.

. . . A little way beyond pleasant Mount Falerno, between ancient Cumae and Pozzuoli, one comes to delightful Le Baie above the beaches, than which there are no places more pleasant 'neath the heavens. . . . Here the most leisure hours are spent, and when more actively inclined, the ladies engage in amorous discussion, among themselves or in the company of the young men; here only the choicest viands are served, and wines nobly aged, powerful not only to awaken sleeping Venus but to resuscitate her, if dead, in any man; how much greater still, in that regard, are the properties of the various baths, only one who has tried them can know. Here the beaches, and the pleasant gardens, and all these places resound continually with many festivities, with new games, with most graceful dances, with an infinity of musical instruments, with songs of love, some played by young men or sung, some by fair ladies. . . . As the weather was very warm, in keeping with the season, many other ladies, and I myself, in order to bear it as comfortably as possible, ploughing the waters of the sea aboard a swift many-oared bark, singing and playing sought out the further reefs, and the caverns in the cliffs fashioned by nature herself, as being the most enjoyable retreats with their shade and the seabreezes ... now here, now there, now this group of ladies and youths, now that other, we went seeking any little reef or beach which offered the shade cast by the heights which intercepted the sun's rays. ... There were to be seen in many places the tables set with snowy linen and such beautiful decorations that the mere sight of them was enough to awaken appetite in anyone who till then had been disinclined toward feasting; elsewhere, as befitted the hour, might be discerned those who were gayly partaking of the matutinal dishes, by whom we and any others who were passing were invited with cheery voices to share their pleasures. But after we ourselves, like the others, had festively eaten, the tables were cleared away and we danced several joyous dances, in the customary style; then, going aboard the boats once more, we went swiftly now here, now there, and in some places something delightful in the eyes of the youths appeared: charming girls, their jackets of sendal removed, barefoot and bare armed, went into the water and pulled sea shells from the hard rocks, and as in so doing they bent over and often revealed the hidden delights of their ample bosom; in other places other girls, with more ingenuity, were seen fishing with nets for the hidden fishes, while others used more modern means ... so now the bosom of that sea was as full of boats, here, there and everywhere, as the sky is full of stars when it appears most pellucid and serene (*Fiammetta*, V, 16, 2; 17, 4-5; 26, 2-9, 13 and see·*Filocolo*, V, 5, 1-2; *Rime*, III, IV, V, VI, VII, VIII).

It is a fanciful society gossip column raised for the first time to the dignity of literature, and which is reflected in the erotic processions of ladies of the Court and of beauties of the middle class, conventionalized in fabled huntresses (*Caccia di Diana*), in the aristocratic and gallant pastimes which in the *Filostrato* turn Troy into a fourteenth-century Naples, in the polite transfigurations of sentimental and intellectualistic conversations in the gardens of Mergellina (*Filocolo*), in the elegant arabesques of feminine coquetry and amorous thrust and parry designed in the Neapolitan *Rime*, and in the varied and impassioned gallant and erotic adventures which dot the early works of this writer "with body brought forth by heaven most appropriate for love" and "from his childhood" with heart "inclined to love" *(Decameron,* IV, Intr. 32).

In this gay and refined society Boccaccio, always athirst for affection, was to form some friendships which would endure throughout his lifetime: with young men, like the pleasure-loving Niccolò da Montefalcone, who later became a Carthusian monk (ep. XV); like Piero Canigiani, a shrewd merchant and businessman in the service of the princes of Taranto, and who was named in the *testamento* as one of the guardians of the heirs (Lett. I; *Decameron,* VIII, 10); like Niccolò da Cignano, representative of the Frescobaldi and then chief of the Arte del Cambio *(Decameron,* VIII, 10); and like Americo Cavalcanti,[8] already in 1334 chamberlain of King Robert, whose younger brother aided Boccaccio himself in his old age (ep. XX and ep. XXI). There were also friendships with older men, like Marino Bolgaro, experienced seadog from Ischia, or Costantino di Rocca, treasurer and intermediary of military loans; these two, in their storytelling, acquainted Boccaccio with the gossip of the Court and of Neapolitan high society *(De Casibus,* IX, 26; *Decameron,* V, 6).[9] And it was in just those years and in the surroundings where he was most at home that he became closely associated with Niccolò Acciaiuoli, the man who for the rest of his life embodied the sharpest contradictions, of loves and enthusiasms, of bitterness and rebukes. They had perhaps met, as boys, at the school of Giovanni da Strada in Florence, and now they were working in Naples for two closely connected Florentine companies, in which we see their respective fathers in friendly cooperation (p. 15, note 29). But they both had gifts and ambitions which made them look beyond the routine of commerce ("Niccola was . . . very handsome, and although unlettered, he was a marvelously fluent man . . . and in the city of Naples . . . he kept a shop, not full of trash but of valuable merchandise brought from many places, and he was planning to do much business" writes Filippo Villani.)[10] Niccolò, three years older than Boccaccio, had arrived in Naples in 1331, "a merchant . . . satisfied with a single servant" (ep. XII), but by 1333 he was the polished counselor and supplier of elegant articles for the chamber of Andrea and Joanna, the young royal couple.[11] By 1334 he was the trusted confidential adviser of Catherine de Valois Courtenay, empress of Constantinople and sister-in-law of Robert, and in 1335, as the king's chamberlain, Niccolò was able to obtain for his father the title of royal vicar and the sovereignty of Prato, and for himself an appointment as "cavaliere" (knight).[12] So, at the age of twenty-five, this lively Florentine merchant had realized his dreams of nobility and was at the center of activity at the Angevin court as the teacher of Louis, son of the empress and future king of Naples, and as "familiar and counselor," administrator general, and seneschal of Catherine. Indeed henceforth Niccolò held the keys to Catherine's heart. ("It was said openly that [Catherine] included messer Niccola Acciaiuoli among her other lovers . . . and made him rich and powerful." So wrote G. Villani, XII, 75, and so also Boccaccio in *Bucc.,* VIII.) Boccacio himself attributed to Niccolò "all the goods and honors which I have received in this world." [13]

Thanks to the constant relations of his father with the Bardi and probably his own relations with Acciaiuoli (and perhaps with Canigiani), young Boccaccio frequented the Angevin court and the Neapolitan aristocracy ("Ne adhuc adulescentulo versanteque Roberti Jerusalem et Siciliae regis in aula. . . ." *De Casibus,* IX, 26). He knew "the customs of the courtiers and their life," but he judged them such that they should not be "followed and observed" (ep. XII). In those circles he encountered the Gran Camerario (first valet de chambre), Don Diego della Ratta, whose sordid avarice is mocked in the *Decameron* (VI, 3); Raimondo and Filippa di Cabanni and their sons, whose incredible rise and precipitous and tragic end is narrated in the *De Casibus* (IX, 26); the Infante Ferdinando, nephew of the king and son of the Princess of Cyprus, whose aspirations to the throne of Majorca he would mention in the *Amorosa Visione* (XLIV, 1-6); Giacomo di Sanseverino, who told him about the retarded intelligence of King Robert as a boy (*Gen.,* XIV, 9); the Coppola, the Barras, the Sighinolfi, the nobles with close business relations with the Bardi (*Caccia,* I, 40; X, 5 and 19); many other important people named in his pages, and all those splendid and bejewelled ladies painted in miniature in the country backgrounds and the legendary formal gardens of the *Caccia,* the *Ternario,* the *Amorosa Visione.*[14] Probably,

Boccaccio also had entrée to the houses of the four heirs presumptive to the throne, "the honorable princes of our Ausonian kingdom . . . whose very tender youth, beguiling handsomeness, and foreseeable virtue . . . made them extremely gracious to all who saw them" (*Fiammetta*, V, 27, 10 and 14).[15]

Even the palace of King Robert very likely was not closed to him. He speaks of the two princesses Joanna and Maria continually and with a kind of gallant familiarity (at least in the *Amorosa Visione*, XLIX and thereafter),[16] and comments on the austere virtue of the pious Queen Sancia *(De Casibus*, IX, 26). But the personage of whom Boccaccio speaks continually from personal impressions is King Robert. From the *Filocolo* to the *Genealogia*, he praises the "lofty prince" who "with the aid of Pallas" kept "these lands in peace" like an earthly paradise *(Filocolo*, I, 1, 14; *Fiammetta*, II, 6, 21; see *Bucc.*, III). He portrays in a graphic manner the king's avarice and greed (*Comedia*, XXXV, 31; *Amorosa Visione.*, XIV, 26 ff.); he shows his valiant efforts in studies *(Gen.*, XIV, 9) and finally, his late conversion to literature *(Gen.*, XIV, 22). As a frequenter of the Court, Boccaccio could admire the noble-mindedness of the king at the death of the prince (September 9, 1328) ("it is magnaminous to bear with even countenance and heart whatever comes"). The sovereign bore the loss of his beloved only son "with unmoved face and words and mind," and "on that very day he attended to the affairs of the kingdom, heard and judged quarrels, dispensed law and order for every need" (ep. XII, p. 169; see *Sen.*, X, 4).

NOTES

1. See Della Torre, p. 102; C. Coulter, "The Road to Alagna" in *Philological Quarterly*, XVIII, 1939; C. Coulter, "A Supplementary Note on the Road to Alagna," ibid., XX, 1941.

2. Impressions, these, of that first journey in which are reflected the descriptions of the displacements between Tuscany and Naples of the heroes of his first romance, *Filocolo* (IV, 1; V, 32), and also of those of the *Comedia* (XXXV, 9, 13, and 73); they recur, interwoven with the impressions of like routes traversed when he was a grown man, in the learned geographical work *De Monitibus, Ad Voces*.

3. Davidsohn, *Forschungen,* II, p. 306.
4. M. Camera, *Annali delle due Sicilie,* Naples [1841-1860], II, p. 77; G. de Blasiis, "La dimora di G.B. a Napoli." *Arch. Stor. Prov. Nap.,* XVII, 1892, p. 93.
5. See *Statuti dell'arte del cambio,* Florence, 1955.
6. It was an accepted custom for the "discepoli" to serve some time also in the other "companies," friendly to, but different from, their regular employments; while the Frescobaldi were located near the Baldi, the Acciaiuoli not only were associated with the Bardi, but Acciaiuoli often appears as an associate of Boccaccino (see docc. citt. on p. 15.)
7. In the first five months of 1337, King Robert engaged six times in tournaments, "equitavit ad justras"; Petrarch, also, describes with amazement a joust of 1343, in which "aderant omnis neapolitana militia, qua nulla comptior, nulla decentior" *Fam,* V, vi; and see Camera, op. cit., p. 507.
8. Torraca, art. cit., p. 146.
9. Torraca, art. cit., pp. 26 ff.
10. F. Villani, *Vite di illustri fiorentini* (in Italian), Trieste, 1858, pp. 452 ff.
11. Doc. cit. by E. G. Léonard, *Histoire de Jeanne Ire,* Paris, 1932, I, p. 150.
12. Documents cited by Torraca, art. cit., pp. 121 ff., and by E. G. Léonard, *Boccace et Naples,* Paris, 1944, pp. 14 ff.
13. It is a phrase in a letter of March 29, 1347: see Léonard, *B. et Naples,* p. 17.
14. For identification of the women of the *Caccia* see V. Branca, *Tradizione delle opere di G.B.,* Rome, 1958, pp. 168 ff.; for those of the *Ternario,* see G. Boccaccio, *Rime,* edited by V. Branca, Padua, 1958, pp. 68 ff.; for those of the *Amorosa Visione,* see *G.B., Amorosa Visione,* critical edition by V. Branca, Florence, 1944, *passim.*
15. Thanks especially to Acciaiuoli, he was at liberty to frequent the Palace of the Princes of Taranto, Roberto and Luigi, where Catherine was dominant; thanks to the goodwill of the other sister-in-law of the king, Agnès de Périgord, hyperbolically extolled in the *Amorosa Visione* ("who for her beauty may be called Phoenix" XLI, 21), he was also admitted to the Hospice of Durazzo (Ospizio durazzesco), near Castelnuovo, where Carlo, the eldest son of the king, was already a power: Carlo, to whom Boccacio seems to address, at least in idea, his first very literate epistle ("Missa duci Duracchii") and to whom, after his tragic end, he composed a deeply felt, plaintive ballad, a final

confirmation of his enduring regard for the Durazzo branch (*Bucc.* IV,
71 ff.). In general, see Torraca, op. cit., p. 158 and art. cit., pp. 128 ff.

16. Certainly not in the *Filocolo,* in which Crescini claimed to see them in
the anagrams of very common names, *Annavói* and *Ariam,* and in which
work he supposed them to represent emblematically the "voluptuous
women": Giovanna and Maria were aged respectively seven and four
years old at the time in which Crescini deemed the *Filocolo* to have
been composed (1334).

CHAPTER 3

Cultural and Artistic Milieu of Naples and His Formation as a Writer (1327-1341)

While Boccaccio was greatly indebted to Acciaiuoli for his aristocratic and courtly experiences, it may be that the example and the successes of his friend in some way served to spur him to gild with fabled splendors his own birth, his own youth, and his own first impassioned experiences of love. The shadow of illegitimacy cast itself on the origins of Niccolò as well as Boccaccio. (The elder Acciaiuoli was an illegitimate son,[1] but Acciaiuoli reacted by aspiring to draw "his generation from the gods of Phrygia" (ep. XIII, 171), and by talking about his Trojan descent, which he inferred from the use of the name of Dardano in his family.) With a similar genealogical snobism, Boccaccio, weaving in those very years the fine fable of his royal birth, claimed to be descended, through his unknown mother, from the kings of France and thus to trace his lineage back to Hector and Dardanus *(Filocolo,* V, 8, 2; also see *Gen.*, VI, 24, *De Mulieribus,* CIII; also *Comedia,* XXIII, 21 ff.). His admired companion had later been raised from his mercantile station, and Boccaccio—as though in imagination he were taking revenge on reality—in his turn enjoyed portraying himself, through easily understood allusions as the one chosen by the love of a daughter of King Robert. The pretty romance is thus made credible for the example of Acciaiuoli and at the same time is emphatically like a fairy tale: the son of the daring and illegitimate union between a woman of the loyal line of Dardanus and a youth, humble but endowed with great qualities, is chosen and redeemed by another descendant of Dardanus, the daughter of a king. It is the ever-evocative fable of the unknown bastard recognized and restored by a princess' love to the rank rightfully his; the beautiful fable, that is, of Florio and Biancifiore which is precisely the one that the royal beloved asks her devoted lover to narrate to her (*Filocolo,* I, 1, 25ff.).

On these sentimental evocations and on the indications of a sound cultural tradition—which had come down from the model Ovidian presentations into the Latin and vernacular literature and treatise writing on love—in that courtly and knightly circle Boccaccio stylized his impassioned amorous experiences by creating the fascinating myth of Fiammetta (it is the mark which points to a certain Maria d'Aquino, an illegitimate daughter of King Robert: *Filocolo,* I, 1, 15—16; *Comedia,* XXXV; *Amorosa Visione,* XLIII, 37-63). But aside from the absence of any indication or reference to so illustrious a personage in the most exact genealogies and in the many documents of the Aquino family, the seductive profile of Fiammetta has revealed itself to be entirely fictitious and constructed according to the most common canons of the love literature of the time, canons which scrupulously dictate the details and the chronology of the story of love set down by Boccaccio for himself and for his Fiammetta (who, in harmony with those traditions, must remain ever young; so that in the *Filocolo* she was born in 1310, in the *Comedia* after 1313, in the *Decameron* after 1321). Freed from the sentimental picture painted by romantic and positivistic biographers according to the usual realistic-bourgeois romance of adultery,[2] Fiammetta, one of the most fascinating figures of Italian literature, has now finally been restored to the purity and power of a shining creature of the imagination, in which a great artist combined and sublimated his various and impassioned experiences of youthful love.

For Boccaccio, while he was living with intensity that mercantile life in Naples, was also engaged in discovering and defining, resolutely, an inner reality most peculiarly his own, the reality which little by little was to develop within him the vocation drawn "ex utero matris." While recalling his boyhood and his youth, in the last part of his magnificent defense of poetry, Boccaccio would write a page delightful in its happy emotion and its modest nostalgia for a time never to be regained:

Verum as quoscunque actus natura produxerit alios, me quidem experientia teste ad poeticas meditationes dispositum ex utero matris eduxit et meo iudicio in hoc natus sum. Satis enim memini apposuisse patrem meum a pueritia mea conatus omnes, ut negociator efficerer, meque, adolescentiam non dum intrantes, arismetrica instructum maximo mercatori dedit discipulum, quem penes sex annis nil aliud egi, quam non recuperabile tempus in vacuum tenere. Hinc quoniam visum est, aliquibus estendentibus indiciis, me aptiorem fore licterarum studiis, iussit genitor idem ut pontificum sanctiones, dives exinde futurus, auditurus intrarem, et sub preceptore clarissimo fere tantundem temporis in cassum etiam laboravi. Fastidiebat hoc animus adeo, ut in neutrum horum officiorum, aut preceptoris doctrina, aut genitoris autoritate, qua novis mandatis angebar continue, aut amicorum precibus seu obiurgationibus inclinari posset, in tantum illum ad poeticam singularis traebat affectio! Nec ex novo sumpto consilio in poesim animus totis tendebat pedibus, quin imo a vetutissima dispositone ibat impulsus. Nam satis memor sum, non dum ad septimum etatis annum deveneram, nec dum fictiones videram, non dum doctores aliquos audiveram, vix prima licterarum elementa cognoveram, et ecce, ipsa impellente natura, fingendi desiderium affuit, et si nullius essent momenti, tamen aliquas fictiundulas edidi, non enim suppetebant tenelle tati officio tanto viris ingenii. Attamen iam fere maturus etate et mei iuris factus, nemine impellente, nemine docente, imo obsistente patre et studium tale damnante, quod modicum novi poetice, sua sponte sumpsit ingenium, eamque summa aviditate secutus sum, et precipua cum delectatione autorum eiusdem libros vidi legique, et, uti potui, intelligere conatus sum. Et mirabile dictu, cum nondum novissem, quibus seu quot pedibus carmen incederet, me etiam pro viribus renitente, quod non dum sum, poeta fere a notis omnibus vocatus fui. Nec dubito, dum etas in hoc aptior erat, si equo genitor tulisset animo, quin inter celebres poetas unus avasissem, verum dum in lucrosas artes primo, inde in lucrosam facultatem ingenium flectere conatur meum, factum est, ut nec negociator sim, nec evaderem canonista, et perderem poetam esse conspicuum (*Gen.*, XV, 10; also see *Corbaccio* 191: "The studies, therefore, appropriate to sacred *philosophia*, were dearer to you from childhood than your father would have liked, and especially in that part which is in the domain of poetry, in which perhaps you have engaged with more enthusiasm of the mind than loftiness of genius").

What stands out clearly, in this deep-felt remembrance, are his early Florentine education ("Nam . . . viris ingenii"), the commercial apprenticeship begun in Florence and continued surely in a more compelling way in Naples from his fourteenth to his eighteenth year approximately ("Satis . . . vacuum tenere"), and finally the five or six years devoted to the study of canon law ("Hic . . . laboravi") with that repugnance and hostility which are patent in a clearly autobiographical page on the *De Casibus* (III, 10). But what is most striking and interesting is the declaration, humble yet peremptory, of his destiny for poetry ("in hoc natus sum"), a destiny which had already been manifest in the years of the poor little school of Mazzuoli, which had persisted in secret in the years—"never to be regained"—wasted in the mercantile novitiate, and which becomes more and more urgent in the years of the juridical studies "in tantum illum [animum] ad poeticam singularis trahebat affectio." Just then, indeed, "iam fere maturus etate et mei iuris factus"—that is to say, after his eighteenth year,[3] while his father was setting him to the study of canon law, Boccaccio, renewing his proficiency in Latin as a necessity for that study, was already devoting himself to the study of poetry "rather more than . . . his father would have liked"; and perhaps he did this all the more freely after Boccaccino left Naples in 1332, to go to Paris for a stay presumably of no short duration.[4]

The Studio Napoletano (university) was renowned in those days for its famous jurists and canonists (for example Lorenzo di Ravello,

Giovanni di Lando, Nicola Rufolo, Giovanni Grillo, Niccolò Alunno, and so on, and perhaps already Pietro Piccolo da Monteforte. Boccaccio certainly alluded to them with the generic phrase "sub preceptore clarissimo," so similar to the preceding expression "maximo mercatori," and for which it is idle to seek any precise identification).[5] But the most celebrated of them all, Cino da Pistoia, was surely the one who exercised on his young Tuscan compatriot a decisive attraction and influence. He was a professor at the Studio Napoletano in 1330 and 1331, constantly quarreling with the canonists and lawyers and their aridity (see ep. IV and *De Casibus,* III, 10), standardbearer of the new poetry, a friend of Dante and of Petrarch. As such he must have appeared as example and lofty guide to Boccaccio,[6] who therefore wanted to studiously note his lessons.[7] Thus in the very bosom of the Studio Napoletano he found a living testimony to that cult of poetry which was growing ever stronger in his soul. Of that fortunate encounter and its subsequent enthusiasms and readings, Boccaccio wanted to leave a record, a sort of emotional commemoration, in the Cino-inspired traceries with which he decorated his very first writings, his earliest poems (*Rime,* XVI, XLVI, LXXI), and the *Filostrato (*V, 62-65). This admiration for Cino is also apparent in the loving care with which he transcribed Dante's great letter to Cino which, as an ardent and impulsive neophyte, he imitated soon afterwards in his own first, very rhetorical epistle.[8] Boccaccio, an attentive reader of the *De Vulgari Eloquentia* (see below, pages 46 and 48), saw in Cino, by the inferences of that very text, the living emblem of great Tuscan poetry, the "amicus," the "other poet" alongside Dante, as he would consecrate him later in the deeply felt apotheosis of his last sonnet (CXXVI: see below, pp. 188-189). And it must have been Cino who confirmed him in the habit of meditative reading and in the cult of the poet of the *Divina Commedia,* strengthening his early boyish impressions in Florence. Leaving aside the echoes and outright quotations (*Filostrato,* II, 80), which are frequent in his most youthful works, the first truly explicit homage to Dante, placing him in the same niche as the greatest poets of Latinity, stands out in the conclusion of the romance that Boccaccio, while still a student of canon law, had declared that he would write.[9] Through Cino, Bocaccio also must have approached the poetry of the other writer highly praised in the *De Vulgari Eloquentia,* that is, the poetry of the "first friend," the foremost friend of Dante.[10] He must also have heard something of the rising young Aretine poet who would one day pay sincere and deep-felt homage to that same Cino, alone of all the poets of the preceding generation.

It is very likely that even before beginning his law studies, thanks to his having frequented the Angevin court, Boccaccio had also begun to visit the other great center of Neopolitan culture, the royal library which Robert, in his passion for books, had greatly enriched. There he certainly met Paolo da Perugia, "gravissimus vir . . . magister et custos bibliotece Roberti . . . curiosissimus . . . in perquirendis peregrinis undecunque libris" (*Gen.,* XV, 6). This man, "multarum rerum notitia doctus," the author of the *Liber Genologie* (which Boccaccio transcribed for his own use in the *Zibaldone Magliabechiano*), of the *Collectiones,* and of the famous commentaries on Persius and Horace, must have appeared to young Boccaccio as the highest example of encyclopedic learning, which, by that time, on the testimony of the *Filocolo,* exercised a powerful attraction on him.[11] In literature and in astronomy, in the study of antiquities and especially in the unusual science of mythological genealogies, Paolo expatiated vigorously with the most varied and subtle implications, enchanting his young admirer ("talium solertissimus atque curiosissimus exquisitor . . . Puto igitur neminem illi in talibus equiparandum fuisse"), so that he, as he would recall with a smile, "iuvenculus adhuc . . . ex illo multa avidus potius quam intelligens sumpsit" (*Gen.,* loc. cit., and Preface). Through Paolo, as well, he somehow approached Greek and Byzantine culture which arrived in Naples from Achaia—so bound to the Angevins—from Calabria, and from Basilian convents. He approached Paolo's friend and his consultant in this field, "Barlaam—Basilii Cosariensis monachus—calabrum hominen, olim corpore pusillum, pregrandem tamen scientia, et Grecis licteris adeo eruditum, ut . . . nedum his temporibus . . . nec a multis seculis citra fuisset virum tam insigni tanque grandi scientia preditum" (*Gen.,* XV, 6). In these impulsive and expansive enthusiams there throbbed that glamourous Hellenic mirage which suggested to Boccaccio the pseudo-Greek dress of the titles and many of

the names and alleged etymologies in his works. Then, too, that
persistent aspiration to penetrate within the boundaries of that
mysterious region of immense and alluring treasures was maturing,
and was to result in the fatiguing graphic Greek alphabet attempts in
the *Zibaldone Laurenziano* and, a quarter century later, in the
enterprising Homeric exploration under the guidance of Leontius, a
disciple of Barlaam who, perhaps, was also present at that time in
Naples.[12]

Along with these prevalently literary or antiquarian preoccu-
pations, the library of Robert, who was passionately interested in
medical and physical sciences (particularly astrology), offered Boccaccio a wealth of opportunities to examine books and meet men
belonging to the glorious tradition of the Neapolitan school of
sciences, through whose agency the scientific and technical
achievements of the Arab East entered the Latin world. Among those
numerous men of learning or precursors of science, the strongest
influence on the budding experimental ambition of Boccaccio was
with his works that of his "concivis," Paolo dell'Abbaco (. . .
"noverim nulli usquam alteri tempestate hac adeo sinum arisme-
tricam, geometriam et astrologiam aperuisse omnem, uti huic
aperuere, in tantum, ut nil arbitrer apud illas illi fuisse incognitum"
Gen., XV, 6).[13] Boccaccio must have heeded and followed Andalò del
Negro, best known for his endless and confused studies, more than
heretofore has been realized. Boccaccio explicitly hailed him as his
teacher, especially in the astrological sciences, and extolled him with
rather exaggerated praise (". . . cum universum fere peragrasset
orbem . . . experientia discursuum certior factus, visu didicit, quod
nox diximus auditu . . ."; "in motibus astrorum doctorem meum . . .
circa ea que ad astra spectare videntur, non aliter quam Ciceroni
circa oratoriam aut Maroni circa poeticam exhibendam censeo"
Gen., XV, 6; "my venerable preceptor Andalò" *Esposizioni,* V, 1, 162;
"cum igitur iuvenis Neapoli olim apud insignem virum atque
venerabilem Andalo de Nigro genuensem celorum motus et
syderum eo docente perciperem . . ." *De Casibus,* III, 1).[14]

Within the circle of court culture, he also encountered Graziolo
de' Bambaglioli, who had been the first to annotate Dante, and who,

exiled to Naples, was working on a moral treatise in homage to a grandee of the kingdom, Bertrando del Balzo.[15] Boccaccio met as often as possible a man who, together with the fine stories of the gods and the heavens, gave him the keys to the most varied stories of men in a densely peopled and voluminous chronicle running from Adam and Eve down to King Robert *(Compendium* and *Chronologia Magna*: the codex Par. Lat. 4939 contains marginal notes from Boccaccio's hand). This man was the Venetian Paolino Minorita, the pontifical penitentiary in Avignon, then nunzio at the Angevin court in 1316, and bishop of Pozzuoli after 1324. He is recorded in the *Genealogia* *(*XIV, 8) as "historiarum investigator permaximus" and for "wordy loquacity" ("dicacitate prolixa"). This is an opinion which on the one hand reflects the almost plagiarist enthusiasm of the author of the *Filocolo* and on the other the severity of the disciple of Petrarch in the *Genealogia* and in the *Zibaldone Magliabechiano* (in which, however, are noted diverse extracts from the *Chronologia*; it was remarked, and rightly, that the vast success of this work was arrested only by Petrarchan historiography).[16] Besides providing him with an infinite amount of gossip and anecdotes, Bishop Paolino must have passed on to Boccaccio some texts intended for the shelves of the sacred writers in the royal library. Among them were the Bible and its great commentaries, *The Golden Legend,* and some writings of Saint Athanasius. These texts, perhaps annotated by the Bishop—together with Father Dionigi (see below, pages 36 ff.)—left their imprint in the *Filocolo.*

In the circle of the learned men gathered in the Library and in the Angevin court, the twenty-year-old Boccaccio, still lacking in culture, found the spring in which to slake his insatiable thirst for the most diverse learning. He developed a liking for that ambitious encyclopedism and for those scientific fancies—from astrology to geography and geology—which unmistakably characterize his culture, as is reflected in the *Filocolo,* the *Allegoria,* the *Genealogia* and the *De Montibus.* At the same time he was attracted by the singular delight of those men of great learning devoted to the rare and unfamiliar word, expression, or piece of information, by their daring and continuous balancing between history and fable, between pa-

raded exactness and easy-going imaginings—a vast and ambitious
erudite chaos from which he would be able to draw with a vigorous
Alexandrine and baroque taste a fascinating rhythm of narrative
fantasy.

These cultural experiences in the University, in the Library,
and at the Court of Naples, impressed upon the life of Boccaccio a
wholly literary sense and obligation, stressed with such vehemence
in the last part of the previously cited passage of the *Genealogia* (XV,
10).

In those years there existed no chairs of rhetoric or poetry in the
Studio Napoletano.[17] However, King Robert had called a famous
and zealous teacher of rhetoric and poetics, a "doctor artium" of
Paris: the Augustinian, Father Dionigi (Denis) of Borgo San Sepolcro
(Bishop of Monopoli from March 17, 1340), who was known for his
astrological and theological culture, as well as for his political capacities (he was a legate at Aquila between 1337 and 1338). Thus
Dionigi was present in Naples, perhaps teaching theology at the
University, as he had previously at the Sorbonne, from 1324. It may
well be that Boccaccio was introduced to this Tuscan, who combined
the culture of Avignon and Paris and who donated the famous "Saint
Augustine" to Petrarch, by his friends of the Galeota family, who, in
fact, were benefactors of Father Dionigi. Or he may have known him
through his compatriot, Father Francesco da Firenze, prior of the
Augustinian convent in Naples, where it is certain that Dionigi was
lodged.[18] Between 1337 and 1340 the "reverend father and teacher
Dionigi" (ep. V), "theologie magister" *(Vita Petracchi,* p. 240), "as-
trologus et theologus Regis," must not only have introduced Boccaccio to the works of Seneca and Saint Augustine but truly become his
teacher in the "hope" of the soul, as he himself declared in an epistle
(V). He also revealed to Boccaccio a poetry and a culture different
from those of Cino or the learned Angevins, directed resolutely both
toward the future and toward the eternal reasons of the spirit. In fact
it was Dionigi who, in his talks, helped Boccaccio to understand the
figure and the work of Petrarch, certainly more directly and perhaps
more completely than Cino da Pistoia, or Pietro Canigiani (who
belonged to the family of Petrarch's mother), or his faithful old

friends Barbato and Giovanni Barrili (even through the medium of Petrarch's protégé, Sennuccio del Bene: Petrarch's sonnet CXII, addressed to Sennucio, is repeated in the *Filostrato,* V, 54-55.)

To Boccaccio, Dionigi offered as a lofty model that young and already sublime writer destined to dominate the culture of his time. He described to Boccaccio Petrarch's literary life in the "Helicon" of Valchiusa (*Vita Petr.,* loc. cit.), induced him to read the great texts, and, especially, all those addressed to Dionigi personally *(Metr.,* I, 4, recopied by Boccaccio in the *Zibaldone Laurenziano; Fam.,* IV, ii, received by Dionigi in Naples, and recalled by Boccaccio in the *Vita Petr.).* Thus the meeting with Dionigi and his literary and spiritual teaching gave solid support to Boccaccio's fervent cult of Petrarch and to that combined literary and spiritual devotion so characteristic of Boccaccio ("et ego quadraginta annis vel amplius suus fui," he would write, perhaps with reference also to the early suggestions of Cino, on the death of the "master and father" "qui splendidissimum tam morum spectaculum quam comendabilium doctrinarum iubar vividum est": *De Casibus,* VIII, 1 and IX, 27; ep. XXIV; *Esposizioni,* XV, 95).

These teachings and these readings—and most of all the example of that model—slowly engendered in Boccaccio an even more direct approach to classical literature and a detachment from the Angevin erudition and the indiscriminate collections of scientific, literary, and historical data characteristic of Paolino Veneto. This is a development which marks the transition from the *Allegoria* and the *Filocolo* to the first literary epistles and the *Teseida.* Also, Dionigi's teachings strengthened Boccaccio's enthusiasm for, and his faith in, the new vernacular forms of poetry which had already been nourished by association with the Frescobaldi, both the merchants and rhymers, and especially by the example of Dante and the school of Cino.

In Angevin Naples, these new forms certainly were available to Boccaccio in Provençal and French. In the library of King Robert were many lyrical collections, song books in the tongue of Provence (lengua d'oc), and France (langue d'oïl), romances and poems, ascetic books "in gallico scripti," "bound in fine crimson velvet, with ornaments and bosses of silver." [19] And at court, where the two

French princesses (Catherine de Valois and Agnès de Périgord) held first rank, both languages were current and the lays and songs of both were listened to with pleasure [20] along with those of the Tuscan "canterini" (ballad singers) and "giullari" (minstrels), great numbers of whom were present in Naples.[21] It is not by chance that Boccaccio speaks of his Fiammetta's delight on reading the French romances (VIII, 7). Nor is it due to chance that his first narrative works are woven on the filigrees of *Fleur et Blanchefleur,* of the *Roman de Troie,* and of the *Roman de Thèbes.*

But, even more than the diverse linguistic costumes, the expressions of the most vigorous "vernacular" culture also spoke with the renewed figurative language of Giotto, "one of the lights of Florentine glory" (*Decameron,* VI, 5):

> "to whom fair Nature hid not that semblance of herself, sealing it in his craft" *(Amorosa Visione,* IV, 16 ff.)

Giotto was painting at Castel Nuovo, in the royal chapel and elsewhere, from 1329 until about 1333; of Tino da Camaino, who from 1323 until his death in 1337 was carving the tombs of Queen Maria and of Carlo of Calabria in Naples; of Tino, of Francesco di Vito, and of Pace da Firenze, who were in those years erecting the Carthusian monastery of San Martino.[22]

NOTES

1. "Born naturally and somewhat less than legitimate" is what F. Villani says (op. cit., p. 452); see also L. Tanfani, *N. Acciaiuoli,* Florence, 1863, p. 10; K. Hopf, *Chroniques gréco-romaines,* Berlin, 1873, p. 476.
2. Naturally such liberation was accomplished together with the wrecking of the romance of her birth; see above, p. 13, note 12. However, fantastic and romantic references dot the pages of the *Lives,* placed ahead of the text in the first editions, beginning with that of Squarciafico; they are missing in the oldest biographers, of the first century after the poet's death (Villani, Bandini, Manzini, Poleton, Munetti).
3. Torraca, art. cit., p. 75.
4. L. de Mas-Latrie, *Histoire de l'île de Chypre,* Paris, 1852, II, p. 164. The

last document showing his presence in Naples is dated March 1331; the first in Paris is of September 1332.

5. G. De Blasiis, "Cino da Pistoia nell'Università di Napoli," *Arch. Stor. Prov. Nap.,* XI, 1886; G. M. Monti, "L'età angioina," in *Storia dell'Università di Napoli,* Naples, 1924.

6. See articles cited in the preceding note; also Della Torre, op. cit., pp. 143 ff.

7. V. Branca, P. G. Ricci, "L' incontro napoletano con Cino," *Studi sul B.,* V, 1968. Evidently Boccaccio attended the lessons of Cino on the Justinian code even though they were not strictly a part of the studies in canon law.

8. Billanovich, *Restauri,* pp. 50 ff. Dante's epistle to Cino is also transcribed in the *Zibaldone Laurenziano,* c. 63r, that is, in the *Cod. Laur. Plut.* 29, 8 autograph of Boccaccio from c. 45v and containing in this second part both texts and transcriptions by him c. 1340-48.

9. *Filocolo* I, 1, 30, "to me, who now spend my time on the holy laws of thy (Jesus') successors," and V, 97, 6, "Have no care [o little book] to wish to be where the measured lines of the Florentine Dante are sung, whom thou, like a small servitor, must follow reverently."

10. The allusions and echoes of Cavalcanti in the oldest *Rime:* I, IX, XI, XIII, XXIV and so on, and in the *Filostrato* IX, 5, 6, 7, 8, and in the *Teseida,* X, 55-57 are the immediate residue of Boccaccio's always enthusiastic and useful readings. But also see some indications to the contrary in A. E. Quaglio's article "Prima fortuna della glossa garbiana," in *Giorn. Stor. Lett. It.,* CXLI, 1964.

11. Torraca, art, cit., pp. 57 ff.; F. Ghisalberti, "Paola da Perugia. . . ," *Rend. Ist. Lombardo Scienze e Lettere,* S. II, LXII, 1929; G. M. Monti, in *Il Mezzogiorno d' Italia nel Medioevo,* Bari, 1930, pp. 129 ff.

12. A. Pertusi, *Leonzio Pilato fra Petrarca e Boccaccio,* Venice, 1964, p. 33; and also in general for Barlaam, pp. 9, 102-103; and see Barlaam, *Epistole greche,* edited by G. Schirò, Palermo, 1954, Intro. with numerous bibliographical references and documents.

13. G. Masini, "Maestro Paolo dell'Abbaco," *Rass. Nazionale,* S. II, XXII, 1919; G. Boffito, *Paolo dell' Abbaco e Fabrizio Mordente,* Firenze, 1931; G. Arrighi, intr. to Paolo dell' Abbaco's *Trattato d' aritmetica,* Pisa, 1964. Boccaccio would meet him later in person at Florence, where Paolo lived until 1374 (he was born in 1281).

14. Della Torre, pp. 49 ff., 154 ff.: Torraca, art. cit., pp. 51 ff. Perhaps it was Andalò del Negro to whom Boccaccio was referring when, in pastoral allusions, speaking vaguely of his studies in the *Filocolo,* he cited

"Calmeta, grave shepherd, to whom most things were manifest" and who "one day . . . began to tell the new changes and the unforeseeable courses of the silvery moon" (V, 8, 16-17). Torraca, art. cit., defended the identification of Calmeta with Paolo da Perugia; Della Torre, Wilkins (*Mod Lang. Notes,* XXI, 1906), Hauvette, and others have proposed the identification with Andalò using persuasive arguments which have been taken up and strengthened by Quaglio (cf. note 16 below).

15. Torraca, art. cit., p. 146.

16. A. E. Quaglio, "Tra fonti e testo del Filocolo," *Giorn. Stor. Lett. It.,* CXL, 1963.

17. G. M. Monti, *L'età angioina cit.*; E. G. Léonard, *Les Angevins de Naples,* Paris, 1954, pp. 282 ff. But perhaps Boccaccio was already in contact with the "summus magister gramatice," Angelo da Ravello, remembered as his friend in the ep. XIX, and who already then was teaching at Naples (F. Torraca, *Aneddoti di storia letteraria,* Città di Castello, 1925, pp. 142 ff.

18. See R. Weiss, "Notes on Dionigi da Borgo San Sepolcro," *Italian Studies,* X, 1953; G. Di Stefano, "Dionigi da Borgo San Sepolcro . . ." and "Per la fortuna di Valerio Massimo," *Atti della Accademia delle Scienze di Torino,* XCVI, 1961 (with an ample bibliography); G. Billanovich, *Petrarca letterato,* I, Rome, 1947, p. 63; V. Branca, *Tradizione,* pp. 181 and 183. Boccaccio owned the commentary of P. Dionigi on Valerius Maximus, dedicated to the cardinal Giovanni Colonna: and probably the impassioned reading of Valerius Maximus in those years is to be connected to the influence of Dionigi.

19. Doc. cit. in Camera, *Annali,* II, pp. 402 ff.; N. F. Faraglia, "Notizie di molti libri scrittori alluminatori ecc. della Biblioteca del re Roberto," *Arch. Stor. It.,* S. V, III, 1889, pp. 357-59. And see Della Torre, pp. 163 ff. (who tends to extend this French culture) and Torraca, art. cit., pp. 106 ff. (who tends to restrict it); E. G. Léonard, *Les Angevins,* pp. 282 ff.

20. E. G. Léonard, op cit., and also *Histoire de Jeanne Ire,* I, pp. 25 ff.

21. Torraca, art. cit., p. 140; G. Padoan, "Mondo aristocratico e mondo communale nell'ideologia e nell'arte di G.B.," in *Studi sul; B.,* II, 1964 (cf. especially for these references, and for those that are made on p. 43, pp. ff.)

22. F. Bologna, *I pittori alla corte angioina di Napoli,* Rome, 1969.

CHAPTER 4

Literary Experience from the *Caccia* to the *Teseida* (1334-1341)

In the decade between 1330 and 1340, Boccaccio progressed toward literary maturity. The childish and indiscriminate enthusiasm of the student at the Mazzuoli school was transformed by the stern experiences of life and the varied yet powerful cultural experiences in Naples, the crossroads of the oriental and occidental cultures. Already apparent is the characteristic bilingualism of the author who, throughout his long career, would constantly interweave Latin and the vernacular in his literary works. The enrichment and strengthening of this mixture grows from the *Elegia di Costanza* and the *Caccia* to the learned works, the *Esposizioni* and the final version of the *Decameron*. Even in this decade two equally important influences dominate his work: culture and imagination. Boccaccio had developed an impassioned and growing enthusiasm for erudition, for "summae," and for every shred of information. This enthusiasm pervaded, in different ways, the *Filocolo* and the *Genealogia*—works separated by a lapse of forty years. The second influence is characterized by a strength of imagination and narrative power that evolved from the *Filostrato* and *Filocolo* to the *Decameron* and the *Esposizioni*. This narrative power could combine

41

elements from the most diverse sources with an utter disregard for repetitions, tracings, or plagiarisms. It had the strength to fuse the most disparate elements into the strictest unity, yet to make everything distinct through its expressive rhythm and its extraordinary representative vitality.

As we have been discussing, imagination and culture characterize Boccaccio's writings of the Neapolitan period, which are difficult to date with precision, probably because of many successive editions. They have the flavor of early and laborious scholastic exercises based on texts proposed as models by the teachers of the time. Boccaccio himself, with smiling *pietas* for his apprenticeship, wanted to preserve two of the exercises in the *Zibaldone Laurenziano* (cc. 60-62). One was an example in poetry entitled the *Elegia di Costanza,* a paraphrase of the famous epitaph of Homonoeia, truly done "cum nondum novisset quibus seu quot pedibus carmen incederet" (*Gen.,* XV, 10)[1] and the other in prose—the so-called *Allegoria mitologica,* in part an adroit cento drawn from the first two books of the *Metamorphoses* in a confused mingling of mythical allegory and history, of paganism and Christianism. Already, however, a surer style and a certain felicity in narration are visible in the two short narrative poems, *Caccia di Diana* (1334?) and *Filostrato* (1335?), which are considered early works of the Neapolitan period because the myth of Fiammetta and her *senhal* [sign, mark], which were to embellish all his other writings down to the *Fiammetta,* are not mentioned in these two.

The *Caccia di Diana,* a narrative poem in eighteen short cantos in tercets (terza rima), tells of a fantastic "hunt," where Diana herself leads the most noted Parthenopean beauties (almost always identified by name and surname), who on the initiative of the "fair lady whose name remains unspoken" rebel against the rule of Diana and turn instead to that of Venus. Actually, what little action there is serves as a pretext for rendering a gallant and courtly homage to the most famous beauties of the time, elegantly depicted against the enamelled and storied background of the Neapolitan landscape.

Probably written immediately afterwards (1335?), the *Filostrato*—in young Boccaccio's approximative Greek it means "the one overcome by Love"—is dedicated by its author to his beloved

Filomena to make her feel his sufferings as a far-away lover. In its nine parts, in fluent octaves he narrates the loves of Troilus, son of Priam, and of Griselda (Cressida: Chryseis), Calcante's daughter (returned to her father, a fugitive among the Greeks besieging Troy), and later of Griselda's unfaithfulness with Diomed and the impassioned laments and utter despair of Troilus, who is finally slain by Achilles while searching vainly for Diomed in order to avenge his betrayal. The principal plot was used previously as a secondary episode in the medieval romances based on Trojan material, and in particular in the *Roman de Troie* of Benoît de Sainte-Maure and in the *Historia Troiana* of Guido delle Colonne.

As we have already mentioned, these works reflect Boccaccio's use of a new poetical style, that of Dante and the "sweet new style." But the change in style and rhythms reveals the influence of other and more humble poetical traditions: that of the "sirventesi," which introduced coveys of ladies, and especially that of the "cantari," which in the first decades of the fourteenth century was gaining in strength and popularity. Thus from Venetia and Tuscany the "fabulationes suas . . . in sonorum cantum productas" were introduced in Naples to gladden even Giovanna and Luigi of Taranto thanks to the famous Giovanni de Firenze.[2] Indeed, in renewing the Dantean "epistola in the form of a sirventese," in which were collected "the names of sixty of the most beautiful ladies of the city" (*Vita Nuova*, VI), the tradition of the "sirventesi" must have been strengthened and amplified, as is attested in those years by the "caudato semplice" *Deo alto pare* (1309) and the "gay sermintese full of love" composed by Antonio Pucci (1335).[3] And in these very same decades the "cantari" (popular poems in octaves or ottava rima) won their most typical public, the landed and mercantile middle class with its yearnings for the days of chivalry and its new cultural aspirations.

With his awakened awareness of middle class taste and with his cultural ambitions, Boccaccio resolutely and decisively engaged in writing his narratives in octaves. He not only broadened the melodic turn of the strophe and made it more variously adequate for its material, but brought into the narration his own sorrowing and direct experience of love and that full and very human sentimental and psychological life which the popular singers, the canterini, who

favored the adventurous and the fabulous, had rejected even when it
was available to them, natural and abundant, in the French sources.[4]
Despite the ingenuous feudal and communal deformation of Trojan
society, despite the various technical and syntactic uncertainties, and
despite the considerable dallying and imbalance of narration and
presentation—obvious weaknesses of a novice in writing—in the *Filostrato* Boccaccio succeeds in finding a voice and a style peculiarly his
own, particularly evocative in its oblivious song of the joys of love and
in its despairing laments and regrets. And with Griselda he succeeds
in sketching the first of those penetrating feminine portraits, all
womenly nobility and impassioned coquetry, which characteristically punctuate his later writings down to the vivid and unforgettable
examples of the Decameron.

    In these early works, Boccaccio seems to consecrate and renew
those traditions of literature which were still current, but undergoing
change. With a firm grasp of tradition, he ventured into the difficult
field of the Italian prose romance (as in the *Filocolo*), and participated
in the development of the Italian narrative. In the *Teseida*, he experi-
mented with the octaves of the "cantari," and with the romance of
chivalry; in the *Comedia delle Ninfe*, he worked with pastoral fables for
the first time; in the *Elegia di Madonna Fiammetta*, he championed the
purely psychological novel; and in the *Ninfale Fiesolano*, he attempted
the pre-Renaissance transfiguration of etiological narration into a
dreamy rustic fantasy. From the time of his very first works, Boccaccio
intended to be a frank and courageous mediator between the most
acclaimed literary traditions and the newer requirements of com-
munication with a public by then very different from that of the
feudal age. Thus, in the *Caccia*, mythological fantasy and moralistic
"contrasto" [medieval poetic dialogue] are bent into a new meaning,
that is, into the portrayal and the glorification of a refined society
which arose between the court and the bourgeoisie, with a form of
joyous and elegant living, visualized with the taste of a miniaturist of
the late Middle Ages.

    The random and weighty cultural baggage Boccaccio accu-
mulated in the years following 1331, which also were the most
romantic in the youthful experience of Boccaccio, is displayed in all
its magnificence in the *Filocolo*, the work first born and fully devel-

oped under [the sign of] the myth of Fiammetta (she appears in the Introduction and asks her lover to write the beautiful story, removing it from the "legendary talk of ignorant people"). It is she whom Florio encounters in the "court of love" in the garden at Mergellina. It is she who in one shape or another recurs in the love stories of Galeone, of Fileno, and of Idalogo. The *Filocolo* (1336-1338?), which in the approximative Greek of Boccaccio is intended to mean something like "weariness of love," is a long romance divided into five books, which for the first time in Italian prose relates the adventures of Florio, son of the king of Marmorina, and Biancifiore, a poor girl received into that court without anyone knowing of her princely Roman origin. It tells of their love from childhood, their cruel separation, the romantic quest of Florio to find his beloved, their splendid joyful wedding, their conversion to Christianity in Rome, and their victorious and joyous return home. But the telling of the famous legend of Byzantine origin (reworked in French as early as the thirteenth century and later in an Italian "cantare") is continually ornamented by Boccaccio with learned digressions, with autobiographical allusions, more or less exact, and with narrative, indicative of the *Decameron* to come. In fact Florio, during his wandering search for Biancifiore, in a beautiful Neapolitan garden, takes part in the refined conversations of an aristocratic group of young men and girls who, in their elegant discussions of "questions of love," illustrate them with examples which are actually novellas (Book IV). Two of these were to be repeated in the *Decameron* (X, 4 and 5). Boccaccio's choice of a great love story is already indicative of a definite taste and poetics, of an art which attempts an escape from daily routine yet still concerns human beings, an art enwrapped in mythical sentiments and heroic adventures (Quaglio) and exalted by culture. The enthusiasm for erudition of the self-taught young man is first manifested in continual digressions, historical and mythological, geographical and geological, scientific and archeological, as well as literary. A cultural X-ray examination of the *Filocolo* reveals zones of direct and unbridled derivation from Paolino Veneto, Andalò del Negro, Paolo da Perugia, and Dionigi da Borgo San Sepolcro. Naturally it also reveals the influence of Valerius Maximus (in all probability still read in a vernacular version), as

well as that—declared in the conclusion, in obedience to the precepts
of the *De Vulgari Eloquentia* (II, vi, 7)—of the classical writers to whose
works the student had most assiduously devoted himself: Virgil,
Ovid, Statius, Lucan, and in whose company Dante was reverently
placed.

In this first great original romance of Italian literature, set in
the sixth century (following the chronology of Paolo and Paolino),
the most striking feature is the thematics already so congenial to
Boccaccio's imagination. He displays a prodigious narrative diver-
sity in all aspects of his work: the epical and the courtly episodes, the
adventures on land and sea, combats and love, the ever so varied
human situation and other situations extraordinary to the point of
the miraculous, the gallant conversations and solemn and even
theological or hieratic discourses, the depiction of famous cities of
west and east (Verona, Naples, Rome, Alexandria, Cairo) and of
lonely stretches of country and seashores, and the delineation of
human characters and backgrounds of the most varied kinds, from
agricultural Tuscan society to harems, from the Papal court to that
singular Neapolitan court of love in which the lyrical schema of
Boccaccio's fancy just appears, and which he would repeat in the
so-called "cornici" (frames) of the *Comedia* and the *Decameron*. In the
romance, also, the amorous material is presented with a most original and felicitous expression, albeit stressing the writer's personal
experiences too warmly and too directly. The material is overwhelming: from the sprouting of passion in Florio and Biancifiore as children and later in their ecstatic abandon and agitations,
in their suspicions and anguish, in their anxious search for one
another and in their ultimate joy; and in the outline of other loves,
in which the sentimental experiences of young Boccaccio are involved. However, the quest of Florio is only the guiding thread of an
extremely confusing narrative plot, and for this reason the *Filocolo* is
not to be read like a modern novel nor with one eye fixed on the
Decameron. As Quaglio says, "it [*Filocolo*] was born and remained a
cento, a medley of a medieval type, of which the framework recalls
either the structure of the thirteenth and fourteenth century epics of
European extraction or the encyclopedias and anthologies of scho-

lastic culture in which anecdotes, legends and proverbs of the Middle Ages are closely packed with classical sources." [5]

Boccaccio first displays his erudition in this early work, in a great variety of styles and with a superabundance of sentiment, which work together to achieve a superior yet sometimes inharmonious general effect. Thus the style of Boccaccio and his particular doctrinal technique both appear at almost the same time. He experiments with adapting models taken from the Latin writers of the decadence (from Apuleius and Servius to Martianus Capella and Boethius), and he creates the first romance art prose by adapting Latin techniques of the *artes dictandi* to the requirements of the new language. They are daring experiments, resulting in aristocratic rigidities in the *cursus* [6] and Alexandrine preciosities and complacent stylistic haughtiness in the rhymed prose. Above all else, Boccaccio pursues a militant culture prompted by the lofty examples of Dante and the poets of the *stil nuovo,* and by the laborious efforts of the *dictatores* of the new language: the popularizers, the narrators composing octaves.

This early experimental work and this diligence, both venturesome, are sustained by Boccaccio's overwhelming ambition to master rhetoric, an ambition which causes him to force rhetorical figures on a difficult milieu. It is precisely the ambition which inspires the rhetorical-literary debauches of the first four epistles (1339), preserved by Boccaccio together with the *Elegia* and the *Allegoria,* and written, perhaps, while he was still bound to his juridical studies ("visis meis decretalium lectionibus" ep. IV). Addressed paradigmatically, the first two epistles follow Dantean models: one to a great nobleman, another to an important author (perhaps Petrarch), still another to an unfaithful friend, and the last to a praiseworthy and consoling one. Recently revealed as obligatory exercises in style, these epistles are often "strangely glossomatic and enigmatic" (Parodi) in their Latin, and in their lofty themes based on models imitative of Ovid and Apuleius. They are very remote from that autobiographical confidence and abandon which until twenty years ago critics—first romantic, then positivist and finally impressionist—wanted to read into them. Even the historical notes and the precise references to some person are examples of Boccaccio's rhetorical art, rather than of his autobiographical interests. Boccaccio always tried to anchor his freest stylistic exercises to a hallucinative exactness and solidity. This is evident in the *Filocolo*, the *Comedia*, the *Decameron*, and in the famous letter written in the Neapolitan dialect and addressed to Franceschino dei Bardi (although in my opinion this letter is of doubtful authenticity).[7] The very attestations on the letter, such as "sub monte Falerno," "apud busta Maronis Vergili," are, however, influenced by passion, as were many incidents in the *Filocolo*. Even his description of himself is "a development of formulary teaching." He describes himself as first humble and completely possessed by his devotion to his high correspondents, and finally as afflicted by poverty and misfortunes (IV), a condition typical of the "querule clausule" used to close a letter. As an appendix to the collections of *ars dictaminis* there constantly appeared one or more formulas with which the student, in prose or verse, bewailed his *questua* of money and aid. At the end of this epistle to Franceschino dei Bardi, the request for a commentary to the *Thebaïd* of Statius seems, therefore, to correspond to a typical theme for closing, that is, to the *petitio*, canonical precisely between the *narratio* and the *conclusio* in every *epistola fucata* and *phalerata* (ornate letter in fine language).[8]

The very interesting and precious rhetorical precepts in the letters of this period, heretofore regarded as conventionally romantic, contradict the assumption that Boccaccio's request for a commentary on the *Thebaïd* of Statius supports the assertion that he wrote the *Teseida* at this time. Although the *Teseida* is written in the style of the school of Statius, it corresponds, in a way, to the prolepses of that high rhetoric which must have occupied Boccaccio at the end of his Neapolitan sojourn. This concern was previously expressed in the *De Vulgari Eloquentia* and reiterated in the conclusion of the *Teseida* ("arma vero nullo latium adhuc invenio poetasse," II, ii, 10, and "but thou, O book, the first to sing to them [the Muses] of Mars dost sustain the anguish, in vulgar Latin nevermore seen" XII, 84).

The dedicatory letter to Fiammetta, analogous in tone to that of the *Filostrato* and to the Introduction of the *Filocolo* but drafted in calm and nostalgic abandon, is clearly related to the Neapolitan period by its evident character of *dictamen* (precept). But the more extensive presence of the "canterina" tradition and especially some references to Florence in the glosses Boccaccio himself carefully appended to the poem make it probable that the completion of the *Teseida* and a good part of the commentary must be assigned a date following his return to Florence (where his poem appears to have been known prior to 1348; it was mentioned by Matteo Frescobaldi, who died in that year).[9]

The *Teseida* (1339-1341?) is a poem in octaves divided into 12 cantos, the classical number for epic poetry (in fact, 9896 verses as in the *Aeneid*). Starting from the narration of Theseus' victorious wars against the Amazons and afterwards against Thebes, Boccaccio sings of the love of Arcita and Palemones—two faithful friends of Thebes held prisoner in Athens—for Emilia, the very young sister of Hippolita, queen of the Amazons and wife of Theseus. After various adventures, Theseus decides that the two rivals will establish by combat who will have Emilia: and in a grandiose tourney in which Greece's greatest heroes participate, Arcita is victorious. But, having been seriously wounded, he dies shortly thereafter: and Palemones obtains from Theseus the hand of Emilia (the poem is preserved in the author's own hand in *Laur. Doni e acquisti* 325).

The *Teseida,* much more than the *Filostrato,* reveals a significant weight of culture and ambition, corroborated and developed in the glosses rich in an erudition, mythological and genealogical, literary and archeological, of a typically Angevin stamp. Indeed, Boccaccio, like Statius and perhaps the author of the *Roman de Thèbes,* probably took the *Teseida* from a Byzantine source, to which the author himself seems to allude when he states that the "ancient story" "has not been translated from the Greek into Latin" (I, 2 and glos.: Is it Digenes Akritas?). There is also a Hellenizing influence in evidence, which certainly favored the translation and success which the poem enjoyed in fourteenth-century Greece.

At the time he wrote the *Teseida,* Boccaccio, by then experienced in rhetoric and stylistic exercises and in the secrets of vernacular poetry, made a choice that would be decisive for Italian literature. In the *Caccia,* he turns the octave from the prevailingly lyrical trend of the *Filocolo* to one firmly narrative and epical. Notwithstanding the long digressions, he lays out the general design of the action with a sureness of development still unknown to the author of the *Filocolo.*

The visualizations of the *Caccia* and certain of the poems seem to have initiated those very elegant descriptions of the Amazons and of Hippolitus and in particular the portrayal of the youthful little figure and the Pisanello-like profile of Emilia (very much a foreshadowing of Poliziano's Simonetta, in the opinion of some critics); the mournful lamentations Boccaccio conveyed through Troilus and some of the sonnets are renewed by Arcita in a more subdued register. In juxtaposing weapons, adventures and loves, characteristic of the *Filocolo,* Boccaccio is in the *Caccia* on his way to achieving a harmonious fusion. For the first time the turbulent, sentimental use of autobiography is bound up and restrained by art: by a literary, cultural, technical and rhetorical preparation and diligence which sometimes makes the expression of ideas heavy and arid, but which represents clear mastery on the part of the the writer.

The many verses also bespeak Boccaccio's mastery of the *rime,* which presumably he wrote during his Neapolitan years (with the exception of some sonnets written between 1373 and 1375, no lyric can be dated with certainty). They are sonnets, felicitous and evocative, especially the nostalgic pictures of Neapolitan shores and countryside, the lively and mordant portraits of feminine coquetry and passion, the cries of a soul prostrated or uplifted by love. The influence of Dante—especially the Dante of the *Vita Nuova* or the poems to a certain Pietra—and of Guido and Cino, is always present and compelling in this lyrical exercise, whereas the new Petrarchan experience is barely touched.[10] Perhaps in the revelation of those very refined utterances Boccaccio experienced one of his impulsive and excessive discouragements, one which led him to burn "vulgaria et profecto juvenilia nimis poemata," which thirty years later he would recall in a very ardent exchange of letters with Petrarch and would repeat later to Pietro Piccolo (*Sen.,* V, 3; ep. XIX; see also pages 141 below and 172).

With these cultural and literary achievements, at a date difficult to determine with any exactness, Boccaccio's critical, decisive Neapolitan experience came to an end. It would be pleasant to believe as some scholars still do that he was among the swarm of scholars of the University and the cultured men of the Court present at the public examination of Petrarch before King Robert in March and April 1341, prior to the latter's crowning with laurel on the Capitoline

Hill and his weaving the praises of poetry and of poets. Dionigi, Barbato, Giovanni Barrili (later the king's representative at the Roman ceremony) were certainly present with the "proceres in facultatibus variis"; Boccaccio himself seems to recall the solemn "conventus," stressing the emotion and literary conversion of King Robert:

> Qui clarus olim phylosophus et medicine preceptor egregius, atque inter ceteros eius temporis insignis theologus, cum in sexagesimum sextum usque etatis sue annum parvi pendisset Virgilium . . . quam cito Franciscum Petrarcam arcanos poematum referentem sensus audivit, obstupefactum se ipsum redarguit, et, ut ego, eo dicente, meis auribus audivi, asseruit, se numquam ante arbitratum adeo egregios atque sublimes sensus sub tam ridiculo cortice, uti poetarum sunt fictiones, latere potuisse.
>
> *(Gen.,* XIV, 22)

Because no other meetings of Petrarch and King Robert are known to have occurred and because Boccaccio did not return to Naples before the king's death in January 1343, it has been thought that this testimony could refer only to that memorable occasion. To the contrary, however, an expert like Hauvette, a Latinist like Hecker, a Petrarchist like Wilkins—followed by a variety of other scholars—noted that the parenthetic *eo dicente* does not seem attributable to Robert (the *eo* would be redundant); more probably it refers to Petrarch, who might have recounted the episode to Boccaccio in one of their various meetings after 1350 (and, besides, he did mention it in the *Posteritati* and reported it in the *Rer. mem.,* I, 37). It may be added that, following a custom very common among the chroniclers and hagiographers of the time, Boccaccio frequently claims to have seen and heard, directly, persons and events of which he had sure and certain information but of which he had learned only indirectly (for example in the *De Casibus,* IX, 21 and 26 and in the ep. IV). We may also add that on none of the occasions on which Boccaccio spoke of his meetings with Petrarch or the Neapolitan examination or the coronation, nor even in the hagiographic biography, did he

ever mention, as he was wont to do under similar circumstances, his
own presence at the crowning, or his direct acquaintance with
Petrarch during the month of the latter's sojourn in Naples close to a
mutual friend like Dionigi.[11] On the contrary, in 1350 Boccaccio
went to greet Petrarch on the latter's arrival in Florence, "miro
nondum visi hominis desiderio" (*Fam.*, XXI, xv), as Petrarch wrote
later; surely Boccaccio, then, when he received Petrarch in his own
house, would not have failed to mention having met or, at least, seen
him in Naples. If not by the stately "conventus," certainly Boccaccio's Neapolitan sojourn and his enthusiastic devotion to Petrarch
were crowned by the happy news that, for the awarding of the crown,
the "magister et preceptor" had preferred Naples and Rome to Paris
(*Fam.*, IV, iv and v, of September 1 and 10, 1340).[12] Boccaccio's stay
in Naples, instead, was darkened by the absence of the dearest friend
of his worldy and courtly youth. Niccolò Acciaiuoli had departed in
October 1338 on the mission to Morea from which would grow his
power and greatness as a politician and statesman; but at that time
the enterprise appeared to be beginning under difficult and worrisome circumstances. This was reflected in the anxieties and sadness
Boccaccio expressed at the time ("Niccola, if any trust is due to the
wretched, I swear to you on my suffering soul that your departure
weighs on me no less heavily than did that of Trojan Aeneas on
Carthaginian Dido": ep. V; see p. 56).

The departure of Boccaccio from Naples, some time late in
1340 or early 1341, may be partly explained by the fact that, in the
years immediately preceding his leaving Naples, the relations
between Florence and Naples had been modified, which changed
the situation of his father and his family. The political and economic
ties which had bound the bankers and the government of Florence
closely to the Angevins had slackened almost to the point of rupture.
With his finances all in order, Robert was no longer as indulgent as
in the past with the "companies." Furthermore, the companies were
weakened by a lack of confidence which was creeping through
Naples (and which led to the failure of the Bonaccorsi and other
lesser companies). The break between Florence and Naples may
have been due to the disappointments the Florentines encountered
from their urgent requests to Naples for help in the long wars over

Lucca. Filled with resentment and hoping for a change in the situation, the Florentines were not averse to overturning their traditional alliances. In these difficult circumstances, in this movement backwards following the period of the expansion of the "companies," Boccaccino appears no longer to have been connected with the Bardi after October 1338.[13]

Since at least August 1333 Boccaccino had been domiciled in S. Felicita, the quarter most frequented by people from Valdelsa, and in which in that same year he had purchased a house for his son Francesco;[14] then between 1336 and 1337 he had been bailor in important dealings and had traded in properties of considerable value, in the name and by the agency of his wife and son (with Biagio Pizzini of Certaldo as guarantor, one of those "merry fellows" portrayed in connection with Frate Cipolla!). But on November 5, 1339 he had to sell a house in S. Felicita (perhaps a part of his own dwelling?) in satisfaction of a debt of three hundred florins which he would have been unable to pay otherwise. In that same period he was obliged to borrow sizeable sums from his sister-in-law (who died prior to June 1340).[15] Perhaps Boccaccino's difficulties had arisen from the general business situation and from his separation from the Bardi company (which, incidentally, passed through a series of difficulties between 1339 and 1340, carrying it to the crisis of 1345).[16] Or they may have ensued on the death of his wife, Margherita, in 1338 or 1339, for she had belonged to a rich and powerful family. In this period, at least after January 1337, Boccaccino had taken a five-year lease "pro se ipso et suo nomine et vice et nomine Johannis ipsius Bocchaccii filii " [17] on property belonging to the church of San Lorenzo a Croce in Capua, with the contracts executed in Florence. Customarily payment was due on the lease in November; however, Boccaccino delayed that of 1340, amounting to 23 florins, evidently because of financial difficulties, until January 1341.[18] It is probable that Boccaccino, having returned to Florence, entrusted the responsibility of obtaining those Capuan leases to his son, still residing in Naples, if, contrary to other deals in which he acted alone or with other men, in this one he wanted him to be associated officially. (This would be another contradiction of the legend of the profound disagreement between father and son, and of that other legend about a Giovanni in a state of extreme indigence in those years and absolutely abhorrent of any business or administrative activity.) In the contract of January 11, 1341, repeating the formula quoted above, the notary added to the name "Johannis Bocchaccii filii," "dicti populi," that is to say, of the people of S. Felicita. This new detail has too easily given rise to the supposition that by that date Boccaccio had already returned to Florence and taken up real domicile in the paternal house, whereas the phrase alludes simply to the legal domicile.[19] In any case it is certain that he was not in Florence during the terrible pestilence of 1340 (G. Villani, XI, 114), as he himself declares (*Esposizioni*, VI, i, 65: "because at that time I was not there, I hear that in this city [Florence] . . ."). However, he had already left Naples by the spring of 1341 because he was not present at the petrarchan "conventus" or at the triumphal return of Acciaiuoli to the Angevin capital in mid-June.

Even ignoring an account of the winter memories of a similar journey accomplished by Panfilo, who is probably a figuration of the writer himself to (*Fiammetta*), it seems in conclusion quite probable that Boccaccio returned from Naples to Florence in the winter of 1340-1341.

NOTES

1. Now definitively attributed to Boccaccio; V. Branca, *Tradizione,* pp. 201 ff.

2. Léonard, *Histoire,* III, p. 412 (a privilege of 1360); E. H. Wilkins and G. Billanovich, "The miscellaneous letters of Petrarch," *Speculum,* XXXVII, 1962, p. 229 (he is Malizia Barattone, in touch with Petrarch also): and cf. p. 40 note 21.

3. V. Branca, *Tradizione,* pp. 195 ff.

4. V. Branca, *Il cantare trecentesco e il Boccaccio del Filostrato e del Teseida,* Florence, 1936; and "Nostalgie tardogotiche. . . ," *Miscellanea Flora,* Milan, 1962.

5. Art. cit.

6. For a discussion of *cursus* (a term of rhetoric) see Part II, Ch. 2, *Prose Structure.*

7. "La lettera di G.B. a Fr. de Bardi," edited by F. Nicolini, *Arch. Stor. It.,* S. VII, II, 1924. Nicolini has been able to confirm the data previously

advanced by Della Torre and Hauvette; Torraca, art. cit., thought the
year was 1361 instead, without serious proofs.

8. Billanovich, *Restauri,* pp. 68 ff.

9. In the canzone *Donna gentile;* S. Debenedetti, "Per la fortuna della
'Teseide' e del 'Ninfale fiesolano,' " *Giorn. Stor. Lett. It.,* LX, 1912.

10. Introd. and notes to the edition of the *Rime* by V. Branca, Padua, 1958.

11. Billanovich has come out strongly in favor of the presence of Boccaccio
at the "conventus" (*Restauri,* pp. 62 ff.; *Petrarca letterato,* I, pp. 68 ff.); he
limits the Neapolitan sojourn of Petrarch to four days; Wilkins rejects
it and holds that Petrarch spent a month in Naples (*The Making of the
Canzoniere,* Rome, 1951, pp. 45 ff.; *Vita del Petrarca,* Milan, 1964, p. 45).

12. Perhaps the decision was prompted by Father Dionigi himself, some
months earlier in Avignon for the "visitatio liminum Apostolorum"
obligatory for each new bishop.

13. From the lists of the Bardi company it would appear that Boccaccino
resigned *in Naples,* July 1, 1338 (Sapori, op. cit., p. 735); documents
cited by Nicolini, art. cit., would indicate that in October Boccaccino
was already separated from the Bardi.

14. Document published by Della Torre, pp. 24-25; and by Gherardi in
Corazzini, op. cit., p. C.

15. Document cited by A. Della Torre, pp. 305 ff.; Hauvette, p. 102; M.
Barbi, op. cit., p. 419; D. Tordi, *Gli inventori dell' eredità di Jacopo Boccaccio,* Orvieto, 1923, pp. 9 and 74 (document of May 18, 1336, concerning the sale of the farm of S. Martino at Mensola, with Biagio Pizzini
as surety. Is this the villa in the parish of Maiano which Baldelli, pp.
284-285, says that Boccaccino owned, or another one?).

16. A Sapori, *La crisi delle compagnie,* Florence, 1926 (for Boccaccino see p.
259).

17. A. Della Torre, p. 345; Hauvette, p. 103.

18. The two contracts already cited by Manni (pp. 20-21) were published
later by Della Torre, pp. 309-310; and 343-344; for the backdating in
January 1337 see Tordi, op. cit., p. 14.

19. Note that the mention "dicti populi" was not essential and in fact does
not appear in the renewal of the lease on May 10, 1342 (Tordi, pp.
51-52). When Boccaccio was sent to Naples, being a boy, he had no
legal status and therefore remained registered (as did every other
member of the family) in the parish where his father resided, that is,
first in S. Pier Maggiore and later in S. Felicita. Even when Boccaccio
would move to Certaldo he would remain legally domiciled in Florence (see page 192, note 5). Also, "vice et nomine" seems clearly to
allude to the absence of the person named from Florence.

CHAPTER 5

Return to Florence and the Assimilation of Tuscan Culture in the Works to the *Decameron* (1341-1360)

The first time we hear the voice of Boccaccio in Florence, on August 28, 1341, it is sorrowful, in a letter directed to the first friend of his Neapolitan youth with an affectionate abandon that prevents any rhetorical stylization:

> Niccola, . . . I am writing you nothing about my being in Florence unwillingly, for that would have to be written with tears rather than ink: only this can I tell you, that, just as Alexander changed the ill fortune of the pirate Antigonus to good, so am I hoping that mine will be changed by you. Nor is this a new hope, but an old one, for nothing was left for me in the world since my reverend father and teacher Dionigi was taken from me by God, perhaps for the best. And let this about me suffice for the present (ep. V).[1]

It is an appeal, both humble and grieving, of this "enemy of fortune" (as Boccaccio signs the epistle) to Acciaiuoli, now famous and powerful. Boccaccio had awaited his return from Greece for two years "with as great desire as that of Penelope for Ulysses"; and he

56

had been happy about it "not otherwise . . . than the holy fathers would have been in limbo when they had heard from Saint John of the coming of Christ, by whom they hoped for their long-awaited salvation in a short time without fail." Now, "in the gloomy darkness of *his* anxieties" Boccaccio, just like a waiting soul, seems to stretch out his arms towards his savior, so that his "ill fortune" be changed "into good." Perhaps the hope was not only for the material succor, but for a return to Naples and a position in the city which would continue throughout his life to be the earthly Jerusalem lost and ever yearned for.

After thirteen decisive years, Boccaccio had returned to Florence changed from an adolescent and immature "discepolo," apprentice, into a man experienced "in the customs of the world," a scholar rich in culture and learning, a writer of Latin and Italian prose and poetry already unequalled in Florence or all of Italy. Yet it must have seemed as though he were plunging back into the meanness and pettiness of the most bourgeois and mercantile life, from which he had dared to hope that he had escaped ("you had always detested being a merchant, a stand about which you had many times boasted to others and to yourself" are words he gives to himself in the *Corbaccio,* 189); he must have felt he had fallen back into that human narrowmindedness which he would enjoy caricaturizing (". . . they, completely ignorant, know nothing but the number of steps there are from the warehouse or the shop to their house . . . their knowledge consists of almost nothing else, except in deceit or gain," 190). From the free Neapolitan cultural life, in which he had won standing and celebrity, he went into the constraint and economic dependence of his father's house oppressed and darkened by family misfortunes and by financial difficulties. From the lively Angevin capital, crossroads of East and West, the seat of a splendid court and a flourishing university, he came to a city culturally depressed (it did not yet have a university), seriously ravaged by the recent plague (according to Villani, XI, 114, a sixth of the population had perished), deeply disturbed economically and politically. The age of the European power of the "companies" was now waning: difficulties, partial failures, humiliating compromises portended the crashes and the failures of 1345. At the same time, after the rule of the Duke of Calabria, the life of the Florentine Commune had become more and more toilsome and wretched because of the unsuccessful attempts to take possession of Lucca and the crisis in the traditional Guelf alliance between Florence and the Angevins. The commune was tending to become a territorial state, without noticing, without heeding, that in this urge to expand it would meet its end. These are the years of the conspiracy of the Bardi and the defeat on the river Serchio, of the disagreements with Robert of Anjou and of the end of the Guelf bloc, of the near tyranny of Jacopo Gabrielli of Gubbio (Villani, XI, 118) and then of that demagogic and stormy tyranny of the Duke of Athens. Both these tyrannies were born of the distrust and the weariness of the many and of the violence of the few grandees capable of arousing the common people to violence.

Truly Boccaccio must have felt that he had passed—as he would repeat years afterwards with sharp nostalgia—from a city "happy, peaceful, abounding in good things, magnificent and ruled by a single king," to another painted by Dante "full of bombastic words and pusillanimous deeds, a slave not to a thousand laws, but to as many opinions as there are men, and always under arms, and at war, as much at home as abroad . . . and filled with proud, avaricious and envious people, and full of numberless worries" (*Fiammetta*, II, 6, 20). He must have felt that he had left behind—as he wrote by implication in the *Comedia* (XLIX, 67 ff.)—"nobility, gentility and valor, graceful pleasantries, example of virtue . . . worldly delights and their sweetness . . . as much of goodness and joy as one can have there . . ." in exchange for "melancholy and eternal weariness," for a "house dark and silent and very poor . . . where the cruel and horrible sight of an old man, cold, rough and avaricious, evermore with anguish saddens me" (in this deprecation the notes of a new capacity for realism are evident).

Even without romantically dramatizing disagreements between father and son, the theme is too insistent in Boccaccio's letters and directly autobiographical passages not to correspond to a reality. Perhaps the trouble in the house was accentuated first by the absence of a "mater familias" and then by the entrance of the new mistress, Boccaccino's second wife, Bice de' Bostichi,[2] and the probable effort of his father to interest Boccaccio again in business and commerce. [3] Also the meetings in November 1341 and the following months with Acciaiuoli, who had come to Florence with Barrili for political negotiations and for the founding of the Certosa (Carthusian monastery), must have sharpened Boccaccio's nostalgia for a time irreparably lost but growing more and more alluring in memory. Boccaccio could not hope for any new Neapolitan post because of the difficult situation of the "companies" in the kingdom and the break between Florence and the Angevins. Boccaccio had to limit himself to keeping close to that beloved fellowship of friends, collaborating in some way as "procurator" or proctor of the splendid achievements of the Acciaiuoli family in Florence.[4]

Notwithstanding his recalcitrant attitude and his protestations, despite his lamenting and invoking an impossible return to Naples, Boccaccio must even by the end of 1341 have begun to have some understanding and sympathy for the Florentine cultural and social world, for he attempted resolutely to gain entry to it. Indeed he clearly wanted to win its regard. The easiest and most natural way open to him for this purpose was a probing of the cult of Dante and of that new, vaguely allegorical and didactic literature, almost unknown in Naples, which in Tuscany was dominant. That movement followed the examples of the Stil Novo or Sweet New Style and Alighieri, the *Fiore* and the *Intelligenza,* Francesco da Barberino and Jacopo Alighieri (son of Dante) and all the repetitions of the *Roman de la Rose.* Also, Boccaccio, so sensitive to the taste and wishes of the public, was attracted by types of literature less aristocratic than those that were in full development at the time: mercantile and domestic memoirs written by middle-class chroniclers such as Giovanni Villani, whose work we see was known to Boccaccio before its "publication." He was attracted by vulgarizations which were appearing in great numbers and bringing within the reach of a new class of readers the texts of the great Latins and the new French writers; attracted by the "cantari" which were soaring to the apogee of their success. Clear indications of Boccaccio's exceptional zeal are given by the laudable collection he formed of rare texts of Dante, or by his interest in Dante, carefully transcribed in the *Zibaldone Laurenziano,* and by the imitations from the *Divina Commedia* which teem in the *Teseida* and the glosses. His interest in Florentine culture is indicated by his allegorizing or borrowing from the vulgarizations, which is so apparent in the glosses—largely written in Florence; by his relations with the popularizers of Valerius Maximus or Ovid themselves (Filippo Ceffi, Carlo Figiovanni?)[5] by the more accentuated "canterine" technique of the octave in the *Teseida,* by Boccaccio's friendship and collaboration with Pucci *(Rime,* LXIX and LXXXI).

Boccaccio's first two works written in Florence are clearly and completely Florentine: the *Comedia della Ninfe* (1341-1342) and the *Amorosa Visione (*1342). Both deal resolutely—although with new and singular intonations and developments—with the great theme of Tuscan literary tradition, that of enobling and transfiguring Love. Both adopt the Dantean tercet, henceforth the typical meter for such themes, and make exceptional use of imitations from the *Divina Commedia.* Both energetically include landscapes, events, and personages of contemporary Florentine life. Besides his acceptance—which has the character of a tribute—of a literary tradition ignored until then, besides the homage of the etiological fable on Florence worked out in the *Comedia,* Boccaccio, by presenting current faces and occurrences, stresses the *militant* character of his works. Indeed for the first time the dedication of the *Comedia* is not addressed to the mythical Fiammetta (who now always hovers on the edges, no longer entreated or cursed) or to other women equally vague and literary ("the fair lady whose name is never mentioned," or Filomena; see above, page 42). It is addressed instead to a prominent political personality, his friend Niccoló di Bartolo del Buono (see below, page 121), with a voice of lament which no longer prefigures literary schemes but, as in epistle V, reveals the sadness of a real situation:

> And thou, O my only friend, and truest example of true friendship, O Niccoló di Bartolo del Buono of Florence . . . take this rose born 'mid the thorns of my adversity, which Florentine beauty by its strength drew from the harsh thornbushes, with me existing in the lowest depths of melancholy wretchedness . . . : I, 3.[6]

Besides, more than a literary atmosphere, a society had revealed itself to Boccaccio. It was middle class to be sure, but gay and gallant and elegant, full of those engaging frivolities, that stimulating tittle-tattle of affection which he had both loved and suffered and celebrated in Naples. The *Comedia* and the last cantos of the *Amorosa Visione* (like the contemporary "ternary" *Contento quasi: Rime* LXX) overflow with his first impressions and enthusiasms and with the gratified knowledge of intrigues and secrets of love. In the alternation and the merging of the figures belonging to his Neapolitan post with those new ones of his early Florentine acquaintance is the most evident sign of the meeting of the two worlds in the imagination of Boccaccio (next to Fiammetta, Giovanna, Agnese there are Lia, Emilia,[7] Lottiera, Alionora, and so on). It is the most concrete testimony of that typically Florentine artistic experience, which in these two works points decisively to the conquest of a new manner, on the technical plane and the poetic.

The *Comedia delle Ninfe* (*Ninfale d'Ameto* to copyists and editors of the fifteenth century) was written towards the end of 1341 and the beginning of 1342 (in the dedication are echoes of the epistle V of August 1341; Lia, the heroine, is mentioned in *Amorosa Visione,* XLI, 35). In imitation of the *De Consolatione Philosophiae* and the *Vita Nuova* (and works of Martianus Capella and Alain de Lille) Boccaccio wrote the *Comedia* in prose intercalated with poems in terza rima. He narrates the transformation of Ameto from a rough, boorish shepherd into a tender and noble lover thanks to Lia and by virtue of the teachings which she and the six other nymphs, her companions, give him by the narration of their loves. Thus within the pastoral framework or "cornice," which was to become so very celebrated a device, there is presented a series of quite varied and realistic tales (at least four of the seven protagonists have been identified as ladies of the upper middle class), "almost a little *Decameron,*" according to the definition of sixteenth-century literary critics.

The *Amorosa Visione* was written certainly after the *Comedia* in 1342 and before the death of King Robert (January 20, 1343) because Giovanna is still presented as Duchess of Calabria (XL, 14-15). It is a poem of fifty cantos in Dantean tercets and crowded with echoes and borrowings from the *Divina Commedia*. The poet

imagines that in a dream he sees successively the triumphs of Wisdom, of worldly Glory, of Riches, of Love, of Fortune which destroys
all, and thus he is made worthy of meeting Fiammetta and of her
"celestial" love, worthy, that is, of the winning of Virtue. The
"triumphs," naturally, serve as a pretext to present the greatest
figures of mythology, of antiquity, of the Middle Ages down to
contemporary personages, and this first example of a series of
"triumphs" morally devised and linked evidently fostered in Petrarch the ideation of his *Trionfi*. In the last period of his life Boccaccio took up this poem and prepared a new version of it (see below,
pages 110 ff.)

The triumph of virtue—and of the Virtues—in both works remains a pure aspiration, an ardent desire, an abstract crowning. But
it contributes also to the most ambitious concern of its author, that
of ennobling the adventures of his characters, always balanced
between the lyric and history, between allegory and chronicle, and
to lift the figure of the woman loved to a cathartical function, to a
superhuman firmness.

In the *Comedia*, Boccaccio mingles novelistic narration, already
essayed in the *Filocolo*, with the versifying, allusive, or absentmind-
edly unrestrained style of the *Caccia* [8] or the *Rime*. He combines
realism with allegorical abstraction, and produces a portrayal of
middle-class society which, for the first time, replaces the heroic or
chivalric milieux with a mannered rustic landscape. More than the
bucolic charm of the picture, or the consciously new conception of
love, what is interesting in the *Comedia*, as Quaglio points out,[9] is the
miracle of a new poetry. The miracle lies in its allegory, which is
obtained by rejecting lyrical bursts, and by dissolving the psychologically keyed theme in the course of narrative development. This
stylistic extremism is interesting, and it, too, has a cathartic value not
found in the overly direct autobiographism of Boccaccio's Neapolitan works. Ovid, Boethius, Martianus Capella, Alain de Lille, *his*
Dante and above all the classical ecologues, laden with medieval
allegorical meanings, inspired Boccaccio in the direction of a new
allegory. (Ameto is often copied from Ovid's Poliphemus yearning
for Galatea.)

Less interesting from a stylistic and literary viewpoint, yet perhaps more decisive in the development of this new literary extremism, is the *Amorosa Visione*. From the beginning, Boccaccio endeavored to establish two emblems of the Florentine culture as he had come to know it. He extolled the work of Giotto, the absolute master of realism (canto V), and raised the figure of Dante to a height above any other artist, ancient or modern (cantos V and VI). For the first time we are aware, in the *Amorosa Visione,* that Boccaccio was attempting to make a systematic arrangement of the erudition he had so enthusiastically accumulated during his Neapolitan years. He systematizes the providential, historical, and moral aspects of his work through the series of five *triumphs,* and orders the literary and cultural elements by drawing rapid characterizations of figures placed in ideal perspectives. The extreme allegorical stylization of the pretty fable of Fiammetta, and the crystallization of her figure in the "acrostic," represent the victory of the rhetorical order over any romantic unseemliness. That is, the reduction of the myth to the patterns of the lyric, and the writing of treatises on love, together with the fashion of acrostics, were dominant in Tuscany at that time. Any excessive use of autobiography is limited in favor of the universal morality of the "legend of Everyman." The poet thus contemplated the passions, objectified in the various "triumphs," which had dominated his youth and pervaded his Neapolitan works.[10]

The "new manner" of Boccaccio the writer is henceforth clear in his aspiration to both master a style and conquer a society through a "militant realism" and a concept of nobility no longer feudal and based on blood-ties, but human and resulting from qualities of the heart (theorized in **XXXIII** of the *Amorosa Visione*). Clear, too, is Boccaccio's commitment to idealize and objectify, in the footsteps of Dante, amorous experiences to the point of delineating an ideal itinerary of man from vain and worldly things, to Love and to Virtue. It is his poetical and humane conception which, after the experiments in the sonnets and the *Fiammetta* and *Ninfale,* Boccaccio would declare in the ideal design of the *Decameron* and later, with more coherence, in the works of his maturity.

But in harmony with the trends and the "acquisitions" of his final Neapolitan period, Boccaccio was also susceptible to the enthusiasms for the glorious apotheoses of Petrarch in Naples, Rome, and

Parma. The admirers of the poet laureate in the land of Tuscany also moved him in the same direction. Among these enthusiasts were: Sennuccio del Bene, who was the first to influence Boccaccio, and who, like Boccaccio, also celebrated Lottiera during those years; [11] Mainardo Accursio; Bruno Casini; Giovanni dell'Incisa; and Franceschino degli Albizzi, the friend and relative of Petrarch. Because of this interest, Boccaccio, while working on his Dantean texts, transcribed one by Petrarch. It was of fundamental importance in his laudable copy-book, the *Zibaldone Laurenziano* (see column 73r, the reference to the crowning with laurel). Perhaps, as well, during the meetings with Barrili and Sennuccio in the winter of 1341 and 1342, when they told him about the Neapolitan and Capitoline solemnities and about their writing devotedly to Petrarch (see *Var.* 57 and *Metr.*, II, 1), Boccaccio's enthusiasm was so sparked that he sketched on the texts dealing with the crowning (collatio, privilegium, etc.) the *De Vita et Moribus Domini Francisci Petracchi*. Like Dante in the conclusion of the *Filocolo,* Petrarch was placed in the long line of the great classical writers, Homer, Terence, Virgil, Horace, Ovid, Lucan, Statius, Juvenal, Cicero, and Seneca. In this biography Petrarch is portrayed with a medievally rational biographical stylization, to which Petrarch himself would be sensitive in his *Posteritati.* His work is given a eulogy, "bombastic, for its rhetoric and indeed its affection ... enlivened by a sincere warmth, which is expressed as stunned admiration, almost that of an unlettered man for the measureless erudition and the complete perfection of one eulogized" (Billanovich, *Petrarca,* p. 75). But alongside these lofty themes, faithful to his linguistic and cultural ambivalence, Boccaccio, the convinced defender of the new literature, places Petrarch's poetry "in suis quamplurimis vulgaribus poematibus, in quibus perlucide decantarit." It was what Boccaccio himself, in the few copies then circulating, [12] harkened to and meditated on in order to filter it into the language of his sonnets (*Rime,* LXXIX ff.) and of the *Amorosa Visione* as well.

While Boccaccio thus broadened and strengthened his literary experience, he also emerged resolutely from the lonely sadness of his first Florentine months. We see him in relations with the most representative personalities of the city's culture (for example, with the "Dantist" Forese Donati and with Franceschino Albizzi, both admired genealogists, and with the poets Bruno Casini and Zanobi da Strada). He mingled with the followers of the *Stil nuovo* (Del Bene, Frescobaldi and Ventura Monachi, Franceschino again),[13] and with the richest and most aristocratic families of the middle class, from the Rinuccini, the Del Buono, the Domenichi and the Rossi (ep. VI and VIII; *Decameron,* V, 9, 4; *Esposizioni,* VIII, 1, 68; XVI, 16), to the families of the ladies introduced and eulogized in the *Comedia,* in the "ternary," and in the *Amorosa Visione* (Gianfigliazzi, Tornaquinci, Nerli, Regaletti, Visdomini, Della Tosa, Peruzzi, Nigi, Manovelli, Scali, Baroncelli, and so on). We hear him passionately engaging in the great civic and economic events of the society in which he lived; now he was far removed from his harsh and very literary disdain.

During that period the disorders of Florentine policies had grown more serious and stormy. Angered, after the Acciaiuoli mission, by the "avarice" and the fickleness of Robert in the matter of Lucca, in those years the crux of the pride of the Marzocco [the emblematic lion of Florence], the Florentines early in 1342 even tried to reach agreements with the Emperor, the traditional enemy of the Guelfs and the kings of Naples (Villani, XI, 138). But forgetting the solemnly ratified law against conferring dictatorial powers on outsiders, a few months later they yielded to the thoroughly Angevin adventure of accepting the rule of the Duke of Athens (nephew of Robert, who, from the start, wanted to direct his uncle's policies: Villani, XII, 4). These perplexities also precipitated the crisis of the "companies" :

> King Robert became so jealous he did not know what to do, greatly fearing that the Florentines might turn to the imperial Ghibelline party. And many of his barons and prelates and other wealthy men of the kingdom, who had entrusted their money to the companies and merchants of Florence, became so worried for the same reason that each one demanded payment, and credit failed in Florence ... and afterwards many good Florentine companies became insolvent (Villani, XI, 138).

In this new situation Boccaccio turned from his old mythical glorifications, like those in the *Filocolo,* and began to make accusations of shabbiness and avarice against Robert, which was the *leit-motiv* of Florentine political publicity. Just while he is solemnly presenting the Swabian Ghibellines *(Amorosa Visione,* XI and XII) he caricatures this new Midas *(Comedia,* XXXV, 32; *Amorosa Visione,* XIV, 26 ff.). At the same time he seems to allude to the crisis of the bankers and merchants ruined by that politics but also by their own cupidity and excessive confidence *(Amorosa Visione,* XII, 62-85 and XIV, 33-36; for *Fiammetta.).* And above all it is in the pages on the tyranny of the Duke of Athens that, in retrospect, we sense both his direct participation (his friend Pino de' Rossi was one of the protagonists of the "cacciata," the expulsion) and an informed judgment on the positions of the Florentine bourgeoisie, even though this is implied by a deprecatory and literary civil dignity.[14]

Notwithstanding the crises and the difficulties, the life of the "companies" remained at the center of Florentine society, and Boccaccio, if he was now separated from the daily routine of the "companies," must not have been a stranger to their problems and their dramas, bound as he was to his own and so many other families of merchants, great and small. He must have felt with anguish the fate of many Florentines (and certainly that of his friends), harassed or even driven out of the kingdom despite the opposition and the defense of the greatly admired Carlo di Durazzo after the death of Robert (January 20, 1343) and the violent end of Gualtieri's domination. He must have contemplated the decline of the "grandi," in whose shadow his youth had been spent, and the waning of the Bardi especially, overturned as they were by the popular uprisings against men of power, who were held responsible for the tyranny of the Duke of Athens ("all the palaces and houses of the Bardi . . . were pillaged by the mobs . . . and by the anger of the people . . . there were burned twenty-two palaces and houses, great and rich" Villani, XII, 21). But at the same time he watched with passionate interest the daring efforts to renew and amplify the glamorous map of the "navigar mercantesco," mercantile ship routes. Early in 1342 there came letters and accounts from an associate of the Bardi, then resident in Seville, telling of a marvelous voyage to the Canaries and to the "insulis reliquis in Oceano noviter repertis." They reported on the customs of the inhabitants of the Canaries and on the commercial

possibilities there. Boccaccio, because he still lived in close relationship with the mercantile society, must have had prompt knowledge of
those reports and must have been ardently interested in them, for he
later included the substance of them in a decorous Latin transcription, *De Canaria*, in the *Zibaldone Magliabechiano* (cols. 123-24). As these
pages reveal, he was prompted not so much by a taste for geography
and discovery as by a sense of participation as a narrator keen on
observing "new aspects of humanity, new specimens of the plant,
man," myths new or old (here, for example, that very old one about the
good savage).[15] Therefore he must have been strongly attracted by
those letters and accounts, not artistic, but nevertheless clear and
trustworthy, and controlled by a critical intelligence extremely alert
to worldly affairs. The output of the pens of that refined class of
businessmen: those "books of memoirs," "secret books," and "domestic recollections," were now becoming numerous in middle-class
Florence, as were the brisk and spirited treatises on economic techniques and geography. One, Pegolotti's *Pratica della mercatura*, a book
emanating from the Bardi circle, attained the rank of masterpiece.

Thus, while resolutely assimilating and mastering a new culture,
while creating a place for himself in a society new to him, and which
little by little he was growing to understand and to admire for his
ability to fuse contemplative with active virtues (symbolized in Lia
and Ameto and later in the two protagonists of the *Amorosa Visione*),
Boccaccio went ahead defining his great vocation, a humane and
universal realism and an epic interpretation of the saga of trade and
commerce.

Notwithstanding the prevailingly sentimental interest revealed
by the title itself, Boccaccio's ideal was already apparent in the *Elegia
di Madonna Fiammetta*, written perhaps sometime in 1343 or 1344.[16]

In the *Elegia* Boccaccio supposes that Fiammetta narrates her
love affair with a young Florentine merchant, Panfilo, and tells of her
worries and her despair—great enough to make her attempt suicide
upon finding that he had first abandoned and then betrayed her. In
contrast Boccaccio, in all his other works and in the *Rime,* had
portrayed himself as being deceived by Fiammetta.

The *Rime,* which have come down to us are approximately 150
components, mostly sonnets, written from the time of his early youth

to the last year of his life, often of uncertain attribution, and never put into a collection by the author. Amid insistent Dantean and Petrarchan echoes, he continually, and almost exclusively, in tones now bantering, now impassioned, now joyous, now despairing, rings the changes on his marvelous and "unique" love unto death for Fiammetta.

In this first modern psychological and realistic novel peopled wholly by middle-class characters, the autobiographical and literary modes of preceding works are almost entirely laid aside. External doings and happenings, the careless and mundane gossip so complex and copious in the preceding works are excluded except for a few data required to develop the secret mutation of a soul from one state to another. The customary relationship between the lovers is reversed and simplified to an extreme, allowing the most subtle motives and the most secret impulses of a woman in love to stand out with exceptional passion and elegance (Boccaccio also relies on classical stimuli and imitations, sometimes heavy and excessive, taken largely from Ovid, Seneca, and Dante).[17] Thus is born Boccaccio's first truly tragical character, his first story all soul and feeling, a story not about amorous joy and glorification but about "a contingency which is often cruel," about a mad perverting passion ("as though, stronger, uncaring, it annuls the laws of others and lays down its own," I, 17, 23); a passion which leads to "martyrdom," to a "sorry pass" like that of Phaedra and Francesca da Rimini (the latter also, like Fiammetta, a reader of "French romances": VIII, 7, 1). In the portrayal of the total life—body and soul—of a real and clearly defined person, more effective than in the preceding didactic and allegorical crystallizations, Boccaccio succeeds in overcoming the dash and disorder of his favored, too-direct surrenders to autobiography; he succeeds in telling a story more freely and at the same time with more composure, thus tending toward the rhythm, if not the tone, which were to characterize the *Decameron*. Precisely because Boccaccio has mastered his narrative, and because of his narrative probing, this story contains a wealth of humanity, which does not manifest itself solely in the inner complexity of the heroine. For the first time, and free of any conventionality, an affectionate light illumines the characters and the environment which surrounds the protagonists: the timorous nurse and the faithful friend, the noble husband betrayed, and the lonely father of Panfilo and even, on another plane, the two houses ruined by the madly amorous passion of Fiammetta. Owing to the abundance and complexity of human motives and interests Boccaccio builds into his story, the references to the Florentine merchants forced to leave the kingdom take on a pregnant allusive significance, as do the gibes and taunts against the commune of Florence, which he had freely expressed in Naples, and the nostalgic recollection of the "good" Guelf peace and its author King Robert, now—purified of his final meannesses—taken up in memory as the symbol of that time forever lost. Boccaccio's new political and social sensibility finds sincere expression in such references, no longer mythical (*Filocolo*) or cryptographic tittle-tattle (*Ameto, Amorosa Visione*), but realistic and concrete symbols, interwoven as they are in the daily existence and the inner life itself of the characters.

A similar simplification of the exterior happenings and a similar wealth of humanity, but freer of literary and erudite juxtapositions and ambitions, characterize the *Ninfale Fiesolano* also, of which the date of composition is extremely uncertain (1344-1346?).[18]

In the classical form of an etiological fable the little narrative poem of the *Ninfale* of 473 octaves recounts the love of the young shepherd Africo for the nymph Mensola who—at first timidly courted and later surprised while bathing—not without secret tenderness yields to the desires of her lover and in due course brings forth a child, Pruneo. But Mensola does not escape the wrath of her goddess Diana, whom she has betrayed by losing her virginity; in despair at her loss, Africo kills himself (and the two brooks running down from Fiesole to Florence, still bear their names). Pruneo, compassionately sheltered by his grandparents, soon gives proof of his valor in deeds which are connected with the origins of Florence and Fiesole (it should be remembered that Boccaccino possessed a house and farm at Corbignano in San Martino at Mensola).[19]

Boccaccio's imaginative creation in the *Ninfale* proceeds more confidently and freely than ever, even though the influence of Ovid and Statius (*Achilleis*) is evident, and even though the whole action develops among nymphs and goddesses, humanized, however, and brought down to the measure of a simple rustic life. The autobiographical experiences are now firmly kept at a minimum, filtered and assimilated in the delicacy with which the passion of love is treated, strongly characterized and seen with new freshness and chasity in two souls almost childishly ingenuous (in the way that Mensola is new in her somewhat dreamy and fragile innocence, in her motherhood, in her death). But at the same time the themes and motifs are multiplied and enriched, ever so much broadened and varied, almost always exactly attuned. Next to the dominant theme (here too love more soulful than sensual) stands the picturization of the Georgic rural environment, not intellectualized as in the *Comedia,* but portrayed in the innocence of the Golden Age. The rapid, light visualizations of nymphs and the hunt dart forth, so different from the ornamentation of the earlier poetry. The lament for virginity lost and the tenderness of motherhood tremble fearfully. For the first time Boccaccio conveys the poetry of family life in the portrayal of those two old grandparents, all tender affection for their grandson. While providing this thematic and human enrichment, Boccaccio's uncertainty seems to diminish, developing a very refined rhetoric distilled from the complex classical and medieval tradition as well as a realistic "antirhetoric" present in the bourgeois or outright popular language urgent in all the youthful works. Thanks to this new sureness of expression and thanks to the experiences he had savored in the more current semicultured literature (besides the *cantari,* the *strambotti, rispetti* and songs for dancing, also present in the *Rime),* Boccaccio succeeds in achieving a spoken style which transforms and assimilates even the imitations of the classics and the *Stil nuovo* and opens the possibilities for the poetic narration of the Renaissance (idyllic in the *Ambra* and the *Stanze,* rustic in the *Nencia* and the *Beca,* romantic in the *Morgante* and the two *Orlandos).* Containing little in the way of descriptive elements, but rich in spoken elements and scenes which reveal states of soul, and clearly controlled as it is by a situation in harmonic and coherent development, the *Ninfale*—as Momigliano remarked—reveals the temperament of a realistic novella writer, not that of a lyricist.

Especially on the eve of the *Decameron,* it would be pleasant to be able to follow point by point Boccaccio's determined technical, expressive, and artistic gains through the cultural, social, and human experiences which prompted or consolidated them. Instead, information on Boccaccio during these years is very scanty and often unreliable, except for general and environmental notes. Family life for Giovanni (who all through his Neapolitan youth had ignored it, and then during those first months in Florence had bitterly deprecated it) must have become enlivened and more agreeable, for after the affectionate mention of it in the *Amorosa Visione* and loving veneration in the *Fiammetta* Boccaccio soon after created the delicate poetry of the *Ninfale*. In about 1344 the house was gladdened by a child, Jacopo,[20] who perhaps lent some of his charm to Pruneo (unless indeed it was suggested by one of Boccaccio's illegitimate children, Mario or Giulio: see below, notes 42 and 43). Despite the difficulties of the preceding years and the economic and commercial crisis, Boccaccino not only was able to acquire a house in the parish of S. Ambrogio (on December 13, 1342)[21], actively to continue his business with the Capuan rentals,[22] and to make contracts amounting to hundreds and hundreds of gold florins,[23] but he was still holding public offices (Ufficiale sopra la moneta, 1345).[24] Boccaccio himself must have participated in some way in his father's activity, perhaps only marginally, and not only in the Capuan leases.[25]

However, in the stormy climate following the expulsion of the Duke of Athens (Walter of Brienne), life could not have been easy, especially for someone like Boccaccio, having connections with the Bardi circle and Angevin friendships. On the one hand the dictatorship of Walter (Gualtieri) had brought onto the stage of Florentine politics a new character, the "popolo minuto" (the common people, the mass). But the grandees (*grandi*), who had skillfully "unhooked" themselves from the tyrant and from associated responsibilities, not only brutally repulsed those dangerous collaborators, but did not permit restoration of the "Ordinamenti di giustizia" (which would specifically have excluded the grandees from government). Thus they provoked angry reactions resulting in those acts of violence, looting and burning of property, to which we saw the Bardi fall victims. On the other hand this "company," while it continued its unpopular pro-Angevin and pro-Neapolitan policies, very inadequately supported by the Consiglio di Reggenza del Regno (Regency Council of the Kingdom), was overwhelmed in early 1345, along with the

Peruzzi, by the unfortunate war waged in France by Edward III of England, the insolvent debtor of millions of good gold florins. "Owing to that failure . . . there came upon . . . the city of Florence greater ruin and defeat than she had ever suffered. And because of this our republic lost and was desolated of all power . . ." (Villani, XIII, 55). In that same year, when Joanna (Giovanna) attained majority and became queen, there broke out in Naples the clash between the Taranto and the Durazzo factions for an eventual succession to the throne. In that "late empire" climate, the struggle culminated in the assassination of Andrew (Andrea) of Hungary on September 18, 1345, who was Joanna's husband, and who, in the eyes of the contending parties, was an obstacle to be eliminated, perhaps not without the connivance of the ostensibly very impartial Acciaiuoli, counselor of the principal suspect, Louis (Luigi) of Taranto. With all this, the kingdom fell into chaos, into the violence between the various factions, into anguish aroused by the announced punitive expedition of King Louis of Hungary [Andrew's brother], as Boccaccio would later mention or narrate in the *Buccolicum Carmen* (III, IV, V, VIII), in the *De Casibus* (IX, 26) and in the *De Mulieribus* (CIII).

Thus Boccaccio's Neapolitan hopes, founded on the Court or on his friend Niccola, and never completely abandoned, fell to the ground tragically;[26] conditions in Florence were getting farther and farther away from those in the "peaceful and prosperous city" dreamed of until the violent reaction against the mayoral effort of Ciuto Brandini and the seditious exclusion laws of October 1346. To Boccaccio, who aspired to a respectable post, who still in 1347 claimed that he was persecuted by misfortune ("nil ultra me michi noverca fortuna reliquit" ep. VI), the courts of neighboring Romagna opened their doors naturally, in contradiction to his feeling. First and foremost that of Ravenna welcomed him where there existed an important family of Boccacci (possibly related to that of Certaldo)[27] and where Florentine culture was known and appreciated due to easy relations and to Dante's long sojourn there, and where Dantean memories were numerous also because of the presence of Suor Beatrice, the poet's daughter. We know with certainty from one of Petrarch's letters (*Fam.*, XIII, xix, 2)[28] that Boccaccio lived in

Ravenna during the lordship of Ostasio da Polenta (cousin and successor to the host of Dante, who died on November 14, 1346).

At the beginning of the Italian version of the fourth decade of Livy, now attributed with extreme probability to Boccaccio, we read the dedication "to the noble knight, Sir Ostasio da Polenta, most especially my lord, at whose request I set about such a great work." Boccaccio lived therefore for a certain time at Ravenna (Probably beginning not earlier than the end of 1345;), in the precincts of the court of Ostasio and, perhaps, after his death, or that of his son Bernardino, whose patronage he was to solicit later. In that period he built up the great Ravenna friendships which would endure throughout his lifetime, for example, that with Donato degli Albanzani, of Casentino, who had a school in Ravenna; that with Dante's old acquaintance, Minghino Mezzani, and so forth.[29] But at the end of 1347 or early in 1348 Boccaccio was in Forlì at the court of Francesco Ordelaffi, "meux inclitus dominus et Pyeridum hospes gratissimus," as he wrote to Zanobi (ep. VI).[30] During those years, Boccaccio, along with Cecco di Meletto Rossi, Francesco's secretary (a nephew of Scarpetta, the host of Dante), engaged in a poetical correspondence in Italian (*Rime*, LXXIX) and in Latin, with allusions to Petrarch (*Carmi*, I and II). In this second Dantean court, naturally, he continued to collect texts and memoirs of the greatly admired poet (the two ecologues and poems of Giovanni del Virgilio—a correspondence already re-echoing in the *Comedia*—the letter of Fra Ilario: all transcribed in the *Zibaldone Laurenziano* together with the poems exchanged with Checco and the ep. VI).

But as the second poem (*Carme* II) and the epistle to Zanobi reveal, Boccaccio was also implicated, though not officially, in the tempestuous incidents subsequent to the killing of Andrew, which involved Florence and the small principalities of Romagna, together with the kingdom. After having sent a vanguard into the Abruzzi in the summer of 1347 (while Acciaiuoli had vainly requested the aid of Florence), Louis of Hungary invaded Italy with his army and by mid-December was already in Romagna. The Signoria of Florence maintained an attitude of neutrality, benevolent towards the king of Hungary, diffident towards the Angevins of Naples, who in recent

times had not measured up to the city's trust in them and who, by
mid-January, were to be rapidly swept away by Hungarian violence
(Carlo of Durazzo was slain; Joanna with her new husband Luigi of
Taranto and their counselor Niccola became refugees in Provence).
The lords of Ravenna were inclined to favor Louis of Hungary, whose
action in humiliating the Pontifical government (which had supported Joanna and still supported her) promised them a position of
greater independence in regard to their sovereign, the Pope. On
December 13, 1347 Francesco Ordelaffi had received King Louis with
great honors and was preparing to follow him into Campania, as
epistle VI of Boccaccio indicates. In it Boccaccio declared that he was
about to depart with Francesco as counselor or secretary or historiog-
rapher, chosen perhaps as one well-versed in Neapolitan affairs:

> . . . nisi itinera instarent ad illustrem Ungarie regem in extremis
> Bruitorum et Campanie quo moratur: nam ut sua ymitetur
> arma iustissima meus *inclitus dominus* . . . cum pluribus Flaminee
> proceribus preparatur; quio et *ipse mei predicti domini iussi non*
> *armiger sed, ut ita loquar, rerum occurrentium arbiter sum iturus,* et
> prestanibus superis, omnes in brevi, victoria habita et celebrato
> triumpho dignissime, *sedes proprias revisuri.*

Disregarding the ambitious disproportion of that "rerum occurren-
tium arbiter"—almost another Acciaiuoli!—the indication is very
clear even though we know little and unreliably of the intervention
of Ordelaffi [31] and nothing at all of Boccaccio's journey to Naples in
that period, while on the contrary everything induces us to rule it
out.[32] Despite the inflections of a literary exercise, somewhere
between the rhetoric of the first epistles and the overt display of
allusion in the eclogues, the letter to Zanobi shows that Boccaccio was
still in the service of Francesco and was planning to remain there.
Perhaps, with the waning of the expedition following the retinue of
the king of Hungary, he deceived himself into believing that he was
still performing a counselor's and arbiter's function in those events,
with those poems to Checco, and with the eclogues. During a time
difficult to determine, Boccaccio, in these writings, showed he was
oscillating from positions favorable to King Louis and from accusa-

tions of Joanna and the Tarentines (III in the twofold version) all the way to deprecation of Hungarian ferocity and kindly judgments of Luigi of Taranto and his followers, to regrets for the good old times of King Robert, to eulogies of the current sovereigns and of Acciaiuoli (IV, V, VI).[33] From invective, he passed in turn to the palinode, to the elegy, to the paean.

Certainly, after so many years, Boccaccio's resumption of writing poetry in Latin, and especially of the very new politically allusive line of the eclogues, must be traced back to his cultural experiences in Romagna, to those within the small humanistic circle of Checco di Meletto and in particular to those prompted by the much-admired Dantean texts and by Petrarch's eclogue on the death of Robert. [34] This new turn in Boccaccio's literary activity —anticipated in some ways, but on an absolutely different plane, by the allegories and pastoral allusions of the *Comedia*—was to be followed throughout the rest of his life, down to the composition of the *Buccolicum Carmen* (sixteen eclogues, to 1366 approximately), through diverse reworkings and essays. Together with similar authoritative texts by Petrarch, Boccaccio was to open the way to a great flowering of humanistic and Renaissance culture, continued even in the following ages.

During these months Boccaccio completed the vernacular version of Livy (decades III and IV). He certainly had started in many years earlier (actually in 1338, according to Casella) in the cultural climate, dominant in Naples, as in Florence, that was demanded by the new audience of middle-class readers.[35] It was an essential and decisive experience for the "father of Italian prose." Rising above the Valerian and Apuleian constructions dominant in the *Filocolo* (and again in the *Comedia*), Boccaccio had mastered the syntax of Livy and the style which he was to impose on Italian literary tradition with his masterpiece. In a narrative sense, he also matured in his historical vision of men and their vicissitudes, as is evident later on in the famous introduction to the *Decameron*.

Furthermore, we already sense that Boccaccio had come to consider the Black Death as a scourge sent "by God's just wrath upon mortals." This providential interpretation, more dominant in the works of Boccaccio than in those of others, including Petrarch's, is evident in the sonnet included in his correspondence with Checco di Meletto, who had raised an anguished question about the terrible disease (*Rime,* LXXIX). If, as it appears, Meletto, during the first occurrence of the Black Death in Italy, January 1348, suggested that the plague was an act of providence, then Boccaccio probably wrote this sonnet after his return to Florence.

Boccaccio must have been disappointed in his Neapolitan hopes by the too speedy return of Ordelaffi, by his more than modest rôle in the Angevin events, and by the dramatic and ferocious turn in the Hungarian expedition, which left no room for cultural or literary praises in its character as a harsh and violent military occupation (moreover, King Louis left the kingdom in May).[36]

Certainly Boccaccio was already in Florence during the terrible plague which began there in March or April 1348 (". . . which, had it not been seen by many eyes and by *mine,* hardly would I have dared believe it, much less write about it . . ." he declares in the Introduzione, 16 to the *Decameron,* and again: "Of which my eyes ... took ... notice," 18, and so on). He could in fact have been kept informed of the details of the tragic situation by his father, who participated actively as "Ufficiale dell'Abbondanza" in the rationing and hygienic measures instituted by the Signoria.[37] The spectacle of human bestiality and human heroism occasioned by the appalling tragedy, by the ruin of Florence, reduced to slightly more than a third of its previous population and in consequence left politically and economically prostrate,[38] and the sweeping away of the circle of his dearest friends (among the dead were Matteo Frescobaldi, Giovanni Villani, Ventura Monachi and Bruno Casini, Francesco Albizzi and soon afterwards Coppo di Borghese Domenichi, followed in the autumn of 1349 by old Sennuccio),[39] all constituted a profound and decisive experience. Nor was the paternal family spared: in 1348 his stepmother Bice died, followed soon afterwards by his father,[40] later affectionately commemorated and almost consecrated by Boccaccio in heavenly glory alongside his grandchildren (eclogue XIV). Thus Boccaccio, as the eldest son, inevitably found himself head of the family with responsibility for the modest but not negligible patrimony left by his father.[41] In this same period, as though to offset the demise of the generation preceding his own (even his uncle Vanni no longer appears in any document), Violante, "nimium dilecta, spes unica patris," was born either in Florence or in Ravenna. She was not the first of his children (there were at least five, all illegitimate),[42] but she is the only one who succeeds in having some physical reality for us, thanks to the beautiful and poetic portrayal of her in eclogue XIV and her father's affectionate memories in two epistles (XIV and XXIII).[43]

The everyday necessities of Boccaccio's family taught him responsibilities and duties, burdensome or consoling, most concretely and realistically. They brought him into contact with problems and persons of the little daily world and measured his ideals against the most time-worn realities. In this situation, where his decisive cultural conquests of Florence and Romagna were converging with his new and varied human and family experiences, and with a deepened understanding of the classics and an extraordinary sensitivity to the voices of the new literature, including its most bourgeois and popular forms, Boccaccio gave shape to the *Decameron,* probably between 1348 and 1351.[44] Boccaccio brought together and arranged elements and tales sketched in the course of his rich career as a writer (at least three novellas were already included in the *Filocolo* and the *Comedia:* X, 4 and 5; II, 10).

In the *Decameron* (this title also is of Greek derivation: δεκα ʿημέρων = *of the ten days*), Boccaccio imagines that seven girls and three youths withdraw to the hills of Fiesole to escape the horrors of the plague of 1348. (This is the classic landscape picture frame Boccaccio used from the *Comedia* and the *Ninfale* onward, perhaps because he was familiar with the views from the houses and farms formerly belonging to his father.) To pass the time, on every day except Saturday and Sunday, each of these ten young people recounts a novella conforming to the theme and order of narration established by the one presiding on that day. Thus 100 novellas are narrated in ten days, intercalated with descriptions of the aristocratic life led by this elegant and refined group.

In this powerful and multiform narrative work Boccaccio depicted the "human comedy" of the communal society, in the autumn of its medieval civilization. He portrayed it especially in its most vigorous and vital expression, which in the preceding century had enabled it to win economic dominance over Europe and the Mediterranean world. That is to say, he depicted the extraordinary saga of its merchant class. But, in accordance with the canons of the most valid esthetics of the time, Boccaccio not only applied the most refined techniques of rhetoric (incuding the *cursus* and rhymed prose), he imparted to his diverse and multicolored descriptions a value above and beyond that of the single episode: that of an example worthy of imitation. Throughout the ten days in which the hundred novellas are grouped, he aimed at symbolizing the measure that man gives of his capacities for good and for evil. And to this end he represented man in an ideal itinerary which, starting with the bitter reproof of vices (day I), ends in the exaltation of virtue (day X). In between, Boccaccio described man measured face to face with the three great forces which, as instruments of Providence, are at work in the world (Luck or Fortune, days II and III; Love, IV and V; Ingenuity, VI, VII, VIII; IX is a day of transition).

Boccaccio thus picked up the themes of love, of adventure, of ingenuity, which had been dominant in all his youthful works. In this progression of "triumphs," almost a "legend of Everyman," he developed them and strengthened them, giving his more vigorous and multiform representation of human reality a universal value and a significance above and beyond that of the particular event. Precisely for this value and this significance, so very new to ancient and to medieval novella writing, Boccaccio produced a masterpiece, the *summa* of Western narrative art. Only a few years after it was completed, it alone of the great works written in one of the new vernaculars, was being spread over all of civilized Europe, in the original or in translation.[45]

NOTES

1. Some doubt remains as to the exact date of ep. V, transmitted to us only in a vernacular version. It was attributed to 1342 also, but without consistent reasons (see Massera, *Nota* to the *Opere minori latine del Boccaccio,* Bari, 1926, p. 324; P.G. Ricci, "Per la cronologia delle opere" in *Studi sul B.,* VI, 1971).
2. She appears as the wife of Boccaccino in a document of May 21, 1343

(Crescini, *op. cit.*, p. 155), and again in one of January 26, 1350 (Manni, *op. cit.*, pp. 13 and 21).

3. The Capuan lease is renewed by Boccaccino together with Giovanni on May 10, 1342.

4. Acciaiuoli entered the picture to deal with the troublesome problem of Lucca. The Florentines had been defeated by the Pisans on October 2, 1341 and had invoked the aid of King Robert, who "was favorable and acted with subtle sagacity, and in November sent to Florence a great mission composed of Sir Gianni Barrile, Bishop of Grufo, and Grand Master of the highest personages of Naples, and Nicola degli Acciaiuoli with a great retinue" (G. Villani, XI, 137). On that occasion Niccola gave to the Carthusians the ground on the Ema where later the famous monastery of Certosa was erected. Barrili was one of the witnesses in Florence of the donation (February 8, 1342). Boccaccio was one of the "procurators" (attorneys) for the transfer of the property to the two priors of the order, who took possession on February 13, 1342 (doc. in Tanfani, *Niccola Acciaiuoli,* p. 47).

5. For Valerius Maximus, see Quaglio, art. cit.; and M. T. Casella, "Il Valerio Massimo in volgare: dal Lancia al Boccaccio" in *Italia Medioevale e Umanistica,* VI 1963 (that tries, without decisive proofs, to attribute to Boccaccio and to his Neapolitan youth the well-known vulgarization of Valerius); for Ceffi, see *Rime,* LXIX, 39 note; for Figiovanni, see his recollection of Boccaccio in the introduction to the Italian version of *Eroidi.*

6. The dedication of the *Amorosa Visione,* in its three acrostics, is the extreme, allusive crystallization of the Neapolitan molds, now bereft of significance.

7. The name already had been used for the protagonist of the *Teseida* and was used again in the *Comedia,* the *Amorosa Visione,* and the ternary (in the form *Emiliana).* Later it was used for a teller of novellas in the *Decameron.* For these reasons Torraca (*Per la biografia,* pp. 112 ff.) and then, more systematically, Billanovich (*Restauri,* pp. 105 ff.) thought that Boccaccio had developed a love for Emiliana de' Tornaquinci. But the hypothesis seems constructed on bases and with criteria analogous to the fine myth of Fiammetta (see Branca, *Boccaccio medievale,* pp. 197 and 244). For identification of these real women presented in the first Florentine works see my notes to the *Rime* (LXIX) and to the *Amorosa Visione* in the editions cited.

8. But in the *Caccia* the allegorical or allusive element was a gratuitous final installment, and external expedient, to conclude.

9. In the Preface to his edition for Mondadori (Milan, 1964).

10. Detailed documentations on these resolutions are in the article: V. Branca, "L'Amorosa Visione (tradizioni, significati, fortuna)," *Annali della R. Scuola Normale Sup.*, S. II, IX, 1942.

11. It is the Mopsa of the *Comedia;* and see *Rime*, LXIX; *Amorosa Visione*, XLIII, 80 (and note in the Branca ed. cit.), and Sennuccio's sonnet *Mirando fiso*. For his relations with Sennuccio in Florence see *Boccaccio medievale*, pp. 247 ff., and the last sonnet of Boccaccio, in which Sennuccio is ranked with Dante, Petrarch, and Cino. For the other Florentine friends devoted to Petrarch see page 83, note 39, also Foresti, *Aneddoti*, pp. 201 ff.

12. Wilkins, *The Making of the Canzoniere*, pp. 81 ff., 287 ff., 350; certainly Boccaccio knew the various sonnets to Sennuccio.

13. See note 11 above and page 55, note 9; notes 17 and 24 below. For the relations indicated later with Rinuccini, See Tordi, op. cit., pp. 78 ff.

14. *De Casibus*, IX: "Cum sumptibus Florentinorum essent attrite vires, frequenti senatu pro salute publica iniere Florentini consilium, et instructo bellorum viro, qui et seditiones civium et hostium coherceret impetus, ampla cum licentia daretur imperium . . . Eam igitur urbem quam non solum a progenitoribus liberam suscepimus sed nec illius unquam memoria cuiquam, exceptis Imperitoribus Romanorum subditam, his artibus iniquissimi cives, exteri, et scelestissimi hominis tyranni impero subiacere, et quasi non suae sed alterius tantum libertati iniecisse vincula, coepere et magnates tripudii subacti populi celebrare triumphos et qui alienum aes debuerant in creditorum papuperiem debachari, sic et plebs inferior discurrere undique . . . Arbitramus enim talia *cognoscentes* . . .".

15. M. Pastore Stocchi, "Il 'De Canaria' boccaccesca. . . ." *Rinascimento*, X, 1959; G. Padoan, "Petrarca, Boccaccio, e la scoperta delle Canarie," in *Italia medioevale e umanistica*, VII 1964. Angelo de' Corbizzi, cousin of one of the representatives of the Bardi and friend of the Boccacci, also participated in this audacious enterprise.

16. No precise date is known; there are only vague indications: the mention of Panfilo at the new wedding of his father might allude to that of Boccaccino; so too Panfilo's return from Naples to Florence which would date more than two years earlier. But stylistic reasons, the maturity of the prose style, the determined inversion of the love story, indicate there was probably an interval of two or three years between the *Comedia* and the *Elegia*.

17. The title itself is Dantean: "per elegiam stilum intelligimus miser-

orum," *De Vul. Eloq.*, II, iv, 6: cf. "with tearful style I shall follow unhappy fates," p. 4: here, after the epic poem *(Teseida)* and the *Comedia*, is the example of a third genre.

18. We can say only that it is prior to 1348, the year of the death of Matteo Frescobaldi, who borrowed a passage from it (S. De Benedetti, art. cit.). Any reference to the autobiographical romance and the myth of Fiammetta is lacking. The narrative poem seems to reflect a new solid experience: Florentine, linguistic, cultural and topographic, and a strong influence of *canterini* (ballad singers) and of rustic Tuscan poetry. Because Boccaccio was absent from Florence in 1346 and 1347, it appears necessary to ascribe the *poemetto* to a date prior to 1346. In point of fact, however, nothing would prevent advancing the date, as proposed by De Benedetti, who was convinced that the original idea was born in the Neapolitan period, as also P. G. Ricci, *Per la cronologia*, cit.

19. Documents cited by F. Corazzini, *Le lettere edite e inedite*, p. XCIX, and by D. Tordi, *Gli inventari* pp. 9 and 89 (see above, page 55, note 15).

20. He was about eighteen in 1361. See Ricci, *Studi* (1959), p. 25.

21. Doc. cit. by Corazzini, op. cit., p. C, and by E. Hutton, *Giovanni Boccaccio*, London, 1910, p. 358.

22. Document of May 10, 1342 published by D. Tordi, op. cit., p. 51: the rental appears stipulated and paid by Boccaccino "pro se ipso et suo nomine et vice et nomine Johannis ipsius Bocchaccii filii." It is interesting to note that, contrary to what has been believed and written, the lease was to continue for at least the lifetime of Boccaccio, for in his will he leaves exactly twenty-five florins, presumably the annual rental, to be paid to Petrillo da Capua, who later prosecuted Boccaccio's heirs, twenty years in arrears (Tordi, pp. 14-15).

23. Document of April 4, 1345 published by V. Branca, "Notizie e documenti per la biografia del Boccaccio." *Studi sul Boccaccio*, III ff., 1965 ff. cit.; documents of 1347 and 1348 published by Crescini, op. cit., pp. 257-58.

24. Manni, op. cit., p. 21; E. Rostagno, "Per la storia degli studi boccacceschi," in *Misc. Stor. Valdelsa*, XXI, 1973, p. 24.

25. A document of 1343 published by A. Aruch, "Ricerche e documenti sacchettiani." *Riv. d. Bibl. e d. Archivi*, XXVII, 1916, p. 87, does not concern the author of the *Decameron* but another Giovanni Boccaccio of the village of San Pancrazio.

26. There has been some discussion about a journey of Boccaccio to Naples in 1345 or 1346, based on the story of Filippa Catanese and her

family told in *De Casibus* (IX, 25-26) with phrases which can be taken as
those of an eyewitness ("quaedam oculis sumpta meis describam"
"que fere vidi iam veniunt"). Although the expressions have been
revealed either as dependent on the usual rhetorical praxis or as
referring to details of the life of Filippa, which Boccaccio might very
well have witnessed in his Neapolitan years, the story in that part
which concerns 1343 seems to be a transcription from Villani (Torraca, pp. 27 ff.; Branca, *Boccaccio medievale,* pp. 235 ff). It is impossible,
however, to rule out absolutely a Neapolitan sojourn, extremely brief
in any case, during this period. Besides, as we have seen, Boccaccio was
in Ravenna in 1346.

27. C. Ricci, "I Boccacci di Romagna." *Misc. Stor. Valdelsa,* XXI, 1913.

28. In introducing Giovanni Malpaghini to Boccaccio, Petrarch wrote:
"ortus est Adrie in litore ea ferme etate, nisi fallor, qua tu ibi agebas
cum antiquo plage illius domino eius ave qui nunc presidet," that is to
say, with Ostasio the grandfather of Guido, lord of Ravenna in 1366
when Petrarch was writing.

29. R. Sabbadini, *Giovanni da Ravenna,* Como, 1924, p. 8.

30. The date of the letter is established by Massera, *Note* to the *Opere minori
latine,* p. 325.

31. Léonard, *Histoire,* cit., II, p. 19; P.G. Ricci, *Per la cronologia* cit.

32. In fact, from Torraca and Guerri to Sapegno and Billanovich, all
scholars now exclude it because the topic taken from the *Esposizioni*
concerning the absence of Boccaccio from Florence during the plague
of 1348 has been dropped (D. Guerri, *Il "lamento" del Boccaccio a Dante,*
Bari, 1926, pp. 137, 179, 247).

33. Long discussions took place on the import of the political allusions (to
Joanna and Andrew, to Louis of Taranto and Louis of Hungary, to
Carlo of Durazzo and the Neapolitan nobles, to the Cabanni and to
Acciaiuoli, among others) on the political and moral coherence and
incoherence of Boccaccio. Events and responsibilities gradually were
clarified and the positions of Joanna, of Louis of Taranto, of Niccola,
improved. As they changed, it is evident that Boccaccio revised and
rectified his own positions and his judgments, either from a better
knowledge of the facts, or in harmony with Florentine politics. Perhaps he changed because of his sympathies and hopes directed toward
the Angevin Court and toward Acciaiuoli (but later violently satirized
in ep. VIII), which is also useful for an understanding of the four
eclogues now mentioned. These eclogues must have been written,
starting with the primitive form of III (it is the "carme" II) approxi-

mately between 1347 and 1351. For a picture of the various discussions see Giovanni Boccaccio's *Il Buccolicum carmen*, Città di Castello, 1914; Hauvette, op. cit., pp. 182 ff.; Torraca, *Per la biografia*, pp. 153 ff.; Léonard, *Boccace et Naples*, pp. 34 ff. Concerning the tone of ep. VI it is to be noted that it is preserved right next to the first four in the *Zibaldone Laurenziano* (c. 50v).

34. It had been sent to him probably by Barbato in that period and was also transcribed in the *Zibaldone Laurenziano* along with other significant texts of the "magister et preceptor": *Metr.*, I, 4, 12, 13, 14; *Var.* 49; episode of the death of Magone: see Billanovich, *Petrarca letterato*, pp. 87 ff.

35. After long discussions, its attribution to Boccaccio is now considered very accurate: see Billanovich, "Il Boccaccio, il Petrarca e le più antiche traduzioni in italiano delle Decadi di Tito Livio," *Giornale Stor. Lett. It.*, CXXX, 1953; M. T. Casella, "Nuovi appunti attorno al Boccaccio traduttore di Livio," *It. med. e um.*, IV, 1961.

36. Léonard, *Histoire*, II, pp. 21 ff.

37. See the document published by Crescini in *Rassegna*, I, p. 245; F. Carabellese, *La peste del 1348*, Rocca S. Casciano, 1898, p. 58; A. Frugoni, "G. Villani, Cronica XI 94" in *Boll. Ist. St. Medioevo*, 77, 1965 (with extensive bibliography). Boccaccino was one of the "Otto di Abbondanza" probably from June 1347 to August 1348. A note by Manni "dai libri delle Riformazioni dell'Archivio del Monte Stanza C . . . Libro dell'Abbondanza," indicates that Giovanni also held the same office; but it is probably a simple confusion with his father, nor is it possible at the moment to identify the original of the document cited so vaguely (cf. E. Rostagno, art. cit., p. 23).

38. M. Villani, I, 2-8; F. Carabellese, op. cit.; A. Sapori, op. cit.; M. Meiss, *Painting in Florence and Siena after the Black Death*, Princeton, 1951.

39. For Coppo, see *Decameron*, V, 9, 4, and ep. VIII; for Franceschino degli Albizzi, whose genealogies Boccaccio compiled and transcribed with Forese dei Donati in the *Zibaldone Magliabechiano* (cod. II, II, 327 of the Nazionale of Florence), see A. Hortis, *Studi sulle opere latine del Boccaccio*, Trieste, 1879, pp. 539 ff. (He was a relative and friend of Petrarch: *Fam.*, VII, XI, XII, XVIII, 5; *Tr. Cup.*, III, 37-38; *Rime* 287.)

40. Doc. cit. by Manni, p. 21. Boccaccio already figured as guardian of his brother Jacopo, approximately eight years old, on January 25, 1350. The document seems to say that his mother had died before his father. See also Latini, art. cit.; Tordi, op. cit.

41. See doc. cit. in preceding note. We find no mention of his brother

Francesco, who must have been of age by then. We cannot determine
with exactness the family hereditament on the death of Boccaccino.
Aside from the personal property, movables or goods and chattels,
which a "mercator" and "cambiator" such as Boccaccino must have
possessed, and in addition to the house in S. Felicita and that at
Sant'Ambrogo (of which we have cited the contracts, pp. 53 and
75), it certainly must have included the paternal house in Certaldo
and the three or four Certaldese farms (see pages 88 and 97), and the
rights and the income from the Capuan lease (pages 53 ff. and 75 ff.),
of which we see registered in 1351 (page 97). Also the taxations of 1351
and 1352 to which we shall refer (page 97) confirm a certain consis-
tence of the patrimony (on the death of Boccaccio his heirs mentioned
five of his farms in the vicinity of Certaldo: see page 187).

42. In eclogue XIV Olimpia (in reality, Violante), pointing to her companions, says to her father: "Non Marium Juliumque tuos dulcesque
sorores noscis, et egregios vultus? Tua pulchra propago est?" (72-73).
The two boys (are their names real, or changed like that of Violante?)
seem older than Olimpia, who is presented as a little girl while they
already have beards, as their father remarks ("Astulit effigies notas
lanugine malas Umbratas vidisse meis": 74-75). There must already
have been two girls, besides Olimpia, for the plural is used.

43. But there has been much discussion concerning Violante also,
achieving little in the way of reliable results. We know with certainty
only that her father saw her for the last time when she was five and a
half years old ("quintum quippe iam annum attigerat et dimidium
dum ultimo illam vidi": ep. XIV) and that she died before reaching
the "age of discretion," that is, before the age of seven (ep. XXIII: "Pro
Olympia intelligo parvulam filiam meam olim mortua ea in etate in
qua morientes celestes effici cives credimus") while her father was
journeying toward Naples (*Bucc.*, XIV, 51 ff.: "Te Fusca ferebat,
Calcidicos colles et pascua lata Vesevi Dum petii"). As we shall see, in
1367 Boccaccio, wrote to Petrarch a deeply felt remembrance of his
daughter, brought back by the sight of Eletta, the granddaughter of
the "magister" (ep. XIV). He had gone to Naples only in the September of 1355 and in the winter of 1362 and 1363. But it seems
unacceptable to believe that Violante died during this latter journey,
for Boccaccio does not record this loss in the enumeration of the woes
which saddened that journey (ep. XIII) and because in the epistle of
1367 to Petrarch he seems to refer to her death as to a long-past

happening. Therefore, if Violante died during the journey of September 1355 before she was seven years old, she must have been born in 1349 or 1350, for otherwise she could not have died before the age of five and a half (ep. XIV). The hypothesis that Violante was born in Ravenna is always based on two allusions in the epistle to Petrarch: that Donato Albanzani and Master Guglielmo da Ravenna had known her (they lived for some time in Ravenna and went there often) and that she did not speak Tuscan, like Eletta. We know, however, that Boccaccio, after having resided there between 1346 and 1347, often returned to Ravenna (so often that Petrarch called him "Ravennate": *Sen.*, V, I; see also ep. VIII: "vetus Ravenna, Forlivium me etiam remuentem vocant"). He was there in 1353 (ep. IX) when he would have seen her for the last time. Her name might have been given her by her unknown mother. Perhaps, however, her father named her in veneration of the first wife of King Robert in that period of renewed devotion to the Angevins. It is reserved for one of the nicest and most chaste girls of the *Decameron* (II, 8). For the discussions of the time and place of Violante's birth, see the dialogue between A. Foresti and F. Torraca in the *Marzocco*, XXXVI, 1931, nos. 6, 7, 9; also Billanovich, *Petrarca*, pp. 202 ff.

44. V. Branca, "Per il testo del Decameron—La prima diffusione." *Studi di Filologia Italiana*, VIII, 1950.

45. This interpretation of Boccaccio's masterpiece to which only a brief mention is made here, will be fully developed, argued and documented in *Part Two* of this volume.

CHAPTER 6

Political Involvement
and the Decisive Encounter
with Petrarch (1349-1351)

If for several months death seemed to have routed factions and hatreds in the City of Flowers, dissent arouse again fiercer than ever, and as before, it was between the two extreme groups of the Arti [guilds] over the issue of the "Ordinamenti di giustizia." The precarious economic condition of the "companies" aroused both uneasiness and desire. Those favored by the privileges of caste or political fortune hoped greedily to profit from the last riches of the formerly powerful "companies" before they were scattered and lost in the bankruptcy settlements. It was a frenzied competition with no holds barred.

Not only because of these internal turmoils but because the Florentines were limited by their constitutional, communal government, they could not bring about political, administrative, and legislative unification in the surrounding districts and in the now extensive territory controlled by Florence. Florence remained weak in the harsh climate of hegemonical struggles which were characteristic of Italian life in mid-Trecento. Florentines felt threatened by the overflow of the Visconti beyond the Apennines. They were unsuccessful in solving the questions and the wars of Lucca and Pisa.

Above all else Florentines were worried by the jurisdictional disagreement with the Church and papal policy of regaining the provinces of Romagna and, still worse, by the ever worsening crisis of the Angevin state. In April 1350 came a new invasion by the king of Hungary and a new siege of Naples. New struggles broke out between Joanna, her husband Luigi (Louis) and her sister Maria, between the factions of Taranto and Durazzo. Finally the Pontifical-Provençal expedition apparently was crowned by success and by an equally apparent triumph for Joanna. Both, however, were cut short by the assassination of the commander Hugo of Baux, instigated by Louis of Taranto who thanks to the astuteness of Acciaiuoli, succeeded in gaining the upper hand and having himself made king (October and November 1350).

In these years we see Boccaccio involved in the play of foreign politics, probably because of the experience he was known to have with matters concerning Romagna and the kingdom, because of the esteem and fame which he had won as an orator and as drafter of official letters, and for his cordial bonds with such personalities who were very influential in the administration of the guilds (Arti) as Pino de' Rossi, Bartolo del Buono, Francesco Benini, Niccolò Frescobaldi, Luca Ugolini, and Andrea dell'Ischia, among others.[1] In August and September 1350 Boccaccio was "ambaxiator trasmissus ad partes Romandiole." [2] We know practically nothing of his errand nor to whom he was sent. (Perhaps he was involved in activities against the aims of the Visconti or against the Papal vicars, particularly at the court of Ordelaffi, his admirer and a relentless enemy of the government of the Church.) But, if not on a diplomatic mission to the Da Polenta lords, Boccaccio certainly went to Ravenna on an assignment to deliver in the name of the Company of Or San Michele—of which on another occasion we see him as a respected counselor (see page 157)—"ten gold florins . . . to Sister Beatrice who was daughter of Dante Alleghieri, nun in the monastery of San Stefano dell'Uliva." [3] It was a gift—homage and compensation almost thirty years after the death of Dante—probably solicited from the Company by Boccaccio himself who, perhaps, accompanied it with a speech of his own and who, on that occasion, garnered memories and data concerning the poet who had illumined his eagerness for poetry since his childhood. Perhaps it was just then, "apud Ravennam urbem," that he met Becchino Bellincione, who was a familiar of King Hugo of Cyprus and well-known to Boccaccio, and who had relatives at the Angevin court (*Amorosa Visione*, XLIV, 1 ff.). Some time previously King Hugo had requested him to compose a work, which finally became a reality as *Genealogia Deorum Gentilium;* in this meeting, Becchino earnestly renewed exhortations in the name of his king (*Gen.*, XV, 13; see below, page 109).

Almost immediately after his return from this mission, Boccaccio received news that his dream of a meeting with Petrarch, the other, the ideal "magister" of his literary youth, would soon be realized. It is certain that a few months earlier he and other admirers had successfully interceded with the Gonfaloniere and the priors of the guilds in support of Petrarch's request that justice be done in the matter of the savage aggression suffered by his friends Luca Cristiano and Mainardo Accursio on the road from the Apennines to Florence, in which Accursio was killed (*Fam.*, VIII, x; see Villani, I, 23). When the long-awaited meeting was at hand, the first visit of the "poet laureate" to the city of his fathers, Boccaccio felt aware, even in his great emotion, that now—after the passing of the generation of such men as Sennuccio and Franceschino Albizzi—he was the undisputed and authoritative leader of Florentine culture, the man on whom fell the responsibility of representing it and presenting it. In that rôle he had that very summer sent a poem to Petrarch imploring that the marvelous writings of the "magister" should not be scattered "inter vulgares etiam profanosque," but on the contrary should be given to his ideal and enthusiastic disciples, such as Boccaccio himself (the poem is lost, but see *Fam.*, XI, ii, 1; XXI, xv, 27, and *Metr.*, III, xvii).

At the beginning of autumn Petrarch had left Parma to travel as a pilgrim to the Jubilee in Rome, and on a cold day in early October ("iam seviente bruma"), he saw "corporis motu celer, miro nondum visi hominis desiderio," Boccaccio coming to meet him outside the gates of Florence to offer him the traditional gift of a ring, and gently but firmly to insist on having him as a guest in his house in Borgo Sant'Jacopo ("amicitie tue penetralibus induxisti": *Fam.*, XI, i, and XXI, xv). In the days that followed, Boccaccio assembled the best representatives of Florentine culture, foremost among them Zanobi da Strada, already a correspondent of his guest and now the appointed secretary of the new sovereigns of Naples (November 4, 1349), the pious and sensitive prior of the Holy Apostles, Francesco Nelli, the young and highly cultured Lapo da Castiglionchio, who revealed to the "maestro" the *Institutiones* of Quintilian and some texts of Cicero, and perhaps Francesco Bruni—who all listened to the poetic and moral reflections of Petrarch, to his learned and literary information, his allusions and quotations from classic texts rediscovered and reinterpreted. And, as Nelli recorded, they listened also to "carmina . . . vocem illam venerandam atque tremendam, motus animi disertissima lingua interprete extollentem."[4] "Now the 'coetus' or the 'schola' of his friends in Florence was established, toward which the affection and the attentions of the poet were directed after death and various fates had dispersed the old friends who at one time had been drawn together in the circle of the Colonna, the bishop and the cardinal" (Billanovich, *Petrarca,* p. 94). In fact Petrarch, as if to establish a hierarchy of human and literary affection, addressed his gratitude and friendship to "Johanni Bocchacci de Certaldo discipulo suo" and the entire Florentine cultural society. The *familiare* of November 2 was the first of those letters written to his friend over the next twenty-five years (*Fam.,* XI, i).

Petrarch had gone to Rome around the middle of October, and on his way back in December, he perhaps decided to stop off at Boccaccio's house to renew the pleasure of those "devoted" Florentines (and also to meet the authorities of the Commune, possibly to talk about the properties of his father which had been confiscated in the past). Then, after he had returned to Parma, on the Epiphany of 1351, Petrarch addressed to Boccaccio the splendid response to his poem (*Fam.,* XI, ii, and *Metr.,* III, xvii) and told him of his codex of the new culture, the new faith in poetry, the *Pro Archia* (he sent it to Lapo in order to request in return the orations of Cicero which he had seen at his house in Florence; *Var.,* 45; see *Fam.,* XIII, vi, 23).

When Boccaccio received these extremely precious gifts and these touching testimonials of affection he was deeply engaged in public life and about to become still more so. Elected to represent the Quarter of Santo Spirito for the months of January and February,[5] as a citizen of flawless probity, he had been named Camarlengo (bursar) of the Chamber of the Commune.[6] And that same February he became Camarlengo and delegate of the Signoria, a position of even greater duty and distinction. In this capacity he opposed Jacopo di Donato Acciaiuoli (the agent for the Neapolitan court) in the matter of the cession of Prato to Florence by the sovereigns Luigi and Joanna on February 23, 1351. This act marked the definitive victory of Florence over the Angevin claims in Tuscany. Perhaps, in some manner, it represented a moral revenge of Boccaccio upon Acciaiuoli, who was the one really forced out of Prato for expressing a preference for Zanobi as literary expert ("letterato") at the Angevin court, which wounded Boccaccio deeply: ep. VIII.[7] The annexation of that neighboring city was one of the actions of the Signoria against the Milanese expansion. Having acquired Bologna in October 1350, Giovanni Visconti now threatened Florence: an action which was developing also, as we have seen, in Romagna, where Boccaccio may have returned in August on an analogous mission or for the usual undeterminable personal reasons.[8]

Boccaccio later was sent on a definitely anti-Viscontean mission as "ambaxiator solemnis" to Ludwig of Bavaria, Marquis of Brandenburg and Count of the Tyrol, to discuss his intervention against the Archbishop of Milan between December 1351 and January 1352. (The letters of his charge are dated December 12.)[9] Ludwig was then maneuvering between the Tyrol and southern Bavaria; thus Boccaccio probably had to traverse the valley of the Adige and Trentino, and to pass through Friuli, "rather a cold country, lovely with its beautiful mountains, its many rivers and bright springs" (*Decameron*, X, 5, 4) inhabited by Certaldese merchants who were perhaps relatives of his.[10]

Certainly, of these successful charges and embassies,[11] the mission that was by far the most agreeable to Boccaccio was that to the son of Master Petraccolo, the companion of Dante Alighieri into exile. The purpose of his mission was to discuss offers which would lead to the return of Petrarch to his "patria" *(Fam.,* XI, v, 13). At the end of March, then, Boccaccio arrived in Padua, the bearer of official letters from the Priors of the Arts and the Gonfaloniere of Justice, penned in all probability by Boccaccio himself. They announced to Petrarch the revocation of the condemnation of his father and the subsequent confiscation of his property (in October 1302), and they invited him to return to his fatherland. As "laureate," and therefore "magister," he was offered a chair in the Studio (university) which had reopened in 1349; Petrarch's acceptance of this chair, they declared, would guarantee the school sure fame and full success. These were decisions and invitations which the Signoria wished to strengthen by having them presented and elucidated by Boccaccio, now recognized as the prince of Florentine culture and the "foremost friend" of Petrarch. They were seconded by epistles of entreaty from the "faithful": Lapo, Zanobi, Francesco, and by precious and delicately chosen gifts: from Nelli, a small breviary to replace, while traveling, the big, heavy one the Florentines had seen Petrarch carrying the previous year; and from Lapo, the greatly desired orations of Cicero.[12] Petrarch, who probably had already decided to accept the invitation of Clement V to go to Avignon, answered with deep emotion and gratitude, but he declined the offer and charged "vir egregius Johannes Boccacci" to transmit together with his epistle "ore disertissimo . . . affectus suos" (*Fam.*, XI, v, of April 6, probably the date of Boccaccio's departure). Norwithstanding Boccaccio's impassioned eloquence, the Signoria, angered, revoked its magnanimous decisions: "pessime factum est nec absque facientium nota" although Boccaccio had noted some degree of "levitas," on Petrarch's part (ep. IX).

The "magister" had received his great disciple in his house near the cathedral in Parma (of which since 1349 he was a canon). While there Petrarch certainly introduced Boccaccio to the circle of the "faithful" which was beginning to form in Padua also; he accompanied him on various humanistic pilgrimages, especially to Santa Giustina to admire the supposed sepulchral slab of *their* Livy (*Vita Livii*, 7-8) and the treasures of the library of the convent and the ancient martyrologies (carefully annotated in the *Zibaldone Magliabechiano*, col. 70r). But above all Boccaccio paid heed to Petrarch, and eagerly copied pages of the "magister," as he was to recall with trembling emotion in ep. IX two years later: "nuntius Patavum ad te veni et commissis expositis dies plusculos tecum egi, quos fere omnes uno eodemque duximus modo. Tu sacris vacabàs studiis, ego compositionum tuarum avidus ex illis scribens summebam copiam. Die autem in vesperum declinante a laboribus surgebamus unanimes, et in ortulum ibamus tuum jam ob novum ver frondibus atque floribus ornatum. Accedebat tertius vir virtutis eximie Silvanus amicus tuus, et invicem sedentes atque confabulantes quantum diei supererat placido otio atque laudabili trahebamus in noctem" (ep.IX). They discussed much-loved texts (those of Cicero, Seneca, and Livy, especially) and the problems posed by those pages. They talked about the collections of letters which Petrarch, whose enthusiasm had been fired by the discovery of the *Ad Atticum* in the Capitulary of Verona, was putting together. He allowed Boccaccio to copy them in part (*Familiari* and also *Metriche*). They debated the great thrilling themes of reason and the value of poetry. Probably Petrarch read to his "disciple" the messages he had already sent out (*collatio, privilegium; Africa,* IX; the epistles to his brother, *Fam.,* X, IV, *Metr.,* II, ii, among others) and went over favorite texts (*Pro Archia* again; perhaps those of Mussato). As the only writer in the vernacular whom he felt to be of his own stature and whose surprising cultural and stylistic fluency he could not but admire, he let Boccaccio listen to some modulations of the *Rerum Vulgarium Fragmenta* (in those days he was painfully transcribing Canzone CCLXX).

With their mutual confidence established, Boccaccio called Petrarch's attention to his more recent writings which seemed likely to interest the "magister" with their classical and moralistic bases (*Amorosa Visione*) or their lofty multiform humanity (*Decameron*), or with their admiring devotion (*Vita . . . Petracchi*), or with literary erudition and the eulogy of poetry (the idea of the *Genealogia*). As a result, Petrarch was prompted by the first to compose *I Trionfi*, by the second *De Obedientia et Fide Uxoria*, by the third *Posteritati* and by the fourth *Invectivae*. Also, Boccaccio must have spoken of Dante, sent into exile with Master Petraccolo and always present in his heart and his imagination. [As an ideal sequel to these Paduan conversations, Boccaccio sent Petrarch a splendid copy of the *Divina Commedia* (now Vat. Lat. 3199) accompanied by an affectionate but entreating poem (carme III).]

The two certainly went on to recall mutual friends and their activities, while Petrarch prepared his answers and thanks to Lapo, to

Zanobi, to Nelli *(Fam.,* VII, xvi; *Var.,* 2 and 29). Boccaccio heard the example of Gherardo eulogized—perhaps by Carthusians who dropped in during his visit (*Fam.* XVI, ii) as well as by his brother— who had become an austere monk after a period of dissipation and had been an heroic figure during the very recent plague. Francesco Petrarca had discussed with his brother Gherardo the meaning and the positive worth of poetry and also the necessity of moral vigilance and religious perfection as the only true goal. Now Francesco was helping his new "disciple," Boccaccio, to single out and to evaluate his own activity and his cultural and artistic preferences, ". . . to accelerate and direct an intellectual upheaval which was in progress" (Billanovich). Boccaccio would repeatedly and humbly trace back this upheaval to the calm and persuasive interventions of the "opti-mum venerandumque perceptorem . . . semper ad virtutem calcar" (*De Casibus,* VIII, I). In the little garden of the Paduan canonry those great spiritual and moral themes (henceforth a conquest for Petrarch, but still an uneasiness for Boccaccio), those sacred and in particular Augustinian texts (on which the "magister" would accustom his "discipulum" to devoutly meditate) illuminated, certainly, the lofty debates and the deeply felt confidences of mind and soul. Between the two great spirits there was established in this way that intimate and fervent colloquy, which—through visits, letters, exchanges of friends, books, news—would not be ended until death, making them ever more "seiuncti licet corporibus, unum animo" *(Sen.* I, 5). This was a meeting which would not only indicate one of the fundamental directives of Boccaccio's life but, auspicious and productive beyond any other in the history of letters, was to begin the splendid spiritual, cultural and literary flowering of the Europe of the late fourteenth and the fifteenth century.

But along with these great and eternal subjects the two Floren-tines also talked about the perils which menaced their native city as a result of Viscontean expansion (ep. IX), of the condition of Italy caught between the wickedness of the tyrants and the wretchedness of the "helpless populace," betwixt the corruption of the clergy and the "Babylonian exile" (Boccaccio made himself a copy of the epistles to the emperor, to Cola di Rienzo, to the doge Dandolo). Even in this field, like Dante, Petrarch revealed himself to be a master of political discernment, even for Florence, the uneasy but now cherished home of Boccaccio.

Truly decisive, then, for Boccaccio, were the experiences of 1350 and 1351: in a civil sense, a moral sense, an artistic sense. That turbulent communal life which, from the time the *Comedia* was written almost to the time the *Fiammetta* was written, Boccaccio had loathed, vexed by snobbish aristocratic and courtly yearnings, he now not only understood and vindicated in contrast to the "tyrannical" forms, but resorted to as a theme for boasting and for intent and animated service, and to formulate a politics which was culture and a culture which was politics (one has only to think of the singular turn of the missions to Ravenna and Padua). His writing, which had been based mostly on satisfied, complacent erudition and was Ovidian and Apuleian in spirit, now was nourished with "moral" Cicero and Seneca, with the great Fathers of the Church. Beginning with the *Decameron* and for the next twenty years, Boccaccio was inspired by great moralistic themes (fortune, nobility, love and death, the legend of Everyman, virtue the synthesis of every dowry, and so on). Boccaccio abandoned literary and stylistic excess of Alexandrian stamp, in part because of his readings of Dante, deeply meditated upon in Florence, and assimilated "non modo memorie sed medullis." In its place Boccaccio developed a vision and writing rigorously inspired by a bold and powerful realism.

Saying farewell to youth and its erratic fancies, Boccaccio, following in the footsteps of Petrarch, planned his life determinedly as a service to studies and to poetry, a service understood as a spiritual fact or, rather, conquest. It was not by mere chance that soon after his return to Florence, Boccaccio developed the great synthesis of the eternal "reasons" of poetry—reasons not merely esthetic but metaphysical, moral, and religious. It became a synthesis inspired by those texts he had copied and discussed, by those unforgettable conversations in the little garden in Padua, that helped Boccaccio to refine the original idea of the *Genealogia* (which goes back to 1350; see page 109). It was not merely by chance that in those same months Boccaccio also began to gather texts for work on his new secret book, the *Zibaldone Magliabechiano,* a singular and precious historical anthology, which reflected his new and thoughtful human, moralistic, and historical interests. Those would also inspire the *De Casibus* and *De Mulieribus*.[13]

NOTES

1. To the first two are dedicated the works of Boccaccio, *Comedia* and *Lettera consolatoria* (in which the two last named are mentioned); for the others and their bonds with Boccaccio, see P. G. Ricci, *Studi* (1959), pp. 29 ff.
2. See document in L. Mehus, *Ambrosii Traversarii epistulae latinae,* Florence, 1759, p. CCLXVIII. He must have begun his mission about August 25, and by September 27 he had already returned to Florence. See A. Hortis, *Giovanni Boccaccio ambasciatore in Avignone . . .,* Trieste, 1875, pp. 6-7; V. Imbriani, "La pretesa Beatrice. . .," *Giorn. Nap. di filosofia, letteratura, scienze morali e politiche,* N.S. VIII, 18, p. 84 (but the calculation to determine the year is erroneous).
3. Document in R. Piattoli, *Codice diplomatico dantesco,* Florence, 1940, pp. 284-85.
4. H. Cochin,*Un amico del Petrarca: F. Nelli* (with letters, etc.), Florence, 1901, ep. XIII.
5. A.S.F. *Tratte 59,* col. 272r; *Volume della "Sega,"* 1-5 (Popolo S. Felicita, Gonf. Nicchio): documents published by V. Branca, *Notizie e documenti.*
6. A. S. F. Camarlenghi della Camera del Commune, 75; col. 129v, "Johanni Bocchaccii de Certaldo et Paulo Neri de Bordonibus laicis civibus florentinis . . ." doc. publ. now by V. Branca, *Notizie e documenti;* a similar heading was used in the copy books 75 and 76, published by Crescini, *Contributo,* p. 258. It was an office or charge of the type of a treasurer's, and was entrusted to citizens tried and reliable morally and financially: A. Gherardi, "L'antica Camera del Commune di Firenze," *Arch. Stor. It.,* S. IV, XVI, 1885.
7. Documents published in L. Tanfani, *Niccolò Acciaiuoli,* cit., p. 82; Léonard, *Histoire,* pp. 480 ff.
8. He was outside of Florence in August, as Nelli wrote to Petrarch (ep. VI); also he was absent from the proceedings of August 18 against the ravagers of his farm (doc. publ. by U. Dorini, "Contributi alla biografia del Boccaccio." *Misc. Stor. Valdelsa,* XXII, 1914).
9. Documents published by A. Hortis, *Giovanni Boccaccio ambasciatore,* pp.

43-48 (see also pp. 8 ff.); G. Gerola, "Petrarca e Boccaccio nel Trentino." *Tridentum,* VI, 1903; V. Branca, *Notizie e documenti,* cit. (letter to the secretary and counselor of Ludwig, the Duke of Teck, who had been in Florence ten years before).

10. A. Battistella, *I Toscani in Friuli,* Udine, 1903; P. A. Medin, "La coltura toscana nel Veneto. . . ." *Atti Ist. Veneto,* LXXXII, 1922-1923; V. Branca, *Per il testo del Decameron,* pp. 80, 86.

11. See also, apart from the previously listed administrative and Florentine documents, the letters of Duke Ludwig (Lodovico) to the Signoria cited by Gerola, *art cit.*

12. For these and other details of the famous visit see in general G. Billanovich, *Petrarca,* pp. 98-164, a volume fundamental to understanding the relations between the two great men of letters.

13. According to the best hypotheses the *Zibaldone Magliabechiano* was compiled between 1351 and 1356 approximately (F. Macri Leone, "Il Zibaldone . . ." in *Giorn. Stor. Lett. It., X,* 1887). Cf. also A.M. Costantini, "Studi sullo *Zibaldone Magliabechiano*" in *Studi sul Boccaccio,* VII and VIII, 1973-74.

CHAPTER 7

Missions of Civil Diplomacy
and Works of Humanistic
Erudition (1352-1360)

The decade from 1352 to 1361, before the withdrawal to Certaldo, is the most Florentine and yet the most European period of
Boccaccio's life and activity. As head of the household—afflicted in
that period by the death of his brother Francesco[1]—Boccaccio now
bore his own and his family's patrimonial and fiscal responsibilities,
both to the Commune [2] and to private persons, especially the
leaseholders.[3] On this account, in the second half of 1352 Boccaccio found himself embroiled in a series of judicial disputes concerning the Certaldese farms belonging to him and his brother
Jacopo. He had either to protect them from ravagers or to keep them
from being abandoned by the peasants.[4] Because of these obligations
and interests and his diverse public assignments away from Florence,
on May 17, 1351, Boccaccio requested the appointment of two
attorneys to help him in the guardianship of Jacopo. Boccaccio was
"variis negotiis impeditus" (and in the drawing up of the petition he
is figured as absent).[5] "Inter publicas privatasque occupationes ultra
velle anxior" Boccaccio wrote again at the beginning of 1353; but he
also rejoiced modestly that "nuper tenuis sibilus iocundioris fortune
repente pacta [paupertatis] confregit" (ep. VIII). And, with a new

97

authoritative bearing of Petrarchan stamp, he assumed a determined position against the laxity of morals which had become widespread since the plague ("nescio utrum dicam ducamur an trahamur a fatis, an potius volentes obviam casus exitio").[6] After attending the impressive funeral of the beloved and admired son of Niccola, Lorenzo Acciaiuoli, in April 1353 (ep. VIII) Boccaccio went to Romagna, perhaps on another mission; by July 12 he was in Forlì, and on the 18th "visitaturus civitatis principem" (ep. XI) at Ravenna, where he spent the rest of the summer. The mission, perhaps informal and not official (the usual administrative traces have not been found), brought him to the court of those who had received him with such esteem in 1346 and 1347 and again in 1350: Francesco degli Ordelaffi and Ostasio da Polenta. Boccaccio's visit probably still concerned the Florentine policy of defense against the Viscontean expansion into Tuscany (M. Villani, III, 2) and which was becoming ever more threatening despite the misleading peace promulgated in April 1353 (M. Villani, IV, 59–60).[7] It was just while preoccupied with these worries on behalf of the "good and holy Commune" and while engaged in this militantly political responsibility that Boccaccio was bitterly surprised, indeed wounded, by the decision of the "magister" on his return to Italy in June 1353 to establish himself at the court of the archbishop Giovanni Visconti. Giovanni was the same "infamis" tyrant that Petrarch himself, in the Paduan conversations two years earlier, had stigmatized as "trucem . . . immanem nunc Polifemum nunc Ciclopem" and "cuius stomacans dampnabat audaciam superbia tyrampnidem . . . infausta omnia imprecans," even because "in . . . Appennini colles etruscosque acuisset dentes et ungues." Boccaccio reminded Petrarch of this with his very own words, writing epistle IX to him from Ravenna "ferventi atque commoto animo," as soon as Boccaccio's candid friend Nelli had shown him actual letters from Petrarch (perhaps *Var.* 7?), which confirmed the news which four days previously he had disdainfully refused to accept from the lips of another friend (perhaps Rossi).[8] Disappointed, certainly by Petrarch's rejection of the offers from the Signoria, for two years Boccaccio had hopefully awaited Francesco's promised return to Italy and to Florence (*Fam.*, XI, vi). In that period he had participated, even in writing, in the struggle against the Viscontean "tyranny" ("Nescis posse meum, que sit mea gloria nescis": words against Archbishop Giovanni which he put in the mouth of the Florentine lion: *Carmi,* IV). Impulsively, but naturally, he could only feel the decision of the "master" as a betrayal, as a political "scelus" "adversus patriam," as a cultural and moral "facinus" towards himself and the other Florentine admirers. In fact "hoc quin factitet negare non potest, scilicet quin una cum Egone [Giovanni Visconti] letetur dum audit ruinas incendia captivitates mortes rapinas et soli patrii desolationes et ignominias, quod grande per piaculum est." [And on the other hand:] "quid tam sublimi preconio liberam vitam atque paupertatem honestam extollere consuetus, jugo alieno subditus et inhonestis ornatus divitiis . . . incestis faciet? . . . nil aliud . . . quam . . . cantare carmen Quid non mortalia pectora cogis auri sacra fames? . . . Mirarer minus si ab eo [that is, by Petrarch] in Ciceronem atque Anneum decantata non audissem . . ." ". . . Credisne quieturos hos ad quos venerit scelus hoc, quin in eum clamitent? Ymo iam clamitant, et conviciis inhonestis veterem eius famam deturpant, falsam, fucatam, fictitio splendore coruscam dicentes: sic et nos adulatores falsidicos mendaces obscenosque esse homines per trivia et nemora asserunt."

In reality, Zanobi and Nelli, Giovanni Aghinolfi and Gano del Colle also rebelled, moved by this same politico-moral reaction (*Var., 7; Fam.,* XVII, x; *Misc., 3*); and Boccaccio foresaw like indignant reactions by Gherado, and Ludwig van Kempen, and their Neapolitan friends Barbata and Giovanni Barrili. Answering Gano, Petrarch himself confessed that "multi similia scripserunt" *(Misc., 3)*, and had to face the blame of Ludwig from Provence (*Fam.*, XVII, 10) and the violent and boorish attacks of the nephew of Pope John XXII *(Invectiva in quendam innominatum)*. This was the sole moment of crisis in the relations of Petrarch with Boccaccio and also with his "disciples" in Florence, Mantua, Provence, Naples and elsewhere; perhaps just because Petrarch observed that Boccaccio, due to the characteristic impetuosity which distinguished him, had expressed himself with the most severe frankness and the most sincere "indignation," Petrarch did not wish to embitter the strife by answering him directly, but sought to calm his friend with mild and persuasive explanations to Zanobi, to Nelli, and to Aghinolfi *(Var., 7; Fam.,* XVI, xi, xii, and xiii;

XVII, x). Thus Petrarch's superior coolness and humane moderation
were able to overcome even the fire and the flame of his "fervens" and
"commotus" great "discipulus." Boccaccio, disinclined as he was to
spite and stubbornness, in those very months increased and enlivened
the tight circle of his literary friends in Ravenna, making it into a
Petrarchan circle. It included Donato degli Albanzani and his
eleven-year-old disciple Giovanni Conversini, whom Boccaccio "sepe
receperat, sepe etiam bellariis allexerat," calling him little Kis; [9]
Guglielmo da Ravenna; Antonio da Ferrara; and again Dante's old
friend Minghino Mezzani. On October 2, shortly after he returned to
Florence, he met with Nelli and Forese and Lapo ("qui nunc aposta-
tavit a musis"), and derived profound enjoyment from the reading of
two admirable epistles from Petrarch to the pious prior of the Holy
Apostles (*Fam.*, XVI, xiv; *Var.*, 56; see Nelli, ep. II). Resolutely
Boccaccio resumed his place as head of the "devout legion" of
Florence to which in the meantime the notary and expert in rhetoric,
Francesco Bruni, had attached himself (Nelli, ep. II, ep. XVI). And
above all, in concert with his friends, with full awareness he assumed
in this period the decisive task of making the excessively Gallic and
Avignonese culture of the "magister" more sensitive to Italian culture, now that he was henceforth established on the Italian side of the
Alps. Indeed, the circle of the most active writers in the vernacular
gathered more and more closely around Boccaccio. Even the "devout" revivals of Pucci and Sacchetti attracted the writers and other
men of high civil and religious responsibilities: for example, before
1348, the chancellor Ventura Monachi, and later, Jacopo Passavanti,
the vicar of Angelo Acciaiuoli. Nevertheless, during those months—
perhaps not without a complacent and literary argument not only
with Zanobi but with Petrarch as well—Boccaccio pictured himself
as modestly poor but with a high sense of personal dignity and of the
dignity of letters: "Viximus et Deo dante vivemus, etsi non splendide,
minus tamen pavide, . . . Michi pauper vivo, dives autem et splendi-
dus aliis viverem; et plus cum aliquibus meis libellis parvulis volup-
tatis sentio quam cum magno diademate sentiant reges" (ep. VIII).

But instead the new year, 1354, brought him new and more
demanding missions: indeed, his first great embassy, that to Innocent
VI at Avignon in May and June.[10] The entry into Italy of the

emperor Charles IV, first petitioned by the Florentines but later
—after the peace with the Visconti—unnecessary and even feared,
made an official approach to the Pontiff opportune. Evidently
Boccaccio had been quite successful in his previous missions since he
was chosen as ambassador in this delicate enterprise (Bernardo was
assigned to him as an assistant).[11] According to instructions, he was
to reveal what great astonishment the entry into Italy of Charles IV
had aroused in the Signoria; but, in case the Emperor should reach an
agreement with the Pontiff, he was to assure the latter that the
Commune of Florence would be faithful to its "inborn devotion" to
the "Ecclesia Sancta Dei ... unicum et singularem refugium" and
request therefore to be taken under papal protection. If then Innocent VI should answer that he knew nothing about it and in turn
attempt to find out what were the intentions of the Florentines, the
ambassador was to respond that "he had no other mission than to
find out the will of the Pontiff " and he was to keep a close watch on
everything.

It was the first time that Boccaccio crossed the Alps and came in
contact with that great "fire" of European political and cultural life
that was the Court of Avignon. Certainly he came provided with
letters of recommendation and introduction from Petrarch; and he
must have met friends and admirers repeatedly in that sojourn in
Avignon (for example Guido Sette, Ludwig van Kempen, Lello
Tosetti and so on). Perhaps, encouraged by them, he made the
pilgrimage, carried out and related to him by Forese Donati two
years previously, to that Valchiusa [Vaucluse] which Petrarch had so
fascinatingly described to him directly *(Fam.,* XI, vi). Perhaps even
then he noted the impressions which he would later set forth in a note
of the *De Fontibus:* ("Sorga ... post eius [of Petrarch] discessum
tamquam sacrarium quoddam et quodam minime plenum eius
hospitium visitantes incole ostendunt locum mirabilem ignaris et
peregrinis: nec dubium quin adhuc filii nepotes et qui nascentur ab
illis ampliori cum honore tanti vatis admiratione vestigia veneren-
tur"). Thus despite the political divisions the correspondence in idea
and spirit continued between the two great men, for in those very
months Petrarch for his part was writing to the doge Andrea Dandolo
in defense of the Viscontean rights *(Fam.,* XVIII, xvi).

The mission must have been accomplished successfully: Innocent VI indeed kept a pleasant remembrance of the Florentine ambassador (see p. 119) and immediately after Boccaccio's return to Florence the Signoria decided to make further use of his experience and authority: not in a great court, but in his own "little fatherland." Accompanied by Cambi, Boccaccio was sent to Certaldo in July to stimulate and organize the resistance of his compatriots against the pillaging bands of Fra Moriale, prototype of the captain of fortune of unscrupulous mercenaries (M. Villani, IV, 14–16).[12] The castle was spared, and soon afterwards Fra Moriale was ordered decapitated by Cola di Rienzo. Boccaccio must have accomplished this civil and military mission with success as well, for we see his status as citizen and his "cursus honorum" growing ever more secure, as testified by the real property tax evaluations between 1353 and 1355 [13] and by his new public offices. Indeed his economic situation must have been particularly comfortable since Boccaccio was able to present to Petrarch (who was customarily in an attitude of poverty before his friend) a gift of considerable value, perhaps in fulfilment of a secret vow formulated four years earlier during the meeting in Padua, that is the extremely beautiful codex of precious antiquity, the *Enarrationes in Psalmos* of Saint Augustine, on which still stands the note of the touched receiver: "Hoc immensum opus donavit michi vir egregius dominus Johannes Boccaccii de Certaldo poeta nostri temporis, quod de Florentia ad me pervenit 1355 aprilis 10" (Cod. Par. Lat. 1989: see *Fam.*, XVIII, iii).

From May 1 to August 31, 1355 Boccaccio was an appointee to the Ufficio della Condotta, charged with checking the "shortcomings of the stipendiaries," that is, of the soldiers in the pay of the Commune, who were numerous and often unruly in that period, troubled even in Tuscany, by the invasion of Charles IV (M. Villani, IV, 44 ff.).[14] Probably for that charge, or for some mission of which we have no information, Boccaccio then saw the Emperor who, before and after the coronation in Rome on April 5, was in Tuscany for some time, and often received, officially or informally, missions of Florentines. At his court Boccaccio must have met Chancellor Johannes of Neumarkt, a good friend of Petrarch ("I remember many times and much more easily to have had entry to the most high Pontiff and to

Charles the Caesar and to many leading princes of the world . . ." he would write to Nelli, ep. XII).[15]

But another encounter was to engage Boccaccio far more, sentimentally and morally, in these months: the meeting with the friend of his brilliant Neapolitan youth—now become creator and arbiter of kings and governments—and with his secretary and confidant Zanobi. Acciaiuoli had come to Tuscany in April and May, either to render homage to Charles IV or to ask him and the Tuscans for help against the Great Company which had invaded the Kingdom at the instigation of Louis of Durazzo.[16] Perhaps Boccaccio participated in such negotiations in Florence as part of his own functions; in the years just past he had not been very tender—nor had the Florentines in general—toward the Grand Seneschal. Aside from the accusations and the judgments in the political eclogues (see p. 74), the epistles to the great protégé, Zanobi da Strada, are bristling with barbs and irony against the "tyrant," the "great,"the "God-man." They stress Acciaiuoli's vain glory and empty pomp, his injustice and cruelty towards his friends, his coldness and incapacity for affection (ep. VII and ep. VIII). Certainly there was, at the origin of these critical attitudes, some resentment for the forgetfulness in which Boccaccio had been left by his now powerful friend, who ignored his impassioned appeals (see pp. 56 and 90). Above all there was the tangle of sentiments and contradictions which come through in the eclogues (see p. 74). Perhaps with intent to prod these attitudes, Acciaiuoli, with his usual heavy sarcasm, persistently referred to Boccaccio as "Johannem tranquillitatum." That is, Acciaiuoli considered Giovanni to be the friend of the good times, the happy times.[17] In this situation, Boccaccio wrote in April 1353 of "adversus me . . . persecutio longa . . . inextricabilis fuga . . . vulnus exitiale" (ep. VIII). Boccaccio wished to stress his own impassioned participation not in the triumphs but in the sorrows of Niccola, in his mourning for the death of the generous and heroic Lorenzo ("ut fere per noctem mediam et fletu solus et eiulans non destiterim"), contrasting it with the inhuman coldness of the father, who was preoccupied with his political ambitions.[18]

But in 1355 the relations between the two former friends seem to have developed favorably, due, perhaps, to the influence of Petrarch (friend and admirer of Niccola and Zanobi), or to the political adaptability of Acciaiuoli, who during those days was bent on winning popularity and sympathy in Florence, especially with any who could influence decisions concerning the requested aid ("in Florence he began to do much entertaining and continued it for a long while in town and country . . . morning and night, and all day long he kept *them* dancing and feasting" Villani, IV, 91). Boccaccio certainly shared the judgment of the Florentines who denied aid to Niccola.[19] And he certainly concurred with the literary circles of the city who scorned the poetical crowning of Zanobi, which they felt was a parody of the Petrarchan laurel, conferred as it was on May 15 in Pisa by the hand of a "barbarian" emperor and obtained by Acciaiuoli for his secretary as an inexpensive recompense for a long and devoted service (*Bucc.*, VIII, 137 ff.; ep. XVIII; Nelli, ep. XVII). Despite these resentments Boccaccio must have arranged for his summer-autumn journey to Naples during that period. Zanobi, weary of the cares and anxieties of court, and perhaps weary as well of the moods and harshness of Acciaiuoli (who ordered him, sometimes brutally, to "stare più firmo in bottega" [20] that is, to "pay more attention to business"), had gladly accepted an appointment as "vicarius in spiritualibus et temporalibus" of Angelo Acciaiuoli, formerly Bishop of Florence and since March 18 Bishop of Montecassino, one of the richest and most illustrious dioceses of southern Italy.[21] In all probability the journey to Naples was planned during Boccaccio's Florentine meetings with Niccola and Angelo and Zanobi (at the same time that pressing invitations were addressed to the cautious Petrarch), and it might have foreshadowed appointment to the post left vacant. After a July and August troubled by a serious illness and violent fevers,[22] upon the conclusion of his duties in the Condotta on September 1, Boccaccio must have left for Naples, to which he was drawn by so many cherished memories, but where, precisely because of his experience and so much of what he had written in the epistles and eclogues, there were so many possibilities for disappointment. What little we know of this journey appears in the typical bucolic allusions of the angry eclogue VIII (and is perhaps alluded to in one of Petrarch's letters: *Fam.*, XVIII, xv). It seems, then, that Boccaccio (Pythias), who had just entered Neapolitan territory and encoun-

tered his friend Barbato (Damon) (at Sulmona? at Naples itself?),
was quickly briefed on some unpleasant new developments at the
Court and was dissuaded from entrusting himself to the promises and
patronage of Acciaiuoli (Midas). Indeed he was advised to renounce
any Neapolitan project he had in view while there was, fortunately,
still time. Certainly the moment was not favorable: Acciaiuoli was at
odds with the Court, which had not followed his counsels to rid itself
of the Great Company; indeed he had disdainfully withdrawn to
Nocera (on October 17 Guido da Reggio, a faithful adherent of the
Acciaiuoli family, and friend and companion of Zanobi as Royal
Secretary wrote: "e dasse bono tempo e non cura se Berta va discalza
poich'ella non volle scarpette," in other words the grand seneschal is
enjoying himself and he doesn't care about the queen's troubles since
she brought them on herself by not following his advice). When the
Grand Seneschal was recalled at October's end he had to throw
himself headlong into negotiations, into war, into the family struggles of the Angevins ("I have come here to Naples," he wrote to
Jacopo on October 31, "after many refusals and pretexts about not
wanting to come and I have already said so many insulting things to
these three friars, our lords, that perhaps another time they won't be
so anxious and solicitous to have me back").[23] Niccola, with his
brusque and expeditious character, certainly had no desire, before or
after, to bother with a writer whom he knew to be antagonistic and
difficult to manage. There was nothing left for Boccaccio (who
perhaps did not see Acciaiuoli nor even reach Naples) except to enjoy
his friends and those of Petrarch, such as Barbato, Barrili, Niccolò
d'Alife, Guido da Reggio (ep. XIV). Boccaccio especially enjoyed
meeting with Zanobi, with whom he appears to have improved
relations, perhaps because of the literary treasures which the "vicar"—in effect governor of the diocese of Montecassino—could authoritatively disclose to him and which, in effect, he put generously into
circulation ("Multas vides et pulchra sedens nunc cernere debes
Librorum in medio quos servant claustra Cassini": *carme* V, 57–58).[24]
In fact perhaps the only positive result of this wretched journey,
saddened moreover by the death of his beloved little Violante (see p.
77 and note 43, p. 84), was the attentive and rewarding visit to the
library of Montecassino. There Boccaccio read texts fundamental to

a comprehension of the ancient world, and he acquired two important manuscripts: the surviving fragments of the *De Lingua Latina* of Varro (V—XXIV), the incomplete *Pro Cleuntio,* the *Rhetorica ad Herennium* (today *Laur.* 50, 10); and, still more precious, fragments of Apuleius and Tacitus (*Annales,* XI—XVI, *Historiae,* I—V; today *Laur.,* 68, 2). These discoveries were promptly and profoundly reflected in the writings of Boccaccio, who was always an avid and sensitive reader.[25] And on that occasion Zanobi certainly spoke with him about the literary projects later expounded in the poem of October 11, *Quid Faciam,* to which Boccaccio, back home in Florence, responded with rather forced cordiality (*carme* V, which was written with their mutual friend Luigi Gianfigliazzi close by: see verses 62–64).

Boccaccio had returned to Florence irritated, because he had been enticed to make the Neapolitan journey by the direct and indirect instances of Acciaiuoli (ec. VIII 24 ff.; and see *Fam.,* XVIII, xv, 1); and while sending the *De Lingua Latina* and the *Pro Cluentio,* copied lovingly in his own hand, to Petrarch, Boccaccio vented his ill-humor in the indignant eclogue VIII. He had Damon-Barbato accuse Midas-Acciaiuoli, who wished to be called "Mecenatem Magnumque deumque," of greed, falseness, and conceited literary ambitions. He concluded forthrightly: "Fur Midas igitur, mechus scelerumque satelles" (ec. VIII, 117) with a clear allusion here to Acciaiuoli's co-responsibility in the murder of Andrew of Hungary, to his foul ties with Corydon (Zanobi?), and to his iniquitous complicity with the "meretrix anus . . . et avara Lupisca" (Giovanna Catherina? Lapa Acciaiuoli?, ec. VIII, 34 ff.). Perhaps some of these accusations and certain more violent tones were added later, after the painful experience of 1362 and after the letter to Nelli (1363): [26] but probably he had addressed similar wrathful outbursts to various friends and certainly to Petrarch (who alludes in Fam. XVIII, xv, 1 to those outbursts?).

But neither for this epistle, nor for the splendid and affectionate gifts of the volumes of Saint Augustine, Varro and Cicero, did he receive any acknowledgment from Milan. For Boccaccio the silence of the master and supreme literary and moral judge must have been particularly inexplicable and worrisome in these last months of

1355. Couldn't Petrarch perhaps in some way have been on the side of that rude and conceited Maecenas, Acciaiuoli, since two years earlier he had been the victim of Boccaccio's attack, "commoto et ferventi animo," precisely for having successfully anticipated his own attempt to take refuge in the shadow of an Italian court (ep. IX). Petrarch, too, was encouraged and praised so obsequiously by Acciaiuoli, and he, too, was a friend of Zanobi, whom he generously eulogized after the crowning in Pisa (*Metr.*,III, 9). Was Petrarch perhaps unwilling to compromise himself by confirming publicly his friendship with the author of that irate eclogue and of those violent writings?

Once again the impulsive Boccaccio wrote to Petrarch an epistle "turbato animo," perhaps tieing together his friend's silence with the haughtiness of one who "imperat ex servo, merces conflavit in aurum" (*Bucc.,* VIII, 58).

The explanations of Petrarch, which finally arrived early in 1356 (after two other letters had gone astray) *(Fam.,* XVIII, iii and iv), must have soothed the bitter thoughts and many doubts felt by Boccaccio, who was always uneasy and readily upset (*Fam.,* XVIII, xv, of December 20). Petrarch insisted on declaring him "poeta," and thus crowned him far more authoritatively than Charles IV and with a laurel far more dazzling and lasting than that granted to Zanobi ("poeta esse voluisti ut poete nomen horreres cum contra multi nomen hoc ipsum ambiant rei expertes. An fort quia nondum peneia fronte redimitus sis, poeta esse non potes?"). Not only did Boccaccio thank him mightily, but without hesitation he took his friend's part against the new "tyrant," whom he branded with a clear and scornful literary allusion. Indeed, with the delicacy of a "preceptor et pater," he wished to be close to him with the shining appellation of "adolescens mei amans" who would offer him encouragement and counsel. Indeed, Boccaccio's emotion and exultation was so great that he copied the text of the letter in his *Zibaldone.*[27] And, shortly thereafter, word of Petrarch's affection must have been repeated to him by Giovannolo da Mandello (the addressee of the so-called *Itinerarium Syriacum*), a highly-placed functionary and a relative of the Visconti family, whom the "magister," writing on Christmas night, had so nobly introduced to Nelli.[28]

The Neapolitan fiasco, which followed fifteen years of longing to settle down in the country of his youth, the affectionate exhortations of Petrarch, and the new readings and discoveries of classics, must have inspired Boccaccio to intensify his studies and to renew his "trade" as a writer, after that extremely busy period of public life (1350 to 1355), in which no organic work had followed the *Decameron.*
And this is perhaps the reason why 1356, 1357 and 1358 are so lacking in external events as to make us suppose they represent a period of rigorous concentration and earnest creative activity. We know only that at the beginning of the summer of 1357 Boccaccio must have been in Florence, where in the Mercato Nuovo he met and welcomed and invited without success to be his guest, Giovanni Conversini, whose acquaintance he had made four years earlier in Ravenna at the school of Donato Albanzani and who was then running away from his family.[29] Also during that summer, Boccaccio returned to Ravenna (evidently for one of the errands which often drew him to that city), where he probably received the *Invective contra medicum,* which he had requested, and which Petrarch sent to him on July 12 (with a codex perhaps of Pliny or Pomponius Mela and Vibius Sequester and a map for his use in writing the *De montibus: Misc.* I; ep. XI).[30]

During these years, aided by the calm and meditative spirituality of Petrarch, the most intense religious and moral zeal of Boccaccio was maturing, and was matched by a humbler and more devoted service to letters and to culture, which he understood as divine truths.

> si quid boni inest, si quid bene dictum si quid votis tuis consonum ... verum scientie mee imputes nolo, nec lauros aut honores alios ob id postulo: Deo quippe, a quo omne datum optimum et omne donum perfectum est, attribuas queso, eique honores impendito et gratias agito, cum ipse more meo semper post exactos quoscumque labores honestos consueverim, qua possum mentis devotione Daviticum illud dicere: Non nobis Domine, non nobis, sed nomini tuo da gloriam (*Gen.,* XV, concl.).

Aside from the eclogues, which would be composed later in the *Buccolicum Carmen,* often, as we have seen, prompted by political or personal occasions, it was around 1350 that the idea for the *Genea-logia Deorum Gentilium* was born and the gathering and elaboration of the immense material began. About 1355 Boccaccio drafted the *De Casibus* and the *De Montibus* and a few years later, the *De Mulieribus Claris*. Foreshadowed in a sense in the studious notes of the *Zibaldone Magliabechiano,* they are works which Boccaccio would recast in successive editions, almost to the time of his death. He reworked them as he was prompted or inspired by new spiritual and literary attitudes, new learned and cultural acquisitions, or by discoveries of new manuscripts and new authors (especially Homer and Leontius Pilatus in 1360 and 1362: see pp. 115 ff.)

The *Genealogia Deorum Gentilium* was begun before 1350 at the request of Hugo IV of Lusignan, King of Cyprus, to whom it is dedicated; the first draft must have been finished about 1360, but the revision and correction, by the evidence of the autograph *Laur.* 52, 9, were continued down to the author's death. The *Genealogia* is a great mythological treatise in fifteen books, constructed with ad-mirable organic unity and, in contrast to similar works of the time, it has a new scientific spirit based on the supposed founders of families. Aside from the narrative and imaginative starting points, and aside from the allegorical and metaphorical framework, the work has a fundamental importance as an imposing compilation of mytho-logical, heroic, epic and general information on antiquity, in which is reflected all the culture amassed by Boccaccio in more than forty years of study. Indeed it was so comprehensive that it constituted one of the most famous reference works down to the nineteenth century, and it was reprinted continually and translated into all the languages of civilized Europe. The *"defense of poetry"* developed in books XIV and XV is valuable for its high ideals.

The *De Casibus Virorum Illustrium* was begun probably around 1355 and completed in its first form around 1360; then in 1373 and 1374 Boccaccio made a new, enlarged edition, and dedicated it to Mainardo Cavalcanti. It is a work intended to demonstrate the transitory nature of worldly goods and the ruin provided by divine Providence for one who rises unjustly and then crashes through pride and folly into an abyss of wretchedness; it is supported by examples from every age, from Adam to the Duke of Athens and Sancia de' Cabanni (and even to Charles IV and the modern kings:

see the Dedicatoria). Distributed through nine books, the tales are framed in an epico-dramatic schema, for the writer imagines that the shades of those illustrious personages pass before him as he sits quietly in his lonely study, and they ask to be heard and recalled to the memory of mankind. Thus, dramatic dialogues are often interwoven, offering a starting point for historical and moralistic considerations.

The *De Montibus, Silvis, Fontibus, Lacubus, Fluminibus, Stagnis Seu Paludibus et de Nominibus Maris Liber* was begun between 1355 and 1357, and was based on the knowledge of Pliny and of the ancient geographers which Petrarch had passed on to Boccaccio. It was brought up to date and corrected up to 1374. It is a catalogue, or rather an inventory, of cultural geography of both classical and contemporary times, conducted out of literary curiosity rather than in a spirit of exploration and discovery.

The *De Mulieribus Claris,* dedicated to Andrea Acciaiuoli, sister of the Grand Seneschal (previously eulogized in the *Amorosa Visione*), was initiated probably in the summer of 1361 and revised in nine successive editorial phases (the first four in 1362) up to 1375 (an autograph remains in the Laur. 90 sup. 98). It includes 104 biographies of famous women, ancient and modern, from Eve to Queen Joanna: in its manifest moralism there is a free and impartial narrative gusto. Boccaccio wrote the work almost as a "pendant," a companion, to Petrarch's *De Viris Illustribus,* and a devoted follower of the two great friends, Donato Albanzani, quite soon undertook to make a vernacular version of it, certainly feeling the spirit of the two "masters" hovering over it.[31]

These are the imposing works which placed Boccaccio next to the Greeks and Latins on the library shelves of civilized Europe, at least until the early 1700's. They were to impress upon the culture of the following age the imprint of his inexhaustible and fascinating erudition and his turbulent and gloomy historiography, tragic in tone and action. These works were to inspire versions of high dignity in the principal European languages, especially the more narrative pages and those dealing with militant current events and politics (for example, *De Casibus* and *De Mulieribus*). And, too, the image of Boccaccio as moralist, as it dominated European culture in the four-

teenth and fifteenth centuries, as it was consecrated as an example by
Santillana, especially in the *Comedieta de Ponça,* as it was made to act in
the *Mystère de la vengeance* as witness of the divinity of Christ, is
imposed precisely by this complex of works conceived or projected
between 1355 and 1361: one of the most fortunate periods of Boccaccio as a writer.

During this period, Boccaccio also continued to develop the
vernacular as the language of the new literature. Along with a
number of sonnets,—more Petrarchan than the earlier ones—using
the meter of those great treatises he made radical revisions in the
Amorosa Visione, the most moralistic of his youthful works, and then
developed the refined ethical declamation of the very successful
Espistola consolatoria a Pino de' Rossi (1361-1362): see p. 129). Above
all, he revitalized the cult of Dante in the *Trattatello in laude di Dante,*
a model of impassioned biography and a masterpiece of its genre
(the exact title is *De Origine Vita Studiis et Moribus Viri Clarissimi Danti
Aligerii Florentini Poete Illustris et de Operibus Compositis ab Eodem;*
autographs in cod. 104, 6 of the Capitolare library of Toledo and in
Chigiano L, V, 176 of the Vatican: for now the most probable
chronology is the following: the first revision after June of 1351; the
second, around 1360; and the third, sometime before 1372).[32]

Stimulated by his return to writing, Boccaccio set off in March
1359 to meet with Petrarch in Milan. The two great men of letters in
this meeting were remarkably different from those in the little
Paduan garden and closer together because of the intimate, enliven-
ing understanding of the last eight years. Boccaccio arrived in a mood
not only keenly anticipatory of the new and fruitful course of his
writing, but humanly enriched by family, political, and civil experiences and disappointments. He was engrossed in that moral and
religious meditation which Petrarch had inspired in him so delicately
in 1351; indeed in all probability he presented himself in that clerical
status which, since 1341, he had praised in the poet laureate (*Vita,* p.
239).[33] During these years, Petrarch had written or continued or
revised his important works *(Invective Contra Medicum* and *Contra
Quendam, De Viris, Familiares, Sine Nomine),* and had devoted himself
above all else to voicing his meditative and religious inspiration (see
the beginning of the *De Remediis, Itinerarium,* and especially the

fundamental revision of the triptych *Secretum, De Vita Solitaria, De Otio Religioso*). He had written some new poems, but more importantly, he had given a clearer form to the design of the *Rerum Vulgarium Fragmenta* (in the studies commonly referred to as "Pre-Chigi" and "Chigi") and, acting on an idea suggested to him by the *Amorosa Visione,* he had begun and made progress in his design for *I Trionfi.* Boccaccio, in his own original way, had approached the "magister's" human ideal of historical and moralistic literature, and Petrarch had not ignored the promptings of his greatest disciple toward a culture and a poetry more harmonious with the new and original Italian tradition. Boccaccio could not have been long in Milan when Petrarch had the idea of planting laurels in the garden of his house near St. Ambrogio, noting, merrily, "Year 1359, Saturday, almost the hour of noon [hora nona] XVI day of March: retentare huiusce rei fortunam libuit ... Inter cetera multum prodesse deberet ad profectum sacrarum arbuscularum, quod insignis vir dompnus Jo. Boccaccii de Certaldo, ipsis amicissimus et michi casu in has horas tunc advectus, sationi interfuit." [34] This act was a symbol of the spiritual and literary understanding which developed and deepened between the two great men in Milan. The days must have passed, intense and calm, as once before in Padua. Boccaccio eagerly copied as many of Petrarch's writings as he could (surely he transcribed the *Buccolicum Carmen,* collated with the author's help, the *Itinerarium,* fascinating for its literary geographical curiosity; the beginning (only the beginning!) of the greatly desired *Africa;* and probably some of the new *Familiari*). Boccaccio admired, studied, and perhaps borrowed some volumes of the exceptional library which he had not been able to see in the temporary quarters of the canonry at Padua (he studied for example, the *Historia Augusta,* which he used in writing the *De Casibus* and *De Mulieribus;* the Pliny, now Par. Lat. 6802—on col. 153 [v] he commented on the data concerning onions with the comic note "nondum certaldenses erant": see "that ground produces famous onions . . ." *Decameron,* VI, 10, 6). Those readings and consultations also enlivened the days' conversations. Boccaccio criticized his friend's reluctance to publish the *Africa,* but Petrarch would not yield and brought forth many arguments in opposition to the vehement eulogies of his friend.[35] Noting a certain evasive tone in Petrarch's answers (see *Fam.,* XXI, xv) Boccaccio boldly evoked the voice of Dante, to whom he attributed a literary excellence equal to that of the ancients. With his exceptional sensitivity to the poetry of all ages and in all languages, Boccaccio was eager to read Homer in his Latin garb, thanks to Leontius Pilatus, whom Petrarch had met the preceding winter in Padua and had engaged to make a specimen of translation (and surely during these conversations Petrarch showed Boccaccio the Greek Homer given him by Sigeros, and the Plato, equally mute for him, but also equally venerable: *Fam.,* XVIII, ii, 10; *Esposizioni,* IV, 1, 252).[36] And, passing from letters to men and their customs, Petrarch disclosed, finally, in the confidential freedom of conversation, that which he had refused to write six years before concerning the reasons for his sojourn in the capital of the Visconti (*Var.* 25). He commented sadly on the ambitious decision of Zanobi to abandon the studious quiet of Montecassino for the agitated and tumultuous life of the Court at Avignon, to which he had solicited appointment as apostolic secretary (see *Fam.,* XX, xiv).

Boccaccio departed, on a dark and rainy day in early April (*Fam.,* XX, vii: by the 11th he had already crossed the Po). Followed by the affectionate anxieties of his host,[37] Boccaccio carried away with him such a great light engendered by this friendship and this literary association that the activity of the following months seems to have been directed wholly to prolonging the ideals of those talks. Boccaccio wrote to Petrarch at the beginning of May, extending his ardent thanks and the announcement of his safe return to Florence. He also resumed his Dantean perorations, and, respectfully but persistently, Boccaccio reiterated the reasons for his admiration and devotion to Dante "primus studiorum dux et prima fax." He appended to the letter the poem "Italie iam certus" (sent previously to Petrarch, but now rewritten) and possibly the Trattatello.[38] (Petrarch answered with the *Fam.,* XXI, xv, but remained vague and equivocal.) Boccaccio drafted the design for his *Buccolicum* on one of the texts which he had copied in Petrarch's library. He followed the examples of Dante, and paid homage to him with quotations, imitations, and a whole language of allusion. Moreover, Dante stood before him in the "de revocatione ad amorem celestem" (XV) in the garments of Phylostropos ("Pro Phylostropo ego intelligo gloriosum preceptorem meum Franciscum Petrarcam, cuius monitis sepissime michi persuasum est ut omissa rerum temporalium oblectatione mentem ad eterna dirigerem, et sic amores meos, etsi non plene, satis tamen vertit in melius" ep. XXIII). Reliving in his memory those colloquies of the soul, Boccaccio bravely resumed the *De Casibus*. He imagined a spectre in his study, opposite a weary, discouraged, drowsy image of himself, "hominem aspectu modestum et moribus venusta facie et miti placidoque pallore conspicua, virenti laurea insignitum et pallio amictum regio, summa reverentia dignum. Quem adhuc tacentem . . . agnovi Franciscum Petrarcham optimum venerandumque preceptorem meum, cuius monita mihi semper ad virtutem calcar extiterat." The spectre appealing to "nostri Hieronymus et Augustinus" and to the Gospels, exhorted him mightily to the work "ut tamquam nobis profuer preteriti, sic et nos posteris valeamus . . . ut juanuam consequamur eternam ut videatur hac in peregrinatione mortali Deo et non vitiis militasse" (VIII, intr.). Finally, heeding the last suggestion of the "magister," Boccaccio devoted himself in 1359 and 1360 to bringing Homer back, not so much to Tuscany as to his fatherland.

The stimulation of Boccaccio's Milanese visit was prolonged by the exchange of affection and views between Petrarch and Boccaccio in the ensuing months. The resulting literary achievements were also encouraged by Boccaccio's increasingly authoritative position in Florence. In July, Giovanni da Mandello, who came to negotiate with the Signoria for the passage of the company of Count di Lando to the Visconti, surely continued to spend some time with Boccaccio and with Nelli. He recounted his journey to the Holy Land, and his description was almost like an illustration of the *Itinerarium* which Boccaccio had copied in Milan.[39] In September, Neri Morando, the eminent Venetian statesman, conversed with the Florentine friends of Boccaccio. He probably discussed the *Buccolicum* with them, and he was entrusted with letters to be handed to the "magister." [40] In those months, moreover, Boccaccio and Petrarch exchanged many letters concerning the text of the *Buccolicum*, which had to be brought up to date, having been revised in the meantime by the author.[41] They also corresponded about the "vulnus ciceronianum," which was inflicted on Petrarch by the enormus manuscript of the epistles to Atticus, according to what Morando himself narrated when passing through Florence.[42]

The records of appraisals, loans, and purchases for this period indicate [43] that it was one of easy circumstances for Boccaccio and his brother Jacopo, who was still under his guardianship. On June 22 Boccaccio, together with Jacopo, received another testimonial of public esteem. He had been chosen as ambassador "ad partes Lombardie" (that is, to the court of Bernabò Visconti, the imperial vicar). But the mission (announced as taking place in eighteen days) must not have been made, since we find no trace of it, as is customary, in political or administrative documents, or even in letters to Petrarch, who certainly would have received his friend on this occasion and would have mentioned the visit in the epistles addressed to him in these months (see, in addition to those cited, *Fam.*, XXI, xv: perhaps the subject of the mission was negotiated and settled with Giovannolo Mandello?).[44]

At the end of 1359 Boccaccio met again Acciaiuoli, who stopped in Florence in mid-December during a journey to Avignon, among other things, to ask the Signoria for aid in winning back Sicily for the Angevins. Perhaps a new reconciliation of the two friends took place on this occasion; and perhaps the "entourage" of Acciaiuoli became interested in the *Decameron*, for Francesco Buondelmonti, the faithful nephew of the Seneschal, acquired a copy of it.[45]

But aside from these literary endeavors and these civil responsibilities, Boccaccio, with his enthusiasm and his literary authority now dominant in Florence, must have devoted the winter of 1359 and 1360 to promoting new translations of Homer. He had learned from Petrarch that Leontius—the Calabrian Greek, a pupil of Barlaam and perhaps already a teacher in Crete [46]—was in Venetia, probably at Padua or Venice. Certainly Boccaccio sent letters to Leontius, directed friends to see him (perhaps he was helped by Morando, then repeatedly passing through Florence?). Meanwhile he arranged to have the new discipline and the new teacher received into the Florentine Studio: the first chair of Greek in non-Byzantine Europe. All of Boccaccio's efforts were crowned with success: "Leontium Pylatum a Venetiis occiduam Babilonem [Avignon] querentem a

longa peregrinatione meis flexi consiliis et in patria tenui . . . illum in
propriam domum suscepi et diu hospitem habui et maximo labore
meo curavi, ut inter doctores Florentini Studii susciperetur, ei ex
publico mercede apposita" *(Gen.,* XV, 7). Leontius arrived in Florence probably at the beginning of the summer of 1360, "aspectu
horridus . . . turpi facie, barba prolix et capillicio nigro, et medita-
tione occupatus assidua, moribus incultus nec satis urbanus homo"
(Gen., XV, 6). As Petrarch wrote, he must have seemed, truly, a
"magna bellua . . . tristior . . . barba et crinibus horridior," with a
"saxeum caput" *(Sen.,* III, 6), carrying everywhere "insolenter . . .
suos mores . . . suam barbam, suum pallium, suam famem . . . , si
tamen homo esset nec se belluam asperitate insigni et novitatis studio
effecisset" *(Sen.,* V, 3). However, Boccaccio, with his sincere and
heroic enthusiasm for culture, received him as a guest in his house;
and he must have been aware that notwithstanding the horrible
appearance and habits of the man, notwithstanding the diffidence
and harsh judgment of Petrarch, he was "uti experientia notum fecit,
licterarum Grecarum doctissimus, et quodam modo Grecarum hystoriarum atque fabularum arcivum inexhaustum, esto Latinarum
non satis adhuc instructus" *(Gen.,* XV, 6). Before the courses began at
the Studio, Boccaccio must have taken lessons in Greek, and must
have tried to stimulate and follow the work of Leontius. Meanwhile,
Leontius, in accordance with the counsels of Petrarch, was reworking
his translation of the first books of the *Iliad,* which he had begun the
preceding winter (see p. 113). He worked from a manuscript which
Boccaccio, with his tireless zeal and at no slight expense, had obtained in Padua, perhaps from a Cretan jurist, guided by information
from Petrarch (who was unwilling to deprive himself—except in case
of absolute necessity—of his own Homer: *Var.,* 25, of August 18). The
work must have progressed by October—Boccaccio was able to send
Petrarch, with a translation of the preamble, an introduction and
numerous notes by Leontius, and "epistolam magnam multaque
continentem sub Homeri poete missam nomine," which formed the
basis of the lofty *Familiare* to the Greek Poet (XXIV, xii, dated
October 9: "Unus vir nostro te latinum seclo revehit . . . Vir iste si
vixerit totum te nobis reddet et iam cepit").[47] Petrarch, moreover,
followed the work not so much with financial aid as with assiduous

consolation and counsels (*Var.* 25; *Fam.* XXIV, xii, 4; *Sen.* III, 6, and XVI,1).[48] Leontius' work was followed with admiration and anxiety by the friends of the Florentine circle, especially Nelli and perhaps Forese or Domenico Silvestri or Domenico Bandini ("fesulana vallis et Arni ripe . . . tres tibi amicos tulerint," wrote Petrarch addressing himself to Homer: *Fam., XXIV,* xii, 4).

On October 18, besides the conversations and the private lessons ("in privato . . . audivi"), Leontius began his public lessons at the Studio (". . . ut legerentur *publice* Homeri libri"). Among his auditors was Domenico Silvestri, an ardent student of culture and a devotee of Boccaccio (Leontius recalled him twenty years later in his *De Insulis,* c. 126).[49] Discontentment and misunderstanding arose because the teaching was not practical nor such as to be useful to merchants and diplomats in the East. But Boccaccio, with his great authority, succeeded in firmly maintaining the cultural and literary character of the daring initiative [50] just as he had persuaded that Leontius, contrary to the usual rules, should be permitted to teach in the Studio although he had no doctor's degree. Leontius spent approximately two and one half years in Florence, teaching through two academic cycles at the Studio (he stayed until October or November of 1362).[51] During that time he translated and expounded Euripides and Aristotle in addition to Homer. That is to say, he included authors who particularly interested Boccaccio for the works he had "on the stocks" (by advice of Petrarch, Plato, on the other hand, had been prudently omitted: *Var.,* 25).[52]

Eventually the translation and commentary of Homer must have proceeded with more effort and less speed, either because they were no longer based on already tested essays of translations (books I–V of the *Iliad*) or because for various periods the coaxing and stimulating presence of Boccaccio was lacking in Florence, as we shall see (only at the end of 1365, after Leontius left for Constantinople with the original translation, would Boccaccio finally have rearranged, copied and sent to Petrarch the oft-entreated Homeric work: *Sen.,* III, 6; V, 1).[53] Despite the judgments of Petrarch, which were severe toward the work and almost cruel toward the man, and which were reëchoed too facilely until recently (*Fam.,* XXIV, xii; *Sen.,* III, 6; V, 3; VI, 1; *Var.,* 25), and in spite of the fatal limits to the haphazard

preparation of Leontius, the translation and the commentary of the
Iliad and the *Odyssey* appear to represent a good medium level of the
Greco-Byzantine culture of the time. And on the same level are the
other translations and notes, which we know directly or indirectly
thanks to the admirable solicitude and tractability of Boccaccio in
annotating them and utilizing them, especially in the *Genealogia*
(some fifty times: "nec infinitis ad eo recitatis, urgente etiam alia cur
animum acrior [perhaps an allusion to his various worrisome vicissitudes in 1361 and 1362?], suffecisset memoria, ni cedulis commen-
dassem": *Gen.*, XV, 6).[54] It was a pioneering and revealing work for
European culture and its future. And not by chance is it due to
Boccaccio "ad poeticas meditationes dispositum ex utero matris"
(*Gen.*, XV, 10): to his passion—tenacious and pugnacious—for the
Greek world which he had lovingly divined from his Neapolitan
youth; to his deeply sensed consciousness of the marvelous and
uninterrupted continuity of intellectual and cultural life, of poetry
and of art, from antiquity to his own days, from Homer to Virgil and
to Dante, from Apelles to Vitruvius and to Giotto. And whereas
Petrarch in the *Secretum* (II) and again in *Seniles* (XII, 2), repeating
Cicero, affirmed the absolute superiority of Latin literature over
Greek, Boccaccio in the *Genealogia* dedicated a whole "capitolo" to
the Hellenic culture:

> Ego in hoc Latinitati compatior, que sic omnino Greca abiecit
> studia ut etiam non noscamus caracteres licterarum. Nam et si
> sibi suis sufficiat licteris, et in eas omnis occiduus versus sit orbis,
> sociate Grecis lucidiores procul dubio apparerent. Nec preterea
> omnia secum a Grecia veteres traxere Latini; multa supersunt,
> et profecto nobis incognita, quibus possemus scientes effici
> meliores (XV, 7).

This is the first time in the neo-Latin world that the two great
cultures of antiquity are felt and relived in their ideal unity; and
Boccaccio is so aware of his decisive discovery that for the first time
he is unable to control a gesture of humble pride. "Ipse . . . fui, qui
primus meis sumptibus Homeri libros et alios quosdam Grecos in
Etruriam revocavi, ex qua multis ante seculis abierant non redituri?

Nec in Etruriam tantum, sed in patriam deduxi" (*Gen.*, XV, 7). Rightly, the most profound and systematic scholar of this episode has been able to affirm recently that "in Boccaccio considerably more than in Petrarch, there is again at work that fusion between Latin culture and Greek culture which from the end of the 6th century to the second half of the 14th century had disappeared as a working element of Western civilization . . ."; and that Boccaccio "foresaw, however dimly, that in order to be truly integral Humanism had to make itself complete with the matrix of Latin culture and 'humanitas,' that is to say, with the culture and the 'humanitas' of the Greeks" (Pertusi).

During this period, through the frequent interchange of letters with Petrarch and with the most eminent men of culture of the time, we feel that Boccaccio and his house—more, in a certain sense, than that of the "magister," aristocratically closed and subjected to frequent transfers—are truly the center of Italian pre-Humanism: the meeting-point of Lombard-Venetian Petrarchism, that of Romagna and that of Naples. In this artistic coterie there developed such men as Silvestri, Salutati, Villani, Marsili, those who would become the loyal members of the Augustinian circle of Santo Spirito which was so dear to Boccaccio (see pp. 183 f.). Wonderful new literary discoveries radiated throughout Italy and all of Europe from Boccaccio's desk. The manuscripts of ancient writers which he promoted, along with those circulated by Petrarch, constituted a new canon of classics.

This stimulation and coordination of Italian cultural life was helped perhaps by the new ecclesiastic dignity which probably was conferred on Boccaccio in this period. On November 2, 1360 Innocent VI—to whose court Boccaccio had come as ambassador in 1354—granted to "dilecto filio Johanni nato quondam Boccacci de Certaldo, clerico florentino," full dispensation "super defectu natalium quem patitur, de soluto genitus et soluta" so that he might receive "omnes ordines et ecclesiasticum beneficium, etiam si animarum cura imminetur epidem . . . etiam si dignatas vel personatus aut officium fuerit et curam habeat animarum et etiam si huiusmodi beneficium canonicatus et prebenda seu dignitas in ecclesia extiterit. . . ." And the broad and honorific concession was made, wrote the Pontiff to Boccaccio, because "vite ac morum honestas et alia virtutum et probitatis merita, super quibus apud nos fide dignorum commendaris testimonio, promerentur ut personam tuam favore specialis gratie prosequamur." Since it is not customary to request—as Boccaccio had requested—a dispensation or a privilege if there is no necessity for using it, it seems natural to think that a man who was already an ecclesiastic and had studied canon law must have obtained some benefice or canonry in those months. In fact, "a note by a most trustworthy compiler of the 18th century . . . seems to present Boccaccio as prior of a church" [55]; and further-more, in his testament there appear (besides many relics) a breviary, maniple, stole and chasuble, various altar hangings and so on; that is, all garments or equipment characteristic of a priest. Even though no document has yet turned up to confirm that Boccaccio used the exceptional privileges granted him by the Pontiff, it is probable that, in 1360 or 1361, he obtained some Church dignity or benefice of no slight importance.[56]

But far more than this natural, and certainly expected, promo-tion, political events in Florence at the end of 1360 and in the first half of 1361 must have profoundly changed the material and moral circumstances of Boccaccio. His economic and civil situation had been in continuous ascent between 1350 and 1358, thanks to the ever-increasing favor he enjoyed with the group directing Florentine politics. The threat of the Visconti, the presence of the Emperor in Tuscany, and the skirmishes with Pisa had persuaded the various parties to accept some kind of truce. But at the beginning of 1358 the factiousness of the Parte Guelfa burst forth and, nothwithstanding the opposition of the Signoria, a bill was passed, under violent pressure, into a law against those who "with the spirit of rapacious wolves under their lambs' skins are constantly trying to get into the sheepfold." Suspects were thus excluded from any public office, anonymous secret accusations were permitted, and the Captains of the Guelf party were authorized to "warn," that is, to keep out of public life, anyone suspected of Ghibellinism (M. Villani, VIII, 24). It was an inquitous law which became a nightmare for the citizens and for the Signoria itself, and an immediate source of civic distur-bances. It had been imposed by "certain great and popular men . . .

[Albizzi and Ricci] for the evil purpose of becoming little tyrants," and they used it continually for personal gain and revenge, especially against the middle class which had with serious difficulty ruled the state after the Duke of Athens was driven out. Under the impetus of these resentments and these nightmares, of aversion to the factiousness of the Guelfs and the Ricci and Albizzi, in the final months of 1360 a movement was outlined for a *coup d'état* on the occasion of the renewal of the priors, on December 31 (M. Villani, X, 24 and 25). Several representatives of the bourgeoisie and of the past regime took part in it (Medici, Del Buono, Bandini, Pazzi, Rossi, Gherardini, and so on, and with them some desperadoes and adventurers, who wove some dangerous agreements with Giovanni da Oleggio, the Viscontian who ruled Bologna, and with the papal legate, Egidio d'Albornoz). As Villani implies (X, 22–23) even the singularly cautious and courteous visit of Niccola Acciaiuoli did not appear casual ("setting a fine table most graciously every day and, without the least arrogance, inviting the citizens and the grandees and the commoners to dine, honoring them in turn": among them were probably Nelli and Boccaccio). Acciaiuoli had returned in mid-December with great success and prestige from his missions to the Papal and Viscontean courts. After the plot for the *coup d'état* was discovered through an informer and the sudden discouragement of Bartolomeo Medici (his brother, the great Salvestro, saved him by reporting his confessions to the Signoria), on December 30 Domenico Bandini and Niccolò di Bartolo del Buono (the dedicatee of the *Comedia*) were hanged; the others took flight and were banished. Among these were Pino de' Rossi, Luca Ugolini, Andrea dell'Ischia—also friends of Boccaccio (see *Epistola Consolatoria*); various others among the conspirators must have been acquaintances of his or at least neighbors, because almost all of them lived across the river, in Oltrarno, and many right in Santa Felicita, the usual quarter of families of Valdelsana origin.[57] Moreover, the bonds of Boccaccio with Acciaiuoli and with highly placed personages of the Visconti court were not unknown in Florence.

Therefore it is not astonishing to see no more public offices assigned to Boccaccio until 1365, since his public position, as well as his economic one, was apparently sharply in decline. It is not as-

tonishing to learn that, on July 2, after having turned over the house
of Santa Felicita to his half-brother, who had just reached his
majority [58] (and with whom there were perhaps disputes: see
Epistola Consolatoria, 81), he retired to his ancestral town, and for
several years looked upon Florence—to which, however, he often
returned—with scorn and suspicion, resolutely intending to settle far
from his city.

NOTES

1. Ep. VIII, of 1353, "mors nuper fratris": it is well known that for
   Boccaccio the "nuper" had a very approximate value.
2. It suffices to see the "estimi" (estimates, evaluations, ratings) for 1351
   through 1355 cited by V. Branca, *Nuovi documenti.*
3. For example, "Mannus calzolarius" (shoemaker), "Sandra treccha"
   (market woman, according to the 1352 documents in *Nuovi documenti.*
4. Doc. cit., U. Dorini, *Contributi,* cit. on August 18 in the first suit, before
   the Giudice dei malefici (Judge of torts), Boccaccio speaks through an
   attorney, Angelo di Ser Andrea; in the second, November 19, he
   personally presents to the same judge an accusation against Francesco
   and Buccio di Pone of Certaldo, who had abandoned the farm of
   Santa Maria at Colline, property of his ward Jacopo, but on November 23 he drops the action.
5. P. G. Ricci, "La pretesa immatricolazione del Boccaccio nell'arte dei
   Guidici e Notai," in *Studi sul Boccaccio,* III, 1965.
6. "Asiatice quondam delitie grecis, asiatice greceque romanis exter-
   minio fuere: nostre nos ipsos pessundant et ex florido culmine in
   sterquilinium redigunt redigentque. Proth mortalium pudor et igna-
   via, proth ridiculum quorundam fastidium, qui effeminates homines
   incestuosissime veneri totis viribus obsequiosos sub acri Marte insulsa
   quodam fictione progenitos volunt!" (ep. VIII).
7. The lords of Romagna, threatened from Bologna, became the opera-
   tional base of the Visconti in central Italy. Their position was favorable therefore, to the Veneto-Ferrarese League of December 1353, and
   they were essential elements for the defense of the rear of the Florentine state.
8. The two identifications are by Billanovich, *Petrarca,* pp. 181 and 185.
9. See the testimony on Giovanni Conversini in the *Rationarum Vite* pub-

lished by R. Sabbadini, *Giovanni da Ravenna,* Como, 1924, pp. 137 and 240; and see *Fam.,* **XXIII,** xix.

10. Documents published and cited by S. Canestrini, *art. cit.,* p. 349; A. Hortis, *Giovanni Boccaccio Ambasciatore,* pp. 48 ff. (and see pp. 13 ff.); V. Crescini, op. cit., p. 259; G. Gerola, "Alcuni documenti inediti per la biografia del Boccaccio," *Giorn. Stor. Lett. It.,* **XXXII,** 1898. The mission, planned in April, was to take 45 days; changed later to 60.

11. He was paid less than a quarter as much as Boccaccio, and a single horse was assigned to him, while Boccaccio had three (Gerola, art. cit.).

12. Doc. cit. by G. Gerola, *Alcuni documenti,* pp. 356–357.

13. See doc. cit. in note 2 above.

14. Doc. cit. by G. Gerola, *Alcuni documenti,* p. 357.

15. I do not believe, as has been said, that Boccaccio was present on the occasion of Zanobi's coronation at Pisa on May 15. Certainly he would have recorded this circumstance, especially in the pointed polemics against Zanobi himself or his patron, Acciaiuoli.

16. Léonard, *Histoire,* III, pp. 154 ff.

17. Evidently "tranquillitatum" is to be so interpreted, in the light of many phrases of epistle VIII as, for example: "An mos iste, precor, bonam suavemque fortunam sequentium esse solet?" and "sed, ut iam supra dictum est, ne felicium septator vocer, timeo ne desistam" (that is, to go to Naples now, after the apotheosis of the Grand Seneschal).

18. An accurate historical-literary analysis of the extremely important ep. VIII and of Acciaiuoli's attitudes has been made by Léonard, *Boccace et Naples,* p. 59, with the usual apologetic interpretations for Niccola.

19. M. Villani (IV, 91) noted scornfully: "then strong and virile things were needed and not vile weakness of women . . . and whereas in the past his person was famous for highmindedness and many virtues, at this time he recalled to the memory of his citizens the detestable life of Sardanapalus."

20. A letter of Acciaiuoli published by Léonard, *Histoire,* III, pp. 507-508.

21. Angelo was a cousin of Niccola: we see him very cordially bound to Boccaccio and his Florentine friends already in the preceding years (Boccaccio called him "noster Angelus," "patrem meum episcopum" in the epistles VI and VIII; and see Nelli, epistles VI and XI).

22. ". . . dum seva Canis injuncta Leoni Stella malum malum finiret iter, stetit ovia febris Incauto mihi dura nimis nil tale timenti: cum qua per menses lucatatus ad omnia vires Exposui . . . Et cecidi, victusque fere inremeabile limen Usque adii mortis . . ." *Carmi,* V, 14 ff.

23. Léonard, *Histoire,* III, pp. 160 ff., 556, 558.
24. It has now been pointed out that it was due to Zanobi in collaboration with Boccaccio that a large part of the classical treasures of Cassino passed on to Florence: G. Billanovich, *I primi umanisti e le tradizioni dei classici,* Freiburg, 1952, pp. 33 ff., 40.
25. The date to be assigned to the acquisition of the Tacitus manuscript was much discussed until very recently: whether that of the Neapolitan sojourn of 1362 and 1363 or that of 1370 to 1371. The first hypothesis was supported with copious arguments above all by De Nolhac ("Boccace et Tacite." *Mel. d' Arch et d' Hist.,* XII, 1892, and *Petrarque et l'humanisme,* II, Paris, 1907,[2] p. 43); the second especially by Hauvette *(Boccace,* pp. 405 ff.) and by Billanovich *(Petrarca,* pp. 389 ff.). All scholars, however, admitted that the last word would be left to the editor of the *De Mulieribus,* in which Tacitus is largely utilized. Since Ricci and Zaccaria (see note 31 below) have now established that the borrowings appear already in the first edition of the *De Mulieribus* datable in 1361, it is highly probable that the codex containing the *Annali* and the *Historiae* was already known to Boccaccio in this 1355 visit to Montecassino. It still remains for Billanovich to clarify the role of Zanobi in the affair, which he termed decisive and promised to illustrate *(Pietro Piccolo,* p. 40), having already pointed out in the manuscript the autograph marginalia of Zanobi himself (cf. J. Stackelberg, *Tacitus in der Romania,* Tubingen, 1960, pp. 46 ff.; G. Billanovich rev. in *Romance Philology,* 17, 1964, p. 696). If it were really necessary to put a later date on the acquaintances with Tacitus, thought might be given to Zanobi's passing through Florence in 1358 or to the transfer of his books, after his death, to the Certosa of Florence in 1361. In any case it remains difficult to explain Petrarch's lack of knowledge of Tacitus, or at least no documentation of it is known, but how many details escape us in the relations between the two great men, and how many of them we are too prone to explain according to the measure of our reason!
26. For the history of the various possible interpretations of eclogue VIII, see Léonard, *Boccace et Naples,* pp. 76 ff. The identification of Zanobi with Corydon is anything but certain.
27 V. Branca, "Un autografo del Boccaccio," *Studi sul Boccaccio,* II, 1964.
28. *Fam.,* XIX, vi, "Hinc quem cernis homuncio Cristo devotus, mundi rerumque fugacium spretor ingens et cupidissimus eternarum ... dimissis frementis aule fragoribus ad illorum [*Apostolorum*] quietissima limina grad*iens* . . .": also XIX, vii; and ep. V of Nelli.

29. See note 9 above. The meeting with Giovanni Conversini in Florence in the summer occurred, I believe, at the end of June or very early in July, if we wish to put faith in that indication of the season. In fact, Boccaccio was already in Ravenna early in July, because Petrarch sent him the *Invective* there on July 12. On the other hand, the encounter cannot be dated after the Ravenna sojourn, because then Boccaccio certainly would have seen Conversini in Ravenna, and on seeing him would not have referred only to his meetings with the "piccino" in 1353.

30. M. Pastore Stocchi, *Tradizione medievale e gusto umanistico nel De montibus,* Padova, 1963, pp. 70 ff.; Stocchi, however, is convinced, as are other scholars, that the *Invective* were sent by Petrarch in 1355.

31. The dates proposed for the Latin works are those held most probable today after the recent studies of Ricci *(Studi,* 1959 and 1962); Billanovich *(Pietro Piccolo)*; Pastore Stocchi (op. cit.); V. Zaccaria, "Le fasi redazionali del 'De mulieribus,'" *Studi sul Boccaccio,* I, 1964 and his edition of *De mulieribus,* Milan, 1970; G. Martellotti, *Le due redazioni delle "Genealogie" del Boccaccio,* Roma, 1951.

32. M. Barbi, *Problemi,* I, pp. 395 ff.; G. Vandelli, *Boccaccio editore di Dante,* Florence, 1933, and in *Studi danteschi,* V, 1922, and XV, 1931; G. Billanovich, *Prime ricerche dantesche,* Rome, 1947; G. Boccaccio, *Trattatello in laude di Dante* a cura di P. G. Ricci, Alpignano, 1969.

33. See the doc. cit. on p. 119 which in 1360 speaks of Boccaccio as a cleric for some time past. But he could not have been a cleric before 1355, since he is called "laicus" in the documents of the Ufficio della Condotta (see p. 102). On the other hand, instead, elected in 1367 to the same office, he is no longer defined as "laicus." (See also note 56 below.)

34. Thus he annotates in the Vat. Lat. 2193: M. Vattasso, *I codici petrarcheschi della Biblioteca Vaticana,* Rome, 1907, p. 233.

35. Perhaps Boccaccio had already written in the *Genealogia,* VI, 53, "labuit Achilles Omerum et Eneas Virgilium, tanta potentes eloquentia ut respective illaudati ceteri videantur mortales, esto evo nostro tertius exsurgat Scipio Africanus non minori gloria, maiori tamen iustitia delatus in ethera versu viri celeberrimi Francisci Petrarce," but later in the ep. XI to Barbato he was to say: "apud Mediolanum et Patavum . . . vires omnes exposui, et hiis fere omnibus rationibus . . . et aliis insuper usus sum ut sacrum pectus mollire flectere et in nostrum desiderium possem deducere, ut scilicet ex conclavi Scipio miris ornarus splendoribus; vidi quidem, emicteretur in publicum; sed frustra. . . ."

36. See A. Pertusi, op. cit., pp. 16 ff., 30 ff.

37. "Boccaccium nostrum suavissimum, et regis fluminum Eridani Comitumque flente, simul et Apennini iuga salvum transihisse cognoveris, ut animo tuo sit quies, quam te integra minime habere posse dixisti, nisi prius ipsum sciveris patriam feliciter attigisse natalem," Nelli would write to Petrarch on May 17 (ep. XXIII).

38. It is a hypothesis of G. Billanovich, *Petrarca*, p. 238.

39. Billanovich, *Petrarca*, pp. 224 ff.

40. Foresti, *Aneddoti*, pp. 364 ff.

41. Nelli's ep. XXIV of September 11 in this connection bears the affectionate notation "Boccaccius noster valet"; the *Fam.*, XXII, ii to Boccaccio advising him not to publicize the little work is of early October.

42. Foresti, *Aneddoti*, p. 168.

43. For example there is the matter of a loan of four gold florins in which Giovanni and Jacopo appear together in the second half of 1359; that of the acquisition of a farm from Paolo di Pace of Certaldo in 1360 (docc. cit. by V. Branca, *Notizie e documenti* and by U. Dorini, art. cit., p. 76).

44. Doc. published by V. Branca, *Notizie e documenti.*

45. See V. Branca, *La Prima diffusione del Decameron*, pp. 21 ff.

46. For the biography of Leontius, see A. Pertusi, op. cit., pp. 30 ff., and in general I refer the reader to the same volume, fundamental for this subject, for the data given in the following pages and especially for the judgment of Leontius' work.

47. Documentation offered by A. Pertusi, op. cit., pp. 22 and 73 ff.

48. He declared "quique [that is, Homer] grecus ad me venit mea ope et impensa factus est latinus" (*Sen.*, XVI, 1); the expense refers to the copy made for him, as is made clear in *Sen.*, III, 6 addressed to Boccaccio: "In futurum autem, si me amas, vide obsecro an tuo studio, mea impensa, fieri possit ut Homerus integer bibliothecam hanc, ubi pridem grecus habitat, tandem latinus accedat."

49. P. G. Ricci, "La prima cattedra di greco in Firenze," *Rinascimento*, III, 1952.

50. P. de Nolhac, *Petrarque*, II, p. 108; A. Pertusi, op. cit., pp. 99 ff., and see *Fam.*, XXIV, xii, 37; also *Gen.*, XIV, 2.

51. "Conversantem fere tribus annis audivi" writes Boccaccio, *Gen.* XV, 6.

52. Besides Pertusi, op. cit., p. 18, see A. Pertusi, "La Scoperta di Euripide nel primo Umanesimo," *Italia medioevale e umanistica*, III, 1960; M. Pastore Stocchi, *Tradizione medioevale*, pp. 80 ff.; G. Billanovich, "Il Petrarca e i retori latini minori," *Italia medioevale e umanistica*, V, 1962.

53. A. Pertusi, *op. cit.,* pp. 24 ff.; *Var.,* 25; his versions are "ceu quedam epule quas gelari oportuit, nec successit, in quibus etsi form non hereat, sapor tamen odorque non pereunt"; but even Petrarch has to admit that in his time "nisi fallor amicus hic noster iam tota in Grecia solus est" to admire and understand Homer (*Fam.,* XXIV, xii, 34).

54. See the detailed particular and revealing documentation offered by Pertusi, *op. cit.,* pp. 295 ff. and 371 ff.

55. The papal bull of Innocent VI is published by G. Billanovich, *Restauri,* pp. 174 ff.

56. Take note however in this connection of some indications or allusions not easy to coordinate. In 1353 (ep. VIII) Boccaccio speaks of Angelo Acciaiuoli as "meum episcopum florentinum," with an expression, that is, more spontaneous and facile in a cleric than in a layman; but in 1355 in an official document, he is mentioned as "laicus" (see pp. 102, 112) In 1366 (ep. XIII) concerning Giandonati, prior of Saints Michele and Jacopo at Certaldo, he wrote: "michi, si ad dignitatem intuear, pater et dominus . . . si ad etatem et dilectionem inspexero, filius meus." The expression seems to indicate Boccaccio as a simple cleric, with no particular rank; unless it refers simply to the fact that, whatever his rank, Boccaccio, as a parishioner of Saints Michele and Jacopo, considered Giandonati as "pater et dominus."

57. Doc. cit. by P. G. Ricci, *Studi,* 1959, p. 31; the judgment was published by A. Cortese in *Studi sul Boccaccio,* II, 1964.

58. Document published by F. Corazzini, *Le Lettere,* p. CII.

CHAPTER 8

Withdrawal to
Certaldo and Religious
and Cultural Reassessment
(1361-1364)

It was not political unrest alone which drove Boccaccio from Florence; his flight was the result of a firm spiritual and artistic choice as well. He did not return to Certaldo in search of lost times; but rather, Boccaccio sought a new peace, an inner silence, and a resolution of spiritual conflicts. Boccaccio sensed a contradiction between his literary and cultural zeal and his active and apparently profane life and the inescapable demands of a firm Christian commitment. Even though his stance as the father of Italian prose and the defender of renewed classicism was firmly established, Boccaccio sought the comforts of solitude and meditation. His retreat borne of anxiety was not unlike Petrarch's hermitlike life in Vaucluse and Silvapiana, where he could devote himself to study and prayer. After having conceived of and, with his narrative genius, created the most lively and magnificent comedy of man and of humanity, now Boccaccio sought the opportunity to find himself. In fact, a few months after his retirement to the castle looking out upon the quiet Valdelsa, he already was writing to Pino de' Rossi:

I . . . have returned to Certaldo and here I have begun, with much less difficulty than I had thought possible, to comfort my life, and the rough clothes and the peasant fare are beginning to please me; and the absence of the ambitions and the unpleasantness and annoyances of our town-dwellers is of such great consolation to my heart that, could I remain without hearing anything of them, I do believe that my repose would increase greatly. In exchange for the anxious and continuous intrigues and occupations of the town-dwellers, I see fields, hills, trees, clothed with green leaves and variegated flowers; things produced simply, by nature, whereas in the towns all is artificiality. I hear the songs of the nightingales and the other birds with a delight no less great than was the nuisance, formerly, of hearing the deceptions and the disloyalties of our citizens all day long; and without any impediment I can commune freely with my dear books whenever I feel like doing so. And, to sum up my state of mind, I tell you that I believe that, mortal as I am, I am enjoying and feeling something of eternal happiness. . . .

In this *Epistola consolatoria a Pino de' Rossi* (written late in 1361 or in the first half of 1362 to comfort his exiled friend)[1] the meditative tone of the moral considerations on the lot of man is more impressive than the political arguments and deprecations. Beyond the natural and evocative presence of the three famous "consolations" of Seneca and the rich consolatory tradition of the Middle Ages, besides the obvious literary attitudes, besides the historical allusions taken directly from the *De Casibus* and the *De Mulieribus,* there is in the letter the clear reflection of intensely meditated personal experiences (see p. 155 f.).

Into this situation of inward and outward uncertainties, of moral and religious anxieties not yet resolved in inward peace and certainty, the episode narrated by Petrarch repeating what Boccaccio had written to him a short time before, must have fallen with a crashing and upsetting roar:

Scribis nescio quem Petrum Senensem patria religione insigni et miraculis insuper clarum virum nuper obeuntem multa de multis, inter quos de utroque nostrorum aliqua predixisse, idque tibi per quendam, cui hoc ille commiserat, nunciatum . . . tu quod ad statum tuum attinet, duo hec (nam cetera sub primis) audisti: vite tue terminum instare paucorumque tibi iam tempus annorum superesse: hoc primum tibi; preterea poetice studium interdici: hoc secundum, ultimumque hic illa consternatio merorque tuus quem legendo meum feci . . . (*Sen.,* I, 5 of May 28, 1362).

There has been much fabulizing on this warning from beyond the grave, especially on the traces of the interpolation made in the life of the Blessed Petroni. Such theories clearly romanticize Petrarch's epistle and give the name of Gioacchino Ciani to the unknown messenger.[2] The warning, as is clear from the sole source (*Sen.,* I, 5), was not at all provoked, as has been generally declared, by scandal over the licentiousness of the *Decameron,* but was addressed to *both* Petrarch and Boccaccio to reprove them for devoting themselves too exclusively to literature and poetry, worldly and decadent sciences. That is to say, Petroni, as though anticipating Dominici and the *Lucula noctis,* wished to enter actively into the polemics against poetry which raged then and in the first part of the following century, and in which Boccaccio had participated and would continue to participate from the opposing camp. This is exactly the point which Petrarch emphasized in his calm and carefully pondered letter, in which not a single word alludes to the writings or to the literary licentiousness of his friend. After having adduced reasonable doubts about the authenticity of the admonition and dismissed any excessive terror of death, Petrarch affirmed fully and energetically the complete legitimacy, indeed the sanctity, of literary studies and of poetry. He even called upon his masters, Augustine and Jerome ("omnium peregrinatio est beata, sed ea certe gloriosior, que clarior, que altior: unde fit ut literate devotioni comparabilis non sit quam vis devota rusticitas; nec tu mihi tam sanctum aliquem, ex illo grege literarum inope dabis, cui non ex hoc altero sanctiorem numero objiciam").

Boccaccio, always sensitive and impetuous, despite his clerical background and probable ecclesiastical rank, rashly thought to abandon his studies and turn over his library to Petrarch when he received the message from Petroni. Petrarch, however, came to his

aid, offering a well-balanced critical experience, that was strengthened with an inner certainty. He accepted the offer of the library, and
quickly turned it to a high and religious purpose ("hec seppellex
nostra, post nos, si votum meum Deus adiuverit, ad aliquem nostri
perpetuo memorem, pium ac devotum locum simul indecerpta per-
veniat"). In that hour of moral and material bewilderment, he took
particular care to encourage his friend to continue his studies and
love of literature, and he cordially invited Boccaccio to live with him
("mecum has quantulascumque temporum reliquias agere, quod et
ego semper optavi . . . sum vero cui in tantum suppetit, quantam
abunde sufficiat duobus unum cor habentibus atque unam domum").

The authoritative reasonings and the affectionate delicacy of
Petrarch must have strongly aided Boccaccio in overcoming doubts
and discouragement. Nevertheless he refused then, as he did later, the
offer of steady hospitality, although it was tendered with affectionate
insistence ("quod amicus totiens te vocantem preveris non laudo
iniuriosus es mihi si fastidis, iniuriosior si diffidis . . ."). He refused it
in a spirit of inflamed independence, and in a strong fear of risking
the spiritual friendship essential to the life of his soul. (Boccaccio
recalled the dangers of cohabitation, which he learned in his experiences with Acciaiuoli.) Impulsive and enthusiastic as ever, Boccaccio nonetheless followed his friend's suggestions and quickly resumed
his literary activities. In his frequent Florentine visits and from
Certaldo as well, he continued to encourage the work of Leontius on
Homer, and in those months he finished the pages to Pino de' Rossi,
the first editorial phases of the *De Mulieribus* and, probably, the *Vita di
San Pier Damiani*, the elements of which he had gathered several
months previously in Ravenna, at Petrarch's suggestion.

In Ravenna, "his own" city, Boccaccio had in fact spent a part of
the winter of 1361 and 1362, as shown by epistle X which tells of a
precious episode of collaboration between the two great men.
Petrarch, who that autumn had resumed work on his *De Vita Solitaria*,
desired information on St. Peter Damian, whose love of solitude he
admired. Having heard that a mutual friend, Donato Albanzani,
was going to Ravenna, the saint's native city, he asked him to carry a
message to Boccaccio to send him that information in Milan. The

"discipulus" immediately undertook to satisfy the desires of the "magister," and having found a "Life of St. Peter Damian" among the "congeries maxima inutilium scripturarum fumosis egesta sacculis" of an old native of Ravenna, he studiously based a careful biography on it and on other documents. This he sent to Petrarch on January 2, 1362 with his epistle X (which was like a preamble relating the story of his research and giving various opinions).[3] Along with presenting information on Albanzani, Boccaccio's epistle seems to allude to the cause of his sojourn in Ravenna and its rather long duration, both evidently known to Petrarch (". . . meque, quod apud eos infortunio meo morer, sollicitas" . . .). The phrase alludes only to his regret or the inconvenience of being in Ravenna ("infortunio meo": "to my misfortune"), emphasized also in the dating ("scripta in cloaca fere totius Gallie cisalpine"). It may also refer to a recent misfortune or sorrow, in view of the repetition of the same phrase in epistle XI, which refers directly to the spring of 1362 ("di questo mio infortunio si fece parola": this misfortune of mine was mentioned). It is possible simply to think of the hardship and harm which befell Boccaccio as an aftermath to the conspiracy of Bartolo del Buono and Pino de' Rossi, or to the unpleasant consequences of the death of Bernardino da Polenta (March 9, 1359) which, as Giovanni Conversini wrote, "Boccacii studia magnifice instruxit" [4] (perhaps loss of benefices?), or of sad events (death, misfortunes, dissensions) connected with people who were bound to Boccaccio by affection in the preceding years (Violante's mother for example?). In any case it is significant that after repeated sojourns over the previous fifteen years, he was in Ravenna for the last time in the winter of 1361 and 1362, and under the shadow of a misfortune which is for us mysterious. At least Boccaccio could take spiritual refuge in the ideal conversation with Petrarch, and comfort in the Damianian praises for that solitude which he had chosen by withdrawing to Certaldo the year before.

The cherished peace of Valdelsa was broken, however, not only by the frequent trips to Florence, but also by persistent and worrisome news: in the summer and autumn of 1361 Zanobi lay dying in Avignon, and Petrarch, asked to take over his post as apostolic secretary, declined the offer but suggested Nelli. After Nelli's apprehensive refusal, Petrarch insisted that Boccaccio should fill the position (*Sen.,* I, 2, 4 and 5). In mid-April a letter from Petrarch (*Misc.* 10) brought not the usual comforting and friendly fondness, but the unhappy news that he was about to cross the Alps on a visit to the Emperor Charles IV. Immediately Boccaccio was filled with fear for the dangers to his "magister" and his precious and still unpublished works ("A desideriis nostris avertit oculos Deus . . . Iam vides," he wrote to Barbato, "quid de homine, nedum de rebus a se compositis, sperare possimus. Hinc dolens merensque sum, et spe destitutus omni studia mea qualiacumque preterita damno, et quod michi vite superest spatium vilipendo,": ep. XI). Shaken and anxious, he was about to rush off to Padua, but the uncertainty of finding Petrarch still there, and the cost of the journey, steep for his now dwindling finances, made him renounce that project. His heart swollen with bitterness and devotion to Petrarch, he wrote to Barbato from Florence, on May 15 (ep. XI). In his letter he promised copies of Petrarch's works to Barbato, and spoke of the journey to Naples which would end this crucial year of his life, and which had been suggested to him by Nelli ("ego cupiebam atque proposueram hiis diebus Patavum ire, et illum ibidem ante discessum viderim et ab eo extrema mandata susciperem, ac vide Neapolim usque pergere nostrum visitaturus Simonidem").

The mild prior of the Santi Apostoli had in fact agreed, in the second half of 1361, to settle down in Naples as the intendant or "dispensiere" (steward) of the Acciaiuoli establishment: the functions once performed by Zanobi. But the latter had shed luster on the little court of the Grand Seneschal with both his title and his activity as "poet laureate." In order to refurbish and increase that honor, Niccola and the southern Petrarchists (Nelli, Napoleone and Niccola Orsini, Barbato) attempted in 1360 and 1361 to get the "magister" to leave the Viscontian court and later Venetia, and come to Naples (see, for example, *Fam.,* XXII, vi; XXIII, xviii; *Sen.,* 1, 2, and 3; *Misc.* 9; ep. Nelli XXVIII-XXX). They insisted so much that Petrarch, after various courteous refusals, finally refused flatly.[5]

Meanwhile, Acciaiuoli imposed himself once more as the true savior and real arbiter of the kingdom. He had just returned to Naples to insure Joanna's possession of the crown after the death of

Louis of Taranto (May 26, 1362). Acciaiuoli had successfully cap-
tured the last of the Durazzeschi, had intervened audaciously at
Messina, and had reinforced the farthest Angevine possession in
Sicily. It must have been during these months, stormy but glorious
for the Grand Seneschal, that Nelli brought forth his proposal to
invite, in place of the crowned poet, the writer most acclaimed after
him, Boccaccio, their mutual Florentine friend ("at Messina, in those
days when our king Lodovico died, it was mentioned . . ." ep. XIX to
Nelli). Notwithstanding the conflicts between Acciaiuoli and Boccaccio in the past (the most mordant eclogues must not have been
published yet), Acciaiuoli accepted the proposal, and Boccaccio
promptly received an "epistle written by the hand of Maecenas,"
inviting him to come at last "to share with him his joys." Every doubt
and every fear which his previous experiences had aroused, was
conquered by the "epistola" and the "conforti" of Nelli ("Finally thy
epistle removed every doubt from me, till then untrusting, and, by
thy Maecenas' leave be it said, in thee I believed").

As we have seen, Boccaccio was in a political and economic
situation both difficult and unpleasant, as is confirmed by epistle XI
to Barbato and the letter to Pino de' Rossi, probably finished just a
short time before. In these difficult and discouraging straits, Boccaccio may have been seduced by the authoritative example of Petrarch,
who had found refuge, peace, and dignity in the shadow of the
various munificent courts. In the letter to Barbato dated May 15, we
already sense Boccaccio's desire for the terms of the invitation to be
made definite. After receiving the insistent letters from Acciaiuoli
and Nelli, Boccaccio set off for Naples at the end of October, accompanied by his half-brother, Jacopo, and transporting his library with
him. His anxious and hopeful departure followed the temporary
conclusion of the Homeric works of Leontius (Leontius was then
transferred to Venice: *Sen.*, III, 6). He was undertaking, therefore, not
the journey projected in his epistle to Barbato (XI), but rather, a
relocation for the purpose of settling down, if not definitively, certainly for some time. Boccaccio's writings were already known and
admired in the Acciaiuoli circle; the *Decameron* was coveted and
sought after ever since 1359.[6] Surely Boccaccio brought with him the
two works whose first editions he had completed during that period:

the *De Casibus,* previously intended for King Louis (and now perhaps
reserved for Niccola), and the *De Mulieribus,* dedicated to the young
sister of the Grand Seneschal. Both of them were important new
works quite in the Petrarchan vein, which Acciaiuoli would have
liked. But hardly had he reached Nocera, the favorite residence of
Niccola, when disillusionment began; for, as Boccaccio wrote in the
spirited grotesquery of his letter to Nelli (ep. XII): "No differently
was I received by your Maecenas than if I were returning from a jaunt
to the towns or countryside near Naples: not with smiling face nor
friendly embrace and gracious words; on the contrary he barely
extended his right hand as I entered his house. Surely, no happy
augury this!" Nor had the situation grown any better when the
Seneschal moved back to his splendid house in Naples:

> Amid these glittering things there was, and still is, a small
> section surrounded and enclosed in a hazy mass of old spider
> webs and shameful dry dust, foul and stinking and which
> would be considered vile by any man, however base, which I,
> quite often with you, called the "bilge," as though it were the
> lowest level of a great ship, the receptacle for any filthy thing. In
> this place, as if it were a great honour, I was interned, like some
> noxious person, not like a friend of long standing . . . to me, a
> tired old man, for my rest in company with my half-brother,
> when it was nearly midnight a cot was assigned, filled with tow
> folded and sewed in the form of small balls and just then
> brought up from the nether regions by a mule driver, and
> half-covered by a stinking bit of rug but without any feather
> spread, and set in a tiny room with gaping holes in its walls. In
> this self-same bilge with its disreputable cot is kept the domes-
> tic ware, the splendid service for dining . . . To those entering the
> house textured with gilded beams, covered with white ivory, a
> small pottery lamp with one burned down candle was visible.
> Opposite it there was a small table not completely covered by a
> greasy, filthy coarse cloth, hanging unevenly down its sides and
> all gnawed by dogs or simply by old age, with a few hazy and
> over-filled drinking cups set out on it; and below the table,
> instead of a bench, a sort of wooden seat lamed by loss of one of

its legs: this I think was intentional, so that, matching the repose of those who sat on it to the joys of the victuals, they would not easily fall asleep . . . In coveys, from hither and yon, came rogues: I mean gluttons, devourers, deceivers, mule-drivers and boys, cooks and scullions, and using a different vocabulary, dogs of the court and domestic rats, excellent gnawers . . . Now talking here, now there, they filled the whole house with the discordant bellowing of oxen, and . . . with foul smells they filled the air of the place. . . .

Over all this wretchedness the Rabelaisian face of the Grand Seneschal stands out, he who

frequently goes into closed assembly and there, so that it may appear that he has much to do with the serious affairs of the Kingdom, he places doorkeepers, according to the royal customs, at the exits of the room, and no one who asks for him is allowed to enter. . . . and in the closet, by his command a seat was placed, for there, no differently than on his majesty's throne, he sits . . . amid very discordant sounds of the belly and the expelling of the stinking burden of the guts, high Councils are held and the proper business of the Kingdom is disposed of . . . the simpletons who wait in the courtyard, think that he, admitted to the Consistory of the Gods, in company with them holds solemn Parliament upon the universal state of the republic (Nelli, ep. XII, pp. 149-161).

From the miseries and nastiness of the "bilge" Boccaccio was rescued by "the liberality of the noble young citizen . . . Mainardo de' Cavalcanti," the brother of an old friend and the wielder of great authority in the kingdom (he was chancellor of the duchy of Amalfi and executioner of a part of the kingdom). Boccaccio "by him with joyful countenance was received at table and in lodgings," and it is to him that Boccaccio would dedicate the *De casibus* with affectionate gratitude. But "while almost separate," restoring his strength "a little in the company of the excellent young man," spurred by the impatience and the insistence of Acciaiuoli, Boccaccio, under the illusion of staying in a quiet retreat with the "new Maecenas," moved with all his books to the Acciaiuoli villa of Triperagoli near Baia. New disillusionment and new humiliations occurred there, such that "a young Neapolitan of very noble blood, who, remembering their past friendship, came to visit him . . . when he saw that bed not fit for a dog . . . jumping hastily upon his horse he flew to Pozzuoli . . . and sent out a splendid bed with pillows for him." But suddenly Acciaiuoli had to return to Naples, and had everything moved out of the villa: and there was poor Boccaccio, "alone, with the load of books . . . left on the shore together with the manservant . . . without the necessities of life and without any counsel." His disillusionment was so strong, that when someone thought of bringing him back to the "bilge," Boccaccio firmly refused, and, since Mainardo had already departed, he withdrew to the dwelling of "a friend, a poor merchant," and vainly waited "fifty days and more" while "he (Acciaiuoli) pretended not to notice." Perhaps during these weeks (or on the journey coming or going), Boccaccio stopped at the greatly admired library of Montecassino (see p. 139). Finally, "not to eat the bread which should be fed to the children of *his* courteous host, and to be no longer tormented by *that* Maecenas, . . . having taken leave of the Great Man with what moderation he was capable of," Boccaccio, sorrowing and furious, abandoned Naples early in March 1363.

On his way to Sulmona, Boccaccio stopped in Aversa, where "one day with great joyousness of spirit he was retained by Barbato and marvelously honored" (for the last time, as his friend was to die in that very autumn). Having passed the frontier of the Kingdom while his brother returned weary and ill to Tuscany,[7] Boccaccio headed, as if to a safe refuge, toward the friendly house of Petrarch, whom he believed to be still in Padua. But the "magister" had been in Venice for some months, so that, after staying for a few days as guest of Pietro da Muglio—professor of rhetoric in the Paduan university (Studio) and a mutual friend of Boccaccio (ep. XIII) and Petrarch (who on March 13 addressed the *Var.*, 39 to him with a letter for "Johannem nostrum")[8]—Boccaccio arrived at last, in the second half of March, at the Palazzo Molin with its two towers ("in hac que mea dicitur, tua domo," Petrarch was to write, *Sen.*, III, 1). It was the luxurious house on the Riva degli Schiavoni, which the Grand Council had assigned to Petrarch "cuius fama hodie tanta est in toto orbe quod in memoria hominum non est iam dudum inter Christianos fuisse vel esse philosophum moralem et poetam qui posse eidem comparare" (according to a resolution of September 4, 1362), accepting in exchange the promise of the collection of books to transform and increase the public library.

The fraternal and kindly welcome of Petrarch must have fallen as balm upon the inflamed spirit of Boccaccio; but it also must have exasperated the bitter recollection of the two Neapolitan friends who had deceived and humiliated him. Boccaccio was so embittered that when a letter of April 22 reached him from Nelli, who deplored his touchiness, his hasty decisions, his sudden flight, and who called him a "man of glass" (with one of those ironical names so dear to Acciaiuoli), he reared up in one of his most wrathful and scornful outbursts. With exceptional irascible and caricatural force, Boccaccio alternated between sarcasm and invective in his response to Nelli (ep. XII). It is a pamphlet which has left a portrait of Acciaiuoli and of his court, perhaps unjust, but with the clarity of a Bruegel. In view of Boccaccio's evident singlemindedness (which he continued later in eclogue XVI), in view of the silence of Petrarch, prudent perhaps but certainly absolute, and that of Nelli himself (who in eclogue XXX to the "magister" in December 1362, did not even mention Boccaccio), it is difficult to establish the rights and the wrongs of the two sides. Certainly Boccaccio, who now had a humble but sure grasp on his own worth, who had dreamed of an authoritative and respected position similar to Petrarch's, must have been deeply wounded by the facile ironies and the coarseness of Acciaiuoli, who was accustomed to treat even those he liked and esteemed (such as Zanobi), even kings and princes, with brusque firmness, as though they were as dependents. On the other hand, in that period of trouble and anxiety for the Kingdom, of political and financial troubles even for his own house, Acciaiuoli must have had neither time nor desire to closely attend and render homage to his old companion, who for twenty years had pursued him with requests both plaintive and imperious.[9] Acciaiuoli would have respected a man of Petrarch's stature, but he did not judge Boccaccio to be of that caliber. He would have welcomed a man of letters, helpful and admiring—if not flattering—like Zanobi or Nelli, but he was unable to accept the new stance of his old and humble companion (and mild Nelli, absorbed and upset by his new and onerous duties, must not have found a way to remedy the neglect and the impatience of the Grand Seneschal). Besides, for a politician as flexible as Niccola, the method "long on promises and short on deliveries" must have been quite usual: a method for which, a few months after Boccaccio's letter, Petrarch himself would offer sharp reprimand (*Sen.*, III, 3).

Certainly Boccaccio explained the reasons for his disillusionment and bitterness to Petrarch, his tactful and affectionate host. By reaffirming the wisdom of Boccaccio's retreat to his house, Petrarch indirectly approved of Boccaccio's decision to leave Naples, and, perhaps, he also approved of Boccaccio's feelings about Acciaiuoli. ("Tu seu humano consilio, seu aliter, id quod constat, duce fretus Deo linques Neapolim et omissa Florentia longiore circuitu me petiisti . . . pia fuit electio . . ." *Sen.*, III, 1.) But perhaps Petrarch's prudence advised against sending the violent epistle to Nelli, since no trace of any reaction has been discovered in the papers of Acciaiuoli and Nelli. Amid the aggrieved Neapolitan recollections, however, Boccaccio may have told Petrarch of his having made a discovery analogous to those which had brightened his 1355 journey: that is, the discovery, probably at Montecassino again, of a manuscript of Martial with the first ten books of epigrams and the *Liber de Spectaculis*.[10]

In the numerous conversations in the house on the Riva degli Schiavoni, it could not escape Boccaccio that the "magister" had become more and more responsive to the literature of the new language. Petrarch had just finished gathering two hundred fifteen poems to make the *Fragmentorum Liber*,[11] and Boccaccio must have read them carefully and perhaps copied them, even if provisorily. The two men probably discussed the malevolent criticisms of certain Florentines leveled against the Magone episode of the *Africa*, which had been made public, and the attacks against the *Buccolicum Carmen* (*Sen.*, II, 1). They must have talked about the Homeric works of Leontius, who was in Venice at least until August, and who certainly gave his two patrons supplementary information and clarifications.

Boccaccio also met old friends (Donato, for example, now a teacher in Venice) and new friends (such as the chancellor Benintendi de' Ravagnani, who accompanied them in delightful outings in gondola: *Sen.*, III, 1). From Avignon, meanwhile, came the good news of the appointment of Francesco Bruini as Apolstolic Secretary (*Sen.*, II, 3), and the sad news of the death of Lelius (Lello Tosetti), which Boccaccio did not have the courage to communicate to his friend (*Sen.*, III, 1). During these months, Petrarch repeated his insistence that Boccaccio should remain as a permanent guest and literary counselor. Boccaccio declined the offer once again, for fear of marring a friendship that had become a reason of life for him (*Bucc.*, XVI, 96 ff., and *Sen.*, III, 1 and 2). Nothing was left for Petrarch but to lament the excessive shortness of the stay ("queror, quod coram quoque sum questus, nimis te hinc abitum properasse"), and to recall those months, later, as a pause of joy and unreal serenity in his life ("Presentiam tuam amico meo gratam et speravi semper et scivi . . . illa vero et fausta erat quandoquidem his mensibus paucissimis nimiunque velocibus . . . inducias videor habuisse cum fortuna nil nisi laetum te presente ausa" *Sen.*, III, 1).

Boccaccio returned to Certaldo in August 1363,[13] after ten stormy months. His renewed self-communion is broken by Petrarch's invitation to visit him to escape the plague (*Sen.*, III, 1, 2), by recollections of the recent visit, and by grief for Lelius and for "nostrum Simonidem," that is, Francesco Nelli, a recent victim of the plague. In his lamentation and his anxious solicitude for Boccaccio's silence, Petrarch seems to have united his two scholarly friends regardless of any previous conflict. They were the two confidants to whom Petrarch wished to entrust the care of the works that death might prevent him from completing.[14] Also during this period, Petrarch and Boccaccio renewed debates that they had begun in Venice over the *Fragmentorum Liber,* on the dignity of vernacular poems, and the opportuneness of preserving and carefully compiling them (*Sen.*, V, 3, to Boccaccio, August 1364).

Petrarch had heard vague chatter and then precise information from Donato concerning the discouragement that might befall the young student of Cino and Dionigi upon reading the oldest *Reum Vulgarium Fragmenta*. Petrarch feared that Boccaccio might go so far as to throw his own youthful poems into the fire (see p. 50). Petrarch used this concern as a pretext for clarifying three points which particularly worried him, especially because during those years he had been accused of arrogance and haughtiness by young Florentines like Pietro Picolo (p. 171). Petrarch spoke of three things: the reasons for his caution in circulating his works; his position with regard to Dante, who was now recognized as "primus" and "nostri eloquii dux vulgaris" (certainly to the delight of Boccaccio); and especially, the quality and value of his obligation as a secular poet in the vernacular. Petrarch could discuss such fine points of literature and its values only with a kindred spirit, with someone whose experience and understanding would be the herald of the "master's" feelings (see ep. XIX). Boccaccio was such a person, and in his conversations, Petrarch confessed his youthful enthusiasms for the vernacular and its poetry, and his passion for the *Rerum Vulgarium Fragmenta*. Indeed, a passion for the vernacular pervades the entire epistle. Petrarch expressed pleasure at placing himself alongside "nostri eloquii dux vulgaris," and at Boccaccio's interest in his early poems. (He scolded Boccaccio for being too severe with his own Tuscan poems.) He spoke of his quest for perfection in the vernacular poetry ("ego ipse . . . de multis feci": that is, "I destroyed many of them"), and expressed satisfaction in excelling in this field also ("si penitus persuasum est vel tibi vel alius et ego te in hoc ordine, velim nolim, superem"). Above all, Petrarch indicates his wish to preserve the vernacular poems, which he feared might otherwise circulate almost at random ("sparsa illa et brevia, iuvenilia atque vulgaria, iam, ut dixi, non mea amplius sed vulgi potius . . . maiora ne lanient providebo"). Such insistent declarations are rare in the writings of Petrarch, but they probably indicate the maturation of his plan to revise and systematize his poetry, perhaps in some definitive form.

The long debate on whether Boccaccio was right or wrong to burn his more youthful rhymes ended with Petrarch's disapproval of the act. In one respect it reflected the conclusion of the long inner struggle which must have preceded the resolution taken by Petrarch on that prophetic night in December 1366. In another, it began the new flowering of vernacular poems in the last decade of Boccaccio's life.[15] It was, in fact, only after this intimate debate, truly decisive for the future of the European lyric, that Boccaccio was to return resolutely to the "vulgaribus poematibus in quibus (Franciscus) perlucide cantavit" (*Vita Petr.*). Following the example of the master, Boccaccio probably formed some small collections of vernacular poems. Besides recopying the Dantean texts, already thrice transcribed, Boccaccio copied the collection of two hundred fifteen Petrarchan poems that he saw in Venice, the *Fragmentorum Liber* (now cod. Vat. Chigiano, L, V, 176), and circulated various copies of it in the course of those years.[16]

Boccaccio also vigorously resumed his prose writing, resolute in that faith in the vernacular that he had communicated to Petrarch. In the light of the debates with Petrarch and his yearned-for recognition, Boccaccio revised the *Trattatello* on Dante (edition III), which he then placed, as though a definitive consecration, in the collection dedicated to the poetry of the two greatest artists of the new literature. And, in or about 1365, he gave shape to that singular misogynous pamphlet, the *Corbaccio*[17] (the title is mysterious: from "corbacchiare" to mock continuously? from "corvo," crow, bird of ill omen?). Boccaccio imagines that, having fallen desperately in love with a coquettish, greedy and sensual widow, it transpires that in a dream he encounters the soul of the husband of his beloved, who mercilessly shows him the shrewd cunning and faults of women in general and those of the widow in particular, with the result that his amorous madness is completely cured.

The *Corbaccio* is a little work balanced between the great medieval antifeminist tradition descended from the *Ad Jovinianum* of St. Jerome and the immediacy of the great realistic novella, between the pensiveness of the treatises and the irascible and vulgar anomaly of the epistle to Nelli. In the *Corbaccio*, certainly, there is also the trace of a disappointment, grievously painful for the man of fifty who, despite his religious and spiritual convictions, was not yet able to detach himself from the world and its pleasures ("let life be dear to you, and do your utmost to prolong it"), who was admonished affectionately by Petrarch for recurring bursts of sensuality (as he himself would recall with emotion in eclogue XV and in ep. XXIII: "ad amorem celestium ab amore illecebri terrenorum" . . . "amores meos . . . vertit in melius" see *Sen.*, VIII, 1). Even more striking, however, is the force of caricature and grotesquery exercised before against Acciaiuoli, the same mordant emphasis on the acrimonious or repugnant, developed with the consummate art of a great narrator. The two invectives, moreover, seem animated by the same scorn of the writer now great, who seeks, wounded and humiliated, the reasons for his life in the profession most peculiarly his own, among his books and his poetry.

> While thou shalt be in the woods and in far-off places, the Castalian Nymphs, whom these evil women try to resemble, will never abandon thee . . . Never will they involve thee in disputation nor discussion . . . but with angelic voice will narrate unto thee the things which have been since the world began . . . and the divine eternal and infinite goodness, and by what steps one ascends to it and by what precipices one is dashed to opposite parts; and to thee, since they will have sung unto thee verses of Homer, of Virgil and of the other great poets, thine own, if thou wilt, they will sing (p. 222).

Thus, even in the acrimony of invective, the voices of the ideals of lofty and contemplative life could be heard—ideals dominant in Boccaccio's life of retirement at Certaldo (and they were scoffed at for the sake of sheer opposition by the wretched widow). The new religious rhythm of his life was revealed in the recitation of the breviary and by an abandoned cult of the Blessed Virgin Mary (pp. 143, 157), which in these years inspired the delicate sonnets to the Virgin and the famous passage in the *Genealogia* (IX, proem). Those explanations of the divine origin of poetry which Boccaccio was then developing in the *Genealogia* were proclaimed. And, there also emerges that ideal, Heliconian image of him on the solitary hill in Valdelsa, absorbed in his renewed lyrical work. It was the image of the writer, who, like Virgil and Petrarch, found his sole recreation in playing the Castalian lyre with the sacred plectrum (ep. XX).

Petrarch also continued to send his confidences. In his letters, he wrote of the various calamities which afflicted him, of the strangeness and the flight to Greece of Leontius, and of his new and already dear friend, Michele di Vanni, who—possibly acting on

Boccaccio's suggestions—would make Petrarch a gift of the famous Madonna of Giotto, which he used thereafter as a "capoletto" (painting hung above the head of a bed), and which he bequeathed at his death to the ruler of Padua (*Sen.*, III, 5 and 6). Boccaccio also found comfort in assiduous attention to his studies. He copied and annotated the "moral" Terentius and various other Latin writers,[18] he revised and rearranged the Homeric work of Leontius, he updated his treatises with the help of new readings and his new cultural acquisitions, and most importantly, he developed and completed the lofty eulogy of poetry which he had conceived and begun fifteen years earlier, and which is not contained in the last two books of the *Genealogia* (XIV is more theoretical and general, XV is devoted especially to an apologia for his own work and that of contemporary writers).

Boccaccio also gave an organic systemization to his meditations on poetry. These meditations were touched on in some epistles (II, IV, VIII) and in the first homage to his great friend, *De Vita et Moribus Francisci Petracchi*. At the beginning of that prophetic year, 1351, Boccaccio's meditations were inspired by the revealing gift of the "magister," the *Pro Archia* (which was the real codex of the new culture, and which Petrarch quoted twice in his Capitoline oration). Boccaccio's new defense of poetry is less cautious, less rhetorical than Petrarch's. It is full, total, impassioned; not restricted to the Latins but extended to all poetry, even that of the first writers in vernacular, of the Stil Nuovo, of Dante, of Petrarch himself: precisely because for the first time poetry is defined and defended *as* poetry.

The attitude in the defense is clearly and frankly polemical. Boccaccio proposes to rout the deniers of poetry: that is to say, the ignorant who boast of that title, the cultivators of divine science who undervalue letters as worldly seduction, the jurisconsults who scorn literature because it does not produce riches, the hypocrites who under pretense of religious zeal and infallible truth accuse poetry of being useless, vain for its fables, perilous for its lasciviousness and the pagan elements in which it delights, condemned by the greatest philosophers, like Plato and Boethius. Such polemics and hostility against literature are all documented point by point in the culture of those centuries, from the *Novellino* to Dante and Petrarch, from

Albertino Mussato to the *Paradiso degli Alberti,* to cite only a few examples.

In confutation of these arguments Boccaccio expounds his concept of poetry: a concept which still adheres in great part to the principles of medieval esthetics. Poetry is fervor in conceiving and expressing things imagined in a lofty and excellent way: and this fervor "qui ex sinu dei procedens" is granted to extremely few, as an exceptional gift. "Huius enim fervoris sunt sublimes effectus, ut puta mentem in desideriu dicendi compellere, peregrinas et inauditas inventiones excogitare, meditatas ordine certo componere, ornare compositum inusitato quodam verborum atque sententiarum contextu, velamento fabuloso atque decenti veritatem contegere." Poetry is the soul of the world, the poet must be a prophet: his task is "reges armare, in bella deducere, e navilibus classes emittere, celum terras et equora describere, virgines sertis et floribus insignire, actus hominum pro qualitatibus designare, irritare torpentes, desides animare, temerarios retrahere, sontes vincire, egregios meritis extollere laudibus" (XIV, 7). But for his high task, divine fervor, that is, inspiration, is not enough; a poet must also possess a knowledge of the laws of grammar and rhetoric and also "liberalium aliarum artium et moralium atque naturalium . . . principia . . . et *secularis glorie appetitus"* (XIV, 7). Rhetoric, a synthesis of all human gifts, is something absolutely different from poetry: "Habet enim, suas inventiones rhetorica . . . satis apparere potest. . . . poesim facultatem esse et ex dei gremio originem ducere et ab effectu nomen assumere et ad eam insigna atque fausta multa spectare." Poetry is characterized by truth composed under a beautiful veil: "mera poesis est quicquid sub velamento componitur et exponitur exquisite" (XIV, 7). Taking up the argument in the *Vita di Dante* (XXII), Boccaccio borrows concepts which Petrarch had repeated many times *(Invectiva in Medicum; Oratio Capitulina; Africa,* IX, 78 ff.):

> It is a manifest thing that all that which is acquired with effort
> has rather more sweetness than that which comes easily. Plain
> truth, because it is quickly grasped, delights with little effort
> and passes into the memory. Therefore, so that it should be
> acquired with fatigue and thus being more highly valued will

be better preserved, the poets hid it under many things apparently contrary to it; and to that end they made up fables, a cover more than anything else, so that beauty would attract those whom neither philosophical demonstrations, nor persuasions, had been able to draw to themselves.

In fact, "poetas illustres sepissime seducere credulos reor et eos facere meliores" (XIV,15). In this respect poetry is similar to the Sacred Scripture, and for this reason, there can be no opposition between poetry and philosophy and theology: "rather I say that theology is nothing but a poetry of God" (*Vita di Dante,* XXII). In fact we see that also the gracious and noble poets "eo usque, quo humanum potest penetrare ingenium, attigisse et absque ambiguitate novisse unum tantum Deum esse; ad quam notitiam devenisse poetas eorum in operibus percipitur liquido" (XIV, 13). Indeed, "etiam Dominus et Salvator noster multa in parabolis locutus est ... et Ipse adversus Paulum prostratum Terentii verbo usus est, scilicet *durum est tibi contra* stimulum calcitrare ..." (XIV, 18).

In this defense and exaltation of poetry, we sense that Boccaccio is fulfilling a mission that is spiritual and religious as well as cultural and civilized. He feels this mission so strongly that he closes those impassioned pages with a gesture of humility and prayer, almost that of a priest who brings a solemn rite to a close: "Non nobis, Domine, non nobis, sed nomini tuo da gloriam" (XV, conclusion; see p. 108).

The full legitimacy of poetry is not only vigorously affirmed, but established through a systematic inquiry which succeeds in setting a record which will not be easily questioned. The concept of poetry defined by Boccaccio still obeys the medieval canon of truth composed *sub velamento;* but in a way it is already humanistic in its universality. It embraces every other expression of morality and of thought, and it emphasizes the "secularis glorie appetitus." These truths are proclaimed with fervent enthusiasm, with the affectionate and continuous calling to mind of Dante and Petrarch, his dearest masters. It reveals the intoxicating ardor of a discovery which has become an indestructible conviction: the conviction that poetry, in the multi-form activity of the spirit and in the broad spectrum of civilized life, occupies a central position that no other faculty could hold.

This intertwining of themes, ancient and new, and the awareness of the eternal worth of letters, are illuminated always by a secret, quiet anxiety for glory. It is an anxiety which is all the more significant in an artist like Boccaccio, so spontaneously given to modesty. Upon him, in the studious and meditative solitude of Certaldo, smiles the great hope, constant and consoling: "nulla est tam humilis vita quae dulcedine gloriae non tangatur" (XV, 7).

NOTES

1. The dating has been determined with certainty by P. G. Ricci, *Studi*, 1959.
2. The life of the Blessed Petroni published by the Bollandists and dated May 29 (*Acta Sanctorum*, Antwerp, 1688, VII, pp. 188 ff.) bases this episode essentially on the *Sen.*, I, 5. Indeed, all of Chapter XI is clearly an interpolation by Fra Bartolomeo, who more than two centuries after the fact made a Latin version of a life of Petroni, written in the vernacular and attributed by that same Fra Bartolomeo to the Blessed Colombini (who died in 1367 and certainly could not have read Petrarch's epistle). See A. Gasparey, "Ancora sulla lettera del B. a F. Nelli," *Giorn. Stor. Lett. It.*, XII, 1888, p. 393; G. Traversari, "Il Beato Pietro Petroni senese e la conversione del Boccaccio," *Rassegna pugliese*, XXII, 1905; Tromby, *Storia critico-cronologica del Patriarca S. Brunone e del suo ordine cartusiano*, VI, pp. 286 ff., CXXVII ff.; G. Petrocchi, *Ascesi e mistica trecentesca*, Florence, 1957, pp. 170 ff.
3. Boccaccio, however, did not always distinguish San Pier Damiani from the escetic Pietro degli Onesti Peccatore, a confusion avoided by Petrarch: *De vita solitaria*, II, 7. For this entire episode and its dating see A. Foresti, "Il Boccaccio a Ravenna nell'inverno 1361-62," *Giorn. Stor. Lett. It.*, XCVIII, 1931. Massera, when publishing the epistle and the biography, assigns them incorrectly to 1357 (*Opere minori latine*, cit., pp. 330 ff. and 368 ff.). The *Life of San Pier Damiani* was written by his pupil, Giovanni da Lodi.
4. Sabbadini, *Giovanni da Ravenna*, p. 190.
5. "Ad id quidem quod Mecenas ipse tuque post illum tanta precum vi me nunc etiam in Campaniam evocatis quid aliud dicam quam mirari

me . . . indefessam hanc instantiam totiens negata flagitantium? Nec rogando enim nec expectando lassamini, cum ego iam non negando tantum sed tacendo ac vivendo prope lassatus sum." *Sen.,* I, 2, probably early in 1362.

6. See the letter of the nephew of the Grand Seneschal, Francesco Buondelmonti, to Giovanni Acciaiuoli, July 13, 1360 with the earnest request for the "book of the novellas of messer Giovanni Boccacci" publ. by V. Branca, *Per il testo del Decameron,* cit.

7. A. Latini, "Il fratello di Giovanni Boccaccio," *Misc. Stor. Valdelsa,* XXI, 1913, p. 34 and document on pp. 38 f.

8. The evidence of this brief stay in Padua was found and illustrated by A. Foresti, "Pietro da Muglio a Padova e la sua amicizia col Petrarca e col Boccaccio," *Archiginnasio,* XV, 1920.

9. A precise narrative of the episode, with new and ample historical documentation, has been provided by Léonard, *Boccacce et Naples,* pp. 84—117; he assumes, however, the rôle of impassioned defender of Acciaiuoli and Nelli, in these pages, and in the articles "Victimes de Pétrarque et de Boccace: Zanobi da Strada," *Etudes italiennes,* IV, 1394; "Nicolas Acciaiuoli victime de Boccace," *Mélanges Hauvette,* Paris, 1934. Cochin and Hauvette also presented defenses of Nelli, *op. cit.*

10. Billanovich, *Petrarca,* pp. 263 ff.: there is still some doubt about whether he knew of this discovery at once.

11. Wilkins, *The Making, cit.,* III, pp. 160 ff.

12. A Foresti, Aneddoti, pp. 425 ff.; and "Fierezza del Boccaccio," *Marzocco,* XXXIII, 1928.

13. E. H. Wilkins, *Petrarch's Later Years,* Cambridge, Mass., 1950 p. 59. In *Sen.,* III, it is said that Boccaccio remained in Petrarch's house more than three months ("mei desiderium . . . trimestri presentia iam lenitum").

14. *Sen.,* III, 1 may also be an indication that the irascible epistle to Nelli perhaps never was sent: note that *nostrum* is used, and that Petrarch always joins Boccaccio in the emotional complaint of his friend.

15. I have gathered and discussed texts and documents of this impassioned debate in *Tradizione,* cit., pp. 289 ff.; and in "Il momento decisivo nella formazione del Canzoniere"; *Studi in onore di Matteo Marangoni,* Florence, 1957.

16. *Rime,* ed. Branca cit., pp. VII ff.; Wilkins, *The Making, cit.,* pp. 90 ff., 160 ff.

17. G. Padoan, "Sulla datazione del 'Corbaccio'" and "Ancora sulla datazione e sul titolo del 'Corbaccio,' " *Lettere italiane,* XV, 1963. The date of the composing of this work had, however, up until now been set as 1354-55.
18. P. G. Ricci, *La prima cattedra,* cit.

CHAPTER 9

New Political and Literary Experiences: Avignon, Naples, Venice, Rome (1365-1373)

The political situation in Florence had entered a period of *détente,* of renewed confidence, of prosperity, thanks to the victorious conclusion of the war with Pisa and the conquest of San Miniato, the benevolent attitude of Urban V, the new pope, the softening of the "laws of admonishment," and the return of the exiles of 1360.

Probably as a consequence of this new political calm, Boccaccio was called to the capital from Certaldo to assume duties similar to those he performed before 1360. Indeed during 1365 he held an office analogous to the one he had in '55, controlling the citizen militia and armory.[1] It is certain that in August he was charged with his most delicate and difficult mission: a diplomatic errand at the court of Urban V. Certainly Boccaccio was called upon as a personality of high prestige, who could avail himself of important friendships at the Papal Court, friendships that began, perhaps, as long ago as the period when the man who was to become Pope had been an envoy to the Angevin Court (1361 and 1362).

Urban V was planning a return to Rome, but was somewhat distrustful of the Florentine commune, which, however, encouraged him in the enterprise. He also distrusted the other ruler of Italy, and it seemed possible that he might solicit the aid and the presence of the emperor Charles IV, who was naturally feared by the Florentines and by the Guelf faction. The Signoria had in fact heard that by "detractors, rivals or other sowers of scandals" the Holy Father, "whose grace, benediction and benevolence we deem ourselves to have merited," had become convinced "that our Commune is a true devoted friend of Holy Church in words" and not in deeds. Therefore in August the Signoria had hastened to send on these "arduis negotiis" "magistrum Johannem Boccacij honorabilem civem florentinum, oratoreum . . . dignum in hiis que retulerit fide indubia" (letters of August 9, 16, 18, 20: there is record of payment on August 20). Boccaccio was charged especially, as his instructions suggest, to clear Florence of any calumny and to prove her fidelity and service to the Church "not in words alone," recalling her aid even in recent times and her sacrifices for the Papacy, documenting them, if it seemed advisable, with facts registered in the chronicles. He was to confirm Florentine devotion by the offer of five armed galleys and five hundred helmeted soldiers with the banner of the Commune as "most faithful escort" for the Pope's return to Italy—aid far more substantial than that expected from Charles IV.

As Petrarch recalled (*Sen.,* V, 1), Boccacio disliked travelling by that time because of "corporis atque animi gravitatem" and of "ocio amicitiam studioso." He also knew the difficulties of crossing the Alps, which he had done eleven years before. In addition to all this, Boccaccio knew that this embassy, like most, would be financially more burdensome than advantageous. He must have undertaken the mission only out of patriotism and notwithstanding the apprehensions which may be read between the lines of the will he drew up just before leaving Florence on August 21.[3] However, he departed promptly, armed with letters of recommendation not only for the Pope but also for the cardinals, for Francesco Bruni, the Apostolic Secretary and for the masters of the Florentine Fraternity of Avignon; and, proceeding along the arduous Ligurian coast road (*Purg.,* III, 49 ff.), he had to stop for another official mission at Genoa. The Signoria, in fact, had instructed him to protest to the doge for the vexations inflicted on the Grimaldi, who had collaborated with the Florentines in recent actions against the Pisans. He was then to report the outcome of his intervention to the Grimaldi themselves, whom as he continued his journey, he would encounter in Nice, where they had taken refuge.[4] Boccaccio must have dispatched this minor mission quickly and continued speedily on his way to Avignon, since the Signoria was sending him messages in that city by August 27 and September 1.[5] With great care and attention Boccaccio was presented and greeted in the Pontifical Court, not only by Bruni but also by Petrarch's great friend, Filippo di Cabassoles, formerly Grand Chancellor at the Angevin Court (1343 to 1347) and now Patriarch of Jerusalem, who "in conspectu Summi Pontificis ac mirantium Cardinalium veri amoris ulnis astrinxerat, post pia oscula" Boccaccio, "hactenus sibi ignotum," but in whom he seemed to see the image of his Petrarch (*Sen.,* V, 1). The Florentine ambassador must have fulfilled his mission by earning the goodwill and the praises of the Pope,[6] for two years later the Signoria sent him on another mission to the same Pontiff (see pp. 162 ff.), and the invasion of Charles IV was cancelled for the time being. When the invasion did occur in 1368, moreover, it took the form of a pious parade ending in rapid withdrawal.

With reason therefore, Petrarch could felicitate with Boccaccio on his new success (*Sen.,* V, 1). It is probable also that Boccaccio had worked to facilitate the annulment of the Florentine canonry requested for Petrarch in April by the Signoria (certainly on the intervention of Boccaccio himself) and shortly afterward inelegantly refused by Petrarch, possibly in order not to renounce that of Monselice.[7]

In addition to his official mission, Boccaccio had also assumed various other tasks and charges: for example, at the urging of the Signoria, he had supported the request of the Dominican, Giovanni di Benci Carucci, who wished to leave the order because of ill health; he defended the old bishop of Pistoia from the harassments of the apostolic chamber instigated by rivals; he helped to further the aspirations of the bishop of Aversa, Angelo Ricasoli, to the diocese of Arezzo, those of Chiaro Peruzzi, bishop of Montefeltro and San Leo, to Perugia or Montecassino, those of Pietro Pileo, bishop of Padua and friend of Petrarch *(Sen.,* VI, 4), to the patriarchate of Aquileia. The last three requests—plus one not clearly defined, for Ristoro, the son of an old and dear friend, Pietro

Canigiani—certainly involved the ambassador personally.[8] Boccaccio also personally advanced requests for benedictions, relics, and indulgences for the citizens of Certaldo, particularly for those who had worked to repair the church which he held most dear, that of the Saints Michael and James.[9] On the other hand, there is not the slightest trace—in this nor in any other embassy—of solicitations for personal benefices or personal privileges, although they were customary then, as now. Boccaccio often lamented his scanty means and the slights of Fortune; and though he was often engaged in promoting friends (from Petrarch to Ristoro Canigiani), there is no evidence of him litigating or begging for himself. He saved one great joy for himself, however, during those days in Avignon: that of lingering in the company of various friends of his own and of Petrarch ("quos mihi reliquos mors fecit": *Sen.,* V, 1), particularly with Francesco Bruni, now highly respected at the papal court and very sensitive to the obligations of culture. Other friends were such men as those sent by Niccolò Acciaiuoli to defend him from the accusations of waste presented to Urban V by his enemies; Pietro Pileo, who had come to press his candidacy for Aquileia; Filippo di Cabassoles, formerly Petrarch's neighbor at Vaucluse, who in their "grata colloquia" plied Boccaccio with questions about their mutual friend, and begged him to get Petrarch finally to send to him, Filippo, the text of that *De vita solitaria* which Petrarch had composed in Filippo's own villa and affectionately dedicated to his friend (*Sen.,* V, 1, and see *Fam.,* XI, v; *Var.,* 14; *Sen.,* VI, 5). Boccaccio also must have spent pleasant and friendly hours with various leading members of the Florentine community in the Papal city: with the Certaldese merchants Leonardo, Giovanni and Chiaro Del Chiaro, with Dato and other members of the family and company of the Berti, with the notary Martino di Giovanni, and with Lanzimanno, who was "king of Porta Ferruzza" (that is, the ward inhabited by the Del Chiaro family), and who must have been a singular sort of person and very well known in Avignon.[10]

It was November before Boccaccio could return to Tuscany (the mission was extended thirty days beyond its planned duration, August 21 to October 4).[11] Boccaccio returned using the Ligurian route which, with its "diffcultatum vie crebris," had so greatly disturbed Petrarch. The latter, on receiving a letter from Boccaccio in mid-December (probably between the 17th and 22nd), thanked him for having ended the worry caused him by knowing that Boccaccio was travelling ("suspensus ad eventum rei manseram usque dum te reducem audirem . . . secura mihi nulla dies, nulla nox"); but he regretted that Boccaccio had not visited the archbishop Guido Sette, his very close friend, during his stop in Genoa. Above all, Petrarch regretted that Boccaccio, who had been within two days' journey of Pavia, had not found it possible to visit him there, "quem vides semper ubicumque terrarum sis." But he understood that because of Boccaccio's "ocio amicitiam studioso . . . talibus curis et negotiis sic adversam" he had been anxious to hasten his return home, where Petrarch pictured him now happy and calm because "quanto autem graviore pelagi periculo rediisti tanto dulcior est reditus gratiorque" *(Sen., V, 1).*

Petrarch's description is in truth a fair image of Boccaccio in his Heliconian retreat. During those months, as the *senile* quoted points out, Boccaccio devoted himself to collecting the letters written to him by his great friend, to revising his own three treatises, and to the drudgery of completing the work on Homer. Before his departure from Avignon, he had sent some advance material to Petrarch, to answer at least the latter's requests for lines on Avernus and on the Lower Regions *(Sen.,* III, 6 of March 1); but the passages sent were not those desired by the "magister," or perhaps they no longer interested him because now he was expecting the complete work (". . . sed quoniam tibi placuit ut mihi postea totum opus illud eximium destinares . . .": *Sen.,* V, 1 of December 22).

In fact Boccaccio had already written to Petrarch (evidently in the November epistle in which he announced his return from Avignon) that he had sent him the "Iliadem totam, Odyssee autem partem" *(Sen., ibid).* But the packet had not reached Petrarch by January 25, 1366, as he wrote anxiously to Boccaccio, informing him of the miserable end of Leontius, who was killed by lightning on his return journey to Italy *(Sen.,* VI, 1).

Not long afterwards, however, just when three important letters of Petrarch to Boccaccio had been lost (see *Sen.,* VI, 1), the anxiously awaited Homer was in Petrarch's hands "meque et omnes seu Grecos, seu Latmos, qui bibliothecam hanc inhabitant *replevit* gaudio atque oblectatione mirabili" *(Sen.,* VI, 2). So great was Petrarch's enthusiasm that he utilized the *Iliad* in his work on the *De remediis,* (completed by October 4, 1366).[12]

Once again, from his meditative and free Certaldese solitude, Boccaccio had to watch and worry about the political involvements of Petrarch (with the doge, with the rulers of Padova, of Rimini, of Milan, and others), and his frequent sojourns at the court of Galeazzo, the new Viscontean "tyrant." Boccaccio expressed his fears in an epistle to their close mutual friend, Donato: "Pone metum," Petrarch answered quickly, "etsi corpore et rebus aliis subesse maioribus sit necesse, sive uni ut ego sive multis ut tu, quod nescio an gravius molestiusque iugi genus dixerim: pati hominem credo facilius quam tyrannum populum . . ." *(Sen.,* VI, 2). In the course of these years there was continual conflict between Petrarch, the aristocrat and courtier although free ("ubilibet animo liber *sum* ubique liber *ago*), and who therefore eulogized Augustus, and Boccaccio, middle-class and even commoner, who scorned any aristocracy of blood and eulogized Marius. Any form of tyranny, even of "signoria," he detested. His criticism of Florentine democracy was therefore not political (indeed the "plebeian law" is eulogized: *Comedia,* XXXVIII, 109) but moral (see p. 129; *A Pino,* 17 ff.) These . . . were, in his opinion, the vices branded of old by Dante as the ruination of the civil life of his city. Although Boccaccio was critical of the internal politics of Florence, he gladly served his fatherland and the communal liberties. Petrarch, on the other hand, aimed with his every act at favoring the "signori d'Italia," the rulers, howbeit "the great-souled few who favor goodness." He acted above all out of a mordant desire for peace, which overwhelmed every aspiration for liberty. Thus whereas Petrarch venerated Charles IV and devotedly and continually urged him to restore the imperial power in Italy, even for the sake of putting an end to the "Babylonian exile," Boccaccio on the contrary shared in the scornful distrust of his fellow citizens for that Emperor, a tippler and a beggar "magnalium maiorum suorum immemorem" *(De Casibus,* dedication) and offered to Urban V the generous aid of the Florentine Commune as the most solid guarantees for the return of the Papacy to Italy. It is also possible that this conflict of viewpoints, while not a flaw in their fraternal intimacy, was at the bottom of the constant and repeated refusal of Boccaccio to make his home with Petrarch.

During this period, in Certaldo, Boccaccio felt with deep emotion the chasm between happy and sad memories; he received the news of the death of the odious-beloved Niccolò Acciaiuoli (November 8, 1365). From Certaldo he continued the action he had started at the Papal Court in favor of Florentine politics. Writing on May 20, 1366 to Leonardo Del Chiaro in Avignon,[13] he hastened to forward the news, to be reported in the proper places, of the capture and incarceration of Anichino Baumgarden, the soldier of fortune and bitter enemy of the Papal government: a piece of news which confirmed the explanations and justifications he had given as ambassador on the temporizing attitude of Florence with regard to the mercenary companies and to Captain Anichino himself. In the same letter he also requested a speeding up of "the privilege which master Francesco Bruni so fully promised us": that is, probably, the indulgences for the rebuilding of the church of Saints Michael and James. Also at this time, with great generosity in view of his modest means, he donated two altar paintings to his favorite parish church in Certaldo [14] and tried to insure a more cultured and more pious prior. During that winter in fact he had attempted to distract the young prior from his enthusiasm for the hunt and to turn him toward studies; then, perhaps in autumn,[15] he sent off this same young canon, Agnolo Giandonati, to his friend Pietro da Muglio. Boccaccio invoked the name of Petrarch as well in his request and he recommended the young cleric to Pietro, a celebrated teacher in Padua, as "scolarem . . . et filium" who should acquire "doctrinam et mores" (ep. XIII). Along with the long and confidential conversations with Giandonati ("multis longis exortationibus hyeme preterita vi ab accipitre canibusque subtractum") Boccaccio must have scheduled, in the winter of 1366, those with Giovanni da Siena, "qui iamdudum gramatice preceptor apud nos scolas regere consuevit," and whom Boccaccio despatched to Pietro with the same letter but a more flattering literary opinion. Boccaccio occupied this free time with these projects, and probably only left Certaldo for the usual flying visits to Florence (where he was a witness in a deed of July 1, 1366.[16]

After another winter in the ancestral town, on March 24, 1367,

Boccaccio left for Florence to undertake one of the Petrarchan pilgrimages which were always most pleasurable for him. Possibly he had vaguely mentioned it to Muglio ("nondum satis certum habeo nunquid de proximo Patavum venturus sim"). Then, besides the always eager "desiderium" of the "magister," prayers and requests from friends about which we have no information ("amicorum spem, qui fidei mee arduum quoddam opus suum peragendum commiserant") convinced him to make the journey. Perhaps it concerned the two students sent to Padua, or Francesco Allegri, who accompanied him and was his host in Venice; or it could have been for some political concern (see ep. XIV). But on reaching Florence "imbres continui et dissuasiones amicorum ac discriminum itineris timor iniectus a redeuntibus Bononia plurimis tamdiu me tenuere." Boccaccio remained in Florence for most of April, and was invited by the Captain of the Company of Or San Michele to meet with other illustrious and influential citizens on April 2 (among them his friends Luigi Gianfigliazzi, Alessandro de' Bardi, Donato del Ricco) to consider "whether or not should be continued the work which for the adornment and safety of the tabernacle of Our Lady has been started in the arch of the building which is above the said tabernacle." The decision reached by this group was "recited" by the leading jurist Gianfigliazzi (*Carme,* V), and was affirmative "on all counts." It was also counseled:

> that for the increasing of veneration and usefulness of the aforesaid Company and the beauty and respectability of the aforementioned tabernacle and even of the whole city, the soonest possible the captains should, with the aid of our lords the priors, undertake to have the grain and fodder market removed and to have the building of the Woolens Guild taken away, . . . its members to build another as beautiful or more so in such place as they find suitable, and where that building now stands shall be an open square as far as the main street.[17]

Once again (as in 1350) we see Boccaccio connected with the company of Or San Michele, and in the role of expert in city planning.

Meanwhile news had reached Boccaccio that Petrarch, called

back by Galeazzo to Pavia, was on the point of departure: "quod cum
dolens audissem, fere a ceptis destiti . . . ; nam, etsi plura ibidem
videre cuperem non me movissent a principio reliqua." However,
because of obligations to his friends and the desire to see the family
and the house of Petrarch again (and, it may be, with a secret hope of
meeting him), in mid-May Boccaccio resumed his journey, and
before reaching Venice, had the pleasure of falling in with
Francescuolo da Brossano (in Padua? Mestre?), the son-in-law of
Petrarch who "post salutationem festivam atque amicabilem" informed him of the safe arrival of his father-in-law in Pavia and
imparted many other news items.[18] The next day Boccaccio boarded
"summo mane in naviculam" and in Venice found there to meet him,
their illustrious fellow citizen and now famous writer, Donato and
"nonnulli ex concivibus" each of whom insisted on having him as a
guest; but he went to the house of Francesco Allegri "cum quo et a
quo mire honoratus a Florentia eo usque deveneram." Actually,
Petrarch would have wanted him to be a guest in his palace, but
Boccaccio declined out of delicacy towards Petrarch's daughter,
Francesca, who was alone at home. Boccaccio was unwilling to take
advantage of the fraternal offer although Petrarch well knew his
"animum integrum" and though "multum suspicionis auferre de-
buissent canum caput . . . et etas provectior atque nimia sagina
corpus invalidum."

However, on the very day of his arrival Boccaccio's first visit was
to the cherished and familiar house of Petrarch. It was a visit which
moved him deeply and which inspired one of his greatest epistles.
The letter reveals diverse affections, all intense but touched with
discrete and measured gentleness (and it must have moved Petrarch,
who kept the epistle, XIV, as "una ex mille" next to some from Nelli
in one of his manuscripts: now Par. lat. 8631). Francesca greeted him:

> . . . que quam primo adventum meum sensit, tanquam redeunti
> tibi letissima venienti michi occurrit, at aliquantisper laudabili
> quodam respersa rubore, vix me viso deiectis in terram oculis,
> quadam modesta ac filiali affectione salutatione decenti et totis
> me suscepit ulnis"; [and then, as though repeating the paternal
> habits] "postquam . . . inter-locuti sumus, in ortulo tuo, assis-

tentibus ex amicis nonnullis, consedimus; ibi explicatiori placidoque sermone domum libros et tua omnia obtulit, et quantum in ea fuit, matronali semper gravitate servata.

Eletta, the grandaughter of the "magister," came forward gracefully, and the sight of her evoked the memory of the ever mourned Violante:

> ... modestiori passu quam deceret etatem, venit Electa tua, delecta mea, et antequam me nosceret ridens aspexit, quam ego non letus tantum sed avidus ulnis suscepi, primo intuitu virgunculam olim meam suspicatus ... eadem que mee fuit, Electe tue facies est: idem risus, eadem oculorum letitia, gestus incessusque, et eadem totius corpusculi habitudo ... In nichilo differentes esse cognovi, nisi quia aurea cesaries tue est, mee inter nigram rufamque fuit. Heu michi! quotiens, dum hanc persepe amplector et suis delector collocutionibus, memoria subtracte michi puellule lacrimas ad oculos usque deduxit, quas demum in suspirium versas emisi advertente nemine.

Next to the gentle delicacy of the little feminine figures, there was the hearty kindness of the huge Francescuolo, who

> ... cum me pauperem novisset, quod ego numquam negavi, in discessu meo a Venetis hora iam tarda in secessu domus me traxit, et cum verbis parum proficeret, manibus illis, giganteis suis in brachiolum meum iniectis, egit ut invitus fere erubescenesque summe liberalitate uterer sua, eoque peracto, quasi fugiens et valedicens abiit (ep. XIV).

It might be said that Boccaccio had found the "house of the soul" in that of his "pater et preceptor"; and the liveliness and tenderness of Boccaccio's expansive and sentimental nature are reflected in this family song for several voices, caressed by the loving veneration for the absent "magister" and deepened by a sharp but calm nostalgia for life and domestic love.

An atmosphere of friendliness and kindness, moreover, must

have surrounded Boccaccio during his Venetian sojourn. He found once again the old familiarity of Ravenna days with Donato Albanzani and Guglielmo da Ravenna; he was honored by Francesco Allegri and by other fellow-citizens; he met "clarum hominem illum magistrum Guidonem de Regio (Guido da Bagnolo), multis plenum effluentemque undique" (ep. XIV). The irony which shadows these words surely sprang out against Guido and his three Aristotelian companions (Leonardo Dandolo, Tomaso Talenti, Zaccaria Contarini) when Boccaccio learned that these supposed friends of Petrarch had spoken of him as a "virum bonum" but "ydiotam" and "sine literis." And certainly he learned, also, from Francescuolo and Donato, that on his recent voyage by water to Pavia, the "magister" had written, against those presumptuous fellows, the most brilliant and significant of his invectives: "*De Sui Ipsius et Multorum Ignorantia,*" dedicated to Albanzani.

Perhaps then—more probably than in the Venetian visit of 1363 or that of 1368—Boccaccio entered on friendly terms with Philippe de Mézières, the chancellor and intimate of King Peter I of Cyprus, son of the King Hugh to whom the *Genealogia* is dedicated. Philippe was in Venice often during those years for the negotiations and action in favor of the daring crusading wars of his king, and he was a good friend of Guido da Reggio, King Peter's doctor of medicine and physics, and of Petrarch *(Sen.,* XIII, 2), to whose mediation is due the imitation of the last novella of the *Decameron* in *Le Livre de la Vertu du sacrement de mariage* of Philippe.[19] It is certain that during that stay in Venice Boccaccio accepted the offer of Francesca and spent many hours among the books of Petrarch, and possibly at that time he placed among them the parts still lacking from the translation of the Odyssey (see p. 154).[20]

After more than a month "quibusdam agentibus incommodis, affectus tedio [afflicted, that is, by the inconvenience of living away from his own house and by homesickness for the domestic walls] eodem labore quo iuverat," Boccaccio returned to Tuscany, arriving in Florence in the last third of June. Here he received ("post dies paucos") forwarded to him by Donato, an epistle sent to him in Venice by Petrarch on May 29, which made him relive the warm and happy welcome he had received in Palazzo Molin. Although Boc-

caccio was losing the hope that he would ever complete the Petrarchan epistolary collections, Petrarch's recent letter inspired him to
gather together at least all the letters which his great friend had sent
him, but which had often gone astray ("quoniam multum in te et in
tuis epistolis loci occupem, . . . certus quia saltem in hoc apud
posteros per multa secula erit venerabile nomen meum . . . iam fere
annus est, eo quod michi ipsi plurime videantur epistole tue ad me, in
volumen unum eo ordine quo misse seu scripte sunt redigere cepi,"
ep. XIV). To complete this book in veneration of Petrarch, Boccaccio
continued to ask for the texts of various letters (*Fam.*, XVIII, iii; XXI,
xv; XXIII, xix; *Sen.*, III, 1 and VIII, 1). He wanted to prolong an ideal
and uninterrupted dialogue, and to continue his spiritual residence
in the house and in the circle of his "pater et magister." Besides writing
to Petrarch after returning to Certaldo, Boccaccio wrote also to their
dearest friend in Venice, Donato Albanzani, recalling the sojourn on
the lagoon and the conversations with Guido "de Regio," and
comparing ideally those days of peaceful study with material cares
and troubles with his very interesting brother Jacopo.[21]

One of Petrarch's epistles to Boccaccio *(Sen.,* VIII, 1), however,
was never sent. It reached Boccaccio a few days later with some
singular explanations (VIII, 8). It had been written exactly twelve
months earlier by Petrarch, on the day he was entering his sixty-third
year, which, according to an ancient belief, was crucial in the life of a
man as a year of catastrophes, of dangers, of death. Knowing the
impressionable character and the emotional nature of his friend,
Petrarch, who claimed to have no faith in such prophecies but to be
ready to face death calmly, had not sent it, feeling at liberty to do so
when the year would have passed. Having now safely reached his
sixty-fourth birthday he could send it remarking that never had he
enjoyed such good health as in the year just past, and rarely had he
been able to enjoy in one single year two such important events as the
conquest of Alexandria by King Peter of Cyprus and the return of the
Pope to Rome.

In the spring, indeed, Urban V had overcome the delays and
resistance on the part of cardinals and dignitaries, of princes and of the
King of France. He had departed from Avignon and, after a pause in
Marseilles, had landed in Italy and established himself at Viterbo

(June 9, 1367). The auspicious news certainly had reached Boccaccio in Venice, but, on his return, he must have been informed by the leaders of Florentine politics of the details of the difficult event. In view of the fortunate contacts he had made two years before with the Pontiff and with his court, Boccaccio was probably consulted on the matter. Perhaps it was during these conversations in Florence that the idea was born in the Signoria of sending someone so authoritative and known to be acceptable as Boccaccio to congratulate Urban V in the name of the Florentine Commune. Urban V appears to have been the Pope best known and most loved by Boccaccio because of their mutual high friendships (from Francesco Bruni to Filippo di Cabassoles), because of their noble dreams of new Crusades (which caused Boccaccio to eulogize King Hugh of Cyprus and Urban V to encourage Hugh's son Peter), and because of Urban V's return to Rome and his Italian policy.

However, the Signoria waited to send its ambassador until the Pope moved to Rome (October 16); and, in fact, early in November action was taken to nominate Boccaccio, and to his name was added that of Giacomino Giani.[22] He must have left immediately and performed this mission in November, since the "breve" of dismissal of the Pope to the Signoria is dated December 1. It bestows high praises on their ambassador [23] (". . . dilectum filium Johannem Boccatii . . . suarum virtutum intuitu benigne recepimus et exposita prudenter Nobis pro eum pro parte vestra audivimus diligenter . . ."). Probably Boccaccio had not restricted himself to the official congratulatory charge, but had once more made himself the interpreter of the thinking of the Signoria concerning the untimeliness of an invasion of Italy by the emperor, and had personally solicited a broad granting of indulgences for those of Certaldo who had contributed toward repairs to his cherished church of Saints Michael and James.[24] Certainly he was also aided this time by Francesco Bruni, with whom he must have talked intimately, as he had two years earlier, and with whom he spoke of a young and esteemed friend, Coluccio Salutati, who was at that time chancellor at Todi and a few months later a co-worker of Bruni himself. Quite naturally, at the court he would have met prelates and dignitaries with whom he had formed, or formed then, friendly relations, for example Filippo di Cabassoles, and the valiant defender of the Pope during his stay in Viterbo, Niccolò Orsini, who was to become a devoted friend of Boccaccio's in later years (see pp. 168 and 170). Boccaccio also revisited the relics and monuments of ancient and Christian Rome which had astonished and moved him ever since childhood (see *Filocolo*, V, 44-52).

Boccaccio's stay in Rome could not have been long, however, for on December 20 he had already returned to Florence, as it appears from a letter written by Coluccio Salutati, who thanked him warmly for having written to him from Rome, as had Bruni, and apologized for not having made a visit of courtesy (ep. I, 19).[25] Probably the shortness of the visit to Rome was determined either by the simplicity of his mission or by the duties in Florence which Boccaccio had accepted during those months: he had been appointed, for the four-month period from November 1367 to February 1368, to the office of the Condotta to check the service and the absences of the mercenaries.[26] Possibly because of the increased need for military forces to meet the dreaded invasion of Charles IV, it was thought desirable to employ the man who had already in 1355 and in 1365 acquired positive experience in similar circumstances, and who by his recent political missions was well acquainted with the general situation. To carry out these duties, Boccaccio had to reside almost constantly in Florence, and could resume life in Certaldo only in the spring (probably in March).

In his "Helyconis ocio," after "res tam turbidas"—as Salutati wrote (ep. I, 19)—Boccaccio surely found again that quota of study and meditation which was now the most cherished condition of his life. It was a commitment which continued even on the journey that summer to Venice, which was to compensate for his failure to meet the "magister" the year before.

Petrarch left Pavia in mid-July[27] and was received with great honor in Padua, where he was now thinking of establishing a permanent residence. Some days later he was joined by Boccaccio at the same house near the beloved cathedral where, in the little garden, they had conversed eighteen years before. Although Petrarch's literary honors were numerous by this time, his domestic life had been darkened by the departure of his daughter's family to Pavia, and by the death of his grandson, Francesco. Now old and alone, the two poets must have derived inward pleasure from their life in common, warmed by an intimate friendship which feared no assaults, and by a firm community of tastes and habits. Italian—indeed, European—literary culture pressed closely around Petrarch and Boccaccio. To hail them thus united their faithful friend Donato came speedily from Venice, bearing letters from Urban V and from Bruni. Side by side the two friends wrote on July 21 to Bruni and Salutati; the latter attributed to his great patron, Boccaccio ("quem studiosissime colere imo adorare consuevi"), his joy, long augured, at receiving first the greetings and then an entire letter from Petrarch (see *Sen.*, XI 1, 2, 3, 4; Salutati, ep. II, 4). While he prepared his answer to the Pope (*Sen.*, XI, 1), Francesco was informed directly by his friend of the difficult Roman situation and of the Pope's character; and perhaps once again, in that period of uncertainty about the invasion of the Emperor, there was a difference of opinion between him, aristocratic and imperial (who in April had rendered homage at Udine to Charles IV, who was entering Italy), and Boccaccio, communal and Guelf (who for three years had been working against the intervention of Charles). But both surely received with emotion the premonitory news of the peace of Modena (August 27) and then, with true joy, news of the elevation to the purple of their dear and venerated Filippo di Cabassoles (September 22).

The cultural life of Padua, moreover, revolved around that house, in which even in those months there gathered the great doctor of medicine, Giovanni Dondi, the two cultured Augustinians, Buonaventura and Bonsembiante Badoer, the enlightened Florentine *condottiere,* Manno Donati, and the very devout Lombardo della Seta. In Petrarch's company Boccaacio visited Biship Pileo, a devoted friend of each of them (see pp. 152-153); he became acquainted with the Maecenas-like lord of Padua, Francesco da Carrara, and seconded his entreaties that his great friend should complete the *De Viris Illustribus* (and perhaps, as an expert in such tasks, Boccaccio helped to promote the work on the frescoes in the Sala dei Giganti). As was the case in each visit, this one was devoted most especially to reading and copying the works of the "magister," in particular those recently completed. During those Venetian months, Boccaccio probably made a copy of *De Vita Solitaria,* to which in a way he had contributed with his research on Damiani (see p. 131 f.). to whom he would at once devote a memoir in the *Genealogia* (XV, 6); the *De Remediis Utriusque Fortune,* already adorned with quotations from his work on Homer and, in the same passage of the *Genealogia* announced as "in lucem novissimus venturus"; and perhaps also the first collection of the *Metrice,* which was recorded also in the *Genealogia* (VII, 29; XV, 6) and in the *Esposizioni* (XV, 99), and the oldest version of the *De Otio Religioso,* which was to become the starting point of a page of the *Esposizioni* (I litt., 91). Except for the last, these are all works which were to appear in the inventory of his library, which was bequeathed to Santo Spirito.[28]

Boccaccio probably also transcribed some of the *Fragmentum Rerum Vulgarium* at this time. Besides their customary literary and cultural debates, and their discussions of Petrarch's settling in Padua while searching for a nearby Heliconian retreat (certainly he had Arquà in mind), and besides their new insistence on a life in common (ep. XVII), Petrarch and his disciple surely must have discussed the problem of the "canzoniere." They debated its validity, its consistency, and its ideal architecture, as they had four years earlier in their letters.

This studious companionship was disturbed and their grief over the loss of Violante and Francesco renewed by the sad news which reached them between August and September—first of the grave illness and then the death of Solone, the son of Donato Albanzani. The two friends wanted to immediately console their faithful companion with a long and affectionate letter of condolence, in which Petrarch spoke also in Boccaccio's behalf (*Sen.,* X, 4). They certainly did not imagine that this compassionate gesture toward their friend and colleague would be their last act in common; nor that the embrace which they exchanged a few days later at the time of their separation would be their last. For in order to be closer to Donato, to distract him from his deep grief, Boccaccio wished to go to Venice, and must have already arrived there by the beginning of October, since Petrarch, repeating his words of comfort to Albanzani on October 3, depicted "Johannes noster" beside the unhappy father (*Sen.,* X, 5). Perhaps at Donato's home Boccaccio finished copying works of the "magister" until his return to Tuscany in October or

November (the exact date is unknown, due to the complete absence of documents or other information on Boccaccio's life until the spring of 1370).

With the difficulties and dangers provoked by the tensions of war, Boccaccio seemed to remain withdrawn—as Coluccio wrote to him on April 8, 1369—in his village, mute even to the appeals and the letters of friends (ep., III, 12). Certainly he carefully revised his treatises, especially *Genealogia*, copied beloved texts (perhaps including those of Dante); but there remains no sure trace of any new and definite undertaking. His solitude and his anxieties were illumined, however, by a gesture and a piece of news, in April 1370, from his "magister," who had also withdrawn upon a hill, that of Arquà ("preceptor meus Euganeos incolit colles," ep. XVII): a generous bequest in the most delicate and loving form, from a brother in studies to a brother in studies, in the testament drafted on April 4 ("Johanni de Certaldo seu Boccaccii, verecunde admodum tanto viro tam modicum, lego quinquaginta florenos auri de Florentia pro una veste hiemali ad studium lucubrationesque nocturnas"); and then the hope of seeing him during his journey to Rome, which Petrarch had finally decided on after so many insistent appeals from Urban V and his co-workers. But having departed from Padova towards the middle of April, Petrarch was suddenly halted by a syncope at Ferrara, whence he was then obliged to return to Padua "in navi iacens" *(Sen., XI, 17)*. Not a trace remains of Boccaccio's anxieties, messages and questions, which must have been very numerous on this occasion. He must have remained at Certaldo, as appears from a letter of May 21, 1370 by Piero del Branca to their mutual friends Leonardo and Chiaro del Chiaro,[29] and at Certaldo he must have been saddened by the accumulation of bad news in the summer months of 1370 (the political situation in Florence was troubled by those opposed to the Visconti and by pacifists; Petrarch's health was failing as was that of other friends like Pietro da Muglio and Donato; and, most especially, Urban V had returned to Avignon at the beginning of September).

In this tired and anxious isolation Boccaccio must have decided on his last journey to Naples, which exercised an irresistible lure to his changeable and impulsive temperament, so typically southern. His

motives for going remain completely unknown: "laboriosam magis-
quam longam anno preterito, peregrinationem intraverim et casu
Neapolim deletus sum," he wrote in June of 1371 (ep. XVII). Perhaps, after the resounding failure of Urban V and of the Florentine
friendship which he always supported warmly, he felt uncomfortable
in the new course taken by the politics of his city ("patriam . . .
indignans liqueram"); perhaps he was worried by straitened economic circumstances (ep. XVII); [30] perhaps he was attracted by the
possibility of a studious and pious settling down in one of the tranquil
southern monasteries rich in goods and books. When he was in
Florence "rumor said that he had become a monk of the Certosa in
Naples" (Sacchetti, *Rime*, CL); [31] and Boccaccio wrote at that time to
his old friend Niccolò da Montefalcone "nescio utrum monacho
dixerim vel abbati " of the Certosa of S. Stefano del Bosco (founded
by Saint Bruno in Calabria), saying that "cum memorum amenam
solitudinem, quorum circumseptum aiebas cenobium tuum, librorum copiam, . . . loci devotionem et commoda . . . monstrasses, *traxisti*
me in desiderium non *vivendi solum,* sed, si necessitas exegisset, *assu-
mendi"* (ep. XV).

Boccaccio certainly remained in Naples for the autumn of 1370
and the spring of 1371 ("Neapoli aliquamdiu fueram vere preterito
. . . desiderio redeundi in patriam quam autumno nuper elapso
indignas liqueram," he would write, after his return to Tuscany in
1371; see ep. XVIII). But even this time, disillusionment and disappointment were his lot, and once again his unhappiness was caused
by one of those companions of his youth in whom he had always loved
to place full confidence. ("Is ergo et senex qui iuvenis fueras: idem
ingenium tuum novi.") After many protestations of affection ("quot
blandientia verba"), Niccolò da Montefalcone suddenly disappeared "in latebram, clam," leaving his friend with only the
possibility of lamentations and imprecations ("O amici confidentia,
o sincera dilectio, o mentis senis et abbatis integritas!"). Boccaccio
wrote these protests and chidings on January 20, 1371 in Naples, and
notwithstanding the "maximum incommodum . . . exitum fere" put
upon him by the incomprehensible behavior of his "friend," Boccaccio refrained altogether from the violence and spirited vulgarity of his
invective against the first Niccolò, the Acciaiuoli. Instead, he wrote to

the second Niccolò, speaking piously of the sudden death of Urban V, without any of the current and widespread disapprobation of this Pope. He kindly informed Niccolò of the election of Gregory XI, which might very well prove favorable to the aspirations of Montefalcone; and finally he asked "quaternum quem asportasti Cornelii Taciti, queso saltem mittas, ne laborem meum frustraveris et libro deformitatem ampliorem addideris." So Boccaccio now had learned from his "magister" inward calm and outward moderation in disappointments and misfortunes, and in addition the willingness and ability to make himself the spiritual and cultural center of life wherever he might be, promoter of new interests and new studies based on rediscovered ancient texts.

During those Neapolitan months, the Carthusian Niccolò da Montefalcone and Niccolò Manganario spent much time in Boccaccio's company, as did the secretary of the Angevin kings, and, later on, of the Papal Curia, Giovanni Moccia,[32] and young Matteo d'Ambasio, notary and then chancellor of Carlo di Durazzo, both of whom were devoted to poetry. There were many others whom Boccaccio saw at this time: Giovanni Latinucci, who was enthusiastic about the *Genealogia;* the famous theologian and preacher, Fra Ubertino da Coriglione; perhaps Count Niccolò Orsini of Nola, a cultured notary and Ciceronian writer, a close friend of Barbato [33] and a correspondent of Coluccio Salutati (ep. II, 2); his friend Monte; the old teachers, Angelo da Ravello, a man of letters and Pietro Piccolo, a jurist; and a number of others whose faces elude us (epistles XV to XX).[34] They are persons who finally were able, in Naples, to create around the old man of literature a circle of affection and of cultural commitment, similar to, but on an entirely different plane from that which thirty years before had aroused his youthful enthusiasms in the time of Paolo, of Andalò, of Dionigi. It was a circle which would have no equal except in Florence, and which was to bring much consolation, with its assiduous correspondence, to the weary solitude of his last years in Certaldo.

Notwithstanding his diffidence and his scruples, Boccaccio could not refuse his warmly devoted group of friends' permission to read and have copies made of what was then his most cherished and compelling work, the *Genealogia.* They worked from the manuscript which Boccaccio constantly revised and brought up to date, and from which he had evidently been unable to separate himself even on this journey. But, like Petrarch before him with his *Buccolicum,* Boccaccio had exacted the promise that the book—not yet ready for publication—would not be circulated nor reproduced in other copies which he had not integrated with corrections, up-datings, and additions. It was a promise which the the enthusiasm and ardor of those readers and their disciples prevented from being kept, with subsequent laments and protests from the author (see ep. XIX and pp. 171 ff. and 177). Besides the support he received from the literary circle in Naples, Boccaccio surely received consolation for the smarting Carthusian disappointment from the affectionate and insistent solicitude of "grandees." He was consoled by Mainardo Cavalcanti and his brother Salice, the executioner and later viceroy, and by his cousin Amerigo. He was comforted by Ugo di San Severino, who also revered Petrarch (*Fam.,* XXIII, xvii; *Sen.,* XI, 9); who "amicis verbis spem prostratam evexerit," and who at all costs wanted him "suis saltem sumptibus, si aliter non daretur, Neapoli retinere" (ep. XVII). Even Joanna caused Ugo to offer him a quiet post ("curabat vir eximius . . . totis vimibus, ut me interveniente subsidio serenissime domine Johanne Jerusalem et Siciliens regine apud Parthenopeos placidos locaret in otio": ep. XVIII). When he was on the point of returning to Tuscany, once again the queen made a great effort to hold him, invoking the direct intervention of her husband, King James of Majorca ("in discessu meo . . . serenissimus princeps Jacobus . . . fecit onorari me precibus ut sub umbra sue sublimitatis ociosus senium traheram, amplissimum ultra regale munus libertati mee offerens spacium": ep. XVII).

In contrast to the wretchedness and humiliation which he had suffered ten years before, Boccaccio was now beset by attention and favors from laureates and crowned heads. Apparently, however, he intended to imitate his "magister" in this regard as well, for he responded in lofty and reluctant words. Indeed, he used Petrarch himself as a shield against all those offers, for never could he have accepted the hospitality of others after having declined that of him who "non ut amicum et socium sed domui sue et substantiis ceteris prepositum dulcissimis precibus et suasionibus . . . , facendiam omnem suam exposuit" (ep. XVII). Boccaccio's jealous love of independence ("non iam patiatur etas libertati assueta colla iuga subicere": ep. XVII) and the desire for meditative and productive solitude which now characterized his life also made him yearn, "senex et eger," for his house and his library. These desires lighted within him "plurimum disiderium redeundi in patriam . . . nec minus revisendi libellos quos immeritos omiserat sic et amicos aliosque caros" (ep. XVII and VIII).

After having written on May 12, 1371 the encouraging letter to young Matteo d'Ambrasio (ep. XVI, "instante discessu meo"), Boccaccio returned to his Certaldo, and on June 26 he sent a letter overflowing with gratitude to Niccolò Orsini (ep. XVII). The illustrious and cultured Count of Nola, whom it is possible Boccaccio had met at Rome in 1367 and at Naples in 1370 and 1371 (pp. 163, 168), had been appointed governor of the patrimony of Saint Peter in Tuscany. When he heard that Boccaccio had refused to stay in Naples, he invited him to be his guest in one of the castles between Rome and Tuscany (perhaps the very one in which a dramatic night is resolved in the *Decameron* [V, 3]). This offer, too, was fondly refused, but for two years, in his "semota camerula" in which he pictured himself engrossed in recitations of the psalms and in meditation on the "ingentia atque innumerabilia divine largitatis in mortales munera," in his fruitful but lonely devotion to study, and in his dignified and chaste poverty ("parvus michi agellus est patrius et hic tenui victui meo satis est": ep. XVII), Boccaccio appears animated more by his ideal conversations with this Parthenopean circle and with the recluse of Arquà than by anything else. Indeed, those contacts had provided him with the means of widening the circle of his correspondents as far as Sicily, including for example, Jacopo di Pizzinga of Messina, protonotary of King Frederick IV, whom Ubertino had praised to him as "gloriosi nominis et longeve fame avidus."[35] In one of his loftiest epistles to him, "ante alios nota dignos," Boccaccio confided the hopes which lighted his spiritual life and his solitude as a priest of poetry:

> . . . in spem venio atque credulitatem, Deum ytalico nomini misertum, dum video eum e gremio sue largitatis in ytalora

pectora effundere animas ab antiquis non differentes, avidas
scilicet non rapina vel sanguine, non fraude vel violentia, non
ambitione vel decipulis sibi honores exquirere, sed laudabili
exercitio, duce Poesi, nomen pretendere in evum longinquum,
conarique ut possint viventes adhuc volitare per ora vivorum et
a corporea mole salutas posteritati mirabiles apparere. A quibus
etsi non integrum deperditi luminis ytalici restituatur columen,
saltem a quantumcunque parva scintillula optantium spes eri-
gitur in fulgidam posteritatem . . . ep. XVIII).

As he had before to Petrarch (*Sen.*, V, 3), Boccaccio also expressed concern about his weaknesses and his discouragement as a
poet, which assailed him sharply in the silence of his meditations on
poetry "anima mundi":

. . . et ipse poeticam aliquamdiu sectus *sum* . . . Ingenti, fateor
animo in stratum iam iter intravi, trahente me perpetuandi
nominis desiderio et fiducia ducis incliti preceptoris mei, et cum
eisdem quibus tu fretus es previus viam arripui. Sane, dum hinc
inde me nunc domesticis nunc publicis occupari permitto curis
et elevatos inspicio vertices celum fere superantes, cepi tepescere
et sensim cecidere animi atque defecere vires, et spe posita
contingendi, vilis factus atque desperans . . . iam canus substiti
. . . nec retro gradum flectere audeo nec ad superiora conscen-
dere queo.

A few months later Boccaccio found a particularly lively and
fervid correspondent in Pietro Piccolo, with whom he debated similar topics. In Pietro's answer of February 2, 1372 to a letter from
Boccaccio, he praised those writings of Boccaccio's which were
highly admired and widely circulated in Naples at that time. He
praised especially a treatise and an epistle to Petrarch on the distinction between the two Senecas and the text of the *Genealogia,* but
he advised against making the latter public because it was still
imperfect (although Piccolo himself had made two copies of it!).
And while he identified himself with the impassioned eulogy of
poetry in the *Genealogia* (XIV, XV), with condescending compla-
cency he communicated the arguments which he personally had

used to defend poetry against the now traditional arguments of a theologian. But in that same epistle, Pietro, who had been introduced twenty years earlier into the Petrarchan cult by Barbato, dared to raise his voice against the proud, jealous watchfulness of Petrarch over his own works. He objected to Petrarch's ambition for absolute literary primacy, and compared it with Boccaccio's modesty and generosity in lavishing his works among his friends. In his epistle of April 5 (XIX), Boccaccio's reaction was firm and magnanimous, notwithstanding the homage to his old master. He had not yet authorized the diffusion of the *Genealogia* because it was still undergoing complete revision (he also thanked Piccolo for his proposals and suggestions and asked him to send more). Boccaccio asserted that Petrarch was quite right in allowing only completely finished works to circulate, and that Petrarch could rightfully claim first place for himself and write "contra appetentiam primi loci" (*Sen.,* V, 3) to him, his "discipulus," who, as a youth, after reading the noble poems of the "magister," had consigned his own first verses to the flames (see pp. 50 and 141 f.).[36] Thus in correspondence and in discussions with his devoted readers from Southern Italy Boccaccio once again gave life to the cult of admiration for his beloved "pater," despite opposition from Piccolo, some young Florentines, and the Venetian Aristotelians. In fact, at the end of his letter to Piccolo confirming his devotion to his "magister," he announced his intention to make a pilgrimage to see Petrarch and to petition again for the release of the long-awaited *Africa* ("disposui circa finem mensis huius vel sequentis principium ad eum usque Patavum ire").

In all probability the visit to Petrarch never took place, if only because of Boccaccio's failing health (p. 174).[37] He continued to correspond with Petrarch, however, and their debates were in a way more productive than ever before. Boccaccio had become more and more sensible to the peremptory demands of the new language of art, not only by his long practice as a writer and his thorough subjection to the discipline of the classics, but certainly also because of the exemplary lesson of the *Rerum Vulgarium Fragmenta.* Some time during 1370 or 1371, after his visit with Petrarch in 1368, Boccaccio had carefully revised and recopied the *Decameron,* and this return to the work of his enthusiastic youth revitalized Boccaccio in his premature old age (Hamilton autograph 90).[38] Petrarch also was prompted to revise one of his earlier works at this time. He had begun his *Trionfi* after Boccaccio had shown him the *Amorosa Visione* in Padua (1351) and now the new edition of Boccaccio's poem inspired Petrarch to return to the *Trionfi*, which he developed in its fullest form.[39] As his writing at this time was largely in the vernacular, Petrarch perhaps also sought suggestions for his own work in the multiform linguistic experiences of his friend. For this reason, he gave special attention to the *Decameron* (probably in the edition lately revised and polished), as he relates in one of the *seniles* of the early part of 1373 (XVII, 3).[40]

The new commitment of the "magister" to the major work of his "disciple" caused him to do something unique in his career as an author. Petrarch's enthusiasm overflows in his translation of the last novella, which he made for his *De Obedientia ac Fide Uxoria*. Immediately he spoke of the "wonderful pages" from Boccaccio to the faithful of his Paduan circle; he showed them to two eminent mutual friends (Gasparo Scuaro dei Broaspini and either Giovanni Dondi or Lombardo della Seta), whose enthusiasm was so aroused that they, too, wished to copy the text.

Petrarch's epistle and the circulation of his translation gave rise to a surge of interest in Boccaccio and his *Decameron* throughout Europe. Boccaccio had a clear presentiment of this, as is shown in his impassioned letter to Francescuolo da Brossano on the death of his "pater et magister." In it he entreated with an insistence made anxious by his long and disappointing wait, "Preterea, summopere cupio, si commodo tuo fieri potest, copiam epistole illius quam ad me satis longam et extremam scripsit . . . sic et copiam ultime fabularum mearum quam suo dictatu decoraverat" (ep. XXIV).

Despite his new fame and the consolations of his friends, Boccaccio's meditative life at Certaldo continued uninterrupted even by civic appointments or missions. After five years of flattering success, the decisive failure of the *entente* with Urban V (the only political activity to which Boccaccio was ever really committed), the sorry chaos, civil, military and religious, which followed upon the election of Gregory XI, the internal tension between the dominant nobles, Albizzi and Ricci, and the middle and lower classes (culminating in 1372 with the creation of the Ten for Liberty and their drastic action), had once again transformed the situation in Florence and Boccaccio was cut off forever from public interests and offices. This situation is reflected and deprecated in the 1373 dedication of the *De Casibus:*

> . . . vidi ex sacerdotalibus infulis galeas, ex pastoralibus baculis lanceas, ex sacris vestibus loricas, in quietem et libertatem innocentium conflare, ambire martialia castra . . . satagentesque adversus veritatis verbum dicentis "regnum meum non est de hoc mundo" orbis imperium occupare . . . Cesarem preponentem Thebani Bacchi vina colentis gloriam splendoribus Martis italici . . . Subiere pectus anxium qui notis insigniti regiis, reges habere volunt, cum falerati sint onagri . . . silvestres bellue rudentes potius quam loquentes.

Boccaccio undertook certain tasks, moved by the solicitations of friends to whom he was particularly devoted, despite the disappointments they had caused him in the past. In the spring of 1372 one of his most cherished Florentine-Neapolitan friends, Mainardo Cavalcanti, now marshal of the kingdom, had returned to Tuscany for his marriage to Andreola Acciaiuoli. He sought counsel on the obstacles of kinship which were impeding his marriage [41] and quite probably he turned to Boccaccio, who was skilled in ecclesiastical law, and who was held in high esteem by Angelo Ricasoli, the Bishop of Florence. Immediately after Mainardo's visit, Boccaccio had fallen seriously ill and therefore was absent from the wedding ("post quam te ultimum vidi, semper vita fuit fere simillima morti": ep. XX).

For a long time Boccaccio had suffered from troublesome obesity, indeed perhaps dropsy, which made movement difficult, as he lamented in an almost caricatural tone ("nimia sagina corpus invalidum," "mole gravatus corporea," "onerosa corporea moles titubans gradus"; "of a man become a goat-skin bottle . . . filled not with wind but heavy lead, so heavy that I can scarce move": ep. XIV; XVIII; XX; *Rime,* CXXII). At the beginning of summer a most annoying scabies developed, like that which had afflicted Petrarch (p. 143), and he developed intestinal and respiratory disturbances and violent pains in the kidneys, spleen and liver ("scabies sicca, . . . ventris ponderosa segnities, renium perpetuus dolor, splenis turgiditas, bilis incendium, tussis anhela, raucum pectus"). And what was worse, these troubles took from him "precipuum solamen": "Muse quarum celesti cantu oblectabatur, obmutuere, et siluit camerula quam consueram sentire sonoram: et breviter in tristitiam omnia . . .". One night after August 12, Boccaccio thought his last hour had come. The violent attacks of fever and the shooting pains made him moan deliriously, while Bruna, his faithful but ignorant "ancillula . . . cuius multis annis obsequio usus sum," could do nothing but cry and try "incompte ac insipide" to "vires in patientiam erigere." At last the country doctor, whom Boccaccio had called in despite his scepticism, gave him relief with vigorous blood-lettings and pitiless cauterization. This put him on the way to recovery, as, in a tone half-anguished, half-humorous, Boccaccio narrated on August 28 in the second part of a letter to Mainardo which he had begun before the crisis. He expressed his congratulations for the wedding, and sent a present of books, but hinted a discreet and secret chiding for having been completely neglected during those very pain-filled months (ep. **XX**).

Mainardo, who must have been still in Florence, caught the hint and hastened to answer affectionately and to express regret and prayers called forth by Boccaccio's sufferings. He sent gifts so that Boccaccio might be able to take good care of himself and protect himself "ab insultu hiemali . . . et misellum fovere corpusculum": first, "aureum vasculum et nummos aureos in vasculo," and immediately afterwards "donum scilicet equum primo." Boccaccio was deeply moved by those proofs of affection, which he had received on September 13, and he wrote Mainardo, "positis pusillanimitatis florentine moribus," and he showed his friendship by his continued concern and by the promises he made about the future. In the central portion of the letter (ep. **XXI**), Boccaccio amiably mocked his friend because he had made excuses for not having read the books sent as a wedding gift: "estivus calor, noctes breves et sponsa nova . . . nedum novum et iuvenem militem, sed etate provectum, canum et scolasticum hominem . . . excusatum redderent." And in the meter of this jocularity, caricaturing himself in abused and

truculent rhetorical language, with mock horror he deprecated the
possibility that Mainardo might give to the women of his household
the "domesticas nugas" of his writing friend to read, because they
would have judged him "spurcidum lenonem, incestuosum senem,
impurum hominem, turpiloquum maledicum et alienorum scelerum avidum relatorem." He ended by excusing himself, making
humorous use of the line to Cicero and Virgil and to the middle-
Latin rhetoricians and poets: "Juvenis scripsi et maioris coactus
imperio." Then, in accordance with the dictates of rhetoric, he
resumed the tone of solemnity and begged Mainardo to remember
him to his relatives and the dear Neapolitan friends, especially to
the noble queen Joanna and to the regent Louis. He exhorted him to
assist not only him but also his "dignioribus amicis . . . Christi
pauperibus" ("Felix equidem es—cum misericordie tanti opificis
organum factus sis et ego eque felix sum, qui a sublimi rerum
Principe audiri mereor clementia sua, et suo iussu ab instrumento
tam placido adiuvari"); he assured him of his deepfelt gratitude and
of his prayer for him and his dear ones "et futuram tibi prolem."

When Mainardo's first child was born in the beginning of 1373,
Boccaccio joyfully accepted the proposal to be its godfather at the
baptismal fount. As a token of gratitude and affection he dedicated
the definitive edition of the *De Casibus* to Mainardo, although in an
earlier time it had been intended for Acciaiuoli (and perhaps later
for Urban V), and which, amid his disappointments and uncertainties, had remained "diu [auctorem] penes ociosum" (ep. of dedication).

By the autumn of 1372, Boccaccio had more or less regained his
health, as he himself wrote (ep. XX). Therefore he could now
perform acts expected of him by his position. He carried the responsibilities of an influential cleric, and was admired for his piety
and historico-canonical learning even by his bishop, Angelo Ricasoli (on whose behalf he had acted in Avignon in 1365, when Angelo
governed the diocese of Aversa). At the end of September he was
charged as fiduciary by the bishop to oversee the proper distribution
of a sum resulting from a legacy.[42]

Also in 1373 Boccaccio continued the careful revision of the
Genealogia, while polishing the *De Casibus* and writing its dedication.

He had finally recovered the annotated copy of the *Genealogia*, which he had left in Naples, and for whose return he had written to the negligent Giovanni Latinucci (ep. XIX and XXI). Warned by the recent failure of his own health and disturbed by the discouraging news coming from Arquà, ever "seiunctum licet corpore, unum animo," Boccaccio sent to his friend an urgent request not to overdo with too much study. Petrarch, surely thinking of the cold winter nights which Boccaccio passed in study (for which Petrarch had made generous provision in his testament), responded with the noble and magnanimous "de non interrumpendo per etatem studio" (*Sen.*, XVII, 2). With this Petrarch seemed intent to end their correspondence with an almost sacerdotal image of himself and his friend as the unconquered and heroic Dioscuri [Castor and Pollux] of the new culture.

NOTES

1. The only source for this information is an archive notice by Manni published by Rostagno art. cit., p. 24.
2. Docc. pub. by G. Canestrini, art. cit., p. 413; A. Hortis, *Giovanni Boccaccio ambasciatore*, p. 50; V. Branca, *Nuovi documenti*.
3. The will was drawn up by Master Filippo di ser Piero Doni; and see Manni, *Istoria*, p. 109 (but the published text is only the vernacular draft of the Latin text of 1374).
4. Docc. pub. by G. Canestrini and A. Hortis, op. cit.
5. Docc. pub. by A. Hortis, pp. 52 ff.
6. We do not know the letter of formal dismissal, but disregarding what Petrarch says in *Sen.*, V, 4, 1, the Pope's praises of 1367 (p. 162) in all probability reflect an attitude which Urban had even in 1365.
7. Doc. pub. by G. Billanovich, *Restauri*, pp. 171 ff.
8. Docc. pub. by Canestrini, Hortis, and Branca in works cited in note 2 above; for Pietro Pilleo, see also Wilkins, *Later Years*, pp. 5 ff. and 74 ff.
9. Hortis, pp. 18 ff; Billanovich, *Restauri*, p. 108; and R. Abbandanza, "Una lettera autografa del Boccaccio," *Studi sul Boccaccio*, I, 1963, p. 9, who thinks that the concession in 1367, published by Billanovich, had already been requested in 1365.
10. See letter published by Abbondanza, art. cit.

11. Doc. cit. by Manni, *Istoria*, p. 39 and by Hortis, art. cit., p. 18. In point of fact, the mission to Genoa could have been accomplished on the return trip, when, we know from *Sen.*, V, 1, Boccaccio stopped in that city. We have absolutely no testimony about the journey out. In view of the urgency of the affair and the mandate to inform the Grimaldi in Nice in the course of the journey, it seems more probable that the mission had been accomplished on the way to Avignon.

12. I follow the chronology now established with precision by A. Pertusi, op. cit., p. 37, instead of that proposed by Wilkins in *Later Years,* who prefers to delay the arrival of the "Homer" at Petrarch's house until the end of 1366.

13. Letter published by Abbondanza, art. cit.

14. D. Tordi, *La chiesa dei Santi Michele e Jacopo,* Orvieto, 1913, pp. 24-25, 34.

15. The year is sure, the month very uncertain; see Massera, *Nota,* cit., pp. 344 f. and doc. cited by Tordi, *Gli inventari,* p. 74.

16. It is the adjudication of tenancy of a house in the parish of St. Felice by Ghino Beverelli to Banco Boticini. Among the witnesses cited is one "domino Johanne Bocchacij." Notwithstanding the existence in Florence in these years of various Giovanni Boccacci (see the note of V. Branca in *Studi sul Boccaccio,* II, 1964) it is probable that the witness is really the author of the *Decameron,* considering the appellation "dominus," his friendship with Banco Botticini, and the location of the house in Santo Spirito.

17. Doc. pub. in part by J. Del Badia, in *Misc. fior. d'erudizione e d'arte,* II, 1887, pp. 31-32; and now completely and with others by V. Branca, *Nuovi documenti,* cit.

18. For this journey of Boccaccio I follow the most probable chronology, which was clearly established by Foresti, *Aneddoti,* pp. 135 ff. and by Wilkins, *Later Years,* pp. 121 ff.

19. See N. Jorga, *Philippe de Mézières,* Paris, 1896, especially pp. 144, 229-385; Wilkins, *The Later Years,* pp. 68, 165 f.

20. Pertusi, op. cit., p. 38.

21. Epistle pub. by A. Campana, "Un'epistola del B. a Donato Alban-zani." *Studi sul Boccaccio,* III, 1966.

22. They gave the prescribed oath on November 11 in the presence of Paolo Accoramboni da Gubbio, "executor of the Orders of Justice": doc. pub. by E. Rostagno, art. cit. pp. 22-23.

23. Doc. pub. by G. Canestrini, art cit., p. 430.

24. Doc. pub. by G. Billanovich, *Restauri,* pp. 168-69.

25. The epistles of Salutati are naturally cited from the Novati edition (Rome, 1891 and subsequently).

26. Doc. pub. by V. Crescini, *Contributo,* p. 259. Note that the stipend is set at 24 lire, while it was 7 lire and 10 soldi in 1355.

27. For this date see Wilkins, *Later Years,* p. 153.

28. For information and documentation see Billanovich, *Petrarca,* pp. 281 ff; Wilkins, *Later Years,* pp. 154 ff. For the bequest to Santo Spirito see Wilkins, *op. cit.* p. 169.

29. Letter cit. by R. Abbondanza, art. cit., p. 13.

30. "Parvus michi agellus est patrius et hic tenui victui meo satis est" he was to write shortly after his return from Naples on June 26, 1371 (ep. XVII); but this may be a primarily literary attitude.

31. Beginning with Manni, scholars have generally attributed the sonnet to the fabled episode of Ciani's visit. On the contrary, it must at least be later than 1369, for the *Sen.* CXLI belongs in 1369, and Sacchetti's poetry is generally arranged in chronological order.

32. See Billanovich, *Petrarca,* p. 288.

33. See Barbato's epistle to Boccaccio published by Massera in *Opere minori,* cit., pp. 332 ff.

34. The date of epistles XVI to XVIII, following recent studies and documentations, is to be brought back from 1372 (indicated in the Massera edition) to 1371, and that of XIX from 1373 to 1372. For the bibliographical data see Ricci, *Studi,* 1962, pp. 3 f.

35. See A. D. Stefano, "Jacopo Pizzinga," *Bolletino Centro di studi filologici e linguistici siciliani,* V, 1957.

36. Piccolo's letter is published by G. Billanovich, "Pietro Piccolo da Monteforte," *Medioevo e Rinascimento. Studi in onore di Bruno Nardi,* Florence, 1955. The article also indicates the copies taken from the *Genealogia* in Naples, the annotations and remarks of Piccolo on the text which were followed by Boccaccio, and it elucidates the relationship between the two correspondents. Boccaccio was so proud of the epistles written to him by the "magister" that he divulged even those which contained opinions and appraisals not at all favorable to Boccaccio himself (*Sen.* V, 3).

37. However, Hauvette (p. 448) and Hecker (pp. 135 f.) did not think it should be excluded. Their opinion forced vague allusions of the *Sen.,* XV, 8 and XVII, 2.

38. See V. Branca and P. G. Ricci, *Un autografo del Decameron,* Padua, 1962.

39. See G. Billanovich, "Dalla Commedia e dall'Amorosa Visione ai Trionfi," *Giorn. Stor. Lett. It.,* CXXIII, 1946.

40. This whole episode is analyzed and elucidated, with various documents, by V. Branca, *La prima diffusione.*
41. See doc. pub. by P. G. Ricci, *Studi,* 1962. The article is very useful for all the relations with Mainardo (and note in ep. XX: "audivi . . . te id iniisse consilium quod tibi quibus potui rationibus suaseram").
42. Document pointed out by Ricci, *Studi,* 1962, p. 9; Ricci himself informs me that the document of September 30, 1372 is in all respects akin to that of March 18, 1374 (see p. 186). It is probably the same document already published in part by Rostagno, art. cit., p. 24 ("die primo Octobris [1372] . . . D. D. Angelus Episcopus florentinus commisit D° Johanni Boccaccio de Certaldo componendi super quodam testamento etc. et exigendi et distribuendi prout sibi placuerit libras 40 etc.").

CHAPTER 10

Lectures and Polemics on Dante and on the Value of Poetry and the Twilight Years at Certaldo (1373-1374)

Boccaccio considered his illness of the summer of 1372 to be a warning that his life would end soon (he emphasizes this in the thoughtful ep. XXI). He wished to close his life uniting, in active veneration, his "pater et preceptor" and his "prima fax et prima lux."

Along with those last affectionate cares revealed in one of the final *Seniles* (XVII, 2), Boccaccio also completed his bucolic poem at this time. It had been undertaken and developed on the exalted model of the "magister," and now he finished it in an even more strongly Petrarchan mode. In a letter to his spiritual director, Fra Martino da Signa (ep. XXIII), he explained its central allegory and its allusive characters.[1] He intended to give firmly moral and ideal meanings to the eclogues, which bore the imprint of sad events and the bristling rancors of his life. Indeed the eclogues have a medi- tative and religious tone which resembles that of the epistle to Fra Martino. In the epistle, Boccaccio paid homage to the provincial father and to the bishop, with fond remembrance of the beloved circle of Santo Spirito (pp. 183 f.). He also quoted the "inclitus . . . gloriosus preceptor Franciscus Petrarca," alone worthy of memory

181

after Virgil, "cuius monitis sepissime michi persuasum est ut omissarerum temporalium oblectatione mentem ad eterna dirigerem." As he faced eternity in his pensive retirement in Certaldo, Boccaccio was thinking, therefore, not so much of the "magister" of culture and poetry, as of the "preceptor" of customs and of life, of the spiritual and religious "pater."

Boccaccio must have turned to Dante, his other "fax et lux," as to a teacher "tam in fuga vitiorum quam in acquisitione virtutum." According to a petition presented in June 1373 by various citizens and approved by the Council of the Commune on August 13, Boccaccio was called to read and to explain "el Dante" in public. The appointment was for one year "with a salary of a hundred florins, which was remarkable" (as the chronicler F. Valori wrote: the decision on the matter had been reached by the Signoria on August 25, certainly not without the influence of the Boccaccian circle of Florence).[2]

This was the last great and courageous task which Boccaccio assumed, despite his precarious health and his increased distrust of city life. He was enthusiastic even though he was aware that there had been, and still were, objections to him in many areas: political and civil, cultural and theological, municipal and domestic, and even personal (from those who had seen themselves branded in the poem). Nevertheless he accepted and bravely undertook the work which—in a moment of cultural crisis and open polemics—was to mark the new direction of Dantean interpretation and of incipient historico-philological criticism itself, especially in its careful attention to the "letter" of the text and in its unusual cultural extension to the Greek and Arabic worlds. Thus the voices of the first and the last great poet of the classical tradition were heard publicly in the culture of the late fourteenth century.

Boccaccio carefully prepared his lectures in the solitude of Certaldo, using his writings and notes on Dante and his own erudite works. He gave the first public reading of "el Dante" in Florence on Sunday, October 23, 1373, in the church of Santo Stefano di Badia, a few steps away from the houses of the Alighieri family.[3] Thus, in a certain sense, the poem was lifted above even the ancient classics, was as though consecrated by the side of ecclesiastical and liturgical texts (though Boccaccio firmly opposed theses on the supernatural inspiration of the work: for example that of Fra Guida of Pisa). The readings, whose audiences must have included some theologians and erudites, must have taken place regularly on week days for several months, since, in accordance with the terms of the resolution, Boccaccio received payment for the first semester of his honorarium on December 31 (for the period October 18 to April 18), and on September 4, 1374, he received the second payment.[4]

These were months of intimate and fertile spiritual communion with the cultural society of Florence, which had undergone many profound changes over the past decade. Now there were writers with vast and varied experience in the vernacular who were bound to Boccaccio by friendship and profound admiration (for example, Antonio Pucci; Filippo Villani, later Boccaccio's biographer and his successor in the Dantean readings; Giannozzo and Franco Sacchetti, then in governorship of a castle near Florence; Agnolo Torini; Ristoro Canigiani, a son of his friend Piero and author of the *Ristorato;* and perhaps Riccardo da Battifolle and Bruscaccio da Rovezzano). There were ardent disciples of his classicism and his Petrarchan moralism (such as Tedaldo della Casa, Benvenuto da Imola, Lapo da Castiglionchio, Guido del Palagio, Giovanni Gherardi) among whom Coluccio Salutati ranked first; he was the Florentine heir of the lofty lessons of the masters of fourteenth century culture (being first notary at Stignano, then from the beginning of 1374 in the Chancellery of the Republic). But especially dear to Boccaccio was the circle "of the soul": that of his beloved Augustinians of Santo Spirito near the paternal house of Santa Felicita, where he probably had resumed residence.[5] In that "cenacolo" two lofty spirits were dominant: Fra Martino da Signa, to whom Boccaccio sent the important epistle interpreting the *Buccolicum Carmen* (XXXIII), and who was later the executor of Boccaccio's testament and the heir to his library; and Luigi Marsili, a young man of high intelligence and piety who, after transferring to Padua early in 1374, became well acquainted with Petrarch and was an intermediary between the two great friends (ep. XXIV). As heir to their spiritual zeal, Marsili initiated the periodical meetings in Santo Spirito which were to develop into the first ardent Florentine academy. With them worked

Onofrio Visdomini (bishop of Florence from 1389), Lorenzo de'
Rinucci (later the provincial father at Pisa), Benedetto di Santa
Maria, Vincenzo Albizzi and Nicola Guadagni, Jacopo Martini and
other monks and laymen whom we see connected in one way or
another with Boccaccio or with his work.[6] During this association
with the Augustinians, it occurred to Boccaccio that he would like to
be buried in his beloved Santo Spirito, should his death come in
Florence. He also matured in his Petrarchan decision to entrust his
writings and library to the care of Fra Martino and the Augustinian
coterie, whom he considered to be his spiritual heirs. He felt that they
would keep his works alive and available to others who might wish to
read or copy them. Through his associations with the Augustinians,
Boccaccio also made contact with other spiritual and cultural
groups. One, which was closely related to Santo Spirito, was that of
the Vallombrosan Giovanni dalle Celle, which inspired certain
friends such as Angnolo Torini, Guido del Palagio, Niccolò di Sennuccio del Bene, Tommaso di ser Francesco di Maso (Boccaccio's
notary),[7] and another, perhaps, was that very active coterie of the
Franciscans of Santa Croce, in which Tedaldo della Casa and Tommaso da Signa spurred interest in the works of Boccaccio and
Petrarch.[8] He also came to know the circle of the Dominicans of
Santa Maria Novella, heirs of the traditions of Passavanti, and their
friend Angelo Acciaiuoli (see pp. 100 and 104).[9]

Some time during 1373 or 1374, when Florentine culture was
flourishing and dominated by the presence of Boccaccio and his
devotion to Dante and Petrarch, Geoffrey Chaucer stopped briefly in
Florence. Chaucer, who had borrowed generously from the works of
Boccaccio and who greatly admired the school of the three great
Italian "Trecentisti," was to change the course of English literature
from a French direction to one definitely Italian.[10] It would be
pleasant to imagine a meeting of Boccaccio with the poet of the
Canterbury Tales.

Despite the flourishing of Florentine culture, and the devotion
to the Dantean readings, which were loved for their lively narration,
their wealth of learning, and their ardent devotion to poetry and
meditative religious moralism, there was also opposition—often
harsh and violent—from several factions. Some came from Guelf

extremists, who—like Lapo da Castiglionchio—were then dominant in Florentine politics. More trouble came from those who feared irreverence and deviations from the righteous path in matters of religion, or even theology. Also, the new culture was opposed by those who entertained a jealously aristocratic conception of literature, too often bound exclusively to the Latin tradition. More than the lack of understanding and the foolish stones cast by the "ingrato vulgo," the ungrateful herd, the accusations that he was prostituting the Muses and their exalted messages must have worried Boccaccio, especially when it seemed that Dante himself would have scorned such vulgarizations ("If I have vilely prostrated the Muses, In the brothels of the sorry mob, And their hidden meanings I have foolishly revealed To the dregs of society. . . . ," "If Dante mourns, wherever he may be, That the concepts of his exalted genius Have been laid open to the unworthy crowd . . .": *Rime,* CXXII and CXXIII). The question of vulgarization is debated with profound suffering in four sonnets (CXXII-CXXV), precisely because his tremulous religious attitude toward poetry had often caused Boccaccio to assume positions apparently analogous to those of the man who now was scolding him harshly (see, for example, *Gen.,* III pr.; XIV, 12; *Bucc.,* XII; ep. XIX-XXIII). Probably this person belonged either to the class ruling Florentine politics, or to one of those circles to which we have seen Boccaccio bound by affection. In any case, he must have been a person of high authority, for there is a tone of respect and progressive humility in the sonnets that is far removed from the outbursts of Boccaccian scorn which marked other such episodes. Actually, the writer made excuses for himself, almost going so far as to shift responsibility on to friends and to invoke his own wretched conditions ("Vain hope and true proverty and the deceived wisdom of friends And their prayers made me do that"; "Apollo on my body has avenged them [the Muses] In such wise that every member feels it" [*Rime* CXXIII and CXXII]). Boccaccio did not always succumb to opposition, however, in an affirmation of courage, he reared up angrily when he felt wounded in his artist's, his scholar's, conscience or when his jealous, umbrageous sense of the dignity of poetry and culture was offended. Boccaccio reacted most strongly when he had the impression that Dante himself was misunderstood and mocked.

("And I, looking in the direction of Heaven, Laughing, shall take some solace for the scorn received, and the deceit; And again, reproaching them [the Florentine people] their ungenerous judgment, and the derided laurel, shall increase their pain and anguish": *Rime* CXXV). Boccaccio continued giving his public readings until early in 1374, and he certainly remained in Florence at least until the end of January, as is proved by the bill of sale of the farm of Santa Maria d'Elmo at Pulicciano.[11] In spite of the extraordinary income of the Dantean "expositions," Boccaccio must have had pressing need of funds if he was selling one of his ancestral farms. His failing health must have caused unusual expenditures, because, after the period of relative good health in 1373, various disturbances, not serious but worrisome, had begun to harass him again in December and January ("iam decimus elapsus est mensis postquam in patria publice legentem Comediam Dantis magis longa atque tediosa quam discrimine aliquo dubia egritudo oppressit . . ." as he wrote on November 7, 1374: ep. XXIV). Probably these ills, plus outbreaks of plague from March to September, were more to blame than polemics and criticism for the decrease and finally the end of the public readings in October 1374 (and in any case they had been requested and approved "for a time no greater than one year").

Before the worsening of his health, Boccaccio must have traveled frequently the twenty-five miles between Florence and Certaldo. Once again, in fact, Bishop Ricasoli "confisus quamplurinum de circumspectione et fidei puritate providi viri domini Johannis Boccacii de Certaldo, civis et clerici florentini," had on March 18 entrusted him with responsibility of settling an inheritance in Certaldo, because "in locis predictis et circumpositis illis iam traxerit moram et conversationem satis domesticam habuerit" and had given him full power of attorney in the matter.[12] Early in July, Boccaccio's condition grew worse, notwithstanding the treatments of the doctors, whom he judged as charlatans (". . . et dum per quattuor menses, non dicam medicorum sed fabulonum . . . consilia sequor continue [egritudo] aucta est"), he was so weak that "exhausta totius pleni quondam corporis pellis hebetatus visus . . . genua et manus tremule facte" he was transferred to Certaldo—the date is uncertain —only with the pitying aid of friends. He spent the summer there "semivivus et anxius, ocio marciens et [sui] ipsius incertus, Dei solius qui febribus imperare potest, medelam expectans et gratiam" (ep. XXIV). Some time between August and September he travelled to Florence, despite his condition: in fact on September 4 he personally drew the second half of his honorarium (no proxy is on record), and had his last will and testament drawn up by Master Tinello, "Florentie in ecclesia et populo Sanctae Felicitatis" (August 28).[13] In the naming of the children of his half-brother Jacopo as sole heirs, in the important bequest to Fra Martino (see p. 184), in the modesty or rather the poverty of the legacies, there is humble but solid proof of the principal motives of Boccaccio's life: the inexhaustible aspiration and the profound fidelity to family affections in spite of discords and disappointments, his truly religious faith in poetry and culture "anime mundi ex gremio Dei originem ducentes," and the generous unselfishness or rather, the noble detachment, which he always kept from any personal gain or enrichment—notwithstanding his many lamentations concerning his poverty. Boccaccio's extraordinary sensitivity to the feelings of the humble is shown by his categorical order to pay any possible debts, by his eagerness to leave all useful objects to his poor and ignorant servant, Bruna di Cianco, and by his gift of the Marian tablet to Sandra, the wife of the faithful Francesco Buonamico. His care for the pious bequests and the scrupulous allotment of numerous relics and priestly articles confirms the image of Boccaccio as a cleric "providus . . . circumspectione et fidei puritate." As a testimony to Boccaccio's openness and faithfulness to the many friendships which characterized his past, Boccaccio was also surrounded at this time by many men who had been close to him throughout his life: for example, Pietro Canigiani and Francesco di Lapo Buonamici, Leonardo Del Chiaro and Ser Tinello da Pasignano, Agnolo Torini and Fra Martino da Signa.

The testament, as if a portrait of the disposition and the life of Boccaccio, had been drawn up "cum nil sit certius morte et incertius hora mortis et hac testante veritate vigilare sit opus cum diem ignoremus et horam qua homo sit moriturus." Certainly it had been planned and drawn with heart made heavy by the most sorrowful news that could now strike it, news which had already been circulated in Florence at the end of July (see p. 192, note 1). During the night between July 18 and 19, his "pater," in his lonely little house in Arquà, had rested his head forever upon his books, perhaps on his Virgil. After his return to Certaldo in September, therefore, Boccaccio must have felt his own material loneliness deepened and darkened by a moral and spiritual loneliness. When a "tearful" letter from Francescuolo da Brossano finally reached him on October 19 with direct news about the death of his "magister," Boccaccio was so grieved that he waited more than ten days before answering (and then it took him three days to pen those few pages). On November 3 he answered with a profoundly sad lament for the lost friend and father (". . . et ego quadraginta annis vel amplius suus fui"), with an unrestrained nostalgic song of gratitude and devotion ("cui quantum habeo tantum debeo"), with a high paean of admiration for the poet, for the scholar, for the spiritual teacher (and passionately invoking his still unpublished writings). But above all, he voiced a kind of liturgical hymn for the mystical "transitum" "ex terrestri Babylone in celestem Jerusalem" of the exalted confessor of Christ, "imitatus humilitate Magistrum et Redemptorem":

> Flevi fere per noctem unam, non optimo viro, fateor, compatiens: certus enim vivo, dum memini honestatis morum ieiuniorum vigiliarum orationumque et innate pietatis eiusdem et Dei dilectionis et proximi, quod dimissis erumnis misere vite huius in conspectu summi Patris evolaverit et ibidem Christo suo et eterna fruatur gloria: sed michi amicisque suis in hoc estuoso solo relictis (ep. XXIV).

Just as the last canonical letter of Petrarch and the last work undertaken by him *ex novo* had been addressed to Boccaccio with exceptional affectionate zeal (see pp. 172 ff., 177), so the recluse of Certaldo ended his epistolary with this lament, his little collection of *carmi,* with the fervid invocation for the *Africa* (carme VII), and his "canzoniere" with the elegiac and heavenly sonnet on the death of his friend (CXXVI):

> Or sei salito, caro signor mio,
> nel regno, al qual salire ancor aspetta

> ogn'anima da Dio a quell'eletta
> nel suo partir di questo mondo rio.
>   Or se' colà, dove spesso il desio
> ti tirò già per veder Lauretta . . .
>   Or con Sennuccio e con Cino e con Dante
> vivi, sicuro d'etterno riposo,
> mirando cose da noi non intese.
>   Deh, s'a grado ti fui nel mondo errante,
> tirami drieto a te. . . .

(Now art thou risen, dear my lord/ unto the kingdom, to mount to which still waits/ every soul chosen [thereto] for that by God/ on its departure from this wicked world./ Now art thou there, where often thy desire/ drew thee to see Lauretta . . ./ Now with Sennuccio and with Cino and with Dante livest thou, sure of eternal rest,/ gazing upon things by us not understood./Ah! if thou didst care for me wandering about here below,/ draw me up to thee. . . .).

In another key, in lines dedicated to the eulogizer of Laura, Boccaccio repeated what he had solemnly written in that almost saintly hymn, interwoven with allusive language and echoes of Scriptures and prayers:

Fecit Silvanus [that is, Petrarch] noster quod nos parva interposita mora facturi sumus; bonorum annorum plenus abiit, immo non abiit sed precessit et sedes piorum sortitus nostris miseriis compatitur orans misericordem Patrem ut fortitudinem itinerantibus nobis adversus vitia prestet et in finem . . . nos ad se recta via perducat (ep. XXIV).

In his freest lyrical outpouring, Boccaccio explicitly united Petrarch and the first mediums of his cult with that other great master, Dante, whose lesson he had begun to meditate profoundly as an exalted message of beauty and truth. He was still drawn to the perpetual and inexhaustible revision of his *Genealogia*, which he was to work on until his death. Although in vain, Boccaccio strove to produce an orderly and definitive edition of the Dantean *Esposizioni*, which at that time was in the form of notes and a comprehensive collection of materials. His work on the *Esposizioni* contains numerous repetitions and extensive borrowings from his other works. There are frequent lapses, with explanatory notes, and many parts surely were intended for a written work rather than for oral treatment (the manuscript is in 24 quartos and 14 small quartos of "carta bambagina" or cotton cloth paper). At his death, Boccaccio left the provisional text of 59 readings, plus the beginning of a sixtieth which breaks off abruptly at line 17 of canto XVII of the *Inferno*. After the *accessus* the commentary on cantos I-IX and XII-XIV deals separately with literal meaning and allegorical meaning; after the expositions of the first cantos, much richer in erudite information and certainly not suited for oral presentation, the expositions of the following cantos, except XIV, become more rapid and less elaborate.

We know little of Boccaccio's life after his final return to Certaldo and the death of Petrarch.

Boccaccio was visited by his devotee Coluccio Salutati, now chancellor of the Republic, and the two men shared the memory of their great friend: "quandocumque dabatur nobis confabulandi facultas, quod rarissimum tamen erat et propter occupationes meas et propter molem et etatem rusticationemque Johannis, nihil aliud quam de Francisco conferebamus. Sufficiebat enim nobis Petrarca solus . . ." (ep. III, 25). Coluccio raised the accord of the Dioscuri of Trecento culture to the Olympian heights of their ancient models when he told Donati in confidence: "Sic, ut antiqua ob nimiam exemplorum copiam, dimittamus, duo nostre etatis lumina, se simul Boccaccius et Petrarca mutuis affectibus dilexerunt." [14] Boccaccio must have spoken of his "preceptor" and "pater" in conversations with Certaldese friends, for example, the prior, Giandonati, who had been recommended to the school in Padua in the name of Petrarch himself, and who certainly assisted his great master and humble parishioner down to the very last hour. Boccaccio probably conversed with the vernacular translator of Ovid, Carlo de' Figiovanni, who remembered having visited "Giovanni Boccaccio several times . . . who then, almost at the end of his days was dwelling here quietly . . . filled . . . with lofty studies of the Muses and of holy Philosophy." [15]

In the solitude of the house in Certaldo, Boccaccio continued his work as a spirit "ad poeticas meditationes dispositum ex utero matris" now bent raptly toward the serene and Christian expectancy of death, for which he was prepared by the lesson and the example of his two great and beloved "fathers" of culture and of life. They seemed to watch, even materially, over the moral and religious obligation of their greatest and most devoted disciple. Dante's presence was felt in the folios of "carta bambagina." Petrarch comforted his vigils with the fur gown which he had bequeathed to him so that he might keep warm at night in the long hours of study and of prayer.

Thus it was that when on December 21, 1375 Boccaccio closed his eyes, for his contemporaries he remained almost hieratically composed in this posture of champion of poetry "ex Dei gremio originem ducens," and the last survivor of the "three crowns."

"Mens sedet ante Deum meritis ornata laborum/ Mortalis vite . . ./ Stadium fuit alma poesis" were the words that Boccaccio wanted written over his grave in San Michele. They were to consecrate the faith and the passion which had grown ever in his soul, which had become more and more the very reason of his existence. As though he were responding to the humble nostalgia of fame which had smiled on him, Boccaccio used the last two books of the *Genealogia* to broadcast to the world his message on the divine origin of poetry ("nulla est tam humilis vita que dulcedine glorie non tangatur." Under that pure epitaph, Coluccio Salutati wrote:

> Inclyte cur vates, humili sermone locutus,
> de te pertransis? . . . Etas te nulla silebit."

Sacchetti also hailed Boccaccio at his death, and he extolled the noble genius of the author of the novellas that were "spread even to France and England." Like Coluccio (ep. III, 25), in the death of Boccaccio Sacchetti mourned the death of poetry itself (*Rime*, CXXXI). In these deeply felt homages to the greatest writer in the vernacular and the most influential classicist and moralist of his time, Boccaccio is raised to a position equal to that of Dante and Petrarch. He received high consecration as the father of Italian prose and Italian narration, and as the hero of the Christian culture of the early humanism.

NOTES

1. The date of this epistle is extremely uncertain. About all that can be said definitely is that the letter was written after 1367-69; that is, it followed the completion of the *Buccolicum Carmen*. Perhaps it was as late as 1370, which is the date assigned to the publication and the diffusion of the work, as Boccaccio was in Certaldo at that time.

2. Doc. pub. by Gerola, art. cit., and later with other useful evidence by D. Guerri, *Il Commento del Boccaccio a Dante*, Bari, 1926, pp. 205 ff.

3. *Istorie pistolesi e Diario del Monaldi*, Milano, 1845, p. 439.

4. Doc. pub. by Gerola and Guerri, see note 2 above, and by Billanovich, in *Italia Medioevale e Umanistica*, VI, 1963, p. 207. The readings must have continued for at least a good part of the second semester, that is, after April 18, 1374.

5. In the documents preceding his will (see pp. 187 ff.) Boccaccio appears to be domiciled still in Santa Felicita (see Branca, doc. cit. in *Studi sul Boccaccio*, II, 1964); but in the act cited on p.   , note 10, he is recorded as "Dominus Johannes olim Bocchaccii Ghelini de Certaldo, comitatus Florentie qui nunc moratur Florentie in populo Santi Jacobi Ultrarni." Either it is an error caused by the contiguity of the two parishes and the position of the house of the Boccacci in Borgo San Jacopo, or there had been changes in the boundaries between the two parishes. Perhaps the houses of the Boccacci had been extended and crossed the line between the two parishes, or for some reason Giovanni had left the old domicile for another in the same district.

6. See in general U. Mariani, *Il Petrarca e gli Agostiniani*, Rome, 1946, especially pp. 66 ff.; V. Branca, *La prima diffusione*, pp. 122 ff. On Boccaccio's will and the library of S. Spirito, see also: D. Gutierrez "La Biblioteca di S. Spirito a Firenze," in *Analecta*, XXV, 1962.

7. For this circle and the men bound to Boccaccio, see J. Hijmans, *Vita e opere di Angnolo Torini*, Leiden, 1957, in particular pp. 15 ff.

8. See V. Branca, *La prima diffusione*, pp. 126 f.; F. Mattesini, "La biblioteca francescana di Santa Croce e Fra Tedaldo della Casa," *Studi Francescani*, LVII, 1960.

9. Perhaps two other sons of Pietro Canigiani already belonged to this circle: Barduccio, author of a work on the *Sermone* of the dying Saint Catherine, and Piero: both of them were among the "most faithful" followers of the Saint of Siena.

10. It is known that Chaucer was in Italy from December 1372 to May

1374, to negotiate with the Republic of Genoa on behalf of the English government for the choice of a British port for Ligurian merchants. On that occasion he was also in Florence (perhaps he had already been in Milan in 1363). The possibility of a direct acquaintance of Chaucer with Boccaccio has been much discussed, and formerly defended with sound arguments (see them summed up, for example, by E. Hutton, *Chaucer and Boccaccio,* and by C. Carswell, *Lollius my Author,* in *The Times Lit. Suppl.,* nos. 1727 and 1769, 1935). These arguments are excluded tendentially by more recent criticism (see such positions summed up by M. Praz in the volume, G. Chaucer, *The Canterbury Tales,* selection, introduction and commentary by M. Praz, Bari, 1957, pp. 61 ff.).

11. Doc. pub. by Tordi, *Gli inventari,* p. 82 (and see also pp. 89 and 98).
12. Doc. pub. in part by D. M. Manni, *Istoria,* p. 35, later completed by Torraca, *Per la biografia,* pp. 237 ff.
13. *Il testamento di Giovanni Boccaccio,* edited by C. Scipione Borghesi, Siena, 1855. For the particulars of the real estate and their derivation from the paternal estate see p. 84, note 41, and see the act concerning the acquisition of Boccaccio's real estate by his heirs on February 5, 1376, pub. by Tordi, *Inventari,* pp. 58 f.
14. Epistle published in part by Billanovich, *Petrarca,* p. 293. And observe that, perhaps in homage to the masterpiece of the master, Coluccio named his two grandchildren Pampinea and Emilia (see L. Ullman, *The Humanism of Coluccio Salutati,* Padua, 1963, p. 3).
15. See respectively D. Tordi, *Gli inventari,* p. 87; and E. Bellorini, "Note sulla traduzione delle 'Eroidi' ovidiane attribuita a Carlo Figiovanni," *Miscellanea ... D'Ancona,* Florence, 1901, pp. 13 ff. The dedicatory epistle continues: "by his loving consolations I was guided to the useful studies of the Latin tongue, and with his help composed and translated many things. ..." Although the Figiovanni family of Certaldo is well known (see *Decameron,* X, 1), the epistle and the very identity of Carlo Figiovanni are seriously suspect.

Part II

The *Decameron*

CHAPTER 1

The Medieval
Tradition

The *Decameron* could not have become known for many years to the cultural and commercial societies of Italy, when Francesco Buondelmonti, the nephew and most faithful agent of the great seneschal Niccolò Acciaiuoli, wrote to Niccolò's cousin Giovanni Acciaiuoli in Florence (at that time archbishop-elect of Patras) in July 1360. The letter indicated the anxious eagerness with which the first copies of the *Decameron* were read and passed around and, sometimes, hungrily purloined:

> Reverend Domine, here is Monte Bellandi writing to his wife that she is to give you the book of the tales of messer Giovanni Boccacci, belonging to me; wherefore I beseech you *quantum possum* that you have it delivered to you; and if the Archbishop of Naples has not left I beg that you send it by him—by his servitors, that is—and he is not to give it to Messere (Niccolò Acciaiuoli) nor to any other person than myself. And if the Archbishop has departed, have it given on my behalf to Cenni Bardella: let him send it to me at L'Aquila or Sulmona; otherwise, do you send it to me yourself by one who you believe

197

will deliver it to my hand; and do be most careful that messer Neri shall not get hold of it, for then never would I have it. I am having it delivered to you because I trust you more than anyone else and I hold it most dear; and do be careful not to lend it to anyone because there are many who would be dishonest. . . .[1]

The same enthusiasm, the same trepidation, the same joy derived from making a discovery, enlivens the prologue, with which in those same years, an anonymous admirer praised writers on love (preserved in the codex Magliabechiano, II, II, 8, in the National Library of Florence). He then continued:

> . . . among others whom I recall at present, who are deserving of fulsome praise and celebrity, there is the worthy Messer Giovanni di Boccaccio, to whom God give a long and prosperous life as he himself may wish. Not so very long ago he has written beautiful and delightful books, in prose and in verse, in honor of those gracious ladies whose high-souled noblemindedness takes pleasure in occupying itself with pleasant and virtuous matters; they take great pleasure and delight in books and beautiful tales, whether by reading them or in hearing them read, whereby for him fame increases, and for you, your delight. And among these books he composed one especially beautiful and pleasurable, entitled *Decameron:* which, you must know if you have heard it read, treats of a gay company of seven young women and three young men. . . .[2]

Insofar as it is possible to deduce from his writing characteristics, the writer of those lines belonged to the Florentine merchant society, in all probability to that gravitating around the company of the Bardi family. That is to say, he belonged, as did the Buondelmonti and the Acciaiuoli, to that upper middle-class society which had founded the great fortunes of the Florentine Commune in the thirteenth and fourteenth centuries.

This upper middle class very promptly disseminated through its thousand channels those works for which its men showed preference. For this reason, the Buondelmonti, the Acciaiuoli, the Bardi, the

Cavalcanti (Boccaccio's epistle XXI) immediately spread the news
of the *Decameron,* which became popular with the middle class because it clearly reflects the enthusiasm and the activity of that society.
As is intimated above, this was nothing new, for copies of more than
two-thirds of the manuscripts written between the late Trecento and
early Quattrocento—so far as my researches have been able to ascertain—were possessed by those families, while, on the contrary, there
seem to be no copies that belonged to famous libraries or to have
come from the more esteemed copyists' shops. As the descriptions of
the codices reveal, copies of the *Decameron* were owned by the most
eminent merchant families of Florence, such as the Capponi (Paris.
It. 482), the Raffacani and the Del Nero, secondhand dealers (Barberiniano, Lat. 4058), the Bonaccorsi (Ambrosiano, C 225), the
Verrazzano (Laurenziano, XC, sup. 106II), the Fei (Laurenziano,
XLII, 4) and the Vitali, all agents of the Bardi company (Paris. It.
62); the Del Bene, the Rosati, the Deti, the Bigati (codices no longer
to be found); or of other cities of Italy such as the Sienese Allegretti (cod.
Ginori), the Franceschi in Arezzo (Laurenziano, XC, sup. 1061), the
Venetian Cabrielli family (London 10297), the Cavalcanti at Naples
(codex now lost). Indeed, copies of the *Decameron* physically were
involved in the complex finances that constituted the adventurous
life of that society. We repeatedly come upon traces of accounts,
rentals, or loans noted on the margins of codices. (For example,
Laurenziano, XC, 1061, Barberiniano, Lat. 4058.) Sometimes we
find modifications of the text, which reveal mercantile interests or
tendencies.

The names of unusual amanuenses are related to the same
mercantile environment. They were persons of the most varied
stations and professions who had turned copyist, who had adapted
themselves to the long, patient work in order to satisfy a personal
desire to have that fashionable text always at hand. Among them
were: Giovanni d' Agnolo Capponi, prior for the higher crafts in 1378
(Paris. It. 482); Piero Daniello di Piero Fei and Lodovico di Jacopo
Tommasini, merchants, as revealed by the very composition of the
codices (Laurenziano, XLII, 4 and cod. Nazionale Firenze, II, II, 20);
Ser Taiuto di Balducci di Pratovecchio, notary (Laurenziano, XC,
sup. 106II); Francesco di Nanni di Piero Buoninsegni, who perhaps

was trying to forget the loneliness of his office at Montalcino by copying the *Decameron* (Laurenziano, XLII, 6); Lodovico di Silvestro Ceffini, merchant, and member of the Opera del Duomo [vestry-board concerned with the upkeep of the Cathedral] (Paris. It. 63); Filippo di Andrea da Bibbiena, probably a well-to-do farmer who transcribed the work "for himself, his relatives, and friends" (Chigiano, M, VII, 46); the Sienese Ghinozzo di Tommaso Allegretti, who sought, in the *Decameron,* solace for his internment at Bologna: "written for himself . . . interned and worse" (Cod. Ginori); and far from Florence in Venetian territory, Domenico Caronelli, an important citizen of Conegliano (Vatican Rossiano, 947). We could continue the enumeration with various manuscripts which, though they bear no note which indicates and verifies their origin, reveal by the handwriting or by occasional notes that they originated in those same surroundings (for example, Laurenziano, XLII, 2; Magliabechiano, II, II, 8; the Palatine of Parma, 24). Even the most famous and most venerated manuscript of the *Decameron,* the one copied by Francesco di Amaretto Mennelli, was inspired, in a way, by this same interest, which is indicated by the character of the copyist's family and the possible destination of the transcription.[3] Also, although a splendid illustrated copy of the *Decameron* was not made until 1467, by Taddeo Crivelli for Teofilo Calcagnini (the codex at present belongs to Lord Leicester), drawings of the usual popular type are very numerous in those manuscripts owned by merchants, among the best of which is the manuscript illustrated with a series of 112 plates that belonged to Lodovico Ceffini (Paris. It. 63).[4]

In contrast to the extraordinary popularity of the *Decameron* in the middle classes, the more properly literary circles remained indifferent to it. That is, even after several years, even after the most official recognition of Boccaccio's fame, one seeks in vain for any evidence in the world of culture corresponding to that explosion of middle-class enthusiasm. The famous judgment of Petrarch in the last of the *Seniles* (XVI, 3) contains his Latin translation of the Griselda story ("Librum tuum quem nostro materno eloquio, ut opinor, olim iuvenis edidisti nescio quidem unde vel qualiter ad me delatum, vidi: nam si dicam legi, mentiar . . ."). Perhaps, as I have shown elsewhere, Petrarch's criticism is strictly literary (he follows

Seneca, *Ad. Lucil.* XLVI), remote from any implied disinterest.[5] His judgment seems, however, to set the tone for the attitude of reserve and almost wilful disregard manifested by that first Humanistic circle. Indeed, the entire following generation seemed to be disinterested in the *Decameron,* although it praised and glorified Boccaccio's erudite output. Filippo Villani, Benvenuto da Imola, Coluccio Salutati, Leonardo Bruni shared this attitude and if they quoted the *Decameron,* it was only marginal and often not even explicit.[6] Certainly it is not merely the question of the language which caused this negative position, for Petrarch himself in another of the *Seniles* (V, 2) appears much more warmly interested in the vernacular poetry of his great friend; at the end of the century those men of letters allude to that same poetry with great interest.

But middle-class enthusiasm remained undiminished in the face of this prolonged cultural diffidence. There is evidence of this in the increased number of copies of the *Decameron,* the ever-more diligent imitation of Boccaccio by others, the repetition of the tales from the lips of the jugglers and the story-tellers in the public squares, to which the public listened eagerly. Sacchetti's *Paradiso degli Alberti* was inspired by the *Decameron,* as was a whole series of songs and of illustrations on wedding chests, which relate tales and themes of the *Decameron.*[7]

This contrast of enthusiasm and of interest is not merely the result of the cultural atmosphere of its time. Instead, it originates from elements characteristic of the work of Boccaccio, which are reflected in its fortunes preceding its full recognition as a literary masterpiece.

This is to say, the *Decameron* appeared during the last decades of the Trecento, not as a work adhering to literary tradition but as a book for agreeable, pleasant reading, as a work created not for the savoring of the refined men of letters but for the joy of less-cultured readers. The merchants of the circle of the Acciaiuoli or the women of the house of Cavalcanti, whom Boccaccio had advised not to read his book (ep. XXI), were the first readers we find poring over the *Decameron,* and they are indicative of this episode in the life of fourteenth century Italy.

The *Decameron* was not written following the style of the classical manner, highly venerated by Italian protohumanists, as it had been earlier by Italian prehumanists; it was not even influenced by the more aristocratic medieval tradition, which imitated the great classical examples, that is, it did not come down from the lyrical tradition. Its antecedents were to be sought, if anywhere, in the exuberant and woodsy narrative production of a middle-class and popular character. Boccaccio wrote the *Decameron* on a lower level, without literary pretensions, in a style which the middle-class society of the preceding centuries preferred to read for entertainment. The *Decameron* was disseminated by word of mouth as well as by the written word. To those readers the *Decameron* appeared as the masterpiece of its type, as the clever systemization of a material beloved but still raw and in a fluid state (although it might have needed a harmonious and stable arrangement). It did not exact the respect and the admiration owed to literary masterpieces but, as the manuscripts show, it evoked a happy and familiar confidence which encouraged alterations and omissions and insertions of new tales, as well as coupling with other narrations. That is, it produced a confidence in the reader so that he would feel free to tailor the book most particularly to *his own,* tastes, needs, and preference.[8] That means the *Decameron* appeared as a completely extraliterary work. Boccaccio himself stressed the idea in the introduction (". . . I mean to relate a hundred tales, or fables, or parables or stories, however they may be called, . . . as a help and refuge for ladies in love.").

Indeed, to that protohumanistic society which already dominated the Italian culture of the second half of the fourteenth century, the work probably appeared to be not only extraliterary but almost antiliterary. Those men, after the "darkening" which followed the great medieval classicism, were laboriously rediscovering the highly venerated classical culture. They entertained the supreme ambition of reuniting themselves to the Latins, while skipping over —as nearly as possible—medieval culture. With passionate trepidation they felt the supreme "dignities" and "reasons" of the spirit entrusted to literature. Such a work as the *Decameron,* on the contrary, tended entirely toward medieval and Romance culture and its world. Boccaccio was intent on collecting and studiously arranging the fancies beloved by the populace. It is this, perhaps, which shows through in the feeling and emotion of the epitaph which Salutati composed for Boccaccio, in the elegant lines of which it is possible to distinguish an implied reproof: "te *vulgo . . .* percelebrem." [9]

Perhaps these interpretations or rather, these attitudes, are only the result of an episodic cultural situation. However, the diverse reactions to the *Decameron* reflect its certain, if not exclusive, reliance on the medieval and Romance tradition.

As has been said, in the extremely varied and complex material of the *Decameron* the classical influence is almost completely absent.[10] The sole tale of a Greco-Roman type, that of Titus and Gisippus (X, 8), is only a conventional setting illuminated by the most characteristic deforming lights of medieval literature. It is but an ornate transcription of one of the most celebrated works of that age, the *Disciplina Clericalis,* enriched with elements derived from a little poem by Alessandro di Bernay. The only two novellas in which some classical influence may be detected, that is, the tenth story of the fifth day (V, 10) and the second of the seventh day (VII, 2), come straight from a Latin writer, Apuleius. Boccaccio himself admitted that one of his inspirations for the two novellas was Apuleius—an author who, like Boccaccio, had lent an ear to the narratives of the people and had deemed them worthy of a literary consecration.

Story-tellers of the Renaissance drew their material from the classical world, even as much as certain narrators of the thirteenth and fourteenth centuries did. They all repeated and adapted the ancient epical or historical exploits. Boccaccio did this as well, but he also decided to yield to his natural inclination for the imaginative. Boccaccio had vast knowledge of classical literature, and, more than any of his contemporaries, was able to draw from that source ample material for narration. Indeed he drew on classical sources for such works as the *Epistole* and the *Teseida,* the *Amorosa Visione* and the *Ninfale Fiesolano.*

In the *Decameron,* on the contrary, even when classical models are available, natural and impressive, Boccaccio seems to avoid them deliberately. Instead he turned to the medieval texts he admired. We have already mentioned this influence in the novellas, V, 10 and VII, 2. Also, Boccaccio's preference for medieval sources over the classics is indicated in the novella of Chynon (Cimone, V, 1), which is much closer to an episode in the story of Barlaam and Josaphat than to the Greek romances proposed by Rohde,[11] and which Boccaccio must have known. In the novella of Andreuccio of Perugia (II, 5) Boccaccio eliminates almost every trace of an episode of the *History of Antheia and Habrocome* by Xenophon of Ephesus (which was known to him). In his version the influence of a fabliau, *Boivin de Provins* is apparent. In the novella of the Angel Gabriel (IV, 2) the possible Ovidian references are blurred by the narration of the pseudo-Hegesippus. It would not be difficult to give many other examples, but one of them marks the *Decameron* beyond any possibility of doubt. This is the famous evocation of the plague in the sombre "overture" of the *Decameron*. Acquainted indirectly with the tragic Lucretian description as found in Macrobius and other annotators of the *Georgics,* Boccaccio modelled his grandiose and terrible pages on those in which Paulus Diaconus —a writer he used frequently—had described the pestilence which tormented various provinces of Italy in the last months of the empire of Justinian (*Hist. Lang.,* II, 4-5).[12]

Even if Boccaccio's use of medieval traditions did not completely overshadow classical influences in his work, his tendency to "contaminate" the latter would suffice to characterize as medieval both his artistic technique and his poetical imagination itself. Moreover, Boccaccio was quite willing to fuse very diverse texts and examples, as I pointed out elsewhere.[13] In his youthful minor poems Boccaccio merged the traditions of the great Latin epic of Virgil and of Statius with the newer and popular tradition of the *cantari,* as he did again in his later works, from the *De Genealogia* to the *Esposizioni*.

Boccaccio's sensibility, his clinging to the literature and the traditions of the immediately preceding centuries—so different from the disdainful coldness of Petrarch and his friends—is indicated by the sympathetically open and frank way with which he adopts the popular art of story-telling in the *Decameron*. Almost two-thirds of the antecedents which can be traced for the tales of the Decameron belong to this literature. The very poetry of the people of those centuries—from the *cantari* to the *lamenti,* from the *canzoni a ballo* (ballads) to the *rispetti*—is given its most illustrious recall and reflection in the *Decameron*. In many cases this has saved it from the oblivion of the centuries.

But even more than in the recapture of the content, the preoccupation of Boccaccio's imagination with this world is revealed in the intonation and the coloring of the narration. The amorous adventures and the salacious jests are related with the carefree and mirthful sprightliness of the fabliaux. The sad and sorrowful stories are patterned after the anguished pity of the *lamenti*. The lofty tragedies of love and death are scanned to the doleful and stately rhythms of the adaptations of French romances. The eventful and risky adventures in far-off places across the Mediterranean or in western Europe have the rapid and straightforward movement of the reports of the Florentine merchants, the real "conquistadores" of that age. The marvellous and fabulous episodes glitter with the fairy-tale lights and the choral enchantment of the *cantari*.

Boccaccio put together and in a certain sense, ennobled, this material, these modes, this complex tradition by means of a technique and style of harmonious writing absolutely congenial to the world in which they were written. He avoids any of the classical drapery or complacent classical starching used by Petrarch and story-tellers of the following age, even for figures and episodes extraneous to the Greco-Roman world.

Boccaccio achieves a dignity of style, a superior harmony (as we point out in the following chapter) from his medieval technique based on the *cursus* and rhymed prose. Also, for ornament he drew from the style of the *De Vulgari Eloquentia*. From the treatises on style and rhetoric of the preceding centuries Boccaccio evolved the literary preciosities which he seems to enjoy scattering through his work like little gems: reference to the canonical numbers, three and ten, the flashing use of names, either allusive to or in rapid correspondence with imaginative periphrases; and the employment of *senhal*, the calculated and scrupulous topographical distribution of the novellas according to a completely literary and medieval geography. (These three facts Billanovich has recently brought to notice and Curtius and De Bruyne have mentioned in their description of the complex world of ideas of that century.)[14] In addition, Boccaccio followed medieval literary precepts when, in outlining his tales, he gave each one a moral-didactic premise. Boccaccio uses symbolic colors (white, green, red, and perse) to indicate the dowries or the sentimental situation of the ladies. He relies on "styles" following the precepts of the most authoritative rhetorical science for writing treatises, from Alberico da Montecassino to John of Garland.[15]

But Boccaccio's objective in the *Decameron* was not merely literary. Unlike later novella writers, he did not organize the diversified material for his novella purely with regard to literary structure. Nor was his intention clearly allegorical. Instead, Boccaccio wished to give his material a coherent development in a rhetorical and moral sense. The *tesserae* [pieces put together to form a mosaic] from the medieval tradition are carefully placed in accordance with the esthetic convictions of that age and of Boccaccio himself, and the precision of the design imparts a metaphysically valid meaning [16] to the work. Likewise in the *Filocolo* and the *Comedia,* the most direct anticipations of the *Decameron,* the "questions of love" and the narrations of the Nymphs were developed with a clear conception of ideas and morality.

The design of the *Decameron,* then, makes it a structurally organic work and not merely a collection of a hundred novellas. As Ferdinando Neri [17] has shown, the structural framework of the tales is the ideal itinerary, which goes from the harsh reprehension of vice (Day I) to a carefully planned eulogy of virtue (Day X).

During the narration, Boccaccio unfolds his version of the "comedy of man." He shows how man can make himself worthy of entrance to the "splendid kingdom of virtue," overcoming the great forces that, like instruments of Providence, seem to govern the world: Fortune, Love, Ingenuity. In orderly succession, Boccaccio presents varied and agitated pictures of mankind; man the plaything of Fortune (Day II); then man victorious over Fortune "by his industry" (Day III). He describes man undergoing the highest ordeals of human joy and sorrow, enduring the rule of Love, the sovereign of the world (Days IV and V). And then, with poignant mirth, he portrays men who use their Ingenuity to distinction (Day VI). He pictures this either in the rapid skirmishes of witty sayings (Day VI) or in deceits and practical jokes which, in accord with the accidents of Fortune and the entire medieval literature, develop and persist in the overwhelming amorous material (Days VII and VIII). Thus, from the initial censure of human vices, through contemplation of the measure which men give of their intellectual and moral endowment under the hazards of Fortune, Love, and Ingenuity, after the pause of the ninth day, Boccaccio presents the magnificent and fabulous epilogue on the tenth day, which describes the most lofty virtues. In the solemn laudatory atmosphere of the epilogue, Boccaccio seems to propose the establishment of the highest motives, the great force-ideas which had governed the unfolding of the magnificent and eternal human comedy. He seems to consecrate them in an almost metaphysical fixity. Thus the epilogue presents Fortune (novellas 1, 2, 3), Love (novellas 4, 5, 6, 7), and Ingenuity (novellas 8, 9) in a new light. In it they are the touchstones of the nobility of man, which are overwhelmed and surpassed by Virtue. Through Griselda, representative of Virtue in the Epilogue, these three great forces find their noblest expression. Fortune turns a poor shepherdess into a splendid lady of the manor; Love transforms Gualtieri and makes Griselda heroic; and Ingenuity is used by Gualtieri to test his wife. Griselda's virtue is portrayed as almost hallowed and stylized, drawn from the traditional concept of the lady "humble and lofty more than any creature." (The echo of the prophecy of Simeone and of the "Ecce ancilla" is clear, for example in the phrases: "Although these words were like dagger-thrusts in Griselda's heart, . . . she answered: 'My Lord, I am ready and prepared.' ")

Thus, Boccaccio wrote the *Decameron* in the form of an itinerary, "a principio horriblis et fetidus, in fine prosperus desiderabilis et gratus." That is, he evolved a plan which "inchoat asperitatem alicuius rei sed eius materia prospere terminatur"; a gallery of figures from Ser Ciappelletto, the new Judas (I, 1, 15) to Griselda the new Mary (X, 10, 28 and 51). He designed and wrote the *Decameron* according to the structure of a "comedy" in the most authoritative medieval tradition, present under Uguccione da Pisa and John of Garland to Dante.[18] This was not only a tradition that Boccaccio revered and loved, but followed exactly as in the *Esposizioni (acc.* 25 ff.) after approximating it in the *Comedia,* an artistic exigency later theorized in Book IV of the *Genealogia* (especially in chapters 9-13).

Boccaccio gave more clearness and solidity to his design, to his setting forth of ideas, by placing it in a framework that somehow emphasizes the important moments, even beyond and independently of the explicit statement of the themes of the various days. This framework, even though it is almost an obligatory poetical schema for Boccacio's imagination, is also characteristic of medieval literature and rhetoric and almost inconceivable outside it. It is not necessary to give examples nor to stress this fact, so constantly has it been brought out by the best criticism of Boccaccio's work. But if any further proof were needed, it would suffice to consider how Boccaccio's design becomes lifeless and loses even its eminent decorative value when it is repeated by the novella writers of the next two centuries. It becomes merely a literary device, a more-or-less wearied homage to the first great example in the literary tradition of the Italian art of novella writing.

Beyond the purely medieval meaning that Boccaccio has instilled in the *Decameron,* he has indicated the rhetorical ideals of that age by the manner in which he realizes his design. Midway between the developments of the "frame," Boccaccio placed the very charming episode in the Valley of the Fair Ladies. The series of the "reigns" of the girls is symmetrically interrupted by those of the young men. The reign of the first day is chivalrously bestowed on the eldest of the girls, Pampinea, just as rule over the last day is allotted to Pamphilus, the senior of the youths. Boccaccio writes the ballads for each day on the paradigm 3:4:3, beginning with an allegorical treatment in the first three, tarrying in a lofty lament of love in the central four, resolving finally in a spacious song of exultation in the final three. Contrary to the more formal and pragmatic manner of the episodes themselves, Boccaccio becomes more imaginative in the "frame, showing the influence of medieval tradition.[19] For example, descriptions of nature fill a large part of the frame." They are always composed with a decorative elegance, in a stylization of precious arabesque. They never have a value taken by themselves; they do not present at all the Panic vitality of landscapes after the example of a Poliziano, although in content they anticipate the elements of his descriptions.

Likewise, the refined and aristocratic humanity of the storytellers in the "frame" is revealed within fairy-tale atmosphere created essentially by the use of an elegant eurhythmy of all the action. This rhythm seems to be controlled by the soft sound of music and performed to a dance step, as in the ideal courtly social groups which serve as a background to the subtle discussions of Andreas Cappellanus, or as in the representations of the chivalric circles of the kings, Arthur and Charles, especially in certain Italian compilations. That is, the action in the "frame" does not represent a human world psychologically alive and real, but only a felicitous visualization of those ideal, longed-for, conditions of life, weightless and remote from any daily concern. This idealized world is both the necessary justification of the art of the *Decameron* and the atmosphere most in harmony with its very exceptional development.

In a way more intimately connected with the philosophical basis of the work, the "frame" clearly reveals the medieval structure of the *Decameron*. Besides providing an organizational principle for the work, the "frame" also discloses the theoretical reasons and ideals which inspire the very diverse and splendid tales.

For example, Fortune and Love are presented as the highest measures and tests of man's capacity. They are also, however, the great themes that link the tales and provide structural and ideological unity; each tale has a theoretical interpretation relevant to its function in the "frame." This structural formulation is firmly rooted in scholastic and medieval traditions.

Pampinea, "the wise," the young woman most gifted with astute human prudence, in the prologues to the third novella of the second day and the second novella of the sixth day, outlines the Thomist and Dantean (Inf., VII, 77 ff.) concept of Fortune. Fortune is not a blind distributor of good or bad luck but is a general dispenser of Providence and of Divine justice. As I have shown elsewhere,[20] Boccaccio conceived of Fortune in the introductions to the *Filostrato* and the *Teseida*, and in *Epistles* IV and V, in a purely fatalistic sense, dwelling upon autobiographical laments. However, he developed a more rigorous and scholastic concept, which is implicit in the whole *Decameron*, and in cantos XXXI-XXXVI of the *Amorosa Visione*. It is a concept which remained a basic idea in Boccaccio's whole work. It was adhered to explictly in the *Corbaccio* (49), the *Esposizioni* (VII, I, 71 ff.), and particularly in *De casibus* (VI, intr.; II, 16; IX, 27). It is a concept absolutely opposed to the humanistic-Renaissance idea which was to be developed from Pico della Mirandola to Machiavelli.

The medieval influence on Boccaccio is also easily discerned in his representation of Love. From the Introduction to the defense [of love] on the fourth day and on to the very end, aside from the merry, facile, carefree, or mundane remarks on Love (always isolated in an atmosphere of middle-class common sense), we get a constant sense of astonishment and almost of dismay in the interventions of the author, who is faced with the total and dazzling power of Love: a dismay which bears the echo of the whole impassioned debate carried on during those centuries. Also, it may bring to mind the anguished astonishment of Dante in the fifth canto of the *Inferno,* which Boccaccio himself stressed. Even Boccaccio's youthful works reflected a human experience dominated almost exclusively by Love. But in it throbbed such a feeling of suspense, such a moral preoccupation with regard to the power of this force, that Boccaccio felt the need to clarify the problem for his own sake. He took recourse, as I have shown elsewhere,[21] in the attitudes and scholastic schemata reflected in the essay writing of Andreas Cappellanus and of Boncompagno da Signa and in the meditative lyric poetry of Guittone d' Arezzo. In cantos XXXVIII-XLV of the *Amorosa Visione* he makes an attempt to compose his thoughts into a more rigorous formulation, in line with those theoretical schemata. Boccaccio does not hesitate to accept the suggestions and more severe distinctions of St. Thomas and Richard of St. Victor.

Boccaccio derived his most compelling declarations concerning the nature and the force of love from his rigorous theoretical formulation, which succeeded in infiltrating even the strictly narrative and imaginative tissue of the *Decameron.* Apart from the interruptions the author makes to comment on love, mentioned above (in Introduction, prologue to the fourth day, conclusion), Boccaccio has Emilia theorize in the prologue to the seventh novella of the fourth day on the contrast between the love of nobles and that of commoners, just as Andreas Cappellanus does in his *De Amore* (p. 235). In the introduction to the sixth novella of the third day and in the conclusion of the sixth of the tenth day, Fiammetta points out the paradigm of the degrees of love, also according to the example of Andreas Cappellanus as revised by Guittone (and see also VII, 7, 25 and IX, 2, 5). Pampinea, by proclaiming the duty of "always loving a lady of higher lineage" (I, 5) and Emilia by her lengthy anticonjugal argument in III, 7,[22] attain the casuistry of the *De Amore* (pp. 38 ff., *Regulae Amoris,* I and VIII). It would be easy to continue to demonstrate how the epilogue is influenced by the discussion on love and charity of Richard of St. Victor; how the subtle allegory of the first three ballads is based on elements of treatise writing which were continued in the lyrical poetry of Guittone; how Boccaccio's particularly frequent references in the fifth and seventh days to the relationship between the rational faculties and love reflect principles expounded by Saint Thomas (*Commentary on the Nichomachean Ethics*) and repeated by Dante (*Convivio,* II, xiii) and so on.

Boccaccio would accept as key themes only those truths that were central and essential to all medieval thought, only convictions that were rationally arrived at, and only problems that were sedulously debated and then victoriously resolved in his own conscience. Also, he used only themes that could symbolize human striving and virtue, tested and measured continually by those higher and almost semidivine forces of Fortune, of Love, of Ingenuity. So, also, although to a lesser degree, had the authors of works dating from the *Golden Legend* to the *Mirror of True Repentance* written examples and narratives devoted to the higher forces; in such a way the authors of the books of virtue and the books of examples arranged complex story-telling material behind a studied theoretical and moral façade. The Aesopic collections were also adapted and slanted toward exemplification in this way. Finally, Dante himself had continually brought the moral and prophetic message of his sacred poem down to the level of human episodes and human examples. Precisely in this manner Boccaccio himself theorized in the middle of his most compelling poetry, thinking perhaps of the novellas of his masterpiece: "Fabula est exemplaris seu demonstrativa sub figmento locutio, cuius amoto cortice, patet intentio fabulantis: et sic, si sub velamento fabuloso sapidum comperiatur aliquid, non erit supervacaneum fabulas edidisse. . . ." He added that this "species tertia [fabularum] potius historiae quam fabule similis est" (*Genealogia,* XIV, 9).

Boccaccio's need to present his narratives in the guise of historical testimonies, with a very particular meaning and value (which is illustrated in Chapter IV), is due to this broad and implied "exemplary" inspiration. It is clearly reflected also by the ideal design of the *Decameron*. This requirement, too, like all the other more elemental requirements of the *Decameron,* is presented in an explicit theoretical declaration in the prologue to the fourth day and in the conclusion; and it is also confirmed from the lips of Fiammetta in the novella IX, 5: ". . . if I had wished or might I wish to wander from the factual truth, I would have been able or would be able indeed to compose and relate it [this tale]; but because departure from the truth of past events, in story-telling, inflicts great loss of pleasure to the listeners, I shall relate it to you in its proper form and aided by the aforesaid reason."

The most active, effective, ideal, and imaginative premises of the *Decameron* also determine the chronological limits of the narrated actions, which were almost without exception (only three in a hundred novellas) the period immediately preceding Boccaccio's own time—that is, the stormy but splendid age of the last Crusades, the struggles of the communes against the Hohenstaufens, the adventurous events in southern Italy, and those decades of chivalry of the thirteenth and fourteenth centuries which witnessed the apogee of the Italian, but especially the Florentine, mercantile power. If the latter period formed part of the more personal experiences of Boccaccio, the former had influenced him through the recollections and the memories of those of his friends who were richest in human experience, such as Marino Bulgaro, Coppo di Borghese Domenichi, Pietro Canigiani (to mention three names as oral sources of the *Decameron*: V, 6; V, 9; VIII, 10). Also, perhaps, he was influenced by some bit of popular poetry, works dating from the time of the *cantari del Barbarossa* to the "laments" of the Anonimo Fiorentino (The Anonymous Florentine) and to the historical ballads of Pieraccio Tedaldi (cf., for example, *Amorosa Visione*, XLI and commentary).

It was the earlier age which had witnessed the formation of a more typically Italian civilization. It had marked the detachment and the differentiation of the political and civil life of the peninsula from that of the rest of the Empire. It was the time when the foundations of the greatest Italian Kingdom were laid, that of Naples (which was particularly dear to Boccaccio on account of his youthful experiences). That time had seen the rise of a new culture and a new literature, which, finally, had firmly established the hegemony of Italian merchants on the Mediterranean and in western Europe. That is, it represented the fabulous and heroic past of a splendid and adventurous present. It seemed to be the refulgent and blazing noon which had prepared the warm lights of an opulent afternoon, of that golden "autumn of the Middle Ages" which Boccaccio lives and pictures with such warm sentiment.

Indeed the history of Italy and of Europe between the eleventh and fourteenth centuries is the background, noble and majestic, of the loftier and more impassioned novellas.[23] The epic deeds, the Crusades in the East, create a more amazing and fabulous framework for the novellas of the Marchesa of Monferrato and of Messer Torello. The great internal and external wars which led to the firm foundation of the kingdoms of France and of England inspired the tragic and surprising tales of the Conte of Aguersa, of Giletta of Narbonne, of Alessandro Agolanti. The fierce struggles between the communes which characterize the Italian history of those centuries come alive again in the burnings and sackings which glow with a sinister light in the novellas of Guidotto of Cremona and of Madonna Francesca. The selfish interventions of foreign kings in the struggles are considered in the tales of Ser Ciappelletto and of Martellino; the feelings of terror which weighed on the life of the coastal towns, threatened by the Corsairs, are echoed in the novellas of Landolfo Ruffolo, of Gostanza, of Restituta. The sadness of a Rome abandoned to the bitter struggles of the Colonna and Orsini families lends its own color to the whole courtly novella of Pietro Boccamazza. The long series of wars and the vicissitudes of the kingdom of Naples and Sicily under the Normans, the Angevins, and the Aragonese—which characterize the history of Italy between the twelfth and fourteenth centuries— live again in the novellas of Gerbino, of Ghismonda, of Teodoro of Madonna Beritola, of Gianni of Procida, of Andreuccio of Perugia, of Nonna de'Pulci, of Re Carlo, of Re Pietro, and so on.

In the course of these novellas, idealized portraits of the protagonists of the history of those centuries are also presented: Tancred and Guglielmo the Good, the two Fredericks of Swabia, and Manfred, the two Charleses, and Robert of Anjou, Pietro and Federico of Aragon and Ruggiero of Lauria, Guy de Monfort and Gianni of Procida; and also Can Grande della Scala and Currado Malaspina, Filippo il Bornio and the "Young King"; Pope Alexander III and the king of Scotland, Pope Boniface and Saladin; the king of Jerusalem, Guy de Lusignan; and Guillaume de Monferrat, Azzo d'Este and Guinigi da Camino. . . . These are figures which always are portrayed in a heroic atmosphere, against backgrounds made precious by a whole throng of admirers; figures which speak their lofty words or perform their noble feats before astonished onlookers, without whom it seems as though those words and those generous deeds could not have come to be. They are epic figures, figures of song and romance, to whom the precious and laudatory atmosphere of the last day is particularly suited.

Boccaccio also includes some notable contemporaries in the novellas: Guglielmo Borsieri and Master Albert of Bologna, Cecco Angiolieri and Guido Cavalcanti, Cimabue and Giotto, not to mention other minor figures of artists, such as Mico of Siena and Carlo Figiovanni. Also, we feel the continual, but implicit, presence of Dante.

The reader of the *Decameron* gradually forms an imposing and very human picture of a decisive period of the history and the civilization of Italy. It is a picture painted in heroic and dazzling colors. It is an epic (that is, an interpretation beyond the events) of that age in which the chivalric and feudal life coincided splendidly with the pulsating and fervid life of the "companies" and the "arts" (trades). The stately structure of the empire was breaking up into many kingdoms, principalities, and communes.

Boccaccio's warm recollection of the immediate past, notwithstanding its fabulous and heroic colors, notwithstanding its gallant figures caught in always nobly statuesque attitudes, is not composed along the nostalgic lines of the Dantean evocations of Guido Guerra or Marco Lombardo or Cacciaguida. Beside the eminent and gilded world of the kings and the knights, Boccaccio sets the industrious and adventurous society of his own age. Federico degli Alberighi and

Lisabetta of Messina have a human nobility not inferior to that of Carlo Vecchio or Ghismonda. They wear no crown, but they possess a humanity perhaps deeper and closer to our own sensibilities; they possess a generosity, simpler but more inward and decorous.[24] Gentile de' Carisendi is no less chivalrous than Re Pietro. Cisti Fornaio is a no less shrewd and elegant jester than Guido Cavalcanti. Andreuola has an aristocratic pride not inferior to that of the Marchioness of Monferrato. The adventures and the conquests of the Florentines are set against broad backgrounds (the vast stormy Mediterranean with its pirate fleets; France, jealous and distrustful of the enterprising Florentines; England cold, and a little mysterious, like an *ultima Thule*).

Boccaccio was deeply attuned to the spirit and culture of the Middle Ages, as has been said. For this reason, he instinctively feels and succeeds in portraying in the *Decameron* the wonderful and ideal continuity between the age of the knights of the sword and the world of the knights of human ingenuity and industry; between those regal figures, solitary and shining with gems, and the heroes of the Italian middle class. Boccaccio linked the age of the Crusades with that of the formation of the free republics and the free communes, the establishment in Naples of a kingdom intermediary between East and West, the great wars of France and England.

In its themes, its structure, and in its imagination the *Decameron* stands as a monument to the highest style of the Middle Ages. But as with epics and literary testaments in general, the *Decameron* glorified an age that was coming to an end.

The massive critical tradition that sees the *Decameron* as the manifest of a new era has erred as the result of two important influences. The first, expounded by Olympia Morata and Pope Blount, was anti-clerical and anti-Roman. Based upon Lutheran polemics, it flourished from the sixteenth century on. The second is a nineteenth-century concept which contrasted the "darkness" of the Middle Ages with the "light" of Humanism. According to this tradition, Dante was the poet of transcendental realities, while Boccaccio was the champion of a new civilization which exalted the earthly life.[25] The divine comedy had bowed to the human comedy.

The critics failed to notice that this theory destroyed the whole design of the *Decameron*—the color and symbolization, the gallant and vibrant humanity. Compared to the new Renaissance poetry, the *Decameron* appeared only crude and violent, its development too tumultuous.

Actually, the *Decameron* does not stand in opposition to the *Divina Commedia;* rather it seems to complement it. That is, each presents an aspect of Italian medieval society, and together they portray the harmony of the eagerness for the real and the quest for the transcendent which characterized that age. The poem of Dante summarizes the intellectual and moral speculation of Italian society and in a way is an intimation and prophecy of the age to come, while the *Decameron* is the representation, or rather the consecration, artistic and, in a sense, metaphysical, of the history of every man and the daily reality of that very human world. It too is a *summa;* the *summa* of the toilsome life, rich in adventures and in snares, in which, every day, man measured his abilities and his strength; it is the *summa* of a world which, according to its own scholastic thought, is no less real and no less sturdy than that which was dominated by the transcendence sung by Dante.

NOTES

1. The letter of Francesco Buondelmonti has been published in its entirety, with ample commentary and identification of the personalities and facts to which it alludes, in the first of my articles, "Per il Testo del Decameron—La prima diffusione del Decameron," *Studi di Filologia Italiana,* VIII, 1950.
2. The pages of the Anonymous Florentine in the Magliabechiana manuscript, from which these lines are taken, have also been published integrally and illustrated in the article cited in Note 1 above.
3. The little sure information available on Mannelli, from among the numerous fabulous stories which created his legend, is collected in the article already cited.
4. For descriptions of the manuscripts of the *Decameron* mentioned in these pages, and for more precise documentation concerning the elements referred to here, see my article cited in the first note and also the second of the series "Per il Testo del Decameron—Testimonianze della

Tradizione Vulgata," *Studi di Filologia Italiana,* XI, 1953. For The First Illustrations of the Decameron, see *Boccaccio medievale,* pp. 219 ff.

5. For this also see the first of my articles "Per il Testo del *Decameron,*" *Boccaccio medievale,* pp. 308 ff. Petrach must have known the *Decameron,* probably as early as 1351. Furthermore, in the same *Senile* of 1373 he states "cum et mihi semper ante multos annos placuisset" (and as I always liked it many years ago), and shows a thorough acquaintance with the book; he speaks with a certain precision of the Introduction, of the prologue to the fourth day, of the copious amorous material, of the joking and merry passages, of the elegiac and tragic novellas. Also, the undertaking of translating a vernacular work into Latin is unique in the activities of Petrarch and emphasizes the exceptional character of his interest.

6. For this attitude and for the precise quotations see in general V. Branca, *Linee di una storia della critica al Decameron,* Rome, 1939, Chapter I, and "Per il Testo del Decameron," 1.

7. For the *cassoni* (chests) inspired by the novellas of the *Decameron* see *Boccaccio medievale,* pp. 219 ff. In the *Paradiso degli Alberti* (ed. A. Wesselofsky, Bologna, 1867) note especially the novella of Bonifazio Uberti (III, pp. 175 ff. and see II, pp. 284 ff.), full of refrains from novella X, 7, and the episode in which a sort of juggler, at Sesto, relates and praises the novella of Belcolore (II, p. 258; see also Chapters IV and V of Wesselofsky's preface and D. Guerri, *La Corrente popolare nel Rinascimento,* 1931, p. 72.) As for Sacchetti, more than the famous canzone on the death of Boccaccio, in which neither the *Decameron* nor any other vernacular work is mentioned, the conclusion of the first period of the Preface in which he sought to justify his work: ". . . and coming at last to a consideration of the excellent Florentine poet Messer Giovanni Boccacci who, describing the Book of the Hundred Novellas as a material thing as regards his noble talent, notwithstanding that it is widely circulated abroad and so sought after that even in France and England they have translated it into their own tongue . . . I, Franco Sacchetti of Florence, as a man of little learning and refinement, have proposed to write the present work. . . ." Amid the high praises, noteworthy is the reflection of the most authoritative circles, where the *Decameron* was considered "a material thing." In the last paragraph of my profile *Giovanni Boccaccio* (Milan, Marzorati, 1956) I have referred briefly to these imitations and to this success of the *Decameron* in Italian and in European literature.

8. For example, Piero di Daniello Fei incorporated in the last day of the *Decameron* a tale derived from one of the most noted of the *Pecorone* (Laurenziano, XLII, 4); other men interwove novellas of Boccaccio with some by Sacchetti (cod. Nazionale Firenze, II, IV, 12) or by Masuccio Salernitano (Mediceo Palatino, XC), by Leonardo Bruni, and others by anonymous story-tellers (Laurenziano, XC, 89; Vaticano Lat. 5337). Still others wanted to join to Boccaccio's novellas tales which had especially delighted them, such as the one about the Grasso Legnaiuolo (cod. of Stockholm) or two anonymous but well-known stories (cod of Modena α 6, 6); Domenico Caronelli, finally, got the idea of prolonging the noble and heroic rhythms of the Tenth Day with an exemplary epistle; and so on. For the entire problem and its related documentation see the articles: "Per il Testo del Decameron."

9. A similar reticence in mentioning Boccaccio's masterpiece appears also in the epistle of Salutati himself. In his epistle III, 25 he carefully names all the Latin works but implies the *Decameron* and the Italian works; in epistles IV, 12 and XIV, 18 he speaks only of the Latin works. When perhaps he must allude to the *Decameron* he uses a very vague formula, "librum illum Boccacci" (*Epistole aggiunte,* IV, Rome, 1891 ff.).

10. The antecedents of the various novellas of the *Decameron* to which there are allusions in this and the following pages are given in the notes to my edition of the *Decameron.* Therefore I give here only brief mentions, referring the reader to those notes for precise documention.

11. E. Rohde, *Der griechische Roman,* Leipzig, 1900, pp. 538 ff.; see also A. Calderini, *Le avventure di Cherea e Calliroe,* Turin, 1913, pp. 203 ff.

12. For these last two examples see *Boccaccio medievale,* pp. 215 and 301 ff.

13. V. Branca, *Il cantare trecentesco e il Boccaccio del Filostrato e del Teseida,* Florence, 1936; see also the introduction and the commentary to G. Boccaccio, *Amorosa Visione,* critical edition by V. Branca, Florence, 1944.

14. G. Billanovich, *Restauri boccacceschi,* Rome, 1945; E. de Bruyne, *Etudes d'esthétique médiévale,* Bruges, 1946; *L'Esthétique du moyen âge,* Louvain, 1947; E. R. Curtius, *Europäischer Literatur and lateinisches Mittelalter,* Bern, 1948 (especially Chapters IV and VIII).

15. On this point see below, pages 207 ff., and Chapters Three, Five, and *Boccaccio medievale,* Chapter Two, especially for the quotations from Joannes de Garlandia. On Alberico da Montecassino, see the Flores rhetorici, III, VII, VIII (ed. Inguanez-Villard, Montecassino, 1938) and for the diffusion of the precept consult likewise the *Liber Decem*

Capitulorum of Marbod Bishop of Rennes (*Patrologia Latina,* Vol. 171), which declares that literary works have the more value the greater the alterations of styles and colors (see especially Chapter I). This is a precept singularly evocative in connection with the structure and development of the *Decameron* and, moreover, quite widely diffused, as is shown by E. Faral *Les Arts poétiques du XIIe et du XIIIe siècle,* Paris, 1923, pp. 86 ff.

16. As in the other references to the laws of medieval Christian ethics from St. Augustine and Boethius to Dante, it would be out of place to give extensive quotations and precise documentation, if, for no other reason, than because after the misunderstandings and misinterpretations which arose especially following Croce it is not always easy to agree on these points. Let us be content to refer to the previously quoted treatises of De Bruyne and Curtius, to which may be added J. Maritain, *Art et Scolastique,* Paris, 1927; H. H. Glunz, *Die Literaturästhetik des europäischen Mittelalters,* Bochum, 1937; M. De Wulf, "L'esthétique du XIIIe siècle," *Art et Beauté,* Louvain, 1943; J. Huizinga, *Autunno del Medioevo,* Florence, 1944; E. Gilson, *L'esprit de la philosophie médiévale,* Paris, 1944, and *La Philosophie au Moyen Age,* Paris, 1947; H. Pouillon, "La beauté transcendentale chez les scolastique," *Arch. d'hist. Doctr. et litt. du Moyen Age,* 1946, with an appendix of hitherto unpublished texts, works which above all others I feel it my duty to name because they have helped me greatly in the general formulation of the problem (see also R. Montano, "Estetica del Medioevo," *Delta,* N.S., 1952 and "L'Estetica nel pensiero cristiano," *Grande Antologia Filosofica,* Milan, 1955 with an interesting anthology of texts). It is perhaps timely, however, to repeat at least, that medieval thought, while it ignored wholly or in part the subjective side of artistic creation, based its esthetics on the consciousness of a double dimension of the beautiful: beauty, that is, as affirmed by Hugh and Richard of St. Victor (*Didascalion,* VII, 4; *De Gratia Contemplationis,* II, 17), Saint Bonaventure (*Itinerarium Mentis in Deum,* II, concl.), Saint Thomas (*Summa Th.,* II, IIq., 180, a.2) and so on, is "of the place, of the motion, of the quality and of the form" of things of the senses, but its value is of a metaphysical order: that is, in so far as those things bring significance of the divine Intellect. Hence the tendency to particularism and analysis, to ascribe them and then enclose them in the Superior Reality: because the consciousness of truths included in even very small things, and which must then be revealed by the acting intellect (such as the colors of the light), is a central position in the esthetic vision of the Middle Ages. "Est veritas in omnibus qui sunt entia quia hic sunt quae

in summa Veritate sunt," St. Thomas himself states (*Opuscoli*, Bari, 1917, II, p. 519), quoting Saint Anselm (*De Veritate*, VII, 10, 13); and, taking positions previously stated precisely by Scotus Erigena (De Bruyne, *Etudes*, I, pp. 359 ff.). Guibert de Nogent insists at length on the concept that "omne illud quod temporaliter speciosum est alternae Illius speciei quasi speculum est" *(Monodiarium*, I, 2 in *Patrologia latina*, vol. 156, col. 840) and Hugh of St. Victor in his Commentaria on St. Denis (II, 1) develops the idea that "visibilis pulchritudo invisibilis pulchritudinis imago est" (in *Patrologia latina*, vol. 175, col. 949). Indeed, for St. Thomas precisely the images and themes "quae magis elongantur a Deo veriorem nobis faciunt aestimationem quot sit supra illud quod de Deo dicimus vel cogitamus" (*Summa Th.,* I, q. 1, a.9); and Richard of St. Victor states that "quod in imo respicit in laudem Creatoris assurgit" and that in works of art "innumera invenimus pro quibus divini numeris dignationem digne mirari et venerari debeamus. Opus itaque naturale et opus artificiale quia sibi invicem cooperantur quasi e latere sibi altrinsecus iunguntur et sibi invicem muta contemplatione copulantur" (*De Gratia Contemplationis,* II, 5, in *Patrologia latina*, vol. 196). Art—daughter of Nature and "almost a grandchild of God"—tries to follow Nature in revealing in men and in their actions, in things, and in their aspects, signs of God and of his Providence. These positions, central to the medieval esthetic vision, were also central to the poetics of Boccaccio, a devout pupil of Dionigi of San Sepolcro, and a reader of St. Augustine, Boethius, Hugh, and Richard of St. Victor, of St. Thomas himself, of whom he personally copied some texts in the present Ambrosiano A 204 inf., in the very years of the writing of the *Decameron)* to such a degree that he repeated them sedulously—albeit without any systematic exactness and with quite literary variations—whenever he went as far as making statements of theory (see for example *Vita di Dante,* Chap. XXII; *Genealogia,* XIV, 7-9 and 13-18; *Esposizioni,* I, 1, 70 ff., and see Chapters II and IV and *Boccaccio Medievale* IX of this book). It must have come naturally to him, therefore, to try to rise from the particularism and the episodic multiplicity of cases narrated (even the numblest and basest) to an "ideal design" which would reveal and arrest their eternal truths: rather, indeed, Truth itself. For these problems in general see: E. Auerbach, *Literatursprache und Publikum in der lateinischen Spatantike und im Mittelalter,* Bern, 1958, and *Studi su Dante,* Milan, 1963; B. Nardi, *Dal "Convivio" alla "Commedia,"* Rome, 1960; D. W. Robertson, "A Preface to Chaucer," in *Studies in Medieval Perspectives,* Princeton, 1963; E. Gilson, "Poésie et verité dans la genealogia de Boccace," in *Studi sul Boccaccio,* II, 1964.

17. F. Neri, "Il disegno ideale del Decameron," *Poesia e Storia,* Turin, 1946.

18. Uguccione da Pisa, *Derivationes* (still unpublished; see the quotations in *Studi Danteschi,* IV, 1921, p. 26); Joannes de Garlandia, *Poetria . . . de arte prosayca metrica et rithmica,* edited by G. Mari, Berlin, 1902 (*Romanische Forschungen,* XIII, pp. 296 ff.); Dante, *De Vulgari Eloquentia,* II, IV, 6, *Epistole,* XIII, 28-32. See also E. Faral, *Les Arts poétiques du XIIe et XIIIe siècle,* cit. (which bears witness to the enormous diffusion of the texts to which we have referred: for example, more than 80 manuscripts are indicated for the *Poetria* of John of Garland).

19. See the interesting documentation presented in this connection by E. G. Kern, "The Gardens in the Decameron's 'cornice,'" *Publications of the Modern Language Association of America,* LXVI, 1951. See also Giovanni Getto, *Vita di forme e forme di vita nel "Decameron,"* Torino, 1958, pp. 1 ff.; A Prete, "Ritmo esterno e tempi spirituali nella cornice del *Decameron,"* in *Aevum,* XXXVIII, 1964.

20. See *Amorosa Visione,* ed. cit., pp. 569 ff., also V. Cioffari, "The conception of Fortune in the Decameron," *Italica,* December 1940; V. Cioffari, *Fortune in Dante's Fourteenth Century Commentators,* Cambridge, Mass., 1944; V. Cioffari, "The function of Fortune in Dante, Boccaccio and Machiavelli," *Italica,* XXIV, 1947.

21. *Boccaccio Medievale,* Chapters 4 and 7, and the commentary on cantos XXXVIII ff. of the *Amorosa Visione* in my edition, cit.

22. These correspondences between the theoretical positions of Boccaccio on love (Andreas Cappellanus, Boncompagno da Signa, Guittone, the Pseudo Egidio) are documented and studied more closely in *Boccaccio Medievale,* Chapter 7, including the development of Boccaccio's thought from the youthful works on down to the *Decameron.* The indicated pages of the *De Amore* are those of the critical edition published by Trojel, Hauniae, 1898.

23. Also for the documentation relating to such rapid allusions to persons and events in the novellas of the *Decameron* as are contained in these pages, see the notes of the commentary previously quoted. An ideal integration of the tableau merely alluded to here will be found in Chapter IV.

24. This very human note on the descriptions in the *Decameron* was first

formulated by Attilio Momigliano, with his penetrating acuteness, in
his commentary on the *Decameron (49 novelle,* Milan, 1924); and later
elegantly stressed by Bosco (*Il Decameron,* Rieti, 1929).

25. Such critical positions are studied in the previously quoted *Linee di una
storia della critica al Decameron* (including the exact quotations from the
works referred to above, together with the names of the individual
authors). It is astonishing to find them again in the brilliant and
evocative, yet impressionistic, synthesis of Auerbach, *Mimesis* (Bern,
1946, especially Chapter IX), in which it is repeated that in the
Decameron the characters live on the earth and only on the earth, of the
flesh and only of the flesh, that the tragic novellas have no immediacy
either of description or of sentiment, that courtly love is missing or is
merely a glimmer, and so on, even to real deafness to the texts themselves. For example, in the analysis of the novellas of Ciappelletto no
moral judgment is to be found. But what of the sinister initial portrait?
Or of Ghismonda? Or of the "eaten heart"? (There is no stylistic unity
but mere rhetorical sentimentality.) See B. J. Layman, "Eloquence of
Pattern in Boccaccio's *Tale of the Falcon,*" in *Italica,* XLVI, 1969.

CHAPTER 2

Structures of the Prose:
School of Rhetoric and
Rhythms of Fantasy

Medieval life, as portrayed in the *Decameron,* becomes completely apparent to the reader only after he has supplied the many elements and techniques that Boccaccio relied on to write each episode. Boccaccio interprets the rules for writing evolved in earlier centuries, but the complexity that he mastered has only recently been revealed through critical reconstruction (it was distorted by its enthusiastic readers from the start).[1]

The prose makes only a few references to the classic models. Rather it has been influenced by Latin prose, such as that of Livy, the idol of the great Italian "rhétoriqueurs" of the thirteenth century, instead of such writers as Cicero, worshipped by Petrarch. It was Livy who influenced Boccaccio's rhythms and narrative (Boccaccio had translated the *Histories* [2] during the same years he was writing the *Decameron*).

In summary, Boccaccio's whole development is influenced strictly by medieval writing.[3] That is, Boccaccio was much concerned with rhetoric.

In his earliest writings we see Boccaccio trying to master the intricacies of rhetoric, which, as a great master has observed, is "le

métier à côté du génie: le métier qui, au Moyen Age, a une importance aussi grande qu'à n'importe quell'époque" (the craft next to
genius: the craft which, in the Middle Ages, has an importance as
great as in any epoch.)[4]

Paolo of Perugia and Dionigi of Borgo San Sepolcro, the most
authoritative guides of Boccaccio's Neapolitan apprenticeship, introduced him to the secrets of rhymed prose. On his table, next to the
classics (from Valerius Maximus to Apuleius and Saint Augustine),
Boccaccio had the great authors of medieval prose and rhetoric
(Boethius, Fuilgentius, Bede, Hilary of Poitiers, Jacopus de Voragine,
the *Speculum Humanae Salvationis*, on down to the *Rettorica* of Brunetto
Latini and the epistles of Dante).

Boccaccio was also inspired by the difficult art of "dittare"
(poetical composition) and *cursus*, when he was writing his first
prose.[5] Indeed, the epistles of 1339, in their strangely "glossamatic
and enigmatic" Latin, reveal a patient and rhetorical work based on
Apuleius, Saint Augustine, Boethius, the *Hisperica Famina*, and the
epistles of Dante, all polished by a rigorous scholastic attention to the
cursus and the *clausulae* most recommended by the *artes dictandi* (for
example, the *clausulae querulae* [peevish stipulations], the versified
clausulae).[6] The prose of the *Filocolo* is characterized by a stylistic
excess and a florid starching of strict rhetorical observance, and by a
predilection for the most acclaimed and showiest *cursus*, known as
velox, although Boccaccio gave it Hilarian refinements.[7] Boccaccio
also attempted to create artificial symmetries and musical cadences,
clearly aspiring to the technique of rhymed prose, which is apparent
in the *Comedia* and the *Fiammetta*.[8]

Boccaccio's concern with rhetoric during his youth,[9] which
dominated his writing right down to the time he began the *Decameron*,
certainly continued to influence that masterpiece as well.

However, just as Boccaccio's tumultuously autobiographical
world and his too undiscriminating and confused cultural enthusiasm find a proper balance and definition in the *Decameron*, so the
suggestions of medieval rhetoric are no longer followed slavishly, but
used with the sure judgment and the freedom of a great artist. The
master "rhétoriqueurs" of the Middle Ages had gradually begun to
use their subtle inventions for ornament. Cassiodorus was the first to

do so. He had proclaimed "Dictio semper agrestis est quae aut sensibus electis per moram non comitur aut verborum minime proprietatibus explicatur. Loqui nobis communiter datus est: solus ornatus est qui discernit indoctos." [10] Alberico da Montecassino also turned from medieval influences as did Boncompagno of Signa, about whom, a few years before, Boccaccio had stated: "dictatoris officium est materias sibi exibitas vel a se aliquando inventas congruo latino et appositione ornare." [11] In the *Decameron* Boccaccio turns from this concept, which he had previously accepted and applied in the minor works. That is, he turns from the utterly scholastic spirit which had shaped that body of literary precepts among the foremost, authoritative masters, the ones he had most admired, such as Cassiodorus and Boncompagno.[12]

He still felt deeply all the force and the worth of the precepts, but he considered them, really, to be a "métier à côté du génie" (a craft next to, on a par with, genius). He no longer tried to use them to ornament his prose but as a means to express his imaginative intuition; he used them freely, deviating from the examples and practice of the most authoritative literary masters.

It is most particularly in the Introduction and in the "frame" that Boccaccio strictly observes the rhetorical canons stemming from the great John of Garland.[13] The *cursus planus,* so dear to Boccaccio, dominates the first lines:

Umana cosa è l'aver compassione ágli afflitti *(planus);* e come che a ciascuna persona stea bene, a coloro è massimaménte richiésto *(planus)* li quali già hanno di conforto avúto mestiére *(planus),* e hannol trováto in alcúni *(planus):* fra' quali, se alcuno mai n' ébbe bisógno *(planus)* o gli fu caro o già ne ricevétte piacére *(planus),* io sono uno di quégli *(planus).*

Boccaccio applies the *cursus* throughout the opening pages of the *Decameron* in a methodical and systematic manner, which he does not do in the novellas themselves. In the novellas, if we except the tenth day, he writes in a free and episodic manner, verging on casualness.[14]

By means of symmetrical constructions and "very sensitive"

clauses, Boccaccio conveys a feeling of gravity in his description of the plague. As he does in so many of the novellas, he begins the narration with the solemn, declarative *Dico* (I say), considered so important in the *Rettorica* of Brunetto Latini and Dante himself:[15]

> Dico adunque che già erano gli anni della fruttifera Incarnazione del Figliuolo di Dio al numero pervenuti di 1348, quando nell'egregia città di Firenze, oltre ad ogni altra italica bellissima pervenne la mortifera pestilenza (note the final *velox*).

But in the novellas we find such a deliberate and scholastic stylistic construction for the most part in the preambles, elegantly tortuous as they are in their intellectualistic or moral circumlocutions. It is enough to call to mind the first lively but colorless tale of Ser Ciappelletto (with one *velox* parallel to another):

> Manifesta cosa è che, sí come le cose temporali tutte sono transitorie e mortali, così in sé e fuor di sé essere piene di noia e d'angoscia e di fatica, e ad infiniti pericoli soggiacere *(velox);* alle quali senza niun fallo né potremmo noi, che viviamo mescolati in esse e che siamo parte d'esse, durare né ripararci, se spezial grazia di Dio forza e avvedimento non ci prestasse *(velox)*. La quale a noi e in noi non è da credere per alcuno nostro merito discenda. . . .

The carefully calibrated prose structure of the Introduction is repeated with even greater rigidity in the discourses of the narrators, speaking with broad and grave circumlocutions, in which the measured, aristocratic reserve of the assembled guests and the image of their embellished and lordly life is reflected.

As has been said, Boccaccio relies on symmetry and, in the final *clausula,* on the most common artifices of medieval literary style (inversions, separations, truncations, and so on). In the solemn opening pages, moreover, he follows a typically medieval model, such as Paulus Diaconus.

E nel vero, se io potuto avessi onestamente per altra parte menarvi a quello che io desidero che per così aspro sentiero come sia questo, io l'avrei volentier fatto (Intro. 7).[16]

That stylistic law is reflected also in a speech by Pampinea, but in her words the inversion and the violent separation are made to serve an anguished psychological state, and seem to suspend the most terrible words and impressions until the outburst of horror is reached in that verb isolated, fearfully, at the end:[17]

E se alle nostre case torniamo, non so se a voi così come a me addiviene: io, di molta famiglia, niuna altra persona in quella se non la mia fante trovando, impaurisco e quasi tutti i capelli addosso me sento arricciare; e parmi, dovunque vado o dimoro per quella, l'ombre di coloro che sono trapassati vedere, e non con quegli visi che io soleva, ma con una vista orribile, non so donde in loro nuovamente venuta, spaventarmi (Intro. 59).

Boccaccio's use of rhetoric in the speeches is, as Schiaffini aptly remarked, "filtered through poetry." The inversions, separations, and truncations are not immediately noticed; only after reading Boccaccio awhile will the reader become aware that the bleak, desolate impression is conveyed more from these rhythms than from things said.

Boccaccio reveals his ability to create the most unexpected and surprising effects in the novellas. Studying the pages of the novellas, solemn and yet dashing, alive, ranging from the heroic to the grotesque, we can see how Boccaccio develops his filigrees, pale and worn, obtains the most imaginative and most overwhelmingly human picturizations. We can understand his determination to search out, to plumb the depths of the fantastic image by means of subtle phonic implications, as well as his struggle with words, his genius for composing the various parts of speech in order to achieve a word order appropriate to his task; not logical, but poetic.

Seduced by the sorcery of an iridescent prose and struck, as if by lightning, by a lofty mirage, Boccaccio had devoted himself to those texts which had established the solemn, artificial style of Isidore of Seville.[18]

Paolo of Perugia probably gave Boccaccio the *Soliloquia* or *Synonyma* of Isidore of Seville, which were considered the best models of prose writing.[19]

He read the writings of St. Augustine, the *Sermons,* that rhetoricians also considered their best model [20] and which caused Boccaccio to transcribe the praise of peace in his epistle *Sacre Famis.* Boccaccio resorted to alliteration, the so-called "etymological figure," puns and plays on words, and the insistent repetition of a given term, following the examples of St. Augustine. Thus Boccaccio portrays the mourning and despairing circle of maidservants around Ghismonda who, "da compassion vinte tutte piagevano e lei pietosamente della cagion del suo pianto domandavano invano e molto più come meglio sapevano e potevano" (IV, 1, 56) (overcome with pity, with streaming eyes begged her in vain to tell them the cause of her sorrow, and a great deal more, as best they knew how). With the mistiest nostalgic indefiniteness Boccaccio indicates how Ghismonda gains hope after hearing that name of good omen, Carapresa (V, 2). Throughout the whole marvelous first novella of the fifth day he reflects the etymology used in *Cimone.* By means of a pun Boccaccio indicates the moral ambiguity of Ferondo's wife facing her tempter, the abbot: "Sooner would I die than say to any one anything that you say to me that I should not say" (mi lascierei innanzi morire che io cosa dicessi ad altrui che voi mi diceste che io non dicessi: III, 8, 12). He renders old Re Carlo's obsession with passion by means of a repetition upon the prophetic word *amor:* "for love of whom the sister . . . *loved,* so in the *amor*ous trap she entangled herself" (per *amor* di cui la sorella . . . ancora amava, s'nell'*amor*ose panie s'invescò: X, 6, 24).

But subtle and magical though it be, Boccaccio abandoned this style in the *Decameron* in favor of one less rigid, to express his freest and most unbiased imaginings. Boccaccio has the priest of Varlungo express himself in free etymological figures, while pursuing and finally convincing Belcolore:

io voglio che tu sappi che egli [questo tabarro] è di duagio infino in treagio e hacci di quegli nel nostro popolo che il tengono di quattraggio: VIII, 2, 35

I want you to know that this cloak is made of *dua*gio, even *trea*gio, and some of our people go so far as to take it for *quattr*agio [this is a play on 2, 3, 4; due, tre, quattro; duagio was a cloth from medieval Douai, in Flanders.]

Buffalmacco too, twitting Master Simon:

voi non apparaste miga l'abbiccì in su la mela ... anzi l'apparaste bene in sul mellone: VIII, 9, 64.

you didn't learn the alphabet on the apple.... rather, you learned it on the melon. ["Mela" means the "a-b-c table" as well as "apple." "Mellone" also means "pumpkin," that is, "pumpkin-head" as well as "melon."]

Boccaccio also uses alliteration comically to emphasize greediness. On hearing the description of the Land of Plenty "cotesto è buon paese: . . . che si fa de' capponi che cuocon coloro?" (VIII, 3, 10), and in word plays, as those which prepare Giotto's thrust at Forese: "credi tu che egli credesse che tu fossi il miglior dipintor del mondo, come tu se'?" ... "credo che egli il crederebbe allora che guardando voi, egli crederebbe che voi sapeste l'abbicci" (VI, 5, 14). Boccaccio also creates the phantasmal and ambiguously grotesque bursts of eloquence of that "great rhetorician" worthy of "Tullius himself or perhaps even Quintilian" who is none other than Frate Cipolla (VI, 10). Finally, Boccaccio created the ludicrous, pompous variations of Maso del Saggio and of Bruno (VIII, 3 and VIII, 9), pinned on these devices, all stretched on the grotesqueness of a rhetoric reflected by the distorting mirror of a grandiose epic of mockery.

From these same masters who followed the style of Isidore, Boccaccio drew also the most complex and most "secret" [that is, "closed" in meaning to all but the literary initiate] laws that he followed during his prose period. That is, he followed those laws for the placement in parallel members, at the beginnings of which the same word is repeated three or four times, and consonances, especially in the final clauses. Boccaccio relates the most lofty moments of the *Decameron* with this rhythm from the tragic and almost hieratic speech of Ghismonda (IV, 1, 52 ff.) and the anaphorical finale—on three rhymed gerunds—of the novella of Re Carlo (X, 6, 36), to the conclusion of one of the most rhetorical tales, that of the tenth day, of Tito and Gisippo. Its structure recalls that of the Introduction,[21] in that Boccaccio uses a succession of waves of groups of three periods cast upon anaphora and homoeoteleuton, intertwining adjectives and nouns. The novella is always governed by the rule of three, by highly elaborated rhythmic parallelisms, by a sequence of *cursus* often linked together:

Quale amore, quale richezza, qual parentado avrébbe 'l fervòre [*planus*], le lágrime e' sospírí [*velox*] di Tito con tanta efficacia fatti a Gisippo nel cuóre sentíre [*planus*], che egli per ciò la bella spósa gentíle (*planus*) e amata da lui, avesse fatta divenir di Tito, se non costei? Quali leggi, quáli minácce [*planus*], quáli paúre [*planus*], le giovanili braccia di Gisippo ne' luóghi solitári [*trispondaicus*], ne' luóghi oscúri [*planus*] nel letto proprio avrebbe fatto astenere dagli abbracciamenti della vaga giovane, forse talvolta invitatrice, se non costei? Quali stati, qua' meriti, quáli avánzi [*planus*], avrebbon fatto Gisippo non curar di perdere i suoi parenti e quei di Sofronia [*planus*], non curar de' disonesti mormorii del popolazzo, non curar delle beffe e degli scherni per sodisfár all' amíco [*planus*], se non costei? E d'altra parte, chi avrebbe Tito, senza alcuna deliberazione, possendosi egli onestamente infígnere di vedére [*velox*], fatto prontissimo a procurare la propria morte, per levar Gisippo dalla croce la quale egli stésso si procacciáva [*velox*], se non costei? Chi avrebbe Tito, senza alcúna dilazióne [*trispondaicus*], fatto liberalissimo a communicare il suo ampíssimo património [*velox*], con Gisippo, al quale la fortuna il suo avea tolto, se non costei? Chi avrebbe Tito, senza alcúna suspizióne [*trispondaicus*], fatto ferventissimo a concedere la propria sorella per móglie a Gisippo [*planus*], il quale vedeva poverissimo e in estrema miseria posto, se non costei? Desiderino adúnque gl'uómini [*tardus*] la moltitúdine de' consórti [*velox*], le túrbe de' fratélli [*trispondaicus*] e la gran quantità de' figliuoli e con gli lor denari il numero de' servidóri s'accréscano [*tardus*]; e non guardino, qualunque s'è l'uno di questi, ogni minimo suo perícolo piú temére [*velox*], che sollicitudine aver di tor via [*planus*] i grándi del pádre [*cursus*] o del fratéll' o del signóre [*trispondaicus*], dove tutto il contrario far si véd' all' amíco [*planus*] (X 8, 113ss.).

Boccaccio has used the technique of the parallelism on *tricoli* or *tetracoli* evolved by Isidore of Seville but which Isidore ascribed to Saint Cyprian and especially to the *Sermones* of Saint Augustine, the devoted disciple of the Apuleian rhetoricians.[22] However, Boccaccio took this technique, created for the gravity of the noblest prose, to create fanciful or ludicrous notes in the *Decameron*, for example in the merrily roguish portrait of the man-servant of Frate Cipolla (VI, 10), which opens with the ternary rhythm of those three nicknames arranged in a rascally crescendo:

... il quale alcuni chiamavano Guccio Balena e altri Guccio Imbratta e chi gli diceva Guccio Porco (15)

... whom some called Guccio the Whale and others Dirty Guccio and some called him Guccio the Pig

Boccaccio finishes the portrayal with a "grotesque short melodic air" *(cabaletta grotesca)*, three cadenced series of three rhymed adjectives:

egli è tardo sugliardo bigiardo; nigligente disubidente maldicente; trascutato smemorato scostumato (17)

he is sluggish disgusting untruthful; negligent disobedient slanderous; careless forgetful licentious

which seems to be echoed, although in less energetic and emphatic tone, in the rhythmed and assonanced presentation of Nuta, the fleshy and malodorous queen of the heart of this servant-Falstaff:

grassa e grossa e mal fatta ... tutta sudata unta e affumicata (21)

[she is] fat and heavy and short and ill-shapen . . . all sweaty
and greasy and smoky

This comic opera rhythm which he superimposes on the rhetoric of Isidore, Boccaccio uses again in the sequences of adjectives
which make caricatures of some of the most immortal blockheads
created in the *Decameron:* whether to emphasize the clumsy, childish
behavior of Ferondo, sent to Purgatory by the enterprising abbot
and by his too tender-hearted wife, "la mia moglie casciata, melata
dolciata" (III, 8, 66) [my tasty honeysweet wife], or, playing in
counterpoint, to mock the reluctance of a silly, presumptuous
woman: "spiacevole, sazievole e stizzosa ch'alcun'altra, che a sua
guisa niuna cosa. . . ." (VI, 8, 5) ([more] unpleasant, sickening and
peevish than any other, who in her way. . . .), or ludicrously to
isolate the figure of poor Calandrino between the ruin of his hopes
and his load of stones, there in his own house turned upside down by
the force of his rage: "tutto sudato rosso e affannato / si fece alla
finestra e pregogli / che suso a lui dovessero andare": VIII 3, 53 (all
sweaty, redfaced and exhausted he went to the window and begged
them to come up to him).

But in these very examples, together with the parallelism emphasized by witty rhymes and assonances, there appears the aristocratic technique of that medieval *gnosis* of rhetoric, versified and
rhymed prose. The use of rhymed prose was encouraged by the
stylistic researches of Saint Cyprian and Saint Augustine. It was
used by Isidore of Seville in the text of the *Soliloquia,* which influenced medieval culture and rhetoric.[23] But it is beginning with
the eleventh century in particular that this technique was perfected
and its use generalized. It was most extensively adhered to in the
twelfth and thirteenth centuries.[24] John of Garland, classing it at
the top of the various *stili,* clearly and authoritatively defined its
characteristics: "in stilo Ysidoriano, quo utitur Augustinus in libro
Soliloquiorum, distinguuntur clausule similem habentes finem secundum leonitate et [vel] consonantiam: et videntur esse clausule pares
in syllabis, quamvis non sint." And he adds: "Iste stilus valde motivus
est ad pietatem et ad letitiam et ad intelligentiam." [25] Evidently, it is

a technique closely connected to that of the *cursus* and the other Hilarian or Isidorian rhetorical styles which we have mentioned.

We can trace the development of rhymed prose to the point when the ultrarefined prose writers no longer speak of lines but of *versus*.[26] [They began a technique which Boccaccio used in the *Decameron* (IV, Intro., 35-36).] During the twelfth century, the form of rhymed prose was diffused in public and private acts and instruments, in letters, in sermons, in theological treatises. It was used most frequently in historiography and especially in hagiographic legends.[27] In these works of a "narrative" character, such prose, either used throughout (for example in the *Speculum Ecclesiae, Speculum Humanae Salvationis*), or as a means of stressing particular moments (as in *Legenda Aurea*), is used more and more, as Poncelet's studies and classifications have demonstrated.[28] It continued to be used into the thirteenth century for writings ranging from the Latin texts to the Romance texts. It is evidenced in France in the translations of Jean Golin and in the most ancient hagiography.[29] In Italy the form of rhymed prose was used first by Alberico of Montecassino [30] in the twelfth century, then by various Franciscan writers and perhaps in the Cantico di Frate Sole.[31] In the thirteenth century, Guittone of Arezzo and Francesco da Barberino were the best known of the Italian writers using rhymed prose.

The tradition and the technique of rhymed prose greatly influenced the cultural formation of Boccaccio, for it appealed deeply to his literary sensibility. The authors whom he venerated most highly, from Saint Augustine and Isidore of Seville to Bede and Saint Bernard, offered him classic examples. He most admired and studied "rhétoriqueurs" such as John of Garland and the *dictatores* of Montecassino as we know from his own epistles (for example, VI and XV).[32] In the persistent search for a lofty type of narrative prose, a search which was the torment of his whole early career as an author, Boccaccio found rhymed prose was used as the form of the texts closest to his prose ideal: the historical and hagiographic texts, such as those Paulus Diaconus, of the *Legenda Aurea*, of the *Alphabetum Narrationis*.[33] He found an approximation of this technique even in the vernacular writers who were his prose models, in Guittone of Arezzo, whose rhetorical examples he relied on for point in III, 5; he found rhymed prose was used especially by the highest master of all, by Dante, who, beside the studies *concinnitas* of the *De Vulgari Eloquentia,* had constructed the noble and sustained prose of the *Vita Nuova* and the *Convivio* using rhymed prose.[34]

When Boccaccio resolved to attempt his most ambitious and in a certain sense, conclusive, prose experiment, his great "comédie humaine," quite naturally he did not neglect these lofty and refined teachings of the richest and most authoritative texts in the narrative tradition.

Although they may not be readily noticed in incorrect versions of the text, Boccaccio used thousands of hendecasyllables and other, lesser verse forms in the *Decameron,* as well as the *cursus* and other precepts of the *dictatores,*[35] to create what is probably the best and most conclusive essay in medieval rhetoric. They have a musical quality arising from the blending of prosaic and poetical cadences. However, they also have a stern and rigid quality, for Boccaccio had carefully written his composition over a long period. Certainly, Boccaccio's careful use of versified prose saves the *Decameron* from being merely an episodic curiosity or a casual story, for he possessed the greatest awareness of the possibilities of this form since St. Augustine. He encountered great difficulty in making a smooth transition from the preludes to the tales into the tales themselves. The change in tempo is most apparent at these junctures, even though Boccaccio tries to smooth them over by repeating expressions, for example the solemn and rhetorical *Dico* (I say), the sharply struck generic references to time or place, the conventional story-teller's beginnings: "You must know, then," "Once there was," "Once upon a time," and so on. But fairly often, Boccaccio successfully makes the transitions in the narrative rhythms, these *impasses* of the imagination, by using the deft and evocative cadences of discursive hendecasyllables, something like the "attack" of a full orchestra, a musical beginning which leads into the fanciful and poetic atmosphere of the tales.

It might be said that through Dioneo Boccaccio wanted to create a separation between the first three novellas and the rest. They are more tightly bound to "exemplary" formulations, whereas his own tale is free and mocking narrative. Boccaccio begins the narrative about the monks of Lunigiana with a pair of hendecasyllables or, rather, with a broken, slow-paced series of little verses (of five and of six syllables). Their rhythmic movements are characteristic of versified prose, that of Barberino for example:

> Fu in Lunigiana | paese non molto
> da questo lontano un monistero . . . (I, 4, 4).

> In Lunigiana, a place not far from here,
> there was a monastery. . .

Or it might be said that Boccaccio makes it seem that Laura wants to avoid the questioning which perhaps she saw on the faces of her listeners. For this reason, she is made to state a theme which might seem tragic and apocalyptic ("how a live man was buried for dead, and how later he was resuscitated"), with an exceptional sequence of nine hendecasyllables and minor verses. They are arranged in strophic structure, in which the final proparoxytones here and there flare like a festive and mischievous wink:

> Fu adunque in Toscana una badia,
> e ancora è,
> posta, sì come noi ne veggiam molte,
> in un luogo non troppo frequentato
> dagli uomini,
> nella quale fu fatto abate un monaco
> il quale in ogni cosa era santissimo
> fuori che nell'opera delle femmine:
> e questo sapeva
> sì cautamente fare
> che quasi niuno
> non che il sapesse ma né suspicava (III 8, 4).

> Once there was in Tuscany an abbey,
> and still is,

built, like many that we see,
in a rather lonely spot,
of which a monk became abbot,
a man in all things most holy
except in the matter of women:
and in this he knew
how to act so cautiously
that almost no one
even suspected him, much less knew.

And the lively and merry tone of the rustic joke played on Calandrino, grown too fond of his hog, or the inspired mockery of the academic prosopopeia Maestro Simone, are announced by the free and easy movements of the particularly happy overtures.

Chi Calandrino Bruno e Buffalmacco
fossero non bisogna che io vi mostri,
per ciò più avanti faccendomi dico
che Calandrino avea un suo poderetto (VIII 6, 4).

Who Calandrino Bruno and Buffalmacco
were there is no need for me to show you,
wherefore, moving ahead, I say
that Calandrino owned a little farm

and the joking movement, in the second case, is stressed by the precious rhymes and the extreme mobility of the accents and the meter of the lines:

Sì come noi veggiamo tutto il dì,
i nostri cittadini da Bologna
ci tornano qual giudice e qual medico
e qual notaio, co' panni lunghi e larghi
e con gli scarlatti e co' vai
e con altre assai
apparenze grandissime (VIII 9, 4).[36]

> As we see all the time,
> our citizens return to us
> from Bologna, as judges or medicos
> or as notaries, wearing robes long and ample,
> trimmed with scarlet and with fur,
> and with airs of pomp and ostentation.

But Boccaccio does not restrict himself to these comic opera preludes alone in starting his novella. The fabulous and magic world of youthful longings for faraway Melisandes, or the unattainable Blue Prince opens magically to the sound of flowing narrative hendecasyllables:

> Voi dovete sapere che in Parigi
> fu già un gentile uomo fiorentino,
> il qual per povertà divenuto era
> mercatante; ed eragli sì bene ... (VIII 7, 4).

> You must know that in Paris
> there was once a Florentine gentleman
> who, because of poverty, had become
> a merchant; and such was his success . . .

Thus Boccaccio begins the most "stilnovistica" [adj. from "dolce stil nuovo"—the sweet new style] tale of the *Decameron,* which tells of Lodovico [Ludwig, Louis] enamored unto death of the very beautiful Lady Beatrix. Using similar rhythms and tones Boccaccio begins the lovely fable of Lisa, hopelessly lovesick for King Peter of Aragon:

> Nel tempo che i Franceschi di Cicilia
> furon cacciati, era in Palermo un nostro
> fiorentino speziale . . .
> ricchissimo uomo il qual d'una sua donna
> senza più aveva una figliuola . . .
> Ed essendo il re Pietro di Raona

signore dell'isola divenuto,
faceva in Palermo maravigliosa
festa co' suoi baroni (X 7, 4).

In the days when the French were driven
out of Sicily, there was in Palermo
a Florentine apothecary . . .
a very wealthy man, who had by his wife
a one and only daughter . . .
And when King Peter of Aragon
had become lord of the island,
he was making wondrous merry with his barons.

They seem verses borrowed from the flowing narrations of the *cantari* [medieval poems in ottava rima or octaves], for they are scanned to create an effect of a mysterious, dissembled awaiting of fabulous events and studded with marvelous names, events, and words, all uttered with calculated delight.

It might indeed have been the subtle nostalgia of the gilded, fairytale world of the Middle Ages which had enchanted him as a youth and illuminated his first experiments as a narrator in prose and in verse[37] which inspired Boccaccio to adopt the lofty, solemn accents of rhymed prose to portray his narrators in the difficult opening strains.

The *canterini,* popular singers, often struck musical chords, at a pause in a poem, to prolong the impressions they had created in the minds of their listeners, or to emphasize them, as does Boccaccio, who often crowns his stories or some important or compelling event in them with the cadenced turn of a line. Thus, the forsaken sigh which dominates the first part of the Introduction, as coming from one who had truly "come out of the sea upon the shore," from the tumultuous agitation of youth to the detached and serene contemplation of the passions, in the final hendecasyllable, is concentrated with its limpid Petrarchan detachment:

dilettevole il sento esser rimaso

I feel it has remained delightful

Boccaccio seems to soften the measured, aristocratic gladness which has illuminated the eurhythmic life of the assembled company with an exceedingly filmy shadow of regret conveyed by the farewell words of the last king (when the last novella has been narrated):

> continua onestà, continua concordia
> continua fraternal dimestichezza
> mi ci è paruta vedere e sentire (X concl., 5).

> continuous uprightness, continuous harmony,
> continuous brotherly intimacy
> is what I seemed to see and hear.

But how many examples of evocative concluding verselines we find in these last pages of the *Decameron,* cited almost symbolically! Thus the slanderous Queen of France ends her wicked life with a confession as full and heavy as that clash between the proparoxytone hendecasyllable and that which ends on an accented final syllable:

> ma davanti a molti altri valenti' uomini
> tutto com'era stato raccontò (II 8, 89).

> but she confessed the whole matter
> before many other worthy men.

The adventures of Andreuccio of Perugia, the lucky horse drover, come to an end after the tumult of so many fearful happenings, with a contrast which gaily recalls the entire theme of the day:

> [parve] che costui incontanente
> si dovesse di Napoli partire:
> la qual cosa egli fece prestamente

e a Perugia tornossi,
avendo'l suo 'nvestito in un anello
dove per comperar cavalli era . . . (II 5, 85)

It seemed that he should at once
depart from Naples:
which he did right speedily
and return to Perugia,
having invested his capital in a ring,
where it was safe for buying horses . . .

Finally, the sinister glow of the infernal hunt—in accordance with
the whole inspiration of Nastagio's tale—vanishes and is transfigured, in the final sentence of the novella, in a roseate light of fable:

. . . e fatte le sue nozze
con lei più tempo lietamente visse (V 8, 43).[38]

. . . and after the wedding
he lived with her happily, for a long time.

As in the narrative atmosphere of the *cantari,* or of novella
writing, Boccaccio spread out and repeated these emphases or,
rather, rhythmical and musical contrasts. They served a quite similar function in the *cantari* and the *Decameron* at critical moments in
the development of the story, that is, at the start of a new episode or
a new situation, or when the culminating action was to approach
the climax. In a way, Boccaccio used them as a musical or literary
transcription of that tone of suspense or astonishment which in such
passages colors the voice of any artist-narrator and gives it warmth
and passion.

Boccaccio describes the four decisive moments of the rapidly
evolving adventures of Landolfo Ruffolo (II, 4), the plaything of
fortune on the stormy and treacherous Mediterranean, by four pairs
of hendecasyllables:

> . . .e già nell'Arcipelago venuto
> levandosi la sera uno scilocco (13)

> . . . and when he had reached the Archipelago
> in the evening there arose a sirocco

The second occurs at the very moment Landolfo enters the fateful gulf:

> fosse e 'l mare grossissimo e gonfiato
> notando quelli che notar sapevano (17).

> the sea was very high and swollen
> and all who could swim were swimming

The third takes place when the pirate ship breaks up,

> il tirò in terra e quivi con fatica
> le mani dalla cassa sviluppatogli (24)

> she dragged him ashore and there with difficulty
> released the grip of his hands on the chest

Finally to stress the lucky salvage with the still unknown treasure,

> ma siccome colui che in picciol tempo
> fieramente era stato balestrato (27)

> but like one who in a brief period
> had been roughly knocked from pillar to post

thus Boccaccio concludes the tale when the imprudent Landolfo recovers his wits.

Boccaccio also resorted to the use of contrast in the novella of Peronella (VII, 2) in two series of verses at the moment when the

lovers are surprised and when the novella reaches its unexpected
and ambiguous ending:

> Ma pur tra l'altre avvenne una mattina
> che essendo il buono uomo fuori uscito . . . (10)

> But then by chance it befell one morning
> that the good man had gone out. . . .

> in quella guisa che negli ampi campi
> gli sfrenati cavalli e d'amor caldi
> le cavalle di Partia assaliscono . . . (34)

> as in the broad fields
> the unbridled horses hot with love
> assail the Parthian mares . . .

Then, after the flare-up of sensuality, the priest of Varlungo falls
back into his sad meditations on his wretchedness, back into the
mean cunning of his daily life, each point in his reflections having its
successive counterpoint in the rhythms of the various hendecasyllables:

> e cominiciò a pensare in che modo
> riavere lo potesse senza costo . . .
> perciò che 'l dì seguente essendo festa
> egli mandò un fanciul d'un suo vicino
> in casa questa Monna Belcolore (VIII 2, 39-40).

> and he began to reflect on how
> he might get it back at no expense . . .
> wherefore the following day, a holiday,
> he sent the young son of a neighbor
> to the house of this Lady Belcolore.

Boccaccio relies on contrast even more to create an atmosphere
of suspense and of waiting for a crisis or to convey the sound of the

amazement at a conclusive or fatal action. For instance, after the urgently pressing, almost cinematic sequence of the varied picaresque scenes, Boccaccio seems to end the description of the adventurous Neapolitan night of Andreuccio with a feeling of impending doom at the unexpected thud of the sepulchral slab falling heavily into place above the poor deluded, twice-tricked youth:

> preso tempo tiraron via il puntello
> che il coperchio dell'arca sostenea,
> e fuggendosi, lui dentro dall'arca
> lasciarono racchiuso (II 5,78)

> choosing their time they pulled out the block
> which held up the cover of the tomb,
> then, taking to their heels, they left him
>   shut up within the tomb

Thus Boccaccio indicates the dismay of gentle Gostanza on finding herself still living, after having timidly sought death. She is comforted by the pitying solicitude of Carapresa, who pronounces her words, as well as those surprising Barbaresque names in a sing-song tone made mannered, euphuistic, by rhymes:

> A cui la buona femina rispose:
> "Figliuola mia
> tu se' vicina a Susa, in Barberia" (V 2, 18)

> To which the worthy woman answered:
> "My daughter,
> You are close to Susa, in Barbary"

Also the silly wait of Egano, when he goes off to inflict punishment and instead, receives a sound thrashing, is given a shading of mischievous suspense by the varied rhythm of three verses all ending in a single rhyme:

> e andossen nel giardino
> e a pié di un pino
> cominciò ad attendere Anichino (VII 7, 36).

> and he went off into the garden
> and at the foot of a pine tree
> began to wait for Anichino

Sometimes Boccaccio used the cadenced movements of only a single hendecasyllable to create an atmosphere of astonished expectancy; as when the most splendid personage of the resplendent group of knights and ladies asked the disheveled, ragged girl:

> Giselda, vuo'mi tu per tuo marito? (X 10, 20).[39]

> Griselda, wilt thou take me for thy husband?

Boccaccio used contrast to convey the anxiety and pressure as well as the insistency and the anguished suspense associated with certain requests, certain prayers, to which last hopes are confided as to the slenderest of threads. For example, the unhappy, emaciated judge from Pisa for one last time addresses tenderly his young wife who has already resolved not to give up the dashing and jovial Paganino:

> Guarda ciò che tu di', guatami bene!
> se tu ti vorrai bene ricordare,
> tu vedrai ben che io sono il tuo Ricciardo (II 10, 26).

> Look well what thou sayest, look well at me!
> if thou wilt indeed recall,
> wilt see indeed that I am thy own Ricciardo.

Also, young Mainardi, lovesick and burning "with love's fires" for the carefully guarded Caterina, in supplication proposes the childish stratagem:

Caterina mia dolce, io non so alcuna
via veder, se già tu non dormissi
o potessi venire in sul verone
che è presso al giardino di tuo padre (V 4, 12).

Catherine my sweet, I see no other way, except if instead of
sleep thou mayest come out upon the balcony hard by the
garden of thy father.

Perhaps Boccaccio's recurring versification of supplications
and prayers is a subtle adaptation of the rich and robust medieval
and rhetorical tradition. Writers of historical and in particular
hagiographic texts liked to use rhyme and rhythm to their words
which might give them the tone and movement of prayer.[40] In the
Decameron itself, aside from the comic exorcisms and incantations of
the tales of Gianni Lotteringhi and Donno Gianni, Boccaccio wrote
one of the most considerable versified sequences in rhythms "da
'breve' volgare" (short syllables of the vernacular). He portrays
Rinaldo d'Esti as he remembers his prayers and popular wayfarer's
devotions, to St. Julian:

nondimeno ho sempre avuto 'n costume
camminando, di dire,
la mattina, quando esco dell'albergo,
un paternostro e una avemaria
per l'anima del padre e della madre
di San Giuliano; dopo il quale io priego
Iddio e lui che la seguente notte
mi deano buon'albergo, e assai volte
già de' miei dì son stato camminando
in gran pericoli:
de' quai tutti scampato
pur son a notte poi stato in buon luogo (II 2, 7-8).[41]

nevertheless, I've always had the habit
while traveling, to say,
in the morning as I leave the inn,

a Pater-noster and an Ave Maria
for the souls of the father and mother
of Saint Julian; after which I pray
both God and him to give me, the coming night,
a good shelter; and many times
by dire perils have I been beset;
escaping from them all,
the next night, then, I am in a safe haven.

Boccaccio's experience as a narrator in verse made it possible for him to create a rhythm entirely suitable to his story-telling. This is apparent in the *Filostrato,* the *Teseida,* and the *Ninfale,* as well as in the allegorical poem *Amorosa visione.* Even his tercets styled on Dante's writing, beginning with the *Caccia di Diana,* show the influence of the ottava rima.[42] These octaves seem to be prose, due to Boccaccio's discursive tone, and because he tied the hendecasyllables together by numerous *enjambements,* but he disrupted any continuity of rhythm by frequently resorting to daring license and to exceptional usages. There seems to be little difference between verse and prose,[43] for Boccaccio almost completely eliminates it with his vigorous narrative, fusing so genially and so freely the lofty and formal technique of the *dictatores* [Lat.: one who dictates; that is, author] of the preceding centuries with that humbler but very live technique of Italian narrative in verse form.

Aside from the narrative rhythm Boccaccio created in the *Decameron,* he also wrote some "filigrees," euphuistic, fanciful cadences in rhythmic modulation. These represent a real discovery on Boccaccio's part, for he evolved themes and styles which were like those used by African writers for a thousand years. They are precisely the motives and themes most expounded in the extremely human world of the *Decameron,* those which Boccaccio presented most frequently in a realistic, unprejudiced, and comic manner as well as in one that is grave, heroic, almost epic.

In summary, there is no representation of moments of an ironic or caricatural nature, ranging from the grotesque to the burlesque, which Boccaccio has not deeply studied and at the same time lightened, by means of an expert counterpoint of verses.

We have previously cited the ways in which Boccaccio has presented Guccio Imbratta, Calandrino, Cisca of Celano—portraits in which the lineaments are in strong and imaginative relief and stressed by sequences of adjectives, either rhythmatic or rhymed. But the gallery of the profiles could be augmented with many of the more unforgettable figures of the comic sub-strata of the *Decameron*. There is the additional portrayal of Guccio Imbratta presented through an idyllic mockery:

> era più vago di stare in cucina
> che sopra i verdi rami l'usignolo (VI 10, 21)

> he had given himself up almost entirely
> than the nightingale of perching 'mid green branches

There is the little picture in the rustic style of Belcolore, with strong chromatic splashes:

> 'na piacevole e fresca foresozza
> brunazza e ben tarchiatra e atta a meglio
> sapere macinare che alcun' altra . . .
> e menare la ridda ed il ballonchio (VIII 2, 9)

> pleasing fresh-cheeked little rustic maiden,
> brown of hair and sturdy of body, and better fitted
> for grinding than any other girl. . .
> and for leading the round dance and the hop

Boccaccio gives us the moral caricature of the cautious husband driven mad by jealousy, previously delineated in some of his own sonnets: [44]

> quasi tutta la sua sollecitudine
> aveva posta in guardar ben costei,
> né mai addormentato si sarebbe
> se lei primieramente
> non avesse sentita entrar nel letto (VII 8, 6).

He had given himself up almost entirely
to watching carefully over her,
nor would he ever dream of going to sleep
until first he had heard [felt] her getting into bed.

The most joyously—and I might say, epically—derisive portrait in the
Decameron, the utmost proof of Boccaccio's genius, in these Leonard-
esque or, rather, Breughelian amusements is the following portrayal:

Aveva questa donna una sua fante
la qual però non era troppo giovane
ma ella aveva il più brutto viso
e il più contraffatto che si vedesse . . .
ella aveva il naso schiacciato forte e
la bocca torta e
le labbra grosse e i denti mal composti
e grandi,
e sentiva del guercio . . . .
E oltre a tutto questo era sciancata
e un poco monca dal lato destro
e il suo nome era Ciuta e
perchè cosí cagnazzo viso avea
da ogni' uomo era chiamata Ciutazza (VIII 4, 21).

This lady had a servant maid
who however was not so very young
but had the ugliest and the most
ill-favored countenance imaginable . . .
she had a badly flattened nose and
twisted mouth and
thick lips and badly shaped teeth
and big ones, at that,
and she was squint-eyed withal . . .
And as though all that weren't enough,
she was lame, and a bit maimed on her right side,
and her name was Ciuta but
because of her cur-like face
by everyone she was called Ciutazza [ugly Ciuta].

Boccaccio continuously interwove the different verses and used strange or grotesque rhymes and assonances—as is found in great realistic poetry—broadened the rhythm by degrees, masterfully creating a crescendo of ugly and repugnant details. He softened it unexpectedly in the septenarius in which, by syllabifying the name, he seems to terminate the capricious image, but intead, opens the way to the *coup de grâce;* it prepares the silence in which the final merry laughter bursts out, spread broadly across those two resounding pejoratives.

Creating whimsy by means of rhythms and rhymes as well as by word, Boccaccio enriches his sketches with the most unexpected and evocative lights and shades. He has a capacity for portraying the soul as he outlines the salient physical features of a person through these surprise cadences. They also, in a related, yet different, direction, penetrate and animate multifarious moments and actions with an ironic and mischievous counterpoint.

Lusca, one of the most unprejudiced champions of panderous eloquence, pursues the hesitant Pirro, whose handsome mistress is yearning for him, with a lash of irony which in our day would be called class prejudice:

> speri tu, se tu avessi o bella moglie
> o madre o figliuola o sorella . . .
> ch' egli andasse la lealtà ritrovando
> che tu servar vuoi a lui della sua donna?
> Sciocco se', se tu 'l credi; abbi di certo,
> se le lusinghe e' prieghi non bastassono
> —che che ne dovesse a te parere—
> e' vi si adoperrebbe la forza (VII 9, 24-25)

> do you think that if you had a lovely wife
> or mother or daughter or sister . . .
> that he the master would bother his head
> about the loyalty which you wish to keep toward his wife?
> If you believe he would, you're a fool; be assured
> that, if flatteries and entreaties did not gain his end,
> —regardless of how the matter might appear to you—
> why, he would just use force

Michele Scalza, the refined "moqueur" of the sprightliest bands of Florentine "good-time boys," is aristocratic, due to his own subtle spirit, in contrast with his noisy, quarelsome companions who love discussion. Boccaccio indicates this by means of the ironic rhythms used for the outburst, tinged with the distaste he has the reluctant dandy express:

> Andate, goccioloni che voi siete!
> Voi non sapete ciò che voi dite!
> I più gentili uomini i più antichi
> non che di Firenze
> ma di tutto il mondo
> o di Maremma, sono i Baronci (VI 6, 6).

> Come now, drivellers that you are.
> You don't know what you are talking about!
> The most noble men, those of most ancient lineage,
> not only in Florence but in the whole world
> or in the Maremma swamps, are the Baronci.

Boccaccio has the merchants, in the long and merry evening in the smoky Parisian inn, express their worldly wisdom as overworked Don Juans in unconventional measures and in rhythms and turns marked by a superficial unconstraint characteristic of traders, topped by facile proverbs:

> "Ma questo so io bene:
> che quando qui mi viene
> alle mani alcuna giovinetta . . .
> lascio star dall' un de' lati l'amore
> il quale io porto a mia mogliere e prendo
> di questa qua quel piacere ch' io posso."
> L'altro rispose: "E io fo il simigliante:
> perciò che se io credo
> che la mia donna alcuna sua ventura
> procacci, ella il fa, e se io nol credo,
> sì 'l fa: e per ciò
> a fare a far sia,
> quale asin dà in parete, tal riceve. . ."

"But this I know full well:
Where I am, when some winsome young thing
falls into my clutches . . .
I lay to one side the love
I bear my wife, and from the one who is *here*
whatever pleasure I can, I take."
His companion replied: "And so do I:
because, if I think that my wife
is intent on some venture of her own,
why, she's doing it; and if I don't think so,
she's doing it anyhow; and therefore
let him who acts be acted upon
like the ass who kicks a wall
and gets it back . . ."

Finally Ambrogiuolo comes to his conclusion:

abbi questo per certo:
che colei sola è casta
la quale o non fu mai da alcun pregata
o se pregò non fu esaudita (II 9, 5-6 and 20).

and of this, rest assured:
that only she is chaste
who never by any man was entreated;
or who, if the entreaty was hers, she was not gratified.

Boccaccio conveys details of the various settings for his tales by means of versified cadences, as well, to help achieve the light, mischievous effect almost akin to comic opera. For example, Buffalmacco has dumbfounded and enchanted Maestro Simone with the marvelous scintillation of his language full of imagery and double meanings, and promises to take him into the home of the Countess of Civillari (that is, stripped of metaphor, into a dark well). He ends the description of the amorous joys which await the poor doctor by exclaiming, with pompous magniloquence:

A così gran donna adunque
—lasciata star quella da Cacavincigli—
se 'l pensier non c'inganna,
vi metteremo nelle dolci braccia (VIII 9, 77)

If our thought is not in error,
we will put you in the gentle arms
of such a great lady
—disregarding the one from Cacavincigli

Boccaccio creates another masterful humorous scene when he describes Master Lizio calling to his wife to look at Caterina, who has
caught the nightingale.[45] The light touch of comic irony, directed in
part at himself and in part toward his daughter, rises out of airy
cadences culminating in the central hendecasyllables, all modulated
on the singing, ambiguous ending:

[lasciami] vedere come l'usignuolo ha fatto
questa notte dormir la Caterina!
Mentre queste parole si dicevano
la Caterina lasciò l' usignuolo (V 4, 31 and 44).

[let me] see how the nightingale
this night has made Caterina sleep!
While these words were being spoken,
Caterina released the nightingale.

Just as in this well-balanced scene Boccaccio uses rhythms of versified
prose to lighten the gestures and the images, in themselves bold and
almost obscene, and to create a fresh and youthful sketch, so he uses
versified prose in his narration.[46]

The introductions to the tales lend themselves most readily to
versified prose. There Boccaccio could depict those refined and

aristocratic conditions of life which make up the atmosphere of the *Decameron*. The elegant eurhythmy with which Boccaccio described the gestures and actions, which seemed to be made to the accompaniment of music in a dance rhythm, is readily composed into hendecasyllables.

At times, Boccaccio uses the hendecasyllables for the measured pronouncements of the rulers of the days, humanly wise and regally composed, like those of Pampinea at the conclusion of the first day:

> [perchè cio che potrà] esser per domattina
> opportuno si possa preparare,
> a questa ora giudico doversi
> le seguenti giornate incominciare.
> E perciò a reverenza di Colui
> a cui tutte le cose vivono . . .
> Filomena, discretissima giovane,
> reina guiderà il nostro regno (I concl., 2-3)

> so that that which for tomorrow may be timely,
> may be prepared,
> at this hour, I opine, should
> the following days begin.
> And to that end, in reverence toward Him
> in whom all things have their being . . .
> Philomena, a most wise young woman,
> as queen will guide our kingdom.

But Boccaccio still more frequently uses the musical rhythm to described the drowsing landscapes which form the background for the aristocratic group. He uses it to describe the leisurely stroll through the countryside accompanied by the sound

> del canto di forse venti usignuoli
> e altri uccelli,
> per una vietta non troppo usata,

ma piena di verdi erbette e di fiori,
li quali per lo sopravvegnente sole
tutte s'incominciavano ad aprire,
prese il cammino verso l'occidente . . . (III intr., 2)

of the song of perhaps a score of nightingales
and other birds,
along a little path, seldom used
but full of green grass and flowers,
which at the touch of the rising sun
all began to open,
the group took its way toward the west. . .

He uses it to describe the pleasant loitering over patrician pastimes:

ma quivi dimoratisi,
chi a leggere romanzi,
chi a giucare a scacchi e chi a tavole,
mentre gli altri dormirono, si diede (III intr., 15).

but here, lingering,
some devoted themselves
to reading romances,
others to playing at chess
and others to other play;
and some indulged in naps.

Boccaccio described the scene, based entirely on visual themes of the very elegant human figures and the sharply etched landscape, in the enchanting picture of the bathing girls in the Vale of Fair Ladies, a picture enveloped in the music of delightsome verse and made still more precious by the Dantean echos (Purg. XXVIII 29):

[il piano che] nella valle era così ritondo
come se a sesta fosse stato fatto . . .
era di giro poco più di un mezzo
miglio, intorniato di sei montagnette . . .

Le piagge delle quali montagnette
così digradando giù verso 'l piano
discendevano come ne' teatri
veggiamo dalla lor sommità i gradi . . .
ivi faceva un picciolo laghetto . . .
e senza aver in sé mistura alcuna
chiarissimo il suo fondo mostrava . . .
un altro canaletto riceveva
per lo qual fuor del valloncello uscendo
alle parti più basse sen correva

The plain which was in the vale was a perfect round
as though drawn with a compass . . .
its circumference was rather more
than half a mile, ringed by six little knolls . . .
of these knolls the sides sloped down,
down toward the plain,
reminiscent of the way in theaters
we see, from above, the rows of seats . . .
there [a tiny brook] made a little lake . . .
and its waters, unblemished by any adulterant,
very clearly showed its bottom . . .
from the vale another little channel led,
through which the water trickled to lower levels

At the center Boccaccio presents that image which charmed Ariosto, the poet of Alcina (VII, 28) and which combines the elegance and the light touch of the most felicitous intuitions of Poussin:

il qual [laghetto] non altrimenti li lor corpi
candidi nascondeva che farebbe
una vermiglia rosa un sottil vetro (VI concl., 2-30) [47]

the little lake no more
their white bodies hid from view,
than would a thin sheet of glass
a vermillion rose

The fascinating and penetrating music that emanates from these waves of verses, making an entire scene gentler and more precious,[48] has its centers of sweet and secret resonances in the varied novellas in the circle of the world most sought for by Boccaccio's imagination: that of the aristocracy of intelligence, of sensibility, of human passion. To express the sentiment of love, he naturally composed the words in rhythms proper to the lyric language, but at times also with a realistic grace and fresh newness taken straight from the poetry of the people.

> trent'anni, fresca e bella e ritondetta
> che pareva una mela casolana (III 4, 6)

> thirty years old, fresh and fair and roundish
> so she seemed a cottage apple

> ella era più melata che 'l confetto (III 8, 51)

> she was more honey-sweet than candy

Or, more often, Boccaccio conveyed the sentiments of love, relying on fables or references to Paradise, by means of the ottava rima of the *cantari:*

> venne crescendo e in anni e in persona
> e in bellezza e in tanta grazia . . .
> ch' era a veder maravigliosa cosa (II 8, 37).

> she was growing both in years and in person
> and in beauty and in such grace . . .
> that it was a marvel to behold.

> ma parendogli oltre modo più bella . . .
> dubitava non fosse alcuna Dea (V I, 10)

> but as she appeared to him incomparably more fair . . .
> he was wondering if this were not some goddess

nelli lor visi
più tosto agnol parvevan ch'altra cosa,
tanto gli avevan dilicati e belli (X 6, II)

in appearance,
they looked more like lambs than anything else,
so delicate were they of countenance, and beautiful

pur sentiva
tanto piacer nell'animo
quanto se stata fosse in Paradiso (X 7, 34)[49]

yet she felt
as much pleasure within her
as though she were in Paradise

Sometimes a faintly stressed cadence suffices to convey a love scene: for example, the precipitous frightened flight of Pietro and l'Agnolella (Little Lamb) resolves into the sweetness of the two scanned hendecasyllables:

amore andando insieme ragionando,
alcuna volta l'un l'altro basciava (V 3, 9).

as they walked along talking about love,
sometimes one would kiss the other.

The highest and most artistocratic tradition of Italian lyric poetry—a tradition to which Boccaccio was especially devoted—goes on living fully not only in his courtly language but in his own "cherished" cadences to arrest the most important moments of each love story.

Boccaccio presents dreamy, sweetly gentle tales of people falling in love through hearsay, like that of the Norman prince for the very beautiful daughter of the King of Tunis:

fama della bellezza parimente
e del valor di lei
e non senza gran diletto né invano
gli orecchi del Gerbino aveva tocchi (IV 4, 7)

fame of her beauty and
equally of her qualities
and not without great delight,
nor in vain,
had reached the ears of Gerbino

He describes silent and secret longings without hope of fulfilment, as in the case of the groom for the almost mythical queen Teodolinda:

E quantunque senza speranza
vivesse di dover mai a lei piacere,
pur seco si gloriava
che in alta parte avesse allogati
i suoi pensieri . . .
come colui
che tutto ardeva in amoroso foco (III 2, 7)

And although without any hope he lived
of ever finding favor in her eyes,
yet within himself he took pride
that he had raised to lofty heights
his thoughts. . .
as one
who was all enveloped in amorous fire

Boccaccio describes hidden desire, such as that of the King of France for the very beautiful and wise Marchesa of Monferrato:

maravigliò e commendolla forte,
tanto nel suo disio più accendendosi
quanto da più trovava esser la donna (I 5, II).

he was astonished, and praised her strongly, in his heart,
growing the warmer in his desire
the more the lady exceeded his former opinion of her.

But Boccaccio reserves the most carefully modulated and cadenced rhythm for the central point in the love stories, that moment
which has been the most enduring in the lyric poetry, that is, the
declaration of love, the pleading for pity:[50]

Che se di là come di quá si ama
in perpetuo v'amerò . . .
che niuna cosa avete
qual che ella si sia, o cara o vile,
che tanto vostra possiate tenere
e così in ogni atto farne conto
come di me, da quanto che io mi sia,
e il simigliante delle mie cose . . .
caro mio ben e
sola speranza dell' anima mia (III 5, 11).

For if one loves on that side of the Alps
as on this,
I shall love you unendingly . . .
for you possess nothing,
nothing whatsoever, either cherished or base,
that you can so surely count on,
call your own,
as you can me, for whatever I am worth,
and for the love I have borne you . . .
my dearly beloved, sole hope of my soul.

Thus Zima, courteous fellow-citizen of Cino da Pistoia, composes his
amorous discourse almost in the metre of a Stilnovistic *canzone*.[51]
Boccaccio expresses the same abandon, the same total dependence of
the lover on his lady, but with a nobler and more magic throb, in the
words of Federigo degli Alberighi. When Monna Vanna unexpectedly appears in his house after so many years of reluctance and

refusals on her part, she can only murmur three hendecasyllables, which seem taken from the most shining love lyrics of Guinizelli or of Cavalcanti:

> che se io mai alcuna cosa valsi,
> per lo vostro valore e per l'amore
> che portato v'ho avvenne e per certo . . . (V 9, 21)[52]

> for if ever I was of any worth,
> it came about, for sure, by your worthiness
> and for the love I have borne you. . . .

Boccaccio broadens the cadences used for the expression of love into grave and sonorous notes in the solemn or dramatic passages of the *Decameron*. Thus just before the tragedy of Gianni and Restituta takes place, Boccaccio launches the passionate assertion:

> quello diletto presero oltre al quale
> niuno maggior ne puote Amor prestare (V 6, 19).

> they took that pleasure, beyond which
> no greater pleasure Love can give.

Likewise, Boccaccio establishes a scornful contrast between the heroines of his patrician world and the covetous and wanton figures of the lower strata of his human comedy:

> affermo cole' esser degna del fuoco
> la quale a ciò per prezzo si conduce:
> dove chi per amore, conoscendo
> le sue forze grandissime, perviene . . .
> merita perdono (VIII 1, 4).

> I assert that worthy of the fire
> is she who brings herself to that for a price;
> whereas she who, for love, knowing its
> enormous forces,
> comes to it . . .
> deserves pardon.

A similar scorn, resounding with a great, an almost inhuman cruelty, seems to congeal the pronouncements of certain stony-hearted grandees in isolated verse lines; witness the sentences which fall heavily upon the heads of timid women in love with the speaker:

> e ove tu non vogli così fare
> raccomanda a Dio l'anima tua (V 4, 43).

> and should you be unwilling to do so,
> commend your soul to God.

Beltramo of Rossiglione makes harsh and mocking answer to the imploring supplications of Giletta, to the prayers of her messengers, lashing his fond wife with awful disdain in impossible conditions:

> Tornerò allora ad essere con lei
> che ella questo anello avrà in dito
> e in braccio figliuol di me acquistato (III 9, 30).

> I shall live with her again,
> when she will be wearing this ring upon her finger
> and holding in her arms a son sired by me.

Tragically bestial, also, sounds the pronouncement of a more famous imitator of Beltramo, namely Gualtieri, when he commands that his daughter be snatched away from her mother; words echoed by Griselda in the terrifying sound of that closing hendecasyllable:

che le bestie e gli uccelli la divorino (X 10, 32).

that the beasts and the birds may devour her.

Boccaccio also relates some of his tales in Dantean lines (Purg., I, 18):

le miserie degli infelici amori . . .
hanno già contristati gli occhi e 'l petto (IV 10, 3).

the miseries of unhappy loves . . .
have already saddened eyes and heart.

That is, the tales of love and death around which the fourth day is woven are modulated on these rhythms now grave and sad, now harsh and pitiless. It suffices to think of the macabre and heroic Provençal legend of the "eaten heart." The first scene of betrayal and bloodshed ends with three heavy and fatal *septenarii,* which broaden out into the final, horror-filled hendecasyllable:

il Rossiglion smontato
con un coltello il petto
del Guardastagno aprì;
e con le proprie mani il cuor gli trasse (IV 9, 13).

dismounting, Rossiglione
with his dagger the breast
of Guardastagno opened,
and with his own hands removed the heart.

The second scene Boccaccio wrote in this manner is entirely centered on the desperate gesture of the woman who takes her own life. It rings with a grandiose affirmation [after she has unwittingly eaten her lover's heart]:

Ma unque a Dio non piaccia
che sopra a così nobile vivanda
. . . altra vivanda vada (IV, 9, 23).[53]

Now may God forbid
that upon such noble food
. . . may other food follow.

Boccaccio conveys the unrestrained sorrow and the passion of Ghismonda with the most mournful notes, composed in continuous poetic rhythms. The conclusion is made in the last image, bleak and grandiose. Ghismonda, dying amid the subdued chorus of her weeping handmaidens, utters her last words:

al suo fine esser venuta sentendosi,
strignendosi al petto il mortal cuore . . .
"Rimanete con Dio, ché io mi parto" (IV 1, 61).

feeling that she had reached the end,
clasping the dead heart to her breast . . .
"Be steadfast in God, for I am going."

Here, Boccacio uses the broad, lyric tempo of the prose to reflect the heroic tension of the protagonist's soul; Boccaccio conveys the extreme firmness of her spirit, as it gives measure and composure to the action, by modulating his words to "the breaking point." The death of her beloved gives a new kind of spiritual ardor to the woman in love; she speaks as though she were already beyond the limits of time, and seems to render audible "the fluttering wings of eternity" in the majestic crescendo of the deeply rhythmed sighs and outbursts:

"Ahi dolcissimo albergo
di tutti i miei piaceri . . .
venuto sei alla fine alla quale
ciascun corre, lasciate hai le miserie
del mondo e le fatiche . . .
Io son certa che ella (*l'anima di Tancredi*) è ancor quicentro

e riguarda i luoghi de' suoi diletti . . .
O molto amato cuore, ogni mio ufficio
verso di te è fornito, né più altro
mi resta a fare, se non di venire
con la mia anima a fare alla tua
compagnia . . ."
E quanto più onestamente seppe
compose il corpo suo sopra quello (IV 1, 51, 54, 57).

"Alas, sweetest refuge
of all my pleasures . . .
you have come to that end to which
each of us hastens, leaving behind the world's miseries,
and its weariness . . .
I am sure that it [Tancred's soul] is still herein,
and gazes upon the lieus of its delights . . .
O dearly beloved heart, my every care
has been lavished upon you, for me naught remains
but to come with my soul
to keep company with yours . . ."
And as modestly as might be
she composed her body upon that other one.

In these rhythms the sentiment of the eternity of the soul and the expression of faith, as Momigliano wrote, rise spontaneously and lyrically, like irradiations of that boundless love; the particularly carnal passion of this tale attains its highest consecration. Thus in this climate of inner and lyrical composure, more spontaneously and more loftily than elsewhere, Boccaccio resolves the prose in the solemn, choral order of the verses. He conveys in its rhythms a tension both solemn and heroic, which makes these pages one of the highest examples of tragic passion.

Bembo noticed it when, in his *Prose,* he remarked that Boccaccio "wished . . . to pour out gentleness . . . and chose . . . words having for the most part their stress accent on the penultimate syllable, and ordered those words in the manner best fitted to draw from them the effect which he proposed to draw from them." [54] But even Bembo, who subjected the prose of the *Decameron* to the most subtle and searching analysis, missed the hidden structure which we have been pointing out only summarily on a few pages of the *Decameron*. Bembo, like almost all later critics, was absorbed and almost dazzled by Boccaccio's attention to the golden Latin models, and by his search for an absolute Ciceronianism. If a few verses seemed to emerge and almost float in the rhythmical prose of the *Decameron*— let Salviati speak for them all[55]—the critics had not penetrated to the secret of prose-poetry. The culture of the Italian Renaissance and of the ages following had thrown away the precious key to that secret, together with those of so many other unrecognized treasures of the Middle Ages, which they branded, even to its very name, as "a desert of barbarous obscurity" amid the pellucid splendors of Classicism and its revival. Even in their consideration of the stylistic material of Boccaccio's prose, the Renaissance writers limited themselves to a largely superficial admiration. They were mainly interested in the linguistics or, rather, the grammar Boccaccio used. They wanted to study the *Decameron* in order to adapt to their own ideas and forms those of Boccaccio, in much the same way they did Dante's *Divina Commedia.*

But three centuries later, the greatest classical and proto-romantic poet of Italy, reading the *Decameron,* noted on the margin: "It appears that here and there Boccaccio was versifying his prose. . . . no one, to my knowledge, noted that Boccaccio, to help himself with the prosody of the Latins, was translating not a few of their verses, and while the harmony was still sounding in his ears, was inserting them into his book." [56] This note remained undiscovered down to our own days. It was an illuminating intuition, like so many others of the first Italian reader and critic of poetry, Ugo Foscolo.[57]

NOTES

1. I am alluding, naturally, to the essay on the critical reconstruction of the text of the *Decameron* presented in my previously mentioned edition and in my article "Per il testo del Decameron."
2. F. Maggini, "Le prime traduzioni di Livio," *La Rassegna,* XXIV, 1916;

"Boccaccio traduttore dei classici," *Miscellanea Storica della Valdelsa,*
XLI, 1933 (studies now collected in the volume *I primi volgarizzamenti
dai classici latini,* Florence, 1952); A. Schiaffini, *Tradizione e poesia nella
prosa d'arte italiana dalla latinitá medievale a G. B.,* Rome, 1943, pp. 151 ff.;
G. Billanovich, "Il Boccaccio il Petrarca e le più antiche traduzioni in
italiano delle *Decadi:* di Tito Livio," *Giornale Storico di Letteratura Italiana,* CXXX, 1953; *Volgarizzamenti del Due e Trecento* edited by C. Segre,
Turin, 1954.

3. E. Faral, "L'Orientation actuelle des études relatives au latin médiéval,"
Revue des études latines, I, 1920, pp. 26 ff.; *La littérature latine du Moyen Age,*
Paris, 1925; E. R. Curtius, *Europäische Literatur und lateinishes Mittel-
alter,* Bern, 1948; E. G. Parodi, *Poesia e storia nella Divina Commedia,*
Naples, 1920; A. Schiaffini, *Tradizione e poesia* cit., and also *Momenti di
storia della lingua italiana,* Rome, 1952. See also M. B. Ogle, "Some
Aspects of Medieval Latin Style," *Speculum,* I, 1926; F. Di Capua, *Il
ritmo prosaico ecc . . . dal IV al XIV secolo,* Rome, 1937-1946, vol. 3; C.
Segre, "La sintassi del periodo nei primi prosatori," *Memorie dell'
Accadamia dei Lincei, Scienze morali,* S. VIII, IV, 1953; F. Quadlbauer,
Die antike Theorie der genera dicendi, Wien 1962; C. Segre, *Linqua, stile e
società,* Milano, 1963; G. L. Beccaria, *Ritmo e melodia nella prosa italiana,*
Firenze, 1964. Such studies on medieval rhetoric and stylistics should,
however, in order that we may fully comprehend their value, be
framed within the esthetic vision of that civilization, for example, as is
defined and illustrated in the works cited in Note 16 of Chapter I.
Only Curtius has called attention to this necessity, besides, of course,
De Bruyne, *Etudes,* cit., II, pp. 3ff.

4. E. Faral, "L'orientation," cit., p. 31; see also E. Faral, *Les arts poétiques
du XII ^eet XIIIe siècle,* Paris, 1923; E. R. Curtius, *op. cit.,* and K. Vossler,
Aus der romanischen Welt, Leipzig, 1942, pp. 5 ff.; L. Arbusow, *Colores
rhetorici,* Gottiingen, 1948; R. McKeon, "Rhetoric in the Middle Age,"
Speculum, XVII, 1942; E. Faral, "Sidoine Apollinaire et la technique
littéraire du Moyen Age," *Miscellanea Mercati,* Vatican City, 1946; and
especially G. Paré, A. Brunet, and P. Tremblay, *La Renaissance du XIIe
siècle: les écoles et l'enseignement,* Ottawa, 1933, pp. 109 ff. Montano (art.
cit.) properly writes at the end of his rapid analysis of medieval rhetoric and poetics in relation to the esthetic vision of that same culture:
"An absolute faith in the validity of certain rhetorical formulas, as
well as of certain rules of logic—the same faith that gave such great
and enduring vitality to the *cursus*—was confused with the consciousness of the *reality* of esthetic facts, of audible and visual harmonies, of

linguistic values. And this could not but be a hindrance to art, just as the excessive use of dialectics inevitably came to hamper the free and creative force of the spirit. And the posterior reaction of humanism and later of romanticism became understandable, in the field of thought as in that of art. But this school so passionately attached to technics, the observation so extraordinarily attentive to the audible and visual play of sounds and colors, the extremely detailed investigations into figures of rhetoric or relationships in the figurative arts, not only gave an unmistakable character to artistic activity, from Gothic sculpture to the *Commedia,* but were invaluable in endowing the West with an incomparable technical skill. Anyone wishing to have an idea of the importance of this fact may consider all there is of chaotic, of monstrous, of abnormal, in all civilizations from the Indian to the pre-Columbian which have evolved outside of this Western School and gave to artistic creativeness a support whose value was easily denied by posterior intolerance but which was of great weight for all art, including the romantic."

5. To the data presented here see *Boccaccio Medievale,* Chapters VII and IX, and A. Hortis, *Studi sulle opere latine del Boccaccio,* Trieste, 1879, especially pp. 473 ff.; F. Torraca, "G. Boccaccio a Napoli," *Archivio storico per le Province Napoletane,* XXXIX, 1915; E. G. Parodi, *Poeti antichi e moderni,* Florence, 1923, pp. 164 ff.; A Schiaffini, *Tradizione e poesia,* cit., pp. 169 ff.; G. Billanovich, *Restauri Boccacceschi,* cit. In addition, and more especially for the knowledge and culture of Paolo da Perugia and of Dionigi, see F. Ghisalberti, "Paolo da Perugia," *Rendiconti dell' Istituto Lombardo,* S II, LXII, 1919; F. Torraca, art. cit., pp. 59 ff.; A. Della Torre, *La giovinezza di G. Boccaccio,* Città di Castello, 1902, pp. 37 ff., 145., 262 ff., 318 ff.; R. Sabbadini, *Le Scoperte dei codici latini e greci,* Florence, 1905-1914, II, pp. 35 ff; U. Mariani, *Petrarca e gli Agostiniani,* Rome, 1946, pp. 31 ff.; R. Weiss, "Notes on Dionigi da B. S.," *Italian Studies,* X, 1955 (with essential bibliography).

6. See *Boccaccio medievale,* Chap. VII especially pp. 219 ff.

7. E. G. Parodi, *Poeti antichi e moderni,* cit., pp. 166 ff.; A. Schiaffini, *Tradizione e poesia,* cit., pp. 160 ff. Guadifredus Anglicus (cod. E, 62 of the Communale of Perugia, c. 388) states that the *velox* is used at the ends of periods for its *gravitas morosa* (also see F. Egidi. *Studi Romanzi,* XXVII, 1937, p. 96).

8. A. Schiaffini, op. cit., pp. 177 ff., and "Autobiografia poetica e stile del Boccaccio dal *Filocolo* alla *Fiametta,*" *Elegia di Madonna Fiammetta,* edited by A. Schiaffini and F. Ageno, Paris, 1954. See also G. Herczeg,

"Boccaccio helye az olasz prózastílus történetében." *Archivum philologicum,* LXXI, 1948.

9. Even his first steps as a writer in verse are marked by a hard apprenticeship in rhetoric. See my article "Il primo carme del Boccaccio," *Tradizione delle opere di G. B.,* pp. 201 ff.

10. Cassiodori Senatoris, *Variae* recensuit. Th. Mommsen, Berlin, 1894 (*Mon. Ger. Hist.,* Auct. XII), p. 3 (praefatio, 3). Exemplary for the canonical authority of Cassiodorus is the judgment of Tommaso of Capua, who as supreme master of the prose art placed him on the level of Virgil, the highest example of poetic style (F. Hahn, *Collectio Monumentorum Veterum et Recentium,* Braunschweig, 1724, I, p. 280).

11. "Rhetorica novissima," ed. A. Gaudenzi, in *Scripta Anecdota Antiquissimorum Glossatorum,* Bologna, 1892, II, p. 257. Also, "orator est vir facundus . . . in pronuntiatione ornatus . . . cum exquisito artificio." On Alberico of Montecassino see particularly the statements in the *Flores Rhetorici* (e.g. II, VII, VIII), ed. Inguanez-Villard, Montecassino 1938 and in the *Breviarium de dictamine,* in *Briefsteller und Formelbücher,* ed. Rockinger, Monaco, VIII, 1863. And for Boncompagno see F. Di Capua, "Per la storia del latino letterario medievale," *Giornale It. di Filologia,* V-VI, 1953-1954.

12. Cassiodorus is one of the authors who figures—even with rare works —in Boccaccio's library. See *Boccaccio Medievale,* Chapter IX and the classical works of Sabbadini and of Hecker mentioned therein. Boncompagno of Signa is one of the treastise writers most in evidence, especially in the juvenile works; *Amorosa Visione,* critical edition, cit., p. 694; also see *Boccaccio Medievale,* Chapter VII. For Alberico of Montecassino see below, notes 17, 31, 32, 48 and note 9 of Chapter IV.

13. See Chapter I and the precept of Matthieu of Vendôme (Faral, *Arts poétiques,* p. 113) on the advantages of beginning with a verb or a sentence "cui consuetudo fidem attribuit, opinio communis assensum accomodat, incorruptae veritatis integritas adquiescit."

14. See below some other analyses of periods of the *Decameron* with indication of the various *cursus;* and *passim* my commentary. As Parodi observed, the *cursus* is generally used in Italian, and in particular in Boccaccio, with extreme liberty as is natural, not to say necessary, in this transference entrusted more to evocative measures than to categorical and circumstantial canons.

15. See for example the beginning of I, 9; V, 2; VI, 2; VII, 2; IX, 1; X, 9; and see *Vita Nuova,* VI and XXIX; *Inferno,* V, 7 and VIII, 1.

16. A period finely analyzed in a stylistic sense by R. Fornaciari, in *Novelle*

scelte del Decameron, Florence, 1930, p. 2. For the borrowings from Paolus Diaconus, see *Boccaccio Medievale,* pp. 304 ff.

17. This too was a technique commended by the most authoritative rhetoricians. For example, Geoffrey de Vinsauf stated:

Si vetus est verbum, sis physicus et veteranum
redde novum. Noli semper concedere verbo
in proprio residere loco; residentia talis
dedecus est ipsi verbo; loca propria vitet
et peregrinetur alibi sedemque placentem
fundet in alterius fundo; sit ibi novus hospes
et Placeat novitate sua. Si conficis istud
antidotum, verbi facies juvenescere vultum.

(*Poetria Nova,* 757 ff.: in Faral, *Arts poétiques,* cit.). Earlier, Alberico of Montecassino stated "Arcem tenet in serie quisquis ex habili iunctura, decus praecium verbis acquirit; verba quasi nimio iam usu vilia bene serendo reddit nova, reddit preciosa" (*Flores,* VII). But perhaps Boccaccio was particularly drawn to the precepts in this sense which he read in the *De Vulgari Eloquentia,* II, vi.

18. Concerning this style, its origin, and its laws, see E. Norden, *Die Antike Kunst-prosa,* Leipzig, 1909, pp. 760 ff.; F. Di Capua, "Lo stile isidoriano nella retorica medievale e in Dante," *Studi in onore di F. Torraca,* Naples, 1922; K. Polheim, *Die lateinische Reim-prosa,* Berlin, 1925, pp. 296 ff. and 432 ff., besides the numerous and fruitful references in the classic work of M. Manitius, *Geschichte der Lateinischen Literatur des Mittelalters,* Munich, 1911 (see the indices of the various volumes under Reim-prosa); Ch. Mohrmann, *Etudes sur le latin des chrétiens,* Roma, 1958-61.

19. The *Soliloquia or Synonyma de lamentatione animae peccatricis* are published in the *Patrologia Latina* of Migne, vol. 83, 826 ff.; for absolute mastery of the rules of Isidore see Norden, Polheim, Manitius, op. cit. (in their indexes); E. Faral, *Les arts poétiques,* cit., *passim*; J. De Ghellinick, *Littérature latine au Moyen Age,* Paris, 1939, I. pp. 24 ff.; *L'Essor de la littérature latine au XIIe siècle,* Bruxelles, 1946, II, pp. 54 ff. For the Augustinian origin of this technique see Norden, op. cit., pp. 621 ff.; Polheim, op. cit., pp. 236 ff.; C. J. Balmus, *Etude sur le style de Saint Augustine,* Paris, 1930; F. Di Capua, "Il ritmo prosaico di S. A.," *Miscellanea agostiniana,* II, 1931; C. Mohrmann, *Die altchristliche Sondersprachen in den Sermones des hl. A.,* Nijmegen, 1932; "Das Wortspiel in den Augustinischen Sermones," *Mnemosyne-Bibliotheca Classica Batava,* S. III, iii, 1935-1936, pp. 33 ff.; J. Schrijnen, *Charakteristik des Altchristlichen Latein,* Nijmegen, 1932; "L'évolution de la langue de S.

A.," *Collectanea,* Nijmegen, 1939, pp. 321 ff.; U. Sesini, *Poesia e musica etc.,* Turin, 1949. Sometimes the coincidence of names of the *Soliloquia* work caused the two authors to be confused (see G. Mari in *Romanischen Forschungen,* XIII, 1902, p. 960).

20. See the studies mentioned in the preceding note, and in particular the volume of Faral concerning the insistence of the treatise writers on these canons, and the article *Das Wortspiel* of Mohrmann for its numerous Augustinian exemplifications of alliterations, word plays on etymologies of proper nouns, puns and plays on ambiguous word endings, paronomasia of simple and compound words, and so on, and also J. Schrijnen, "Die Namengebung in Altchristlichen Latein," *Mnemosyne,* II, 1935.

21. "O quanti gran palagi, quante belle case, quanti nóbili abitúri [*velox*], per addietro di famiglie pieni, di signór' e di dónne [*planus*], infino al menomo fante rimaser voti! O quante memorabili schiatte, quante amplissime eredità, quante famose ricchézze si vídero [*tardus*], senza successor débito rimanére [*velox*]! Quanti valorosi uomini, quante belle donne, quanti leggiadri giovani, i quali non che altri, ma Galieno Ippócrateo Esculápio [*velox*] avrieno giudicáti saníssimi [*tardus,*], la mattina desinarono co'loro parenti [*planus*], compágn' e amíci [*planus*], che poi, la sera vegnénte, apprésso [*planus + planus*], nell' altro mondo cenárono con li lóro passáti [*velox + planus*]" (Introduction, 48).

22. See for example the Augustinian exemplification collected by Norden, *op. cit.,* pp. 621 ff., by Mohrmann in her article on pp. 52 ff., by Balmus, *op. cit.,* pp. 129 ff. (Chapters III and IV). For the Apuleian and African rhetorical tradition see Norden, *op. cit.,* pp. 586 ff.; Bernhard, *Der Stil des Apuleius,* Stuttgart, 1927; P. Junghanns, *Die Erzählungstechnik von Apuleius Metamorphosen,* Leipzig, 1932. For Isidore see Polheim, op. cit., pp. 296 ff.

23. For the origin and developments of this technique, in addition to the mentioned works of Manitius (in the indexes), of Norden (*passim* and especially pp. 757 ff.), and Polheim (especially pp. 382 ff.), see: K. Burdach (and G. Bebermeyer), *Schlesich-Böhmische Briefmuster aus der Wende . . .,* Berlin, 1926 ("Vom Mittelalter zur Reformation," V); J. Marouzeau, *Traité de stylistique appliquée au latin,* Paris, 1935; J. Schrijnen, *Charakteristik des Altchristlichen Latein,* cit. (in the index, *Prosarhytmus*); J. Leclerq, *Revue du Moyen Age Latin,* I, 1945; E. R. Curtius, op. cit.

24. In addition to the works mentioned in note 23 above, see for this, E.

Faral, *Les arts poétiques,* cit.; J. De Ghellinck, *Littérature latine,* cit., II, pp. 158 ff; *L'Essor,* cit., passim and especially II, pp. 54 ff., 195 ff.; Di Capua, *Per la storia,* cit.

25. G. Mari, "Poetria magistri Johannis anglici de arte prosayca metrica et rithmica," Romanischen Forschungen, XIII, 1902. The quotation is on p. 929 and continues with the exemplification: "pre timore genus humanum obstupeat, de communi dampno quilibet abhorreat; admirentur servi, stupescant liberi; dum vocantur ad cathedram elingues pueri, conformantur magistri leves discipuli. . . . See also the passage (with some variants) in L. Rockinger, "Briefsteller und Formelbücher des XI bis XIV Jahr-hunderts," *Quellen und Erörterugen zur bayerischen und deutschen Geschichte,* IX, 1863, pp. 483 ff. For the high and widespread authority of John of Garland, in addition to what was said in Chapter I, see also: G. Mari, "I trattati medievali di ritmica latina," *Memorie dell' Istituto Lombardo,* XX, 1899, pp. 373 ff. (on pp. 407 ff. is published the part II of the *Poetria,* that is, the *Ars rithmica);* E. Faral, *Les arts poétiques,* cit., pp. 40 ff.; C. S. Baldwin, *Medieval rhetoric and poetic,* New York, 1928, pp. 191 ff.; J. De Ghellinck, *L'Essor,* cit., passim (see the indexes). In the *Ars rithmica* Johannes defines *leonitas*: "rectas consonantias in fine dictionum que dicuntur leonitates a Leone inventore" (p. 419, ed. Mari, cit.); and for such definition see also Polheim, op. cit., p. 341; C. Erdman in *Corona Quernea,* Weimar, 1941, pp. 55 ff.

26. See, for example, Honorius of Autun, "Speculum Ecclesiae," *Patrologia latina,* vol. 172, columns 829-830. The remark is by Perdrizet and Schiaffini.

27. In addition to the works mentioned see P. Perdrizet, *Etude sur le Speculum humanae salvationis,* Paris, 1908, pp. 9 ff.; Th. M. Charlund, *Artes praedicandi,* Paris, 1936; F. Di Capua, *Sentenze e proverbi nella tecnica oratoria,* Naples, 1947.

28. Still unpublished so far as I know but the results are reported by Perdrizet, p. 13, and by De Ghellinck, *L'Essor,* cit., p. 196.

29. Perdrizet and De Ghellinck, op. cit.; for the translations of Golin, see A. Thomas. *Mélanges . . . de l' Ecole de Rome,* 1881, p. 267.

30. For Guittone, see Schiaffini, op. cit., pp. 37 ff.; F. Meriano, *Introduzione alle lettere di Fra Guittone,* Bologna, 1923. For Francesco da Barberino see O. Antognoni, *Giornale di Fiologia Romanza,* IV, 1894, p. 78; F. Egidi, "Per una nuova edizione del Reggimento e costumi di donna," *Studi Romanzi,* XXVII, 1937; G. E. Sansone, "Per il testo del Reggimento," *Giornale Storico di Lett. It.,* CXXVII, 1950. For the Franciscan writers

and the *Cantico* see V. Branca, *Il cantico di Frate Sole,* Florence, 1950, pp. 58 ff. Certain translations are not lacking in examples of versified prose, for example, those from Aesop in the Tuscan text, which is best represented by the Riccardiano, 1645 (see for example the fables XXXI, L, LIII, LV, LX), as I have been able to ascertain during the researches which I am making on the translations from Aesop in the Italy of the thirteenth and fourteenth centuries (see "Un Esopo volgare veneto," *Miscellanea Ferrari,* Florence, 1951).

31. In the previously mentioned *Breviarium de dictamine* see the careful analyses of it in Rockinger, op. cit. pp. 1 ff. (with texts); Manitius, op. cit., III, pp. 301 ff.; De Ghellinck, *Littérature,* cit., pp. 165 ff., and *L'Essor,* cit., II, pp. 57 ff.

32. See, for example, Torraca, *G. Boccaccio a Napoli,* cit.; P. de Nolhac, "Boccaccio et Tacite," *Mélanges . . . de l' Ecole de Rome,* XII, 1892; V. Branca, ed., *Amorosa Visione,* cit., pp. CIII ff. and 427; G. Billanovich, "Petrarca e Cicerone," *Miscellanea G. Mercati,* Città del Vaticano, 1946 (p. 17 of the extract). For the tradition coming down from Alberico and still alive in Montecassino in the thirteenth and fourteenth centuries see De Ghellinck, *L'Essor,* cit., II, pp. 60 ff., 80.

33. For knowledge and imitation of Paulus Diaconus, see *Boccaccio medievale,* pp. 301 ff.; for the *Golden Legend* and the *Alphabetum* see *passim* the commentary on the *Decameron* in my previously mentioned edition.

34. G. Lisio, *L'arte del periodo nelle opere volgari di Dante,* Bologna, 1902; E. G. Parodi, reviews in *Bulletino della Società Dantesca* (new series), X, 1903, pp. 73 ff. and XXVI, 1919, pp. 16 ff.; A. Schiaffini, op. cit., pp. 85 ff. Petrarch also, moreover, was not insensible to the charm of the *cursus* and of rhymed prose. See E. Raimondi, "Correzioni medievali . . . ," *Studi petrarcheschi,* I, 1948; G. Martellotti, "Clausole e ritmi nella prosa narrativa del Petrarca," *Studi petrarcheschi,* IV, 1951; also M. Boni, *Studi petrarcheschi,* III, 1950, pp. 242 ff.

35. They are carefully scrutinized in the previously mentioned writings of Parodi on Boccaccio, and more exhaustively—especially for the minor works—by Schiaffini, pp. 151 ff.

36. Other analogous examples may be seen in I, 4, 3; II, 9, 4; II, concl., 1; III, 4, 7; III, 7, 4; III, 9, 4; IV, 5, 4; IV, 7, 6; VII, 2, 10; VII, 4, 5; VIII, 7, 2; IX, 5, 2; and so on. Naturally in all these illustrations it is necessary to keep in mind the very free technique used by Boccaccio in this versification, subject to the most daring license (dialeph, synaleph, dieresis, sineresis, among others) and to the less-used accentuations, a phenomenon stressed in like cases by Egidi also (art. cit., in

Francesco da Barberino); phenomena illustrated and widely studied in the mentioned critical editions of the *Teseida* and *Amorosa Visione*. And one must not neglect the fact that in the flow of the prose natural elisions occurred between those members of which we give in these pages the disposition of the verses, only as illustrating examples, and I might say didactic examples; and that opportune or necessary dropping of final syllables could be indicated only by the dot written under them. The examples presented in these pages naturally represent only a sparse selection. More systematic indications are to be found in the notes of my previously mentioned commentary.

37. For the broad and decisive influence of the *cantari* on the youthful works of Boccaccio and in particular on the *Filostrato* and *Teseida*, see V. Branca, *Il cantare trecentesco e il Boccaccio* cit. I refer the reader to this little volume and to one by Ezio Levi (*I cantari leggendari del popolo italiano*, Supplement 16 to the *Giorn. Stor. Lett. It.*, Turin, 1914) for more details of my remarks on the customs of the *canterini* in the following pages.

38. See for example other endings terminated with verses in II, 9, 75; II, 10, 43; V, 4, 49; V, 10, 64; VI, 7, 16; X, 8, 52; X, 9, 113 among others.

39. See analogous examples in I, 7, 16; II, 1, 17; II, 2, 19; II, 8, 97-98; III, 7, 64; III, 8, 37; V, 3, 35; V, 4, 43-44; V, 5, 27; V, 6, 8; VI, 2, 17, and 28; VI, 4, 8, and 16; VI, 8, 13; VIII, 1, 13-14; VIII, 7, 19; X, 8, 49; X, 9, 59 and so on.

40. For a general treatment of this tradition see the works mentioned in notes 23 ff., and that of Perdrizet in particular; also A. Wilmart, *Auteurs spirituels*, Paris, 1932; G. De Luca, "Un formulario di cancelleria francescana," *Archivio di storia della pietà*, I, 1951.

41. For other similar examples see II, 8, 35; II, 9, 52; VI, 4, 9; VI, concl., 15; VII, 1, 27, and 32; IX, 10, 16, and others.

42. See G. Boccaccio, *Amorosa Visione*, critical edition by V. Branca above (especially pp. CXLVII ff. of the Introduction and the commentary *passim*); V. Branca, "L'*Amorosa Visione*: tradizione, significati, fortuna," *Annali della Scuola Normale di Pisa*, N. S. XI, 1942. And for the *Caccia di Diana* see V. Branca, *Tradizione delle opere di Giovanni Boccaccio*, Rome, 1956.

43. See V. Branca, *Il cantare trecentesco*, cit.; G. Boccaccio, *Teseida*, critical edition by S. Battaglia, Florence, 1937, pp. CXLIX ff.

44. See, for example, sonnet LVI, *Se quel serpente che guarda il tesoro*, filled with imprecations against the constant oppressive watchfulness of the husband of the beloved.

45. B. Croce, *Poesia popolare e poesia d'arte,* Bari, 1946, pp. 81 ff.

46. For examples analogous to all those presented in these last few pages, see also III, 1, 20; V, 6, 38; VII, 5, 3; VIII, 1, 14; VIII, 2, 34; VIII, 3, 15; VIII, 5, 7; VIII, 9, 33 and 47 among others.

47. For other versifications in the introductions see, for example, III, intr., 6; V, intr., 1; VI, concl., 15 and so on.

48. And for this use of rhymed prose it would be easy to recall the most authoritative texts of medieval rhetoric, from the precepts of Alberico of Montecassino (for example, *Flores,* cit., VIII: "Tenendum etiam censemus esse summopere ut non tantum pulchritudini vel sonoritati, verum etiam tam verborum quam sententiarum insudes dulcedini," *Breviarium de dictamine,* VIII-XIII) to those already mentioned of Johannes of Garlandia.

49. For this language and these expressions, of the people or of the *cantari* themselves, may I be permitted to refer the reader once more to my *Il cantare trecentesco,* cit., pp. 36 ff.

50. In this connection see *Boccaccio Medievale,* Chapter VII and its documentation.

51. Echoes of the "stil nuovo," and in particular of Cino da Pistoia, are not rare in the lyrics, and in the love poetry of Boccaccio: see G. Boccaccio, *Rime . . .,* edited by V. Branca, Bari, 1938, pp. 326 ff. (notes); *Amorosa Visione,* critical edition, cit., in the index (Stil Novo); *Filostrato,* V, 62-63; and also G. R. Silber, *The Influence of Dante and Petrarch on Certain of Boccaccio's Lyrics,* Menasha, Wisconsin, 1940; *Boccaccio Medievale,* pp. 114 f., 257; V. Branca-P. G. Ricci, "L'incontro napoletano con Cino" in *Studi sul B.,* V, 1968.

52. For other similar examples see II, 6, 52; II, 7, 42, and 48; III, 2, 8; III, 9, 15, and 20-21; V, 3; IX, 5, 58; VIII, 9, 112; X, 4, 2 and others.

53. For other solemn declarations in verse for example II, 7, 86; IV, 2, 27, and 36; V, 6, 38; VII, 5, 3; VIII, 9, 112; X, 4, 2 among others.

54. P. Bembo, *Prose della volgar lingua,* edited by C. Dionisotti, Turin, 1926, p. 63.

55. L. Salviati, *Degli avvertimenti della lingua sopra il Decameron,* Naples, 1712, p. 111.

56. Ugo Foscolo, "Discorso storico sul testo del Decamerone," *Saggi e Discorsi critici,* edited by C. Foligno, Florence, 1953 (vol. X of the Edizione Nazionale delle Opere di Ugo Foscolo), p. 347. The same idea is in the "Discorsi sulla lingua italiana," *Prose Letterarie,* Florence 1939 (Vol. IV of the *Opere edite e postume di Ugo Foscolo),* p. 205.

57. Further documents and details useful for the understanding of the

techniques and problems discussed in this chapter, not without references to Boccaccio, are provided by: F. Quadlbauer, *Die antike Theorie der "genera dicendi,"* Wien, 1962; C. Segre, *Lingua, stile e società,* Milano, 1963; G. L. Beccaria, *Ritmo e melodia nella prósa italiana,* Firenze, 1964; V. Branca, "Poetica del rinnovamento e tradizione agiografica nella *Vita Nuova,"* in *Studi in onore di Italo Siciliano,* Firenze, 1966; C. Margueron, *Recherches sur Guittone d'Arezzo,* Paris, 1966. D. Rastrelli has developed my analyses for other novellas of the *Decameron* in "Letture boccaccesche" in *Studia Ghisteriana,* S.II, II, 1957.

The attribution of the Vulgarization of Livy to Boccaccio (see p. 223) has now been confirmed by M. T. Casella, "Nuovi appunti attorno al Boccaccio traduttore di Livio," in *Italia Medioevale e Umanistica,* IV, 1961.

CHAPTER 3

The Mercantile Epic

Boccaccio pictures the very sumptuous mercantile life of Italian civilization at the end of the Middle Ages in a series of daring and spirited tales comprising the *Decameron*. This society was led by a handful of men bent on the conquest of Europe and the East. They were men of initiative and perseverance, who, having been misunderstood and distorted by Sombart, are only now being revealed as men of exceptional stature.[1]

Furthermore, they were disdained by Dante as "la gente nova e i subiti guadagni"—upstarts and profiteers. They were ignored as being inferior or alien to the refinements Petrarch represented. Compagni mentioned them very little in his historical works, nor were they considered in the stylized narrations of the *Novellino*. Boccaccio was just the writer to recognize the mercantile society in the "human comedy" of his *Decameron*. The life of this society dominates the whole work with an exuberant vitality. Boccaccio did not use the mercantile class merely to provide the themes, backgrounds, characters, and customs that color more than half the novellas, but because of its exemplary significance in both a human and artistic sense. That is, the presence of this social class in the narrative is an irreplaceable necessity in the development of the *Decameron*.

276

No other class could be used to portray the measure which man can give of his endowments and his capacities when confronting the great forces which seem to dominate humanity—Fortune, Love, Ingenuity—Boccaccio could not find examples in that age of a more powerful and more overpowering representative eloquence. After the era of the knights of the sword, henceforth cherished only in memory and tinged with a subtle nostalgia, it is the world of the Italian merchants which, in the late Duecento and the early Trecento, provides the most vital, aggressive champions in the struggle against those superhuman forces.[2] It is in that world, to quote Stendhal, that the "plant, man," was then growing most vigorously. Those people were traveling all over the known world, always endeavoring to avoid the ambushes of Fortune, always tensed to overcome with their own ingenuity the initiatives and the pitfalls of other men's ingenuity, and always ready to prove their readiness in the most varied adventures of love.

These were the real pioneers of the waning medieval civilization: pioneers—to quote the most authoritative student of their period—"with open minds, with ready intelligence, with a solid culture, with aspirations which verged on ambition and on pride, tenacious and persistent." They imposed everywhere "such a personality as invited the flattery of princes and aroused populations to rancor; pioneers who returned home laden with experiences and riches, both of which were devoted to further their political ambitions" and to sublime creations of art in the splendid private and public palaces, in the churches and the temples which have preserved the civilization of that century for future generations.

The very description of the sumptuous life of the Bardi and Peruzzi has almost the colors of a golden legend.[3]

The Italian society of the time was resounding with this magnificent and eventful undertaking which was centered in Florence and based on the strength of the florin, which had supplanted the Byzantine hyperper and the Arabic dinar.[4] During this time, in the very heart of his own family, Boccaccio had lived through the earliest and most dazzling and enthralling episodes of his existence. His family served as agents in their own right and as *fattori* [bailiff-farmers] of one of the most powerful "companies," that of the Bardi family—who with their allies the Peruzzi and Acciaiuoli constituted the "pillars of Christianity" as Villani called them. Boccaccio's father and uncles for more than forty years had traveled the highways of European traffic, between Florence, Naples, Paris, and the great French fairs. In his Latin works Boccaccio recalls with emotion the tales his father had told him of his own adventurous and often fearsome experiences during these travels.[5] And Giovanni himself, having become a skilled computer with the abacus at an early age, had begun work in Naples, in the shadow of the Bardi bank. He worked next door to the warehouse of the Frescobaldi family in that zone of commercial transactions which he was to use as the bewitching background of the picaresque nocturne of Andreuccio. He spent these years in the bank, receiving its customers, having the "exchequer," and keeping the books: ledgers, cash, drafts, and letters of change, and real estate, which he bought and sold. He drew up "audits of the books" to be used in "settling the accounts," that is, arriving at the final balance sheet for the *compagni*. Those were years spent in all the other tasks proper to an "apprentice" such as he. Boccaccio lived and tried to forget the weariness and the risk of that existence devoted to shrewd deals, daring moves, and pitfalls,[6] for he was given a chance to enjoy a singularly close contact with the mercantile world. Boccaccio constantly made new contacts with men from the most diverse countries who met in the warehouse, not only to talk business but to await messengers bringing news of the various markets to be compared and discussed. The colorful and fabulous tales told by friends and relatives were nourished and given substance by direct experience, that is, by a firm truth which made them humanly and imaginatively real and definite.

The fascination of the mercantile tales of the *Decameron* lies in their sharp outlines and clear references based on Boccaccio's personal knowledge of the business world. Because of his experiences in the mercantile adventures of his time, Boccaccio was able to develop and "bring alive" the business world to a point that it almost became a character itself. Ciappelletto's cold, calculated impiety dominates Boccaccio's description of impartial and mercantile pitilessness which, to judge from historically documented customs, governs the actions of Musciatto Franzesi and his usurious brothers.

The frustrated ingenuousness of Andreuccio, which begins the fantasmagorical sequence of increasingly romantic events, is arrested in an imprudent but customary gesture, in that same Neapolitan market place which was one of the most animated and famous centers of the horse trade. Boccaccio describes the rapid alternation of the fortunes of Landolfo and Martuccio, which flashes the more stormily and suddenly against the background of the seafaring custom of the "mude" (that is, of convoys), and of the facility with which the most casual traders and merchant adventurers indulged in piracy, as documents attest for the men of Lipari, such as Martuccio. The poetry of the theme of love and death in the figures of Simona and Silvestra is dominated by the environment of the merchants. Boccaccio places his tale in a humble world of labor and of affections, imaginatively depicted and defined through the action of "masters," "agents," and "apprentices." The story takes place amidst "disciples" (who like Boccaccio, go abroad "to perform the duties they had learned"), "shop boys," "artisans," "spinners" (Simona is the first elegiac spinner in Italian literature!). Boccaccio could develop the mocking, roguish rhythm of the web of deceits between Salabaetto and the fair Sicilian with unerring certainty only because he had a minutely detailed knowledge, or rather direct experience, of the mechanisms used in the ports for deposits, warranties, and advance payments.[7]

Boccaccio fuses all the elements together with his mobile, shifting narration. In turn, through his narratives, Boccaccio made this mercantile world seem alive and present as no other writers were ever again to do in Italian narrative literature. From Sercambi on down to the story-tellers of the sixteenth century narrative was reduced merely to imitating the many literary paradigms inherited from the dazzling example of the *Decameron*.

His mercantile experience had allowed Boccaccio to observe contemporary life, but life as it was beyond the commune, the region, beyond Italy itself, over civilized Europe, and over the eventful Mediterranean. Nevertheless, Tuscany and Florence (and Siena and Pisa) are always at the center of the ideal geography of the *Decameron*, as they also were of commerce and finance. However, he used other locations as well. He described Piedmont (I, 6; X, 10), on the edge of Italy, which was still tightly enclosed in an archaic feudal life amidst a mountain austerity (except for Asti). It is delineated almost as though it were part of a fairy tale. He describes Friuli at the other end of the Alps, as "a rather cold land, joyous with beautiful mountains, many rivers and clear springs." It is colored with the impressions of merchants who were fellow townsmen (and perhaps relatives of Boccaccio), Lapo and Lodaringo from Certaldo (X, 5).[8] Boccaccio becomes more complete and more precise when he describes the regions which participated more actively in European traffic, sometimes in sharp and direct competition with the Florentine and Sienese companies. Naturally there are echoes of these rivalries and of the opposing alliances (often projected on the political plane) which give light and shade to these environmental glimpses. Boccaccio describes Venice, noisy with trade, suspicious, and jealous of the Florentines, through a veil of scornful animosity with the usual "blazon" of corruption, of treachery, and of talkative frivolity current in Tuscan commercial circles and undoubtedly confirmed by Boccaccio's friends in Romagna (IV, 2; VI, 4 and even II, 1).[9] Boccaccio represents the great rival of Florence, Genoa (whose friendship in the enduring struggles with Pisa was one of the pillars of Florentine politics in the fourteenth century), by a gallery of hardworking, tenacious merchants, stubborn to the point of stinginess but open to more generous impulses, and faithful to the ancient, invincible honesty, which is matched by the exalted virtue of their womenfolk (I, 8; II, 8 and 9; II, 10).[10] Boccaccio broadens his descriptions even more when he writes about the two great republics: on the one hand the courtly life of the cultured cities of the Venetian sphere from Treviso to Verona (I, 4; II, 1), and on the other the harsh beauty of the eastern and western Rivieras studded with castles, with busy towns, with lands cultivated by the merchants themselves (Mulazzo, Lerici, Finale, Albenga, Monaco: I, 4; II, 6, 8, 9 and 10; VIII, 10). Boccaccio does not describe Lombardy and Milan to so great an extent, probably because their financial and commercial activities were not yet powerfully developed. Furthermore, he may not have held so great a sympathy for these towns for their trade was directed toward lands such as Switzerland and Germany, somewhat outside the prevailing interests of the Florentine companies, and because Florentine politics of those years were particularly suspicious of, even hostile to, that region and its rulers. Boccaccio, however—in addition to other, fleeting mentions (III, 5; VII, 3; X, 9)—does make Milan the background of a tale involving a German and one of those Lombard moneylenders famous throughout Europe (VIII, 1). He uses Pavia as the setting for the story of Teodolinda, as well as for a tale describing the loftiest and noblest idealization of merchant life and contacts between Christian kindness and Arab generosity (X, 9). (The Brescian background of the novella of Andreuola stems from another origin.) Boccaccio uses other locations in the Po River basin—which are still Lombardian in the more common meaning of the term[11]—to portray the ambitious Emilian partners, "companions," and their rich and active cities, each so vital in its characteristic life. He describes Piacenza which had launched its men into France in competition with the Florentines and which appears in all its sanguine vitality through the impartial arrogance of Ambrogiuolo (II, 9).[12] He portrays Modena and Bologna, rich in commercial transactions, learned and aristocratic (I, 10; II, 2; VII, 7; VIII, 9; X, 4). He describes Ferrara, which in the eleventh century had been a marketing center for the silks imported from the Orient and which in Boccaccio's time was a point of departure toward the Venetian lands, notwithstanding the troubles of wars and the insecurities of the roads (II, 2; also VIII, 10). He mentions Faenza, Forlì, Ravenna, Imola, Rimini, and other minor towns, and the lands of Romagna so dear to the Florentines and so familiar at first hand to Boccaccio himself (IV, 2; V, 4, 5, 8; VII, 5; III, 7).[13]

Even the regions left more in shadow by history do not escape the close observation of the author of the *Decameron,* just as they did not escape penetration by the Florentine companies. The Marches and Abruzzi which were strategic strongholds for the Acciaiuoli, the Peruzzi, the Bardi (who had branches in Ancona and Aquila, see III, 7; IX, 4), as well as for those who operated between Florence and Naples,[14] appear dimly, half way between fable and mockery, in the speeches of Maso del Saggio and Frate Cipolla purposefully farcical deformations of commercial echoes (VIII, 3; VI, 10; III, 7; V, 5; VIII, 5; IX, 4). But Boccaccio's memories of the other areas of central Italy are more directly tied to mercantile customs, such as Perugia, which furnished messengers and drovers to the kingdom of Naples. Perugia is the home town of "Andreuccio the horse dealer"; its piazza is sketched as the background of the incredible adventures of the Vinciolos, governors in Terra d'Abruzzo by designation of the Acciaiuoli company (II, 5; V, 10). Rome and Latium, upset and abandoned during the period of the Avignon Captivity, are brought to life in the desolate glimpses of them in the story of l' Agnolella and the livid portrayal of the Roman Campania, full of ambushes and surprises for the Florentine merchants who crossed it on their way to Naples (V, 3; of course all recollections of Rome as the Papal See are considered separately, from I, 2 to X, 2).[15]

Just as in the activity of the Florentine companies and in Boccaccio's own life, so in the *Decameron* the kingdom of Naples is certainly, after Tuscany, the part of Italy whose life and presence is most felt by the reader. Boccaccio reserves his sparkling, almost fairy-tale-like evocations of knights and princes especially for "The Kingdom." But the vitality and the same concrete aspects of the portrayal of those ambiences go back, on the contrary, to the customary impassioning experiences of commerce. Boccaccio describes the thronged fairs of wine-rich Puglia in the tales of Landolfo Rufolo and Donno Gianni (II, 4; IX, 10). His description of landscapes and environments is based on his experience when he lived there as an "apprentice" of the Bardi company.[16] From impoverished and deserted Calabria there comes only the fearsome echo of the terror caused by pirates (V, 6). But, as is natural, the two centers Boccaccio gravitates toward—concerning both the mercantile life and the novellas—are on the one hand Naples and the Campania and on the other, Sicily. Besides his amazingly precise reconstruction of the activities around the port of Naples in the novella of Andreuccio (and in other aspects, in that of Catella and Peronella), in the halo of the ancient commercial prosperity there lies the whole "coast of Amalfi, full of little cities, of gardens and fountains, of rich and industrious men engaged in mercantile pursuits" (II, 4). There are the dreamy gulfs of Salerno, of Naples and Gaeta, with their islands: Ischia, Procida, Ponza; with their fairs (that of Salerno being famous: VIII, 10); with their lively cities, from Ravello to Capua,[17] which unfold fresh beauty over a whole series of novellas (II, 4 and 6; IV, 1 and 10;

V, 6; VIII, 10; X, 5 and so on). And Sicily, dominated by Florentine merchants at Palermo and Messina, at Trapani and Catania, looms up with the enchanting visages of these and other cities and with its harsh and sun-baked isles: Ustica and Lipari. It dazzles like a rich, familiar land stretching out toward the feared and fabulous countries of Barbary (II, 5 and 6; IV, 4 and 5; V, 2 and 6 and 7; VIII, 10; X 7; and so on). Even the other great Italian island, Sardinia—where the Bardi company had agents and factors specializing in the grain trade—peers out of the pages of the *Decameron,* although veiled in a rather indefinite and legendary aura, as an obligatory point of navigation in the western Mediterranean, between Africa and the ports of Provence and Catalonia (II, 7; IV, 4; also III, 8; VI, 10).

It might be said that wherever the initiative of Italian business-men was directed, there too the imagination of Boccaccio, nourished by direct or indirect mercantile experiences, wished to tarry and to sketch persons, environments, and landscapes. And this he did with such exactitude and such evident knowledge, such experience of the men and the affairs of the most active section of the middle class, as to become himself the subject of many Italian legends. The legends relate his adventures in those very places of which he writes, from Udine to Ravenna, from Ferrara to Palermo, and they are so vast, so bizarre, so fanciful and enduring, that they are comparable only to those of Dante.[18]

But that vast European and Mediterranean background on which is embroidered the adventure, or rather the heroic *quête* of the merchants, widens the horizons of landscapes and environments to an extent unprecedented in Italian literature. They begin beyond the Alps with the visual description of the Italian regions, the vastness of the fields and the riches of the cities of France, of Provence, of Burgundy and Flanders (I, 1, 2, 5; II, 3, 8 and 9; III, 9; IV, 2, 3, 8 and 9; VII, 7; X, 2, and so on). Boccaccio tells of exploits across the Channel, in England and even in Scotland and Ireland (II, 3 and 8). That is, he includes all the lands of conquest of the Italian companies—and particularly those of the Bardi and Peruzzi families—lands of rapid, rich and inexorable conquest. By exposing the pitiless cupidity of the Franzesi and the calculating coldness of Ciappelletto and the usur-ious brothers, Boccaccio projects a livid light upon the mercantile affairs in these countries (I, 1). The arrogant and laughing chatter of the merchants gathered in the famous Parisian inn or the alternating vicissitudes of the Lamberti give a rhythm of unprejudiced and ever-fresh enterprise to the picture of this region (II, 9 and II, 3). The courtesy of young Alessandro or the dreamy amiability of Lodovico unexpectedly illuminate this fierce and expeditious world with the light of that magnanimity and courtliness which were the leaven of the great civilized and artistic prosperity born of that prodigious economic vitality (II, 3; VII, 7). Boccaccio also includes the faithful customers of the Italian moneylenders (VIII, 1; II, 1): Spain and Catalonia (II, 7; IV, 3; X, 1), obligatory points of trading and dangerous for navigation (and where the Peruzzi were the dominant leaders), and Germany, still somewhat shut in and as violent as her mercenaries.

But the truly broad field opened to Boccaccio by his Neapolitan experiences and by a famous voyage of the Acciaiuoli, is the sea of Greece, with its famous ports of the Morea,[19] and the eastern Mediterranean, dotted with islands, whipped by gales, beset by wars, by pirates and by the most varied happenings and acts of violence. He was familiar with the great sea power of Constantinople, clearing center for all the Levantine trade, which stretched toward the Black Sea and the wealthy port of Caffa (II, 4 and 7; III, 7; V, 1; VIII, 10). He knew the western Mediterranean in detail through the regular commercial relations with Provence, Catalonia and the Balearic Islands (where the Bardi company had branches, and the Angevins important interests: II, 7; III, 9; IV, 3 and 9; X, 7). In addition to European centers, Boccaccio was familiar with Africa, mysterious and feared, from which Tunis and Alexandria emerge as Meccas of the Italian "companies" (IV, 4; V, 2; I, 3; II, 6, 7 and 9; VIII, 2; X, 9) and with the distant Orient of the Crusades, of Saladin. There the great hope or, often, illusion, of Italian commerce developed along the still fresh tracks of the Crusaders, and the merchants were more successful than the Crusaders in dominating those precious outposts of Asia. They had business interests in Rhodes, Crete, Chios, Smyrna, Acre, Antioch, and especially in Laiassus where, as Marco Polo writes, "all the drugs and all the cloths of silk and of gold from the interior with all the precious merchandise, and the merchants . . . of every country come." Laiassus was an emporium at the crossroads of Syria and Egypt, of Persia and Armenia, and the Bardi concluded advantageous agreements with its king through the intermediary of Francesco Pegolotti. (See I, 9; X, 4 and 7; V, 1; X, 9; II, 7; II, 9; X, 9; V, 7; IX, 9 and so on.)[20]

It is a geographic penchant (confirmed from the *De Canaria* to the *De Montibus*) which answers, in its own personal and original way, the rush of Italian merchants in the thirteenth century toward unknown lands and new markets. There is not, one may say, any land marked by the exploits and achievements of these persistent and daring conquistadores of the late Middle Ages which does not elicit a precise testimony and a vivid narrative transfiguration in the *Decameron*, in this marvelous "book of merchants' navigation."

To this new unlimited broadening of geographical horizons there corresponds a widening of human perspectives equally rich and audacious. In the sprightly series of tales in which Boccaccio exemplified the ideal theme of his "comedy," those intrepid merchant figures have a central place as protagonists. In order to present witnesses, living and authoritative—in either a positive or a negative sense—of the great human truths on which the *Decameron* is built, it was natural for the writer to turn to the representatives of that humanity which, to repeat Renan, gave "la plus grande leçon d'énergie et de volonté de l'histoire."

In the bitter reproof of vices on the first day, Boccaccio uses the pitiless cupidity of the Franzesi, the calculated impiety of Ciappelletto, the mean avarice of Erminio Grimaldi to give greater depth to the harshly polemic portrayal of the "greats" of the century. By contrast the subtle and lightning-flash shrewdness of Melchisedech or of Abram and the good-humored wisdom of Giannotto or the merchant persecuted by the Inquisitor put into relief the cupidity of the mighty. Boccaccio shows these men to be masters of crafty prudence and subtle polemics, and through their art, capable of eluding the traps set by the greedy mercantile giants. After this *quasi* prelude, in which the most striking and unforgettable figures come straight from the world of commerce, there follows the quickly-moving diptych of Fortune, dominating or dominated (second and third days), in a world crowded with these pioneers of the Italian

economic seignory. From free-and-easy Sandro Agolanti who keeps
a tight grip on commerce in Treviso, to the cluster of Italian merchants cleverly sketched in their after-dinner jocundity at the inn,
there is a whole gallery of powerful and colorful portraits, of ambiences, minutely studied and impressionistically painted, which on
the second day constitutes a magnificent, action-filled mercantile
sequence. There is Rinaldo d'Esti, a rather ingenuous but pious
trader plying between Emilia and Venetia who, after the most
unexpected misfortunes, receives from his Saint Julian the grace of a
pleasant hospitality. There is the rapid alternation of failures and
unhoped-for luck of the Lamberti, always galloping between Florence and England. There are the comic vicissitudes and happy
endings of imprudent and frustrated youths such as Landolfo and
Andreuccio. There is the smiling, astute awareness of the merchants
who sagely complete the incredible, sorrowful pilgrimage to Alatiel.
There is, finally, the rapid, merry picture of Monaco, free port of
pirates and Calvary of merchants (see also VIII, 10). If all the
novellas of the second day, except the eighth, bear a mercantile
stamp, on the third day also this mercantile epic develops in the
subtle scornful contrast between the lady of high lineage and the
nouveau riche woolens merchant to whom she has been given in
marriage (III, 3), in the cautious shrewdness of Zima who profits
from the niggardliness of the noble Vergellesi, in the Oriental adventure in which a Florentine patrician, Tedaldo Alisei, tries to
forget love. It is almost as though Boccaccio wishes to illuminate the
conflict between human ingenuity and Fortune with a light allusive
to the antithesis so dear to him: the antithesis of fortuitous nobility
and nobility won in the continuous struggles of an existence constantly exposed to the most sudden and serious risks, made always
taut by decisive and total commitment. That the characters of the
drama between man and Fortune were chosen from the bourgeois
and merchant classes reveals a new, impassioned attention to that
society. For medieval literature traditionally evoked kings, princes,
knights, with their battles and their military, political and civil
vicissitudes to show that antithesis. Boccaccio himself followed the
medieval conventions in *De Casibus Virorum Illustrium*.

The influential force of the mercantile world on Boccaccio's imagination is even more clearly revealed in the diptych concerning Love, the supreme proof of the nobility or the baseness of men (fourth and fifth days). If Boccaccio's use of figures from the mercantile world in the tales concerning Fortune seems natural despite contrary medieval traditions, his use of bourgeois characters for the diptych on Love is entirely gratuitous. And yet it is almost always families or persons of the middle class who carry the action during the fourth and fifth days. For example, there are the Balducci, agents of the Bardi, protagonists of the famous apologue in the introduction to the fourth day; the great Venetian "mercatanti" "di ca' Quirino," who trade with Flanders; the "Civada" of Provence "of splendid faith," who travel through Spain; the Florentine Sighieri or the men of Lipari given to piracy; and the Sicilians and Genovese in the novellas of Gianni and of Teodoro. Indeed, whether in the great symphony of love and death of the fourth day or in the festive lightness of the musical comedies of the fifth, the noblest, the most impassioned heroines, those most caressed by the imagination of Boccaccio, belong to that very world still ignored by the "sweet new style" and by Petrarch. Lisabetta is shut up in her silent grief until death; Simona, girlishly unwitting, throws her life like a flower on the grave of her beloved; Girolamo and Silvestra are bound indissolubly by love in childhood and then, later, by sudden death; Gostanza is timid and trembling as she faces the unknown and yet does not draw back from the desperate amorous "inquiry." All these unforgettable figures of lovers seem illumined by a more fearful fascination as they stand so very fragile and slender, outlined against the dark background of a world dominated by money, by greed, by the inexorable pitilessness of economic expediency. In their unadorned, almost weary beauty they exercise a power of seduction more subtle than that of the begemmed and haughty feudal ladies, and they are certainly not a whit inferior to them in the nobility and heroism of their sentiments.

The exposition of mercantile life is brought to its fullest development in that vast triptych of "Ingegno" (wit, ingenuity) of the sixth, seventh and eighth days. Again, instead of drawing on traditional medieval sources, Boccaccio turns to bourgeois society for his characters. In the beginning of the triptych, for example,

Boccaccio presents Cisti, a humble trader, who, by virtue of the prudent keenness of his wit, rises above the nobles and grandees. The mercantile world continues to dominate through the eighth day, which evokes the unscrupulous and knavish world surrounding Salabaetto and Canigiani. It would be tiresome to elaborate the examples of the dominance of mercantile characters and themes because they are too obvious and because the point has been made enough times, although with different connotations. It will suffice to recall the powerful mock-heroic resolution of the contrast between nobles and merchants that occurs in the center of the triptych. In the grotesqueness of the invective of a mother-in-law directed at a "petty trader of asses' dung" there seems to be a plebeian transcription of Dante's scorn for one who "cambia e merca" (VII, 8).

Thus, after the pause of the ninth day—when the refined and wealthy world of the Florentine companies is contrasted with the wretchedness and misery of the traders Apulia (IX, 8 and 10)—Boccaccio imparts to the idealized portrayals of the middle class the same literary dignity that medieval tradition gave to nobility. After the lordly prudence and subtle weariness of Gilberto, after the sorrowing blazing profile of Lisa in the novella of Torello, there emerges a most aristocratic depiction of the figure of the merchants, "sage and eloquent."

So from one extreme to the other of the precise and carefully calibrated Gothic structure of the *Decameron*, along the great double or triple arcades which develop it organically and complete it coherently, this mercantile "constant" is revealed as continuous and necessary in the dynamics and in the very values of that carefully planned architecture. Without this urging of a world new to literature, without this highly original life of a social class portrayed and described in its own technical or, rather, expressive language,[21] the *Decameron* would have neither its driving "exemplary" force nor its eloquent, multiform human richness. It could not be *the* poem of the autumn of the Middle Ages in Italy were it not also the epic of the men who have stamped its civilization most powerfully, carrying it to the center of European life.

The mercantile "constant" in the *Decameron* opens unexpected perspectives in the imaginative structure of many of the novellas. It is an invitation to a new reading of this rich and mobile comedy of mankind.

We have already seen this influence in the picaresque tales, like those of Andreuccio da Perugia or Salabaetto (II, 5 and VIII, 10). The flavor of the mercantile society is also apparent, although in a different way, in the adventurous enterprise of the Lamberti (who were closely allied to the Bardi) in England which ended in a fairy-tale apotheosis (II, 3).[22] We also see it in the colorful and emotional portrayal of an unbiased circle of merchants, always—as witness the creation of the *Universitates Mercatorum*—both solidary yet inimical, always present and always competing at the great French fairs, in the rich Italian cities, or in the legendary emporiums of the Orient (II, 9). This mercantile world is also portrayed in the humiliating life of wretchedness and snares of the petty traders of Apulia, the real human dregs of this powerful and enterprising class (IX, 10). But beyond these sequences (and so many others which we have simply pointed to) in which the reflections of that commercial civilization now appear evident to us, the reading "in a mercantile key" reveals in an exemplary way its validity and its power of suggestion when it is applied to famous texts traditionally illuminated by other lights.

The poetry of the elegiac, amorous raving of Lisabetta of Messina, silent unto death in her mourning, palpitates so timorously and so pitifully for the very reason that it rises like a fragile flower of goodness in the pitiless environment of Tuscan merchants.[23] Lisabetta's brothers are brutally absorbed in their trafficking and their money and have neither a glance nor a thought for their sister. They abandon her quiet awaiting of a love, and give not a thought to the heart-breaking dreams of a girl already become "matura virgo," or a care for the needless fading away of her youth. Between the sentiments of the heart and these reasons of narrow self-interest, of stubborn pursuit of gain, there is no possibility of mutual understanding. The brothers in their boundless strength cannot but suffocate the trembling heartbeats of Lisabetta. The pitifully tragic and elegiac rhythm of the novella arises precisely from this antithesis, which is all the more grave because this love of a woman of the class of the partners, the "soci," for a poor apprentice lad seems to aim at sweeping away the implacable laws which govern the life of the "companies." Scandal is a threat to mercantile reputation which may compromise deals: therefore the elimination of Lorenzo is rapidly decided, as a necessary mercantile operation (". . . after long discussion, they decided to pass over the matter in silence . . . until such time as without damage or disgrace to themselves they could remove him from their sight"). The brothers show no concern for their sister, but only for "the damage or disgrace to themselves." And in fact the crime is hastily executed as an unpleasant but necessary business, without a shadow of hesitation ("they took Lorenzo with them and, having reached a very solitary and remote spot, seeing a propitious opportunity . . . they killed Lorenzo and buried him in such wise that no one was aware of their act"). After the murder, the brothers opposed an impenetrable wall of silence to the anxious queries of their sister, who "very often and solicitously" inquired as to the whereabouts of Lorenzo: a wall that echoed darkly an obscure threat ("if you ask us about him any more we will give you the answer you deserve"). Repulsed into the iciness of her anguish and her solitude, Lisabetta takes refuge in her world of anxious fantasies, of obsessive visions, even to the heroism of that macabre and loving gesture ("from that torso she plucked the head . . . then took a fine large flower pot . . . and put it therein wrapped in a fine cloth; and having thrown earth upon it she planted there some clumps of lovely Salernitan basil, and thereafter never did she sprinkle them with any water other than dew or orange water or her very own tears"), until—like a Shakespearian Ophelia—she failed, in a calm and disconsolate raving of which death would be only the final, conclusive episode. But this final elegy of love and death, abandoned and very gentle, fearful, the more chaste and enchanting because it too is projected on the background of the brutal self-interest of the brothers, who have no eyes to see the crescendo of Lisabetta's tender madness until their mercantile interests are threatened ("whereat they were greatly astonished and feared lest the matter become known; and [Lorenzo's head] being buried, with no more words, cautiously leaving Messina and having made arrangements how to extricate their business, they departed to Naples"). The only thing that they worry about is the ordering of their business: henceforth their sister is removed forever from their world and is abandoned to her fate because she has put herself outside of the inexorable laws of their life. The theme of the novella is really the piteous, disconsolate withering of the flower of love and its death in ground hardened by the absolute domination of the "ragion di mercatura."

This is the newest aspect which Boccaccio so acutely portrays in his presentation of this powerful and industrious class: a society in which feelings, passions, and the moral, civil and political laws themselves risk being subordinated to and dominated by this "ragion di mercatura," as implacable and inexorable as two centuries later the "ragion di stato" was to be. It is the great, immeasurable force of these men for whom the laws "constituted . . . only providential screens behind which and under cover of which they could carry on any activity which would lead them to their goal." It is the force of these men who, "when in spite of everything, they perchance encountered in the law a real obstacle, even though this law was of their own creation, and to hide or justify its violation appeared absolutely impossible, they audaciously and unscrupulously suppressed the hindrance." [24]

To illuminate this world where the "ragion di mercatura" is absolute, Boccaccio opens the *Decameron* with the tale of Ser Ciappelletto. Too often and too exclusively critics have considered this tale to be an impious mockery of the cult of the saints or a portrait in high relief of a hypocrite of exceptional rascality. Thus it has gone unnoticed that the narrative starts with an exasperated portrayal of the extremely hard life of merchants and contractors in France. It pictures the life of jailers continually watched with hatred by the populace, or the life of *conquistadores* encamped in foreign lands, subject to pitfalls and snares amid people always ready to break out in revolt and rioting. In the appalled dismay of the two Florentine usurers (I, 1, 26) there is at work that unrelenting circle of deep-seated malice and hostility which surrounds and threatens them. The fires of pogroms and the massacres during the persecutions which took place in France (1277, 1299, 1308, 1311, 1312, 1329 and so on) emit fearsome flashes, while in that sharp-edged epithet of scorn, "these Lombard dogs," there seem to echo and reëcho the curses and the jests which were the constant counterpoint to the name of "Italian merchants" in everyday speech, in songs and chronicles ("The Lombards are very crooked men . . . traitors they are and full of guile . . . they devour and lay waste . . . not only men and beasts, but also mills and castles, lands, fields, woods and forests . . . they bring . . . only a piece of paper in one hand and a pen in the other and thus clip the wool from off the inhabitants' backs and pay them taxes with the natives' own money . . . they are fat to bursting at the expense of the needy and are like wolves devouring the people . . ."). Only after this introductory narrative does the absolute law which determines the action of the characters in the novella become intelligible: whatever the cost, they cannot and must not permit that their inexorable tyranny suffer the smallest crack, lest they suffer a total collapse of their power and the loss of their very lives. It is this iron law of trade which colors their portraits with sinister power: Musciatto Franzesi, a selfish man "of great cunning" (Compagni), does not hesitate to jeopardize the life of his old friend, unemployed and ill, for the sake of strengthening his own power in Burgundy and of keeping a curb on those "Burgundians . . . full of deceit . . . intractable" about paying the heavy tribute. The Florentine usurers who take Ciappelletto into their house are concerned only with the harm which might befall their business and have not the slightest thought for the illness, the death, or the damnation of the soul of their guest (remember the inhuman concluding words after the sacrilegious confession: "seeing that he would be received into a church for burial, they had no care concerning the rest"). An extreme example of man's subjugation to the "ragion di mercatura" is Ciappelletto himself, who chooses to damn his soul for eternity rather than to endanger the domination of the Italian bankers in Burgundy. It is this "reason" which leads him, a believer (and not a sceptic as has been alleged), to the sacrilegious confession at death's door (22-28). This is the motif for the admiration of the usurious brothers for Ciappelletto's incredible impiety, akin to that of Capaneo [one of the seven against Thebes; see Inferno XIV, 46-71; XXV, 15] and for his superhuman (or rather, inhuman) strength ("What manner of man is this, whom neither old age nor infirmity nor fear of the death which he sees approaching, nor even fear of God before whose judgment seat he expects shortly to stand, have been unable to deter?"). And then, too, the famous sinister portrait of Ciappelletto which opens the story with its dark uncompromising lines and gloomy sharp-edged enumerations does not appear to be an oratorical delay nor a piece of bravura, but rather a coherent and necessary premise to the enormous, calculated impiety which is the heart of the novella and which is portended in the shudder of the words which end the sinister profile with the echo of the evangelical horror for Judas ("Bonum erat ei si non esset natus homo ille"). The entire sacrilegious confession obeys this premise: even the satisfaction of Ser Ciappelletto, fully engrossed at a certain point in his mocking and impious game, is but the full development of those motives presaged in the introduction. This confession also ends on two notes of horror: the quoted words of the brothers, and the vision of him "in the hands of the devil in perdition."

The portrait of Ciappelletto is sinister because at the center of Boccaccio's attitude there is a certain hesitation. As he extolls this new mercantile epic, Boccaccio also calls attention to its limits or rather, to the inhuman aspects of this powerful civilization. The figures of Musciatto and Ser Ciappelletto, for example, are tinged with gloom and blame. Boccaccio's hesitation and dismay may recall similar feelings in Dante, which Boccaccio emphasized (*Esposizioni* V, I, 177 ff.), and they are occasioned by sinners such as Paolo and Francesca, for example, and by the strength of the passions and influences which brought them to damnation ("When I heard those wounded souls . . ."). Boccaccio's awareness of the destructive aspects of the "ragion di mercatura" allows him a certain detachment and prevents his writing a passionless eulogy or panegyric. This consciousness, although perhaps painful for Boccaccio permits him to present the mercantile world in all its contrasts, in the merciless harshness and the ineluctable necessities on which the European empire of that handful of invincible men was founded. To this end, side by side with the splendid fairy-tale adventures of the Lamberti in England and of Tedaldo and Torello in the East (adventures softened in the courtly light of great love), side by side with the generous daring of the undertakings of Martuccio and Landolfo (illuminated perhaps by the creation of unforgettable works of art),[25] side by side with the subtle *trouvailles* and wit of Melchisedech, Cisti, Salabaetto, and Piero Canigiani, Boccaccio sets down the livid finales of actions dominated by the monstrous "ragion di mercatura." And in order to present this harder and cruder aspect Boccaccio follows the directives and the inspiration of his narrative art (see Chapter IV, pp. 312 ff.) He chooses exemplary figures; for example the Franzesi brothers (and their agents, collectors of tithes and tribute in France), who are the prototypes—for public opinion and for Florentine historiography itself—of mercantile origin, from Compagni to Villani. They are prototypes of speculators risen to the summits of power by trampling every scruple, every civil and moral law, going so far as to falsify the coinage and betray the traditional solidarity between Italian merchants.[26] That youthful unscrupulousness, that boldness in pioneering, that expeditious daring, so often admired and colorfully portrayed with warmest sympathy, are caught here in their shady, cruel deformation and degeneration, in an inhuman if not Satanic extreme, whose enormity may dumbfound but cannot attract—as is true of certain Dantean figures, from Capaneo to Vanni Fucci. Ser Ciappelletto himself, who with a maximum of impiety brings a life of rascality to a close, seems to be depicted as an example, as a dark and fearsome stand-in for the traditional portrait of the wise and wary merchant who—like those presented in various other novellas of the *Decameron* (I, 2; II, 7; X, 3)—reached the end of a difficult life serene on his deathbed, with the most humble and pious utterances, leaving most generous legacies.[27] The end of the agent of the Franzesi seems the diabolical caricature of the end of a great champion of the early felicitous mercantile dynamism: of Scaglia Tifi, who also enjoyed the confidence of emperors and the king of France, and who was also a true ruler of finance and commerce in Burgundy. Just like Ser Ciappelletto, gravely ill and having dictated a pious testament, Tifi had himself carried into the Church of the Holy Spirit in Besançon and laid naked on the bare earth, like Saint Francis; and, surrounded by the praying monks, his hands joined together to form a cross upon his breast and his gaze fixed on heaven, he serenely awaited death.

One might indeed say that in those sinister portraits and those inhuman extremes, Boccaccio somehow foresees the limitations of that great movement which started the capitalistic organization of society. He sees them clearly just when, for that Odyssean spirit of research and conquest of new spaces, there is substituted as sole mover and sole law the search for the greatest and quickest possible profit. The epic and imposing *quête* of the Italian merchants setting forth on the conquest of East and West, who had been able to subordinate their personal gains to the common good and to a greater solidarity, to the point of sacrificing their lives for the great ideals of the fatherland and the Crusades,[28] seems then to fall miserably into the mortifying circle of cupidity and avarice. Boccaccio had pointed scornfully to this as the most total negation of every dignity and every virtue of mankind in the *Filocolo* (IV, 106) and the *Filostrato* (III, 38), and later in the *Comedia* (XXXV, 31 ff.) and the *Amorosa Visione* (XII ff.). Indeed, in the *Decameron,* his constant and meditative contemplation of human truths and abilities seems to have nourished with a substance distilled from his own sufferings that scorn which in his youthful works was in large part merely literary. The novellas most polemical in this sense—from that about Erminio Avarizia (I, 8) to the episodes of Vergellesi, Diego della Ratta, Gulfardo and so on (III, 5; VI, 3; VIII, 1)—are vibrant with the realization that mean, unbridled cupidity constituted one of the perils which were degrading contemporary society. It was perilous because, as we read in the correspondence of one of the great merchants of the time, Francesco di Marco Datini, "God wants measure in every thing and no immoderate thing ever pleased that eternal equity."[29] It is a conviction which takes on deeper moralistic and deprecatory tones in the *Corbaccio,* in the letters to Nelli and Maghinardo, and in *De Casibus* (III, 1), and which is affirmed more systematically in some pages of the *Esposizioni* in which it is easy to hear an echo of the epic sung in the *Decameron.*[30]

But already in the *Decameron,* even before the sinister portrayal of the "ragion di mercatura" in the Franzesi brothers and Ciappelletto, it might be said that this conscience is present in the appalling picture of the plague " . . . sent by the just wrath of God upon mortals for our castigation because of our iniquities. . . ." With these words Boccaccio gives literary expression to a widespread conviction reëchoed by experienced merchants turned chroniclers, such as Stefani and Villani.[31] And again, taking statements from the same surroundings and the same writers, Boccaccio does not hesitate to stress, among all those iniquities, the explosion "of avarice" and every

"most cruel sentiment" scornful of the most sacred values of friendship, family, and religion.

Indeed, in the grave and dignified gesture which concludes that
triumph of death and divine wrath, in the sadness for the end of so
many "great palaces . . . fine houses . . . memorable families . . . rich
inheritances . . . famous treasures," an elegiac regret palpitates and
trembles, a mournful and most human emotion, reminiscent of
Tasso, for the eclipse of a rich and stately civilization; that of the first
generation of the great Italian merchants whose decadence, already
begun in the crises and difficulties of the preceding years, seems to
have been inexorably hastened by the terrible scourge of 1348.[32] It is
the conclusion of the pioneering period which in the late thirteenth
and early fourteenth centuries had started the great Italian
mercantile expansion in the civilized countries of Europe and the
Mediterranean, east and west. It is the twilight of the splendid epic
enterprise into which the best representatives of the new middle class
had thrown themselves, looking for profit to be sure, but with a broad
spirit of adventure and human generosity—as Boccaccio notes fondly
in a letter (see below, pp. 326f.). They were men who truly had spread
civilization and opened the way to progress, without arms, without
violence, adopting as the supreme law of their activities not a "ragion
di mercatura" which had become quite inhuman, but the lofty, very
humane standard which stands at the beginning of their statute: "No
enterprise, however small, can have beginning nor end without these
three things: that is, without *potere,* without *sapere* and without *con
amore volere.*"[33] From this generous class went forth the avantgarde
of the new European and Mediterranean unity; the genial evaluators
of global situations and economies, ready to embrace even the most
complex and remote opportunities, like those offered by the
Crusaders and by the great Mongol migrations, in order to expand
their commerce and bring to a higher level of efficiency the civil life of
their communes;[34] the champions of that invincible initiative, of
that insatiable curiosity about men and countries, champions who
might bear such names as Marco Polo, Guido and Ugolino Vivaldi,
or Niccolò Acciaiuoli.

Just in the sunset of this society which at the end of the Middle
Ages had created the presuppositions of the new civil and social way

of life, just when a more cautious and systematic organization was on the point of replacing the adventurous and heroic impetus of the pioneers, Boccaccio created his multiform and very human "comedy," with a feeling for the values and limitations of that grandiose movement, an alert and vigorous feeling which, however, does not diminish his admiration and nostalgic longing for the vital energy of those exceptional men. In the *Decameron,* Boccaccio is the enthusiastic rhapsodist, the inspired *trouvère* of those first heroes, whose confidence in the strength and destiny of their society compelled them toward new horizons, "foursquare to the blows of fate." In the *Decameron,* the epic of the autumn of the Middle Ages in Italy, the boldest precursors of modern society could not be absent; the *chanson de geste* of the paladins of commerce could not be wanting.[35]

NOTES

1. The great adventure of Italy's merchants has been amply documented and explained in the last decades by Armando Sapori in a series of studies, of which I shall mention only the most important: *La crisi delle compagnie mercantili dei Bardi e dei Peruzzi,* Florence, 1926; *Una compagnia di Calimala ai primi del Trecento,* Florence, 1932; *I libri di commercio dei Peruzzi,* edited by A. Sapori, Milan, 1934; *Mercatores,* Milan, 1931; *Studi di storia economica medievale,* Florence, 1956; *I libri della ragione bancaria dei Gianfigliazzi,* edited by A. Sapori, Milan, 1946; *Le marchand italien au Moyen Age, Paris,* 1952 (with ample bibliographies). For all references to the mercantile and economic life of that century, to the customs and the prevailing practices, I have made much use of these volumes based directly on the study of the Tuscan "companies" which were central to Boccaccio's experiences, without of course neglecting other general treatises: for example, A. Doren, *Storia economica d'Italia nel Medioevo* (1914), Italian translation by G. Luzzatto, Padua, 1937; G. Luzzatto, *Storia del Commercio,* Florence, 1915; A. Segre, *Storia del commercio,* Turin, 1923; M. Weber, *Gesammelte Aufsätze zur sozial-und-Wirtschaftsgeschichte,* Tubingen, 1924; J. M. Kulischer, *Allegemeine Wirtschaftsgeschichte des Mittelalters und Neuzeit,* Berlin, 1928 (translated by G. Luzzatto, Florence, 1955); Y. Renouard, *Les hommes d'affaires italiens du Moyen Age,* Paris, 1949 (and also "Le compagnie commerciali fiorentine del Trecento," *Archivio Storico Italiano,* XCVI, 1938). In particular Luzzatto's studies (and the one in *Nuova Rivista Storica* V, 1922) and those of

Sapori confute the thesis of Sombart which, based on data taken from the commerce of German cities, reduces the activities of Italian merchants to petty enterprises of scant importance *(Der Moderne Kapitalismus,* Munich, 1922; Italian translation by G. Luzzatto, Florence, 1925). A broad and precious panorama of the diverse problems of the economy at the end of the Middle Ages has recently been traced by R. S. Lopez, Ch. E. Perrin, M. Mollat, P. Johansen, M. Postan, A. Sapori, Ch. Verlinden in the 3rd and 6th volumes of the *Reports of the 10th International Congress of Historical Sciences,* Rome, September 4-11, 1955, published by the Ed. Sansoni, Florence, 1955. In view of the literary character and content of this essay, from now on I shall refrain almost entirely from specific quotations or documentation of economic history, implying reference to the above mentioned works.

2. Of course using the term "mercante" (merchant) I allude always to the figure of the "mercator" (dealer) or "mercatante" (merchant) which are much more complex than that which the language of today indicates with the noun "mercante." In that not yet specialized or differentiated economy the merchant, it is known, engaged in several lines of activity: that of lender and banker, of merchant and trader, of treasurer, of contractor and so on. Indeed by engaging in one activity he was necessarily forced to assume others: to collect taxes and credits in England, for example, he was led into involvement in the trade and then the industry of wool. "The members of the Bardi and Peruzzi families who engaged in huge foreign lending operations, at any rate banking, accepting deposits by third parties ('arte del cambio'), then invested interest and deposits to acquire woolens which they sold in various markets and had wools made up in their own warehouses ('arte della lana'), and invested also in the purchase of foreign unbleached cloths which they dyed in their own dyeing establishments, decorated, stretched and dried in their own 'tiratoi' or stretching plants ('arte di Calìmala'), and they did not disdain trafficking also in 'spices,' which term included drugs and chemicals, especially raw materials for dyes, as well as a wide range of other associated articles ('arte dei medici e speziali'). Thus the famous escutcheon of the "pears," emblem of the Peruzzi, and that based on the rhombus, the 'losenges' boasted by the Bardi, hung in the streets of Calìmala above warehouses crammed with scarlet goods from Ypres; serges from Caen; arras, draperies from Arras (tapestries); and in via Santa Cecilia shops packed with more modest goods woven in Florence; they were

hoisted like a banner over the fair banks in Champagne, where money changing and the sale of currencies were carried on; they loomed over the great mansions at whose doors there came knocking the ministers of an Edward III of England, of a Philip of France, of a Rupert of Anjou who was lord of Naples, to provide for the expenses of the royal houses and even the wars" (Sapori, *Mercatores,* op. cit., p. 6).

3. See Sapori, *Studi,* p. 1098 and *Le Marchand,* p. xxxv. See also the interesting and significant *Dit des Marchands* by Gilles li Muisis.

4. For this splendid event which made the florin—rather than the Venetian ducat—the monetary basis of commerce, the real dollar of the Middle Ages, see especially C. M. Cipolla, *Money, Prices and Civilization,* Princeton, 1955.

5. Concerning information on the family and the youth of Boccaccio, to which I refer on this page, see the references in Part I of this volume. From 1327 to July 1, 1328, while in Naples, Boccaccio's father received the annual salary of 145 lire (Sapori, *La crisi,* p. 259). Concerning the paternal recollections mentioned by Boccaccio, I allude particularly to the Parisian and Neapolitan tales in the *De Casibus* IX, 21, and IX, 26.

6. In addition to the works referred to in note 5 above, see in particular for the duties of the beginner, Sapori, *Studi,* pp. 695 ff.; and for the correspondences between the places in the novella of Andreuccio and those familiar to Boccaccio in his mercantile activities as a youth, see my notes on the novella itself (II, 5). In the "Ruga Cambiorum," "juxta Petra Piscium," King Carlo II had assigned free of cost to the Bardi, next to the Frescobaldi, "unus ex cambiis suis . . . absque iure pensionis seu quocumque diricto" (De Blasiis, "La dimora di G. Boccaccio a Napoli," *Archivio Storico per le Province Napoletane,* VIII, 1882, p. 93).

7. I shall not pause, as a rule, to give bibliographical documents or references to confirm the real or allusive data here passed over rapidly, since I have pointed them out for the individual novellas in my commentary on the *Decameron.* I refer my readers to it for this study as well as the other studies in Part I of this volume.

8. On this interesting detail see in general A. Battistella, *I Toscani in Friuli,* Bologna, 1898 and Udine, 1903; P. S. Leight, "Note sull'economia friulana del secolo XIII," *Memorie Storiche Forogiuliesi,* XXXIII-XXXIV, 1937-1938; and especially A. Hortis, *G. Boccaccio ambasciatore,* Trieste, 1875; idem, *Studi sulle opere latine del Boccaccio,* Trieste, 1879, pp.

237 and 948. Also G. Bini in "Atti della Società Colombaria" 1908-1909, and P. A. Medin in "Atti Istituto Veneto" LXXXII 1922-1923 for documents on Tuscan merchants—some from Certaldo itself in Friuli and Veneto.

9. For the Venetians the escutcheon of bad faith was of Genovese origin. For all this, in addition to the notes to the novellas cited, see B. Chiurlo, "Per Chichibio 'bergolo viniziano' e per 'i vinziani tutti bergoli,' " *Atti 1st. Veneto,* XCVIII (1939); V. Branca, "Boccaccio e i veneziani bergoli," *Lingua nostra,* III, 1941; and *Esposizioni,* XIV, 1, 59.

10. It should be remembered that, as I point out in the notes to I, 8, Boccaccio was sent by the Florentine Signoria on a mission to the Doge of Genoa on behalf of Genoese merchants who had acted against the   Pisans, in concert with the Florentines. Also, the slave trade carried on by the Genoese is mentioned (II, 8; V, 7), but not condemned, by Boccaccio because it was accepted in those centuries; see also R. Livi, *La schiavitù domestica nei tempi di mezzo e nei moderni,* Padua, 1928; A. Damia, *Schiavitù romana e servitù medievale,* Milano, 1931; L. Tria, "La schiavitù in Liguria," *Atti della Soc. Ligure di Storia Patria,* LXX, 1947; Ch. Verlinden, *L'esclavage dans l'Europe médiévale,* Bruges, 1955.

11. As is known, the terms Lombard and Lombardy in the fourteenth century still had a geographical meaning covering a greater territory than now; Boccaccio himself indicates this (see commentary on *Amorosa Visione,* XL, 40 ff.; *Eclogue,* XVI, 79). The generic term "Lombards" is excluded from the foregoing; on the other side of the Alps it was applied to the lenders (A. Segre, *op. cit.,* I, pp. 215 ff.; G. Piton, *Les Lombards en Frances et à Paris,* Paris, 1892-1893), as is also proved by the *Decameron* (I, 1, 26 "These Lombard dogs . . ." said of the two Florentine brothers who were usurers).

12. In the last decades of the thirteenth century there were at least thirty-seven merchants from Piacenza at the Lagny fair; in 1278 it is a native of Piacenza who as "capitaneus universitatis mercatorum lumbardorum et tuscanorum" confers with the French sovereign concerning the return to Nîmes of the expelled merchants (F. Bourquelot, *Etudes sur les foires . . . ,* Paris, 1865, I, pp. 164 ff., 185; A. Sapori, *Mercatores,* p. 99).

13. For Boccaccio's experiences and residences in Romagna—even during the time of the composition of the *Decameron* (between 1345 and 1350) especially at Ravenna and Forlì—and for the relations of these lands with Florence and Tuscany, in addition to the works cited in note 5

above, see: A. Hortis, *Cenni di G. Boccaccio attorno a Tito Livio,* Trieste, 1887; C. Ricci, "I Boccacci e il Boccaccio a Ravenna," *Miscellanea Hortis,* Trieste, 1910; idem "I Boccacci di Romagna," *Miscellanea Storica della Valdelsa,* XXI, 1913; F. Torraca, "Cose di Romagna in tre egloghe del Boccaccio," *Atti e Memorie della R. Dep. di Storia Patria per le Romagne,* S. IV, II, 1912; G. Billanovich, *Petrarca letterato,* pp. 86, 181, 201, 208 ff.

14. In addition to the general works already mentioned, see the numerous indications in the three volumes of E. Léonard, *Histoire de Jeanne Iᵉ,* Munich-Paris 1932-1936 (in index). In L'Aquila or Sulmona we find one of the oldest copies of the *Decameron* sent by agents of the Acciaiuoli (see pp. 3 ff. and *La prima diffusione,* op. cit.); we find a great friend of Boccaccio and Petrarch, Barbato of Sulmona, making use of the continuous passage of couriers and merchants between Naples and Florence for his correspondence (M. Vattasso, *Del Petrarca e di alcuni suoi amici,* Roma, 1904, p. 14; A. Foresti, *Aneddoti della vita di F. Petrarca,* Brescia, 1928, p. 400; Billanovich, *Petrarca letterato,* pp. 251 ff.); right in Abruzzo Niccolò Acciaiuoli was to hold a very important meeting of his friends (Vattasso, op. cit., pp. 404 ff.; Branca, *art. cit.,* p. 26).

15. See the references and quotations in this regard from Boccaccio's own works, on pp. 312 f.

16. The direct experiences of Boccaccio show especially in the description of particular usages of Apulia in the *Comedia* (XXVI, 70); and in the detailed knowledge which one of his letters (IV) reveals about the factions and the struggles taking place in Barletta, the city of Donno Gianni and the principal branch of the Bardi and Peruzzi companies, near Trani (II, 4), formerly a great emporium but in complete decadence in the fourteenth century.

17. Boccaccio had several friends at Ravello, among them Angelo da Ravello "summus magister grammaticae" (F. Torraca, "G. Quatrario," *Arch. Stor. per le Prov. Napoletane,* XXXVII, 1913); at Capua he engaged directly in financial activity, with the rental of the property of San Lorenzo in Croce: see *Relazione della Commissione Conservatrice dei Monumenti e oggetti di Antichità e Belle Arti di Caserta—Verbale della tornata del 6 luglio 1891,* pp. 419 ff.

18. The reconstruction of this "legend" would be truly informative, as testimony not only of the tremendous success and popularity of Boccaccio even in the natural deformations from which his work suffered, but also in a singular and instructive burgeoning of fantasy, partly erudite, partly popular. And so, beyond any document, we would see

Boccaccio, like a new Rinaldo d'Este, "in a journey from Ferrara to Verona" spend a pleasant night at Castelguglielmo "in an old house belonging to the Castle, which still today is visible" and pointed out (P. Mazzucchi, *Memorie storiche di Castelguglielmo*, Badia Polesine, 1903, p. 7; because of the extreme anthropogeographical exactness of the references to roads, canals, and the adherence to the historical reality of the desolation of the zone during the Polesine war under Azzo VIII—all this in II, 2); we would witness his unsuccessful love affairs in Ravenna and his literary arrows consequent thereto (V, 8; see Borgognoni, in *Domenica letteraria*, III, 1881, n. 13); we would enjoy his pranks and vendettas in Perugia, with none other than Pietro di Vinciolo (V, 10; see Manni, *op. cit.* pp. 638 ff.) and so on.

This strength of fantasy in the location of places has also called forth a legend, similar but in a different direction: that is to say, the identification or the creation of places or details or figures which are at the center of certain novellas: such for example as the secular tradition which, influenced by the Aretine novella (VII, 4) gave the name "of Tonfano" to a well in Arezzo in via dell'Orto, opposite the so-called house of Petrarch (A. del Vita, *Guida d'Arezzo*, Arezzo, 1923, p. 57; U. Tavanti, *Arezzo in una giornata*, Arezzo, 1928, p. 106; A. Chiari, "Una novella aretina del Decameron," *Atti e Memorie dell' Accademia Petrarca*, N. S. XX, 1936), or that which since the fifteenth century, based on hints of Boccaccio (VI, 2), indicated the location of the oven of Cisti near the Florentine church of Santa Maria degli Ughi (Richa, *Notizie istoriche delle Chiese fiorentine*, Florence, 1754, III, pp. 182 ff.; Manni, *Istoria, op. cit.*, p. 392) or the pleasant tissue of notes and fantasies which was, for example, around popular and grotesque heroes of the mirthful novellas of the *Decameron* such as Caladrino and Guccio (one need only, for example, see the lives outlined by Manni, *Veglie piacevoli*, Florence, 1815, I, pp. 11ff.; II, pp. 3 ff.). And along a similar line of ideas and research one might consider also the ample series of novellas which were used and related as events or actually as historical documents by the most diverse writers and scholars: from commentators on Dante to chroniclers, from learned men of the seventeenth and eighteenth centuries down to more modern historians (see, for example, the novellas II, 1 and 6; V, 4; VI, 6, 7 and 9; VII, 3, 6 and 9; VIII, 3, 4, 5 and 8; X, 2 and 6, together with the pertinent notes in my commentary).

19. A single example must suffice, in order not to weigh down these rapid notes: the eventful wanderings of Alatiel (II, 7) seem to be developed on the slender and fanciful filigree of the vicissitudes of the Angevin

princes in Morea, and the adventurous voyage of Niccolò Acciaiuoli between 1338 and 1341, hailed by Boccaccio himself in an epistle (V). When the action of the novella, after the first phrases, shifts to the eastern Mediterranean, the fixed ports of call are: first, the great emporium of Chiarenza (33) frequented by Genoese, Venetians, Florentines—where after its conquest by the princes of Majorca, closely bound to the Angevins—there took place the wedding of two august personages of princely rank celebrated by Boccaccio, Ferdinand of Majorca (brother of Sancha, the wife of King Robert) and Isabella of Ibelin (sung in the *Amorosa Visione*, XLIV, 1 ff., cousin of Hugh of Cyprus, to whom *Genealogia* was dedicated: Rodd, *The Princes of Achaia*, London, 1907, pp. 136 ff.), and where Acciaiuoli embarked for his return to Naples, after his great undertaking (Léonard, *op. cit.*, I. pp. 98 ff., 185, 327; II, p. 121; III, p. 6); then the Morea (44 ff.) where Acciaiuoli's expedition took place, when he was accompanying Robert and Luigi of Taranto to take possession of the principality. These two princes were not esteemed by Boccaccio and were quite effeminate, just like that "prince of Morea" who gets Alatiel in his power (*Egloghe*, III and IV; Villani, XII, 52; Rodd, *op. cit.*, II, pp. 180 ff.; Léonard, *op. cit.*, I. pp. 100 ff.; then Athens and its duke (49 ff.), with probable allusion to Walter VI of Brienne, duke of Athens and lord of Florence in 1343, exactly—as is said in the novella (49)—"friend and relative of the prince" of Morea, he too occupied with continual expeditions in Achaia (see *De Casibus*, IX, 24); immediately afterward Constantinople (63 ff.) with Costanzio and Manovello, respectively son and nephew of the emperor, just as Constantius and Manuel were of Andronicus, emperor in the first years of the fourteenth century, and not alien to those Angevin aspirations and undertakings; then Chios (75), one of the most usual ports of call of Italian merchants in those seas; and finally (76 ff). Asia Minor, under the great shadow of Ozbek, khan of the Golden Horde, who in those very years (1313 to 1340) favored the Genoese on the Black Sea and in Crimea, and was extolled by the associated Florentine and Neapolitan circles (R. Lopez, *Le colonie genovesi nel Mediterraneo*, Bologna, 1938, pp. 299 ff.); leaving aside the imaginary figure of Basano (78 ff.) in which it would be possible to see a souvenir of Basano, faithful associate of King Andrea and enemy of Robert and Luigi Taranto-Acaia (Léonard, *op. cit., passim;* see index).

20. For all this see W. Heyd, *Storia del commercio del Levante nel Medioevo*, Turin, 1913; J. Hatzfeld, *Trafiquants italiens dans l'Orient hellénique*, Paris, 1919; G. M. Monti, *Le crociate e i rapporti fra Oriente mediterraneo e Occidente*

europeo, Rhodes, 1936. The Marco Polo quotation about Laiazzo is taken from *Il Milione,* translated by L. F. Benedetto, Milan, 1931, p. 9. For the frequent and interesting relations between Sicily and Armenia and Tunis, mentioned in V 7 and V 2, see the article of C. Traselli, *Sicilia Levante e Tunisia nei secoli XIV an XV,* Trapani, 1952.

21. The presence of this exceptional, almost jargon-like language (already mentioned on pp. 279 ff.) may suggest another evocative itinerary for a reading in a mercantile key. The event-filled liveliness of the fairy tale doings of the Lamberti in England (II, 3) also results from insistence on terms used in an expressive sense and not in the current meaning ("credere," "to give mercantile credit"; "accattare," to borrow money"; "merito" and "vantaggio," "interest"; "cessare," "to fail"; "accostarsi, accontarsi," "to enter into commercial agreements"; the mocking irony provoked by merchants, who, presumptuous "because they are rich" wish to "become refined or ennobled by marriage alliances" (III, 3; VII, 8); it frisks and crackles in the continuous pizzicato of terms used by artisans and in commerce which, almost like a comic opera counterpoint, accompanies in caricature the acts and gestures of those conceited personages ("artefice lanaiuolo"; "mescolato," mixed textiles; "ordire una tela"; "disputar del filato"; "i lucignoli"; "i pettini"; "gli scardassi"; "romagnuolo," a coarse cloth; "civanzarsi," to advance; "mercatantuzzo di feccia d'asino"; "mercatantuolo di quattro danari"; and so on); the profile of Rinaldo d'Este (II, 2) as a simple, rather ingenuous merchant results directly from his characteristically sententious phraseology ("lascio correr due soldi per ventiquattro denari," "dicendo questo non esser della fede" that is, not worthy of the credit extended to him, and so on); the deceit by thrust and parry between Jancofiore and Salabaetto (VIII, 10) acquires its mercantile exemplarity from the extreme precision of the sparkling linguistic coloring of all those strictly technical terms or expressions ("fondaco," "dogana," "doganieri," "dare per iscritto la mercatantia," "il pregio," "scrivere in sul libro della dogana a ragione del mercatante," "trarre la mercatantia," "i sensali," "ragionar di cambi, di baratti e d'altri spacci," "radere" and "scorticare," that is, to get money by sharp practices and without mercy; "i maestri," that is, the heads of a commercial bank, "i pannilani," "dare, pagare il legaggio," "aver gran fretta dello spaccio," "bucherame cipriano" that is, a particular species of byssus, "accivire" to borrow, "servire" to lend, "balle ben legate e ben magliate," "tirare a pochi" to aim at little

money, "fare fondaco"; "il legno è stato preso da corsari di Monaco e riscattasi diecimila fiorini d'oro," "aver delle due derrate un denaio," "non ne vuol meno che a ragion di trenta per centinaio," "sicurare" and "far sicuro," to give security for a loan, "pregio ingordo," "fare scrivere la mercatantia in uno," "fatte loro scritte e contrascritte," "rimandare buona e intera ragione", etc.); and so on. Such language exercises even subtle evocative or allusive suggestion in entirely aberrational and unforeseeable ways. It is probable, for example, that the great fame and high esteem of the "lana di Garbo" (from which derived "lanaiuolo di Garbo," "panno di Garbo" extended to the wool and textiles of the whole Iberian peninsula and a part of France) caused the "reame di Garbo" to be chosen from among all the Moorish kingdoms in the novella of Alatiel (II, 7) and in the grandly roguish prayer of Frate Cipolla (VI, 10), initiated and weighed on the double meaning of mercantile expressions, "i privilegi del Porcellana," "in Truffia e in Buffia" "vendere a rítaglio," "moneta senza conio" and so on); and it is clear that the play on words with which the priest of Varlungo tries to deceive Belcolore (VIII, 2) is developed on "duagio," that is to say, the current commercial term for the fine cloth of Douai, highly esteemed in Florence and dealt in by the Bardi company ("io voglio che tu sappi che egli [il mio mantello] è di duagio infino in treagio e hacci nel popolo nostro che il tengono di quattragio,": see *Purgatory*, XX, 46). But this is a research project which merits much more detailed investigation and which I expect to develop in another time and place on the basis of documentation already provided by my notes on the *Decameron,* and with the help of the very useful, and already utilized, *Glossary of Medieval Terms of Business,* Florence Edler (Cambridge, Mass., 1934).

22. Consult especially, for the English vicissitudes of the Italian merchants, besides the general works previously cited, A. Sapori, "Le compagnie italiane in Inghilterra," *Moneta e credito,* VIII, 1949.

23. As I have already noted, there existed right in Messina—in whose siege the Florentines took part with the Angevin troops—a colony of merchants of San Gimignano, like Lisabetta's brothers. It would seem that this colony was flourishing, since Charles II addressed himself in 1296 to the men of San Gimignano to obtain help against his enemies and thus protect the interests of that colony (S. Gimignano, Archivio Useppi, Libro di Provisioni, N N 23). And a curious coincidence has been observed also: some Sangimignanese merchants, the Ardinghelli,

transferred from Messina in mid-fourteenth century to Naples, as Lisasbetta's brothers, or rather as was probably a natural custom (see *Nel VI centenario della nascita di G. Boccaccio,* Poggibonsi, 1913).

24. Sapori, *Studi,* p. xix; and the following quotations of songs and chronicles are taken from Sapori, *Mercatores,* p. 97.

25. I allude to the magnificent Arabo-Sicilian palace of the Rufolo family at Ravello, and to the tradition which attributes the splendid ambo of the cathedral and the allusive mosaic to Landolfo.

26. Compagni, II, 4; Villani, VII, 147 and VIII, 56. It is said that Musciatto was the man who persuaded Philippe le Bel (Philip IV) to debase the currency and to plunder the Italian merchants; later most likely he was the evil genius of Charles de Valois in his undertaking against Florence. See in general the study of F. Boch, "Musciatto dei Franzesi," *Deutsches Archiv,* 1943.

27. See Sapori, *Mercatores,* pp. 113 ff.; idem, *Studi,* pp. 839 ff., 101 ff. (also for the end and the will of Scaglia Tifi).

28. See the ample and eloquent documentation supplied by Sapori, *Le Marchand Italien,* pp. xii ff., xlix ff.

29. Lapo Mazzei, *Lettere d'un notaro a un mercante del secolo XIV,* edited by Cesare Guasti, Florence, 1880, II, p. 142.

30. "There are some, then, who, without being in need, become so inflamed with the desire to become rich, that crossing the Alps and the mountains and the rivers and to reach foreign nations by sea, seems a mere trifle to them, despising entirely what Seneca writes to Lucillius about these labors, where he says: *Magnae divitiae sunt, lege nature, composita paupertas. Lex autem illa nature scis quos terminos nobis statuat . . .*" "And if these men were satisfied when they have reached some respectable end, or if they were satisfied to reach this objective with honest labor and laudable profit, perhaps some excuse could be found for the natural appetite which is innate with us: but because we are unable to put some moderation in this, all of us exceed in the wretched vice, that is to say, in inordinate wishing for more than is proper." *Esposizioni,* VII, 2, 58 ff.; and also III, 2, 25 ff. and *Lettera a Pino,* p. 179.

31. Marchionne Stefani, *Cronaca,* in R.R. II. SS², XXX, 1; G. Villani, XII, 84; M. Villani, I, 2. And, in general, for merchants who became writers, see C. Bec, *Les Marchands écrivains,* Paris, 1967.

32. For this, see the important conclusions of Ch. Verlinden, "La grande peste de 1348 en Espagne: contribution à l'étude de ses conséquences économiques et sociales," *Revue belge de Philologie et d'Histoire,* XVII, 1938; Y. Renouard, "Conséquences et intérêts démographiques de la

Peste Noire en 1348," *Population*, III, 1948; E. Perroy, "A l'origine d'une économie contractée. Les crises du XIV siècle," *Annales d'Economies, Sociétés, Civilisations*, II, 1949; C. M. Cipolla, I. Dhont, M. M. Postan, Ph. Wolff, *Rapport au IX Congrés International des Sciences Historiques:* section I: Anthropologie et Demographie, Paris, 1950.

33. See Sapori, *Mercatores*, p. 533 and especially pp. 155 ff., 619 ff., 1013 ff., for the above-mentioned passage from one to the other of the two "moments" of the mercantile economy.

34. This is the vision on which Renouard was particularly insistent, and more recently in the article "Le rôle des hommes d'affaires italiens dans la Méditerranée," *Revue de la Mediterranée*, XV, 1955.

35. For a Marxist interpretation of this mercantile epic which I have pointed out, see: Z. Rózsa and G. Sallay, articles in the volume of miscellany *Renaissance Tenulmáyok*, Budapest, 1957; and for an acute historical point of view: G. Getto, *Letteratura e critica nel tempo*, Milano, 1968, pp. 359 ff. And see also the volume of the *Cambridge Economic History* (ed. M. M. Postan and H. J. Habakuk) entitled *Economic Organization and Policies in the Middle Ages*, Cambridge, 1963. For the voyages of the merchants: J. P. Roux, *Les explorateurs au Moyen Age*, Paris, 1961; V. Bertoloni, "Le carte geografiche nel *Filocolo*," in *Studi sul Boccaccio*, V, 1969 (concerning the geografic-mercantile culture of Boccaccio and the possibility that he knew the maps of Marin Sanudo).

CHAPTER 4

The New Narrative
Dimensions *

In the spring of 1351, Boccaccio met with the man who was to
be his "preceptor" and his "magister," Francesco Petrarca. That
meeting in Padua proved to be the most fortunate encounter in the
history of Italian literature, one that was decisive for all of European
culture. Two years afterwards, Boccaccio recalled it with timid
emotion:

> I believe you will remember, illustrious preceptor, for the third
> year has not yet passed since I came to you at Padua as a nuncio
> (messenger) from our Senate, and having completed my mis-
> sion I spent a few days in your company, and almost all of that
> time we spent in just one way; you busy with your sacred
> studies, I eager to possess your compositions, making copies of
> them. As the day was waning into evening, as though by
> mutual understanding we arose from our labors and went into

* In order not to weigh down with notes the discourse which necessarily proceeds at
a rapid pace, I advise the reader that all the documentation relating to historical or
factual references in the novellas mentioned is to be found in the notes to my
edition of the *Decameron.*

your little garden all verdant with leaves, and flowers of early
spring. Then a third man would join us, your friend Silvanus,
and sitting there conversing in quiet and pleasant leisure we
passed the remainder of the day and on into the night. (Ep. IX)

It was the first time since the hurried and rapid conversations in
Florence in 1350 that the two great spirits could discuss their in-
nermost spiritual and literary convictions. Boccaccio, who was
"eager to possess the compositions" of Petrarch, but too poor to hire
a scribe, tirelessly copies the works of Petrarch. And, naturally
(Petrarch's constant interest in Boccaccio's work has been over-
looked for too long), Petrarch inquired about his friend's latest
writings. Boccaccio was concluding his draft of the *Decameron* at this
time, and it is more than probable that he discussed it with Petrarch
during this meeting (the foremost authorities on the two great
Trecentists now seem convinced by the argument I pointed out
some years ago).[1]

The memory of those confidences lingered with Petrarch for
more than twenty years. He devoted more solicitous and thoughtful
attention to them now, as by this time he was more concerned with
life than with letters, more intensely experienced in "human vices
and value" (as he recalls insistently in the last three *Seniles*). Petrarch
let his emotions "arouse him to tears" over various pages of the
Decameron; he even reread them admiringly to his closest friends. He
spread throughout Europe the novella of Griselda, which he translated into the noblest Latin.[2] In his renewed interest and participation in the dissemination of the *Decameron,* Petrarch's imagination
also acted in obedience to the ever more powerful promptings of his
historical-romantic inclinations. From the pages of the *Familiares* to
those of the *De Viris,* his instinctive genius as a story-teller had given
repeated though marginal proof of this side of his imagination. This
influence had transformed the life of Joseph into a novella of sinuous
feminine seduction quite similar to Boccaccio's novella of the Count
of Anguersa. As he pored over the *Decameron,* Petrarch's imagination
was attracted most strongly to those novellas which assumed the
form of a historic tale where history and fancy, reality and invention
seemed to reflect one another. In his last three *Seniles* Petrarch wrote

about the problem of the historicity of the action in the novellas, and
the discussion is one of those impassioned literary-moralistic debates
which characterized the Petrarchan circle. The central judgment in
the *Seniles* resembles the interrogation which stands at the end of his
letter to Boccaccio: "an historiam scripserim an fabulam" (Whether
I wrote history or fable"). Petrarch, a story-teller in love with the
deeds of the great characters of history, sought to confer a more
distinguished patent of nobility upon the novella of his friend when
he referred to it as "historia" rather than "fabella."

Petrarch's preference for "historia," moreover, was not merely
the result of his aristocratic prehumanism and his strictly observed
classicism. Rather, it was a thirst for real or at least plausible
references, which characterize medieval literature. Among the few
progammatic declarations or "poetics of narrative" which Boccaccio
put into the mouths of his cultured story-tellers, the one which is most
striking, as we have seen, is that of Fiammetta: "Had I wished to
diverge from factual verity, or should I wish to do so, I would have
been able and would be able to compose [the novella] and to recount
it using other names; but because departure from the verity of things
which have occurred greatly diminishes the delight of the listeners of
the novella, I shall tell it to you in its proper form and aided by the
reason just given" (IX, 5, 5).

Fiammetta's words are a clear statement of the relationship
between reality (or history) and imagination on which Boccaccio
would continue to insist in the *De Casibus,* in the *De Mulieribus Claris*
and in the *Genealogia.*[3] As with almost all of his most explicit confidences regarding poetics, this position reflects the widespread and
authoritative canons of medieval esthetics.[4] Boccaccio proclaimed
that the novella "exemplaris seu demonstrativa" (that is, of the same
"species" as those of the *Decameron)* is "potius historia quam fabula
. . . veritati simillima."

Boccaccio's affirmation of "historia" rather than "fabella" was
an ideal response to the insistent questionings of Petrarch. It also
reveals a long-ignored aspect of the daring and successful structure of
the *Decameron.* That perspective is not one of strict historical truthfulness as interpreted in the eighteenth century by such men as
Manni, Salvini, Bottari, and Lami, who approached the *Decameron* as

a document whose every detail should be identified and verified as factual truth. Nor is the perspective exclusively literary, as critics such as Bartoli, Landau, Gröber, and Di Francia would have it. Their approach, which was popular in the last century and even in recent years, was to identify the literary "source" [5] of each novella. If the first approach intended to "nobilitate" the *Decameron* in obedience to the great historical enthusiasm of the eighteenth century, the other tended to relegate it to the margins of actual life and real environments, in order to consider it the last link in the chain of literary or popular themes from the fabled Orient.

Although in different ways, both of these were defensive positions. They looked to entirely extraneous themes to find an escutcheon for a work which was highly admired but, in a certain sense, was "irregular," held almost in suspicion by the more orthodox literary traditions. They necessarily remained at a standstill in considering the material and the episodes which they sought to trace back to historical or cultural origins. They did not concern themselves—at least not explicitly—with *how* those elements had come to attract the narrative imagination of Boccaccio and how, in a certain sense, they had determined the forms which it was to take.

In comparison with the structure of episodic clusters of tales which characterizes the collections of novellas which preceded it, the *Decameron* appears as a unified work, firmly governed by a plan based on ideas, a work grounded in a precise moral structure of which the so-called "frame" is an essential element. As we have shown, the novellas develop from the first to the last day according to a clear, preëstablished order which obeys the canons of the most authoritative medieval poetics. That is to say, they illustrate a moral itinerary of ideas which moves from the harsh and bitter reproof of vices on the first day, through recognition of the tribulations which afflict men in their daily struggles, and culminates in the epilogue of the tenth day in praise of magnanimity and virtue. To depict these pragmatic truths of the medieval vision of life, Boccaccio embellished his portraits with historical references which, in a sense, would create a relationship between them and life: a strong bond from which there was no escape. He had to find a language which would enlarge the meanings of those portraits by employing names, faces, and facts that were familiar and charged with sentimental impact. That is to say, what was needed were terms or, rather, in this book where men were more important than landscapes, figures, eminently allusive figures which, somewhat like the heroes of the Greek rhapsodies or medieval epics, could become a focal point for portrayals, facts, or particularly significant sayings. Boccaccio resorted to this technique just as Dante, in order to confer the force of prophetic admonition upon his wonderful vision, had above all evoked persons "known to fame." [6]

The portrayal of the meanness of petty and avaricious nobles would not be so meaningful if the aristocratic and peaceful atmosphere of the novella of Bergamino (I, 7) were not dominated by the disdainful and now legendary figure to Can Grande della Scala. The seductive tales of love and death (Day IV) would not reach such great and austere proportions were they not modulated and intoned on the glamorous names of Norman princes, such as Tancred and William the Good, or of Provencal knights or troubadours such as Rossillon and Guardastagno (IV, 1 and 4 and 9). The panegyrical splendor of the final day would be both less fabulous and less convincing if the most illustrious characters of the history of those centuries did not march through them from Frederick Barbarossa and Saladin to Charles of Anjou and Peter of Aragon, from Alfonso of Castile to Pope Boniface.

Indeed, new research into the figures used by Boccaccio to embellish his portraits constantly brings to light the meaning that they must have had for Boccaccio and his contemporaries.[7] For example, the danger and surprise of the tale of Pietro and L'Agnolella (V, 3) comes to life with the imagery of an Ariosto if we know how to interpret the historically allusive language. Dense with surprises and ambushes, that forest is not an artificial, mannered forest in the style of the enchanted woods of the romances of chivalry. It is the forest of Aglio near Frascati, on the route over which the Florentine merchants and Boccaccio himself traveled constantly between their city and Naples. It was a "silva latrociniis incolarum accomoda" (a wood well adapted to the safe operations of brigands), as Boccaccio defined it in his *De Montibus*. And the fortress where the anxieties of the two lovers finally are dispelled is one of the Roman castles to which Boccaccio had often been invited by his friend and admirer, Niccolo Orsini, protector of the Florentines, who was actually a member of the family of that Liello Orsini da Campo di Fiore, named in the novella as lord of the castle. Indeed, in addition to the effect of these particular references, the whole fearsome and anxious weaving of the tale derives a certain tragic eloquence of its own from the insistent allusion to a Rome abandoned and a prey to factions, as it is sorrowfully presented in the *Filocolo* (p. 21), in the epistle to Jacopo di Pizzinga, and in some of the *Familiares* addressed to Boccaccio (II, 12; VI, 8; XI, 1).

It is not just singular historical figures and events which enrich the *Decameron* through realism and allusion. The entire epic of thirteenth and fourteenth century Italian mercantilism and its conquest of Europe is reflected in the heroes and settings of the novellas. The changing fortunes of the Lamberti, which motivate the fabulous adventures of the third novella of the second day, must have had special import to readers of the Florentine merchant society. The incidents in the novella correspond with many which are reported in the registers of the Arte di Calimala and in the Exchange report, where the Lamberti are described as "cessantes et fugitivi," just as they are in the novella. The novella which ends the eighth day, with its tale of the merchant trapped and deceived by the beautiful courtesan, who is later tricked herself, must have been a familiar story to its readers. The tale is based on documented mercantile usages—such as the deposits and warranties—and its characters are drawn from portraits of royal or illustrious persons. Young Salabaetto, so vain in his foppish handsomeness, loses his head over two beautiful Sicilian eyes dewy with tears. His personality is taken directly from descriptions found in the Archives of Florence; he is a typical merchant, the son of a family of priors. Even more authentic is his slyly mischievous counselor, Pietro Canigiani of the powerful Acciaiuoli company, who is honored with the most important offices at the Angevin court and in the Florentine Republic. The novella must have acquired a joyfully allusive flavor (with a touch of smiling admonition) from the depiction of those two personages, very much alive at that time, and well known. It must have come alive in that dubious environment of courtesans and swindlers, procurers and unscrupulous merchants.[8]

While the figures "known to fame" serve a solemnly admoni-
tory function in the *Divina Commedia,* they add more varied and subtle
meanings to the *Decameron,* where they are often used in novellas of
mirth and amorous intrigue.[9] The equivocal situation prepared for
Catella by Ricciardo in the dark bedroom (III, 6), where she expects
to find her husband, but finds instead a rejected but unresigned lover,
is enriched with a scale of mischievous allusions. The setting is a
characteristically Neapolitan "stufa," and the plot revolves around
easily identifiable personages, from Ricciardo Minutolo, knight and
counselor of King Robert and Queen Joanna of Naples, captain and
viceroy of the Land of Otranto, to Filippo Sighinolfi, an authentic
courtier of that same queen, who belonged to a family with which
Boccaccio was on friendly terms. Catella herself is based on the
impetuous, passionate, and jealous woman whom Boccaccio had
already numbered among the most famous beauties of the Neapolitan court in the gallant arabesque of *La Caccia di Diana.*[10] Even the
lover, who has indiscreetly knocked at the door, has the recognizable
features of the respectable Giovanni di Nello, the apothecary, consul
of his guild in 1345 and devout Dominican Tertiary of Santa Maria
Novella, where he provided for his interment in a splendid chapel
(VII, 1).[11]

Thus, from the generic and trite motivations of the vast medieval literature dealing with the cunning and trickery of women, the
novella enters the circle of the piquant town chronicle. Indeed, it is
from this very circle that Boccaccio draws one of the great themes of
the *Decameron:* the contest between men to outdo one another in the
swift and subtle game of astuteness and intelligence. From the
immortal adventures of Calandrino, perennially robbed, soundly
beaten and even mocked, to the animated linguistic skirmishes of the
sixth day there is an animated gallery of municipal figures and places
which is developed all through the *Decameron.* Thus, in the history of
novella writing, Boccaccio daringly opens the doors to the contem-
poraneous world. He does it with that same sharp sense of the
continuity of human and cultural values which permits him—rather
more than Petrarch—to observe the uninterrupted tradition which
binds the culture of classical antiquity and of Greece itself to that of
the century of Dante.[12] By drawing his figures and settings from his

own world, Boccaccio lends a quality of spaciousness to his narrative, and it is all the more rich in perspective because the figures are raised to a plane equal to that of the ancient and traditional literary forms. Boccaccio avoided the sterility which marked the works of other Italian narrators who drew from contemporary sources (the tradition began with Sacchetti and continued through the anecdotage of the following century, which is found especially in the works of Poliziano). While the works of those writers seemed to exhaust themselves in the exclusive use of contemporary figures, Boccaccio's writing thrives on these techniques precisely because they are articulated within a framework of more traditional figures and sources. Boccaccio's work is created by deeply felt motivations of narrative poetics, and allusive references are used not for their own sake, but rather for their contribution to the rigorous and complex imaginative design of the *Decameron*.[13]

Since the *Decameron* is not an episodic collection of novellas, but is rather a unified work based on an inner moral structure, many of the tales are "exemplary." They exemplify the ideated motivations, or the key themes and human symbolism which integrate the design of the work as a whole. As Boccaccio shuns theoretical pronouncements, he turns instead to a representative language of exemplary character. This language demands the support of reference to historical reality and immediately recognizable elements representing fixed values. This "exemplary" inspiration, moreover, is not so much a characteristic peculiar to the design of the *Decameron* as it is a constitutional inclination of Boccaccio's imagination and medieval poetics in general.[14] Indeed, Boccaccio relied on "exemplary" techniques in several of his other works: the *Filocolo, Comedia, Amorosa Visione, De Mulieribus Claris,* and *De Casibus Virorum Illustrium.* The special nature of the *Decameron,* however, requires a full spectrum of narrative techniques: they range from abstract schemata and events outside of history to figurations "exemplary" not only for the action which is going on but also for precise allusions to the identity of the characters and their surroundings. That is to say (as we saw in the pronouncement from the *De Genealogia)*, these figurations create narrations "exemplares seu demonstrativae ... potius historia quam fabula, veritati simillima."

In the *Filocolo*, the impressive generosity of the lover who re-
turns to her husband, intact and honored, the beloved lady believed
dead and buried as such, sounded like a beginner's rhetorical attempt to tell of nameless men and women, living in an unnamed
country (XIII, question of love). When this same tale is recast in the
imaginative design of the *Decameron*, it is not an abstract event or an
oratorical exercise; it acquires direction and reality in both language and references. Its new form is based on the lives of the
well-known Bolognese families of the Carisendi and the Cacciane-
mici, who held highly important offices at that time (X, 4). If in the
Filocolo the novella was merely the vehicle for the amorous casuistry
of aristocratic conversation, in the *Decameron* all resources are drawn
upon to compose a picture of perfect courtliness and knightly
refinement which would be quite pale and unsubstantial if left in
abstraction or anonymity.

In the *Decameron*, all the most clearly "exemplary" novellas seek
in historical allusion the center of gravitation of their most decisive
meanings.

The exemplary figures often are placed in frameworks opposed
to their nature, and out of the contrast Boccaccio creates depth and
meaning in his tales. The figure of Agilulfo, for example, based on
Paulus Diaconus, represents prudence and the high discretion of
authority and intellect which are necessary endowments for a ruler.
His aristocratic virtues are all the more exemplary within the
framework of violence and barbarity (III, 2). Similarly, Boccaccio
exemplifies the struggle between the passion of the senses and the
God-given mission of justice of kings by setting the figure of Charles
d'Anjou beside the seductive beauty of Iseult and Guinevere (X, 6).
The novella assumes its exemplary value through antonomasia; the
princely moderation of the central figure, the king, achieves noble
eloquence when framed by the crowd, astonished and exalted by the
grand gestures of its lord.

These novellas which are filled with historical allusion do not
remain enclosed within the splendid circle of kings and heroes of the
sword. The solitary figure of Guido Cavalcanti (VI, 9) creates an
unforgettable image of the primacy of the spirit and the immortal-
ity of thought. His noble agility and elegance of wit rise above the

noise and pleasure-seeking of his companions. As he suddenly takes flight, his enigmatic witticism hangs suspended in air with a definite epigrammatic value precisely because the fascination of the meditative poetical solitude of the "amico primo" of Dante is concentrated and summed up in it.

Always more powerfully individuated in the memory and fantasy of the readers are those figures who by their presence put a definite seal on the reality long planned by Boccaccio in composing the grandiose ideal design of his masterpiece, a truth not claimed but *figured* in all of their most human values.

The long "exemplary" tradition, which in the Middle Ages was too abstract and given to fragmentation, at last finds adequate expression in the depiction of the great forces which govern life in the *Decameron*. Also, the traditional novelistic themes and middle-class anecdotage of the *fabliau* type are redeemed from their dispersive episodicity. The *Decameron* unites these two great traditions—the "exemplary" and the anecdotal—which were separated and unrelated in the Middle Ages. Boccaccio renews them and gives them an appropriate language by eliminating their abstract episodic character and placing them within the context of history.

The narrative power gained by Boccaccio in his use of historical context is clearly apparent in the so-called "frame," which is historical rather than mechanical. Rather than rely on conventional narrator's figures for his "frames," Boccaccio surrounds his tales with a framework that begins with the scourges which ruined Florentine prosperity in 1348, and ends with the calm hills of Fiesole, sacred to an aristocratic way of life and to the poetry of literature and the arts. This new narrative power is especially decisive in those novellas where traditional material is most evident.

Certainly there was no theme more worn by constant use in oriental, classical, and medieval literature, than that of *agnitio* (recognition). It is the theme of the child whose courage and virtue under the stress of a series of persecutions and misadventures is crowned by the miraculous revelation of his or her illustrious birth, until then unknown. Rather than a theme, it had become, in theater and narrative, a useful artifice, a *deus ex machina*, from which any trace of the imagination and its language was absent. In the *Decam-*

eron, however, this exhausted expedient comes alive. Its meaning is coherent with that of the action and even casts light on the action itself. The recognition of Giusfredi Capece is not the mechanical conclusion, but the artistically necessary and inevitable heart of the pitiful novella of Madonna Beritola (II, 6). The rhythms of the narrative, which span the political events in Sicily between the Angevin conquest and the Vespers, reach their climax in the miraculous recognition, which is no longer a pretext or a gratuitous happening but the final and exemplary event in that riot of precipitously overthrown fortunes. It is precisely the exact historical dimensions within which it is set which give it this extraordinary reality and this central significance. Against the background of the warfare of Swabians, Angevins, and Aragonese, two great Neapolitan families, the Capece and the Caracciolo, provide the heroes of the novella. The *agnitio* occurs in the midst of the aristocratic life in a castle belonging to Corrado II Malaspina, hero of the famous episode in *Purgatorio,* who manifests that same generosity for the exiles and that too exclusive and proud affection for his family which are at the heart of the Dantean portrayal: "ai miei portai l'amor che qui raffina" ("toward my family I bore the love which here is purified") (*Purg.,* VIII, 120). All of the environmental and topographical details correspond so closely to reality that when criticism of the text suggested the phrase "il Capece in cattività per lo re Carlo guardato," it immediately found its justification in the structure of the novella, because a Capece, vicar-general of the Swabians and a rebel against the Angevins, was imprisoned and tortured.[15] The recognition is of further exemplary significance because it is the solemn consecration of a reality already implicit in the love choice which Corrado's daughter, Spina, had made of Giusfredi (the foundling): a choice, Boccaccio emphasizes, determined by the feminine divination of the "generous soul [of the youth] determined by his origin." With this the novella assumes aspects typical of medieval society: it becomes a lofty example of the indomitable force of family stock and of the meaning of love, which chooses men and causes them to act according to their worth and not their appearance. The overworked expedient of *agnitio* is consigned to oblivion in the absolute coherence of narrative motivations and rhythms, of symbolical and exemplary significations, of allusive and figurative language.

Many traditional themes find new life at the touch of a narrative imagination which distinguishes them in the context of reality and then connects them in the ideated architecture of the *Decameron*. It is, for example, the theme (which had become a rhetorical *topos*) of the woman calumniated unjustly, whose innocence is recognized only after piteous odysseys. It is renewed in the novella of Ambrogiuolo and Ginevra (II, 9) in a precise and vivid mercantile framework, with desolate and elegiac intonation. It is the mechanical expedient of the choice between two mysterious strong-boxes, one of them filled with base material and the other with treasures, an expedient which regains its vividly exemplary tone in the interplay between King Alfonso of Castile (previously extolled by Dante for "his royal beneficences" equal to those of Saladin and Alexander) and Ruggiero Figiovanni, a member of a family of Certaldo with which Boccaccio was on most friendly terms (X, 1). It is the theme that had become a dead paradigm in the storytelling of both East and West of the deceiver deceived (feminine in this case) which in the novella of Salabaetto (VIII, 10), is transfigured through historically allusive language into a vivid portrayal of the adventurous life of the Florentine merchants.

A perhaps extreme example of Boccaccio's use of traditional themes and techniques is the figure of Nastagio degli Onesti, in the novella about the daydream of love interrupted and in a sense resolved, by the infernal hunt in Chiassi (V, 8). In this tale, perhaps more than in any other, the literary antecedents are most clear, and at the same time most reduced by a long tradition to pure expediency, to wearied oratorical artifice. Following Nordic mythologies, visions of infernal hunts had run through western literature for centuries; eventually they came to denote punishment for particular crimes. They had been used as a *topos* of the most cultured and acclaimed oratory by such authorities as Caesarius of Heisterbach and Elinandus, Vincent of Beauvais and Passavanti. The tradition of penalties for women cruel in love was just as illustrious and canonical. It had been used in the *Disciplina Clericalis,* the *Speculum Morale,* and in the most authoritative and systematic treatises on love, including that of Andreas Cappellanus, whom Boccaccio greatly admired. In this novella (as in all of the *Decameron*), Boccaccio substitutes the liveliness of contemporary people for the mannered figurines of the literary antecedents. Instead of stylized and colorless artifice, he presents an entire society that is alive and fascinating. The infernal hunt is contrasted to the gay and refined life of the Ravenna aristocracy, which is portrayed as it was in the first part of the thirteenth century. This life had been recalled by Salimbene of Parma and in the *Novellino,* and even Dante nostalgically described it with the very names used by Boccaccio in his novella:

> . . . la casa Traversara e li Anastagi
> (e l'una gente e l'altra è diretata),
> Le donne e i cavalier, li affanni e li agi,
> che ne 'nvogliava amore e cortesia . . . (*Purg.* XIV, 107 ff.)

> . . . and the Traversara house and that of the Anastagi
> (and this house and that are without male descendants),
> The ladies and the knights, the perils of war, the pleasures
>   of peace,
> desire of which love and urbanity aroused in us . . .

This aristocratic society moves in dreamy abandon, in courtly conversation, against a background full of charm made precious by Dante himself:

> . . . divina foresta spessa e viva . . .
> tal qual di ramo in ramo si raccoglie
> per la pineta in sul lito di Chiassi
>   (*Purg.* XXVIII, 2 and 19-20)

> . . . divine forest dense and ever green . . .
> just as it swells from branch to branch
> through the pinetum along the shore of Classis

In this environment so historically and evocatively particularized, the unexpected and violent apparition which twice destroys the silent solitude of the forest no longer resembles the symbols of an abstract casuistry or any mythological or moralistic schemata. It is a great and terrible human apparition which, with its language of impassioned loves and generous courtesies, of splendid living and magnanimous chivalry, steps into the colorful portrait of a vanished society.

> Now it befell that one Friday almost at the beginning of May, in a spell of very lovely weather, when he had fallen into thought of his cruel beloved, after having given strict orders to his whole family to be left alone, to be thus the freer to meditate, step by step, thoughtfully, he betook himself into the pinetum, and the fifth hour of the day having almost passed, when he had penetrated a good half mile into the pine grove with no concern for food nor other matters, suddenly he seemed to hear great weeping and lamentations uttered by a woman; whereupon, his gentle thought thus broken into, he raised his head to see what might be the cause, and was astonished to find that he had strayed into the pinetum; and not only that: for looking before him he saw, coming through a copse of close-growing shrubs, running toward the spot where he was standing, a most beautiful young woman nude, and all scratched by twigs and sharp thorns, weeping and loudly crying mercy; and besides all this he saw at her flanks two great fierce mastiffs which, running hard after her were biting her as occasion offered; and behind her, riding a black charger, a dark-complexioned knight, his strong features contorted by anger, rapier in hand, with frightful and rude words threatening her with death (V 8, 13-17).

"Here the infernal tragedy is as tangible as an earthly tragedy" (Momigliano); the depiction is neither vague nor abstract, suspended as it is "in the evidence of the hallucinations which grip the gaze and seem isolated in nothingness." The hunt does not remain a marginal pretext, an episode from which to draw consequences. It is the very heart of the novella, it is a myth in which the protagonists are reflected and become fully recognizable, because the feelings of those who are no longer pretext-figures but living and identified men and women are fully fused into the hellish vision. The ardent and despairing passion of Nastagio, his vain and dream-like desire "to hate the girl as she had hated him," are mirrored in the vision, as is the resistance of the beautiful Traversari girl, who is on the verge of yielding and accepting her defeat. In those persons and those surroundings, both historically and figuratively allusive, and in this eloquent presentation of portraits and scenes so real and so valid as to stand on their purely visual merits, the hellish hunt has found its own coherent and persuasive language. The effect is like that achieved in the spectral wood of the Dantean suicides, with its macabre thorny brambles and the lightning flashes of the "nere cagne bramose e correnti."

Boccaccio's creation of a historically allusive language is de-cisive not only for the exemplary structure of the *Decameron,* but also for the expression of his narrative imagination in general. The references to real people and events are not merely episodic or incidental; rather they are structural motifs, or narrative constants, and as such they offer entirely new possibilities for portrayal and narration.

Throughout the whole literary tradition of antiquity and the Middle Ages—in the East as in the West—portrayals of human life were written in pure forms, in stylized symbologies, or they were arranged in the various types of chronicle or legend as sequences of events set paratactically on a single plane. They were the two directions in which narrative experiences developed, the two ex-treme poles of attraction and of opposition: between the symbol and the event no meeting nor synthesis was possible. This quality, this *dichotomia,* moreover, constituted another of the more constant limits of the imaginative language of Boccaccio's youthful works: they oscillated between laborious constructions using overly complex symbols and allegories (*Filocolo, Comedia, Amorosa Visione*) and the monotonous depiction of human realities (*Caccia, Filostrato, Teseida*). By the time of the *Fiammetta* and the *Ninfale,* however, Boccaccio's narrative imagination was finding at last the rhythm which in the *Decameron* would make the descriptive synthesis of the two forms possible, using a historically allusive language common to both of them. Symbol and chronicle, example and legend thus can meet at last, can reconcile and illumine their different dimensions, previously opposed or rather alien to one another, in this new descriptive, figurative dimension; a dimension in which descriptions, without losing any of their exemplary and eternal value (outside of time and space), are on the contrary set down with power and identified precisely *within* time and space. The chronicle, whether of episodes or of sentiments, is thus adopted to the subject and to the forms; the events and the symbology are historicized simultaneously, they meet at a point of convergence which renews them and artistically and intellectually clarifies them.

This is the solution of Boccaccio which makes it possible for him to create in his *Decameron* the great *summa* of medieval narrative and at the same time to open the ways to the completely new techniques of the following age, in which that contrast and opposition between symbol and episode is not only overcome but forever obliterated.

That ideated structure of the *Decameron,* based on the ideas-force of the medieval vision of life, the urgent need to depict these working forces above all in figures "known to fame" (that is, immediately identifiable by the reader), that opening up of the art of novella writing to include contemporary municipal life, that lofty, pellucid exemplification in which traditional themes and plots are composed and renewed, that wealth of possibilities discovered in historically allusive language, all these elements which we have been identifying as constitutional motifs of Boccaccio's very new and felicitous narrative technique, find their figurative and expressive meaning in this new dimension.

If the play of the imagination is thus enriched by those perspectives and possibilities which have been pointed out, the new language is demonstrated most daringly and in a sense, most extremely, in the novellas in which the historically allusive meanings are carefully concealed in the adventurous flow of purely imaginary events. Then historical allusion renounces its most determinable functions, aiming instead at more subtle, more surprising meanings. The effect is something like a hallucinatory play of shadows and lightning flashes between two different planes, almost a state of suspension, miraculous and enigmatic, between reality and dream, which gives new descriptive depth to the narration.

Boccaccio creates such a balance in the sinister atmosphere of

Naples at its most picaresque, which both envelops and scans the urgent and surprising rhythm of the incredible adventures of Andreuccio da Perugia (II, 5). In the unexpected flare-up of the strangest episodes (which precipitate Andreuccio from love's paradise into a foul-smelling abyss, from which he is dragged at the voice of the terrifying Mangiafoco, thrust into a well and caused to resurface suddenly like a devilish apparition, and then is dumped sprawling into a tomb in a macabre embrace, from which he is made to pop up unexpectedly as a sort of mocking spectre), in all this phantasmagoria of startling surprises, the outlines of things and of very solidly identifiable persons flit by in succession like fabulous grotesques, made unreal by their very reality. This fabulously dense and oppressive night in which the most unbelievable surprises acquire a precise consistency of their own, floats in stagnation amid the ambushes of the narrow streets and alleys in which Boccaccio had spent the adolescent years of his mercantile apprenticeship. The astute Sicilian courtesan seems to have the profile of the "Flora sicula" who was a "pensioner" of Malpertugio himself in 1340 and 1341. The ogre-like face of a "Camorrista" finds his imaginatively mock-heroic name accurately spelled out in the Angevin archives for May 1336: beetle Buttafuoco. The embalmed cadaver which suddenly becomes the *deus ex machina* of the whole novella, still shows today, in the cathedral of Naples, its finger despoiled of the precious ring. Here the play of fantasy has become more tightly knit: the allusive language suspends all the portrayals in an atmosphere of hallucinating clarity and makes them bounce back and forth between reality and imagination in a refraction of constantly receding lights and facets. The most imaginative portrayal, in the daring and auspicious play, becomes more real than reality itself.

Sometimes the location of a landscape, mentioned so casually that we hardly notice, suffices to create the allusive high-tension atmosphere of some novella. The depiction–surely the most surrealistic Boccaccio has given us—of the white body of Elena which stands out in the moonlight atop a solitary tower, so shining and spellbinding because it is suspended on the verge of the destruction and ruin of the flesh, would not have that quality so intensely visual as to surpass reality, if it were not standing in a landscape of the

Arno valley described in minute detail with the patient realism of a
Flemish background (VIII, 7). Nor would the fabulous experiences
of Messer Torello surpass the limits of the most ordinary fable to
create instead an evocative and exemplary figuration of courteous
kindness, if his magical nocturnal flight from Cairo to Pavia in that
bed resplendent with gold and jewels did not end suddenly inside
the solid walls of Pavia's S. Pietro in Ciel d'Oro, and evaporate in
the daily round of weary chores of the sacristan and the sleepy
monks coming down to say matins (X, 9).

Boccaccio also uses an inverse technique, that is, by stressing a
precise allusion, he illumines a figure or event in a highly real and
exemplary sense.[16] For example, Boccaccio evokes the name of a
citizen of proverbial honesty, Coppo di Borghese Domenichi, as the
source of a novella (V, 9). He also uses the name of the Alberighi
family to create nostalgic echoes of the memories of Cacciaguida:

> Io vidi li Ughi, e vidi i Catellini,
> Filippi, Greci, Ormanni e Alberichi,
> già nel calare, illustri cittadini (*Par.* XVI, 88 ff.)

> I saw the Ughi, and I saw the Catellini,
> Filippi, Greci, Ormanni and Alberichi,
> already in decadence, illustrious citizens

echoes which lend an air of history to the calm and chivalrous elegy of
Federico degli Alberighi, and give the story the rhythm and the flavor
of an ingenuous primitive legend. All of Federico's traits and
deeds—the virile melancholy of his suffering, his renunciation, his
willingness to sacrifice his cherished hawk to his reluctant beloved—
comprise a wealth of human sentiment, which in its simplicity and
plainness is perhaps greater and certainly is more inward than that
depicted in the great tales of the generosity of kings and princes.
Federico's gesture clearly takes on a solemn exemplary quality in no
way inferior to to the heroic combat of a paladin for his lady. He is the
knight of arduous inner renunciations and silent struggles, the knight
of a spiritually noble humanity who takes his place alongside the

knights of the sword and of courtly war, with an exemplary dignity that is similar, but more inward and more persuasive.

Thus in the new descriptive dimension, Boccaccio has effected not only the convergence of two literary traditions, but also the imaginative conciliation of two societies. He has united the feudal society, with its solemn nobility and rites of warfare, and that of the more splendid communal age, whose human wisdom and courtliness were reflected in the elegance of their words and deeds.[17] Because he situated the most varied human values concretely in history Boccaccio could express the continuity between the world of the knights of the sword and the one of the knights of wit and measured subtlety of mind. Boccaccio seemed to stress it more explicitly when he confided anxiously to Jacopo da Pizzinga: ". . . in spem venio atque credulitatem, Deum ytalico nomini misertum, dum video Eum e gremio sue largitatis in ytalorum pectora effundere animas ab antiquis non differentes; avidas scilicet non rapina vel sanguine, non fraude vel violentia, non ambitione vel decipulis sibi honores exquirere, sed *laudabili exercitio,* duce poesi, nomen pretendere in evum longinquum, conarique ut possint viventes adhuc volitare per ora virorum" (ep. XVIII).

Boccaccio was conscious of having in some way depicted in his masterpiece the anxious—and discouraged—lyric exhortation of his Master to the Lords of Italy, to the "magnanimous few who care for good works":

> . . . Piacciavi porre giù l'odio e lo sdegno
> Venti contrari a la vita serena;
> E quel che 'n altrui pena
> Tempo si spende, in qualche atto più degno
> O di mano o d'ingegno,
> In qualche bella lode,
> In qualche onesto studio si converta:
> Così qua giù si gode,
> E la strada del ciel si trova aperta. . . .
> I' vo' gridando: Pace, pace, pace.

> . . . May it please ye to abandon hate and scorn,
> Winds contrary to the life serene;
> And may time spent in harming others
> Be converted into some more worthy act,
> Either of the body or the mind,
> Into some beautiful praise,
> Into some honest study:
> Then here below life is good,
> And the road to Heav'n lies open. . . .
> I go about crying: Peace, peace, peace.

NOTES

1. *Per il testo del Decameron—La prima diffusione, cit.,* and see for example G. Martellotti, "Momenti narrativi nel Petrarca," *Studi petrarcheschi,* IV, 1951.
2. See *Boccaccio Medievale,* Appendix concerning the diffusion of Petrarch's free translation.
3. Read for example in the *De Casibus Virorum Illustrium,* the Introduction; VI, intr.; VIII, 1, where Petrarch is brought in to state: "Agit et in preteritos istud desiderabile bonum fama, ut gibbosos claudos torvos et quacumque vis deformitate deformes, decoros, splendidos augustosque posteritati demonstret: et si sic alios omnes putas, fac si possis, quin mentalibus oculis fame splendoris superaddas aliquid . . . si voce aliud dignum, non fingendo, dignitati superaddimus aliquid phanthasie." And see the *De Mulieribus Claris,* Introduction: "ratus sum et quandoque hystoriis inserere nonnulla lepida blandimenta virtutis et in fugam atque detestationem scelerum aculeos addere, et sic fiet, ut immixta hystoriarum delectationi sacra mentes subintrabit utilitas." Also see *De Genologia,* XIV, 9-10 and 13, from which the above quotation was taken; and see note 6.
4. See also the works cited in note 16 of chapter I. The texts of Hugo of St. Victor *(De Scripturis . . . ,* III and *Didascalion,* VI, 3 and *passim:* "fundamentum et principium . . . historia est"), those of St. Bonaventura (in *Lib. Sententiarum,* I d. 2a 1 q.4 and d.31 p. II a. 1 q.3), those of John of Garland *(Poetria,* ed. cit., pp. 886 and 926), and those of Dante himself *(Convivio,* II, 1: see B. Nardi, *Dante e la cultura medioevale,*

Bari, 1942) are of particular value. Keep in mind that often for the treatise writers historical sense and literal sense are equivalents, as they are also for the medieval rhetoricians (see *Convivio*, ed. Busnelli-Vandelli, Florence, 1953, I, p. 96, note, with various meaningful quotations; also Dante's Epistle, XIII, 22; see also St. Thomas, *Summa th.*, I q. 1 a. 10, and *Quodlibet*, VII a. 15-16). In the pages of the *Genologia* cited above the presence of the distinctions of John of Garland is clear; history for him is "tout récit, toute relation d'événements ou de péripéties dont la succession éveille l'intérêt" (any recital or account of happenings or vicissitudes following one on the other which awakens interests) (De Bruyne, *Etudes*, II, p. 20).

5.   For exact information about the works of the authors cited above, and for others along the same lines, as well as for a more detailed history of these two questions, see my *Storia della critica al Decameron.*

6.   In this connection, see also notes 3 and 4. And again in the *De Casibus* "lepiditate historiarum . . . ratus sum quid Deus omnipotens seu, ut eorum loquar more, fortuna in *elatos* possit et fecerit . . . consternatos duces illustresque alios . . . in medium succincte deducere" (Introduction): and then Fortune says: "ex his videlicet quos meae manus ad sydera evexere et demum mersere sub inferis et casus eorumdem describis" (VI, intr.). Fortune also warns that she works on the most humble; but Boccaccio answers that the examples of the great are more effective. In the *Commedia* all the personages who act are historical, exactly according to the needs of an artist who wants to construct a "comedy," a vision of life: for history insofar as it is willed by God, as it is a portrayal of Providence, in a certain sense is sacred history, in which the data foreordained by God himself speak; this was well illustrated by Bruno Nardi *(Dante e la cultura medioevale, cit.,* IX; and *Nel mondo di Dante,* Rome, 1944). We are in the sphere of history not in a physical sense alone, and not only in a symbolical or allegorical sense, but in the precincts of narrations which try to be earthly and corporeal history and at the same time allusive and metaphysical history; that is to say, narrations which, in different directions, are equally the *Divina Commedia* and the *Decameron* (for Dante in this connection, in addition to the Nardi volumes see: Gilson, *L'esprit de la philosophie médiévale, cit.,* and *Dante et la philosophie,* Paris, 1931; and also Montano, art. cit.).

7.   Naturally the searching out and the study of the historical ornaments and their meaning have a particular value for the *Decameron,* and not merely for those reasons of poetics which we have indicated. That is to

say, we must not forget the convictions which Boccaccio himself expressed at different times (see notes 3 and 6), the atmosphere of realism in which the work was conceived and which was characteristic of the civilization of the late Middle Ages (Huizinga, op. cit., pp. 295 ff.), or the "exemplary" architecture of the collection of nevellas that intend to represent eternal verities and which therefore had all the more need to be solidly anchored to history (see pp. 319 ff.).

8. Here, naturally, we stress the historicity of the characters; for the typical mercantile precision of the customs and language we refer the reader back to Chapter III.

9. Besides, Alberico da Montecassino earlier cautioned that there are three kinds of history: great—of wars, or divine matters; medium—for physical concerns; and humble—for the games of youth and the lusts of love affairs. And he added that the writer must consider which degree or manner is to be chosen for each kind in order to befit the plot (*Flores,* ed. cit., II); similar distinctions and similar precepts are found also in the *poetria* of John of Garland, loc. cit.

10. To the information in my commentary there should be added the data on Catella Sighinolfo collected in *Tradizione delle opere di G. Boccaccio.* Also, the Sighinolfo family had become related, during the period of Boccaccio's Neapolitan sojourn, with the Barrili family, since Perillo Sighinolfo married Regale Barrili, daughter of the great Giovanni Barrili, a personal friend of Boccaccio (De Blasiis, *Racconti di storia napoletana,* Naples, 1906, p. 144).

11. Naturally it would be easy to multiply the examples each time, because practically all the novellas of the *Decameron* are based on some historical or realistic reference, and some of the very few exceptions are such only because of our ignorance or of the disappearance of pertinent documents.

12. See *Boccaccio Medieval,* Chapter IX. Especially significant is the presence in the novellas of persons who not only actually existed but were known by Boccaccio and were perhaps still living at the time of the *Decameron:* for example, I, 10, Alberto da Bologna; IV, 10, Montagna; V, 6, Marino and Restituta Bulgaro; V, 9, Coppo di Borghese Domenichi; V, 10, Pietro da Vinciolo (?); VI, 10, Biagio Pizzini; VII, 1, Gianni di Nello (who died in August 1347); VIII, 10, Pietro dello Canigiano, and perhaps Niccolò da Cignano, and so on. This tendency to set contemporaries and acquaintances by the side of historical and illustrious personages is constant in Boccaccio. Just think of Robert of Anjou, of Ruggiero of Lauria, of his father himself,

presented next to the mythological heroes and the greats of the past in the series of triumphs of the *Amorosa Visione* (not to mention the Neapolitan and Florentine beauties who parade through the same poem); and then think of the examples of the Duke of Athens, of Filippa and her relatives in the *De Casibus,* and of those of Robert and Joanna of Anjou and of Camiola in the *De Mulieribus:* not even remembering Petrarch, evoked not only in the *De Genologia* (see especially XV, 6 and 13; XIV, 22) next to the ancient writers but even brought into the *De Casibus* (VIII, 1).

13. For this very reason the historical and factual elements should not be sought and studied for their abstract anagraphical truthfulness, but only as references chosen to give concreteness to the ideal and artistic themes which we have examined above.

14. See in general notes 3, 4, 6, 7; Nardi (*Dante e la cultura medioevale, cit.*) justly remarks that Dante, abandoning all allegorical fiction, gave his poem an eternal value by basing it on the historical *sense* which, for him, as in the Scriptures, coincided with the literal sense (see Epistle to Cangrande, 22): "All those who act in his drama are historical personages: the material is *sacred,*" as in the examples of the Bible (Montano, art. cit.).

15. The Capece must have been well known to Boccaccio since he named them in the early *Caccia di Diana* (I, 29); new light is cast on the troubles of the Capece rebelling against Carlo I by documents noted in the recent work edited by Filangeri, *I Registri della Cancelleria angioina,* Naples, 1953, II and III *passim,* see Index; IV, pp. 80, 109, 176; V, pp. 62, 193. In Corrado's time the Caracciolo were fierce adversaries of the Angevins, so that Pietro was hanged on an accusation "de proditione" (of treachery) (Archivio di Stato di Napoli, *Notamenta ex registris Caroli II,* II, I, cc. 1612 ff.). There existed a Biancofiore or Beritola Caracciolo, daughter of Ligorio Caracciolo Pisquizi (executioner in Terra di Lavoro who lived between 1230 and 1280), mentioned as living in 1295, and according to Fabris she was indeed the wife of Corrado Capece (Fabris, *La famiglia Caracciolo,* table XXI in the *Supplementi* to Litta, *Famiglie celebri,* Milano, 1819 and later published in Naples, 1902 and after).

16. Naturally, for these two perspectives also it would be easy to multiply the particularly significant examples: for example, in I, 4 the reference to the Convent in the letter of Brother Ilario; in I, 6 the fusing of the real data and of imaginary creations in the figure of the Inquisitor; in II, 7 the imaginatively unrestrained adventures of Alatiel located

point by point in places associated with the Durazzeschi; in II, 8 the drops of tenderness hidden in the dear and familiar names of Giannetta and Violante; in IV, 4 the insertion of the non-existent figure of Gerbino just at an uncertain point in the genealogy of the Norman princes; in IV,7 that precisely and vivaciously sketched background of the life of the Florentine woolens craftsmen; in V, 5 that banal and canonical intrigue, which develops from a historical episode such as the siege of Faenza, which had so vast and fearful an echo in Tuscany; in VII, 2 the precise references to the Neapolitan environment for a transcription from Apuleius; in IX, 1 that background of historic factional struggles given to one of the most hallucinating and phantasmal episodes, and so on.

17. The problem studied in this chapter is enriched with new perspectives and documentation in *Boccaccio Medievale,* "Registri strutturali e stilistici" (pp. 86 ff.), also for the aspect mentioned on pp. 325 f.

New archival documents and new environmental indications continue to confirm the insistent historical allusions of many novellas. Let it suffice to cite the volumes of the *Registri della Cancelleria angioina* which appeared after 1956 (VI-XX) and already used by me for this purpose in the commentary to the *Caccia di Diana* (Milan, 1967), for example for II, 6; and the "Notizie e documenti per la biografia del Boccaccio" published in *Studi sul Boccaccio,* III and ff.

Index Nominum